The premise of this book is simple and sound: we have a great deal to learn about prayer from the prayers offered by our forebears in faith and recorded in our canonical scriptures. Dr. Ward offers us a book on prayer that has been informed by careful study of these prayers in conversation with biblical scholarship, refined in ongoing conversations within faith communities seeking to learn how to pray more faithfully themselves, and, of course, bathed in prayerful conversation with God throughout the process. Sitting with these prayers and listening to the wisdom Ward has gathered concerning what they reveal about the sacred crucible of prayer cannot fail to enrich readers' practice of one of the cardinal disciplines of the Christian life.

David A. deSilva
Trustees' Distinguished Professor of New Testament and Greek
Ashland Theological Seminary

Nathan Ward has written a book on numerous biblical prayers that is wondrously accessible and instructive. He divides his discussion of each biblical prayer into three parts:

- Context that probes the ancient historical setting of each prayer;
- Content that looks to the specific articulation of faith; and
- Connection that lets Ward draw lines to our contemporary faith and practice of prayer.

This is a rich and wise commentary on biblical prayer. Those who take it up may expect interpretive surprises, and may anticipate growth in their own prayer life as well. A most welcome read designed for close study!

Walter Brueggemann
Professor Emeritus of Old Testament,
Columbia Theological Seminary

This book was "like a treasure hidden in the field" that unexpectedly appeared in my life. It expertly guides us on a tour of prayers in the Bible so that we better understand the wondrous mystery of prayer but also meaningfully enhances our own life of prayer. It is a marvelous gift that I will read and re-read.

David E. Garland
Professor of Christian Scriptures
George W. Truett Theological Seminary
Baylor University

The Bible's prayers are not only reports of what people prayed. Their presence in the canon of Scripture means that they also teach us about prayer, providing a school of prayer as we read them. Tracing these through the canon, Nathan Ward provides readers with a rich exploration of biblical prayer that teaches about prayer and encourages reflection on how and why we pray. All who read will thus be challenged to explore the riches of prayer once more.

David G. Firth
Trinity College Bristol/University of the Free State

This book provides a lucid and compelling examination of biblical prayers in all their variety. It models a sound and rigorous approach to biblical exegesis—starting with the context of each prayer and then moving on to look at its detailed content before drawing out some key application and learning points. The text incorporates the insights of numerous biblical scholars, but the author has adopted a style and approach which makes such insights accessible and meaningful. I commend this book because it compels us to stop and reflect afresh on some of our presumptions about prayer. At the same time, it contains practical wisdom about the practice of prayer and is rooted in a theological approach which honours the will and purposes of the God to whom we pray. It is impossible to miss the emphasis which the author draws our attention to in the concluding chapter: biblical prayers reveal to us people who know who God is and who acknowledge his will, care and reign. This fact alone should make reading biblical prayers a priority for people who pray today, and Nathan Ward's book provides excellent guidance as we do so.

Debra Reid
Spurgeon's College, London

Nathan Ward reminds us: if we want to learn to pray, we have no better tutor than the ancient saints on their knees. Read this book, but read it slowly. Each chapter's foray into a Bible prayer contains gold you will only appreciate fully if you take your time, mull it over, and then practice it on your own knees.

Edwin L. Crozier
Author of *Plugged In: High-Voltage Prayer*

"Teach us to pray" is a request every believer can identify with. In *Our Eyes Are On You* Nathan Ward points us to the rich resources of the prayers of the Bible. In this comprehensive study of the wide variety of prayers in the Bible, Nathan

Ward explains 35 prayers across the whole Bible in light of their immediate and covenantal contexts, and with much practical help. Read this and you'll find yourself informed, edified, and praying more!

Alan J. Thompson
Head of the New Testament Department,
Sydney Missionary and Bible College, Australia

Nathan Ward engages in a sensitive and humble exposition of biblical prayers, useful for anyone who wants to model their own prayers on biblical examples.

Michael F. Bird
Academic Dean,
Ridley College, Melbourne, Australia

This is a beautifully clear and profound and wide-ranging and thoughtful and illuminating book on prayer in the Scriptures. The people who read it and put its insights into practice are going to have their relationship with God transformed.

John Goldingay
Senior Professor of Old Testament
Fuller Theological Seminary

This well-written, accessible book roots Christian prayer in the right soil—in Holy Scripture, both Old and New Testaments. It will prove to be an excellent companion for those who are now on the same journey as the ancestors in faith whose conversations with God form the foundation for the author's helpful reflections. As he says: we can indeed "learn to pray better by seeing how the faithful men and women of history have prayed."

Iain Provan
Founder of the Cuckoos Consultancy
Retired Professor of Biblical Studies

OUR EYES ARE ON YOU

Our Eyes Are On You

A Study of Biblical Prayer

Nathan Ward

Our Eyes Are On You: A Study of Biblical Prayer
© 2023 by DeWard Publishing Company, Ltd.
P.O. Box 290696, Tampa, FL 33687
www.deward.com

All rights reserved. No portion of this book may be reproduced in any form without written permission from the publisher.

Cover design by Barry Wallace.

Cover photo by Jason Hardin,
https://thingshopedforphotography.pixieset.com/portfolio

Epigraph quotes are from:

Barclay, *The Letters of James and Peter*, 299.
Calvin, *Commentaries on the Four Last Books of Moses*, 4:75.
Carson, *Praying with Paul*, 177.
Kaiser, *Have You Seen the Power of God Lately?* 26–27.

Full information can be found in the bibliography.

Unless otherwise noted, Scripture quotations are from the ESV® Bible (The Holy Bible, English Standard Version®), copyright © 2001 by Crossway, a publishing ministry of Good News Publishers. Used by permission. All rights reserved. The ESV text may not be quoted in any publication made available to the public by a Creative Commons license. The ESV may not be translated in whole or in part into any other language. Any emphasis in Bible quotations is added by the author.

Reasonable care has been taken to trace original sources for any excerpts and quotations appearing in this book and to document such information. For material not in the public domain, fair use standards and practices were followed. Should any attribution be found to be incorrect or incomplete, the publisher welcomes written documentation supporting correction for subsequent printing.

Printed in the United States of America.

ISBN: 978-1-947929-26-5

To My Parents,

Keith and Dene Ward,

who first taught me to pray

There is nothing more efficacious in our prayers than to set His own word before God, and then to found our supplications upon His promises, as if He dictated to us out of His own mouth what we were to ask. **John Calvin**

The first necessity of prayer is the earnest desire, not to get what we wish, but to discover the will of God for ourselves. **William Barclay**

The promises of Scripture were not meant to excuse us from prayer or to let us know what it was in the kingdom of God that we could take for granted. Instead, they were given so that we might be taught what it is that we ought to pray for and what it is our faith could cling to. **Walter C. Kaiser, Jr.**

It is a wonderful comfort, a marvelous boost to faith, to know that you are praying in line with the declared will of almighty God. **D.A. Carson**

Contents

Preface xi

Abbreviations xvii

1. Far Be It from You! (Gen 18.22–33) 1

2. You Have Shown Steadfast Love (Gen 24.12–14) 8

3. Please Deliver Me (Gen 32.9–12) 15

4. Please Bless Me (Gen 32.22–32) 21

5. Please Pardon This People (Num 14.11–23) 26

6. I've Poured Out My Soul (1 Sam 1.10–11; 2.1–10) 34

7. Who Am I? (2 Sam 7.18–29) 44

8. I Have Sinned Greatly (2 Sam 24.10–14) 52

9. Direct Their Hearts Toward You (1 Chron 29.10–19) 60

10. Give Me an Understanding Mind (1 Kgs 3.3–14) 66

11. Open Your Eyes Toward This House (1 Kgs 8.22–61) 73

12. Our Eyes Are on You (2 Chron 20.5–12) 82

13. Out of My Distress (Jon 2.1–9) 89

14. You Alone Are God (2 Kgs 19.14–19) 98

15. How Long Will You Not Hear? (Hab 1.2–4) 107

16. Why Do You Idly Look at Traitors? (Hab 1.12–2.1). 114

17. In Wrath Remember Mercy (Hab 3). 121

18. Nothing Is Too Hard for You (Jer 32.17–25) 130

19. Because of Your Great Mercy (Dan 9.3–19) 138

20. We Are Before You in Our Guilt (Ezra 9.6–15) 148

21. Let Your Ear Be Attentive (Neh 1.5–11). 156

22. Turn Back Their Taunt (Neh 4.4–5) 165

23 You Have Dealt Faithfully (Neh 9.6–37) 173

24. Now My Eye Sees You (Job 42.1–6) 183

25. My Eyes Have Seen Your Salvation (Luke 2.22–35). 190

26. Teach Us to Pray (Matt 6.5–15) 197

27. The Hour Has Come (John 17) 206

28. Not My Will but Yours Be Done (Matt 26.36–46) 215

29. Grant Your Servants Boldness (Acts 4.23–31) 222

30. Increase and Abound in Love (1 Thes 3.9–13) 229

31. The Lord Glorified in You (2 Thes 1.11–12) 238

32. Know the Hope, Riches, and Power of God (Eph 1.15–23) . . . 245

33. Exceedingly Abundantly Beyond (Eph 3.14–21) 252

34. Pure and Blameless for the Day of Christ (Phil 1.9–11) 261

35. Knowledge to Walk Worthy (Col 1.9–14) 268

36. Conclusions 276

Appendix A: Praying to Jesus 282

Appendix B: Use of the Lord's Prayer 288

Appendix C: Some Important Prayer Passages 292

Bibliography 305

Preface

Most Bible classes on prayer I am familiar with study various prayer principles from verses mentioning different things about prayer. Several years ago, when I suggested our congregation study prayer, I envisioned something different: a class studying the prayers that occur in the Bible rather than another Philosophy of Prayer class. I tried to convince someone there to teach a class on Biblical prayers, but found no takers. A few years later, when I helped organize the adult Bible class curriculum, I put that class on the schedule—and no one signed up. Eventually, I said, "Fine, I'll do it myself," and did.

Honestly, I didn't know what to expect as I began preparing for it. I didn't know what prayers I would use, how many there would be, or what sorts of points I might be able to make from them. Surely, I had read them all many times before, but I had never studied them in any depth nor tried to use them as exemplars. Eventually I settled on 20 or so prayers and, despite not knowing what to expect, the class went well. Later, I had the opportunity to teach a Selected Topics class at Florida College, where I am a part of the Biblical Studies faculty, and returned to the material, adding more prayers and adjusting it for a collegiate audience. It was again received well and I have taught it a couple of times in that setting since. Eleven years later, I upped the count to 35 prayers, added new resources to my own reading list, and taught it again at church, which was the impetus for converting outlines to manuscript.

Reflecting on my time with this material, two things stand out: first, the lessons are simple, self-evident, and highly repetitive; second, the material impacts students deeply. The former is rooted in the fact that so many people in the Bible pray in the same way. Even though they pray in drastically different contexts and have quite different aims in their prayers, they keep coming back to the same themes. This, incidentally, may also be the grounding of the latter: the profundity of the simple; the constancy of the method; the sameness in the prayers despite the difference of the needs. There is, indeed, something impactful about seeing it again and again, regardless of the situation. Prayer seems to be a mystery to so many Christians; "I wish I had a better prayer life," countless people say or think daily. But in this study, the mysterious becomes obvious. Prayer, it turns out, is not that complex. It is the overwhelming positive reception I have received from these classes that has driven me to write this book.

A book of this type inevitably has limitations, and I want to acknowledge them at the outset. It cannot be exhaustive, either in its study of Biblical prayers or its study of the prayers included herein. First, many prayers in the Bible are not covered.[1] I have selected 35 in an attempt to have a broad representation of Old and New Testament prayers from various time periods. Even though a few are quite brief, the prayers I have selected are longer than some that are not included. Second, selecting 35 also means that those prayers cannot be discussed in every detail. Even limiting myself as much as possible and making the book a slightly larger size has produced a book eclipsing 300 pages. Third, there is simply no room for technical or academic studies on matters that arise. I have included footnotes throughout to direct an interested reader to more resources for further study on those matters. Fourth, you will notice that this book lacks a discussion of any of the Psalms. There was simply no way to select only three or four psalms for inclusion. Even a study of a representative psalm from each "category" (lament, praise, thanksgiving, etc.) would have made this book unwieldy. In the end, a study of the Psalms as prayer is its own book—which is not a promise that I will ever write such a volume. Finally, the applications made throughout are not exhaustive. They are intended to be conversation starters and individually thought provoking and should lead you to think beyond

---

[1] In the Old Testament alone, Greenberg, *Biblical Prose Prayer*, 59–60n3 lists 97 prayers in which the wording of the prayer appears and another 43 that mention prayer without the wording.

what I have suggested. I am quite certain the 35 prayers this book discusses contain theological depth to be mined far beyond what these pages contain.

I should also note the methodology I use throughout. Generally speaking, I avoid formulaic teaching or writing. Trying to cram all sorts of different material into the same canned blueprint seems like a poor approach. Preachers and teachers who always use the same schtick either cannot preach on certain things or wind up with bizarre lessons where their content does not match their formula. Commentary series that require a certain formulaic methodology can be uneven even within the same volume. I am a firm believer that content should determine delivery, not a predetermined formula. That said, this book is formulaic. I don't know if that makes me a hypocrite or just someone who can see that things I generally don't like can sometimes be necessary. Further, not only is it formulaic, but it is *alliteratively* formulaic at that! So much for avoiding schtick. In this case, however, I have found that the formula—context, contents, connections—is helpful in managing the different amounts of material in the different prayers. It will lead to some unevenness, as different prayers are different lengths or have simpler or more complex contexts, but, in general, I believe that it works well for this particular study—and I hope that you will agree.

I also want to say a word about the name of God. As most Bible students are aware, the name of God in the Old Testament is not usually transliterated in English versions, and there is no consistency when it is. For that matter, we cannot even be certain of just how it would be spelled or pronounced in English, since Biblical Hebrew is entirely consonantal, and God's name went unspoken for so long. The modern scholarly consensus is "Yahweh," but that is a best guess. The Hebrew Scriptures simply have the consonants (YHWH/YHVH),[2] but a Jewish tradition was to substitute the word "Lord" when reading the text. This tradition has found its way into most English translations, which translate God's name as

---

[2] Alternate Hebrew alphabets and pronunciations designate the letter ו as either *vav* or *waw*, which explains the W/V change. The J/Y change behind "Jehovah" has to do with how modern languages deal with the י, which in English is *yod*, or a consonantal Y sound. A J/Y switch in one direction or the other is common in different modern languages.

"LORD" in small caps to indicate it is God's name, rather than the normal word for "master" or "sir."

A common lament among modern Christians is that God's name has fallen out of use. He gave us His name so that we might know it, so the reasoning goes, and our failure to know and use it speaks to something deficient about our religion—or at least it betrays a failure to have a personal relationship with a God whose personal name we do not know or use. While it is hard to argue with the logic—and a book on prayer might seem like the perfect place to go to the mat for this very cause—I have not taken up this issue and quote the ESV as it is translated throughout, rather than replacing "LORD" with any of the versions of God's name. My reasoning is quite simple: although substituting "Lord" was well established in the first century, Jesus never sought to correct the Jews of His day on the issue; although Paul regularly quoted the LXX in his epistles, he never changed its "Lord" to reflect the personal name of God. If Jesus did not make this a battleground issue in His teaching, I do not know why I should; if "Lord" is good enough for Paul when quoting a translation, it's good enough for me. Where I do use the name of God in discussion, I default to the contemporary standard "Yahweh."

Finally, I wish to offer my sincere gratitude to those who have been a part of this work coming to fruition. My classes at Florida College and the 58th Street church in Tampa sat through early versions of the material, giving me a chance to study it, teach it, continue to think about it more deeply, and hone it further. Evan Blackmore assisted with proofreading of the whole manuscript in a later stage, which helped trim my writing and clarify further my points, and offered valuable alternate perspectives on some of my points along the way. Jerold Redding provided an eleventh-hour check of every Scripture citation, catching more errors that I would prefer to admit were present. The shortcomings of this book, which will surely be many, are all my own doing.

The first proofreaders of almost all my writings have been and will continue to be my parents, Keith and Dene Ward. Their knowledge of Scripture, grasp of good writing, and willingness to look at a draft that probably should have been self-edited another three times before they received it make them the perfect first stop. It is to them, the ones who taught me about God and talking to Him in prayer, that I dedicate this book.

Now I offer you this fruit of my labor with the prayer that its simple, repetitive messages will be as impactful to you as it has been to so many others.

Nathan Ward
January, 2023

Abbreviations

Commentaries, Journals, and Reference Works

AOTC	Apollos Old Testament Commentaries
AYB	The Anchor Yale Bible
BCBC	Believers Church Bible Commentary
BCOT	Baker Commentary on the Old Testament Wisdom and Psalms
BDAG	*A Greek-English Lexicon of the New Testament and Other Early Christian Literature*
BDB	*A Hebrew and English Lexicon of the Old Testament*
BECNT	Baker Exegetical Commentary on the New Testament
BLS	Bible and Literature Series
BS	*Bibliotheca Sacra*
BST	The Bible Speaks Today
BTCB	Brazos Theological Commentary on the Bible
CAD	*The Assyrian Dictionary of the Oriental Institute of Chicago*
CBQ	*The Catholic Bible Quarterly*
CC	Concordia Commentary
cf.	*confer* (compare)
ch	chapter
chs	chapters
DCH	*The Dictionary of Classical Hebrew*
DSB	The Daily Study Bible
EBC	The Expositor's Bible Commentary

EC	Epworth Commentaries
e.g.	*exempli gratia* (for example)
et al.	*et alia* (and others)
etc.	*et cetera* (and the rest)
HALOT	*The Hebrew and Aramaic Lexicon of the Old Testament*
Ibid.	*ibidem* (in the same place; the same source previously cited)
i.e.	*id est* (that is)
INT	Interpretation: A Bible Commentary for Teaching and Preaching
IVPNTC	The IVP New Testament Commentary Series
JETS	*The Journal of the Evangelical Theological Society*
JSNT	*Journal for the Study of the New Testament*
NAC	The New American Commentary
NCB	New Century Bible Commentary
NCBC	New Cambridge Bible Commentary
NCCS	New Covenant Commentary Series
NIB	*The New Interpreter's Bible*
NIBC	New International Biblical Commentary
NICNT	New International Commentary on the New Testament
NICOT	New International Commentary on the Old Testament
NIDOTTE	*New International Dictionary of Old Testament Theology and Exegesis*
NIGTC	The New International Greek Testament Commentary
NIVAC	The NIV Application Commentary
NSBT	New Studies in Biblical Theology
OTBT	Studies in Old Testament Biblical Theology
PNTC	The Pillar New Testament Commentary
PTW	Preaching the Word

REBC	The Expositor's Bible Commentary, revised edition
REC	Reformed Expository Commentary
SOGBC	The Story of God Bible Commentary
TB	*Tyndale Bulletin*
THNTC	The Two Horizons New Testament Commentary
THOTC	The Two Horizons Old Testament Commentary
TNTC	Tyndale New Testament Commentaries
TOTC	Tyndale Old Testament Commentaries
TTCS	Teach the Text Commentary Series
TWOT	*Theological Wordbook of the Old Testament*
UBC	Understanding the Bible Commentary Series
v	verse
viz.	*videlicet* (namely)
vv	verses
WBC	Word Biblical Commentary
WTJ	*Westminster Theological Journal*
ZECNT	Zondervan Exegetical Commentary on the New Testament
ZECOT	Zondervan Exegetical Commentary on the Old Testament

Bible Translations

CSB	Christian Standard Bible
ESV	English Standard Version
KJV	King James Version
LXX	Septuagint
NASB	New American Standard Bible
NET	New English Translation
NIV	New International Version
NJB	New Jerusalem Bible

NKJV	New King James Version
NRSV	New Revised Standard Version
REB	Revised English Bible
RSV	Revised Standard Version

Bible Books

Gen	Genesis
Exod	Exodus
Lev	Leviticus
Num	Numbers
Deut	Deuteronomy
Josh	Joshua
Jdg	Judges
1 Sam	1 Samuel
2 Sam	2 Samuel
1 Kgs	1 Kings
2 Kgs	2 Kings
1 Chron	1 Chronicles
2 Chron	2 Chronicles
Neh	Nehemiah
Ps	Psalm
Pss	Psalms
Prov	Proverbs
Ecc	Ecclesiastes
Isa	Isaiah
Jer	Jeremiah
Ezek	Ezekiel
Dan	Daniel
Hos	Hosea
Jon	Jonah
Mic	Micah
Nah	Nahum
Hab	Habakkuk

Hag	Haggai
Zech	Zechariah
Mal	Malachi
Matt	Matthew
Rom	Romans
1 Cor	1 Corinthians
2 Cor	2 Corinthians
Gal	Galatians
Eph	Ephesians
Phil	Philippians
Col	Colossians
1 Thes	1 Thessalonians
2 Thes	2 Thessalonians
1 Tim	1 Timothy
2 Tim	2 Timothy
Phlm	Philemon
Heb	Hebrews
Jas	James
1 Pet	1 Peter
2 Pet	2 Peter
Rev	Revelation

ONE

Far Be It from You!

Genesis 18.22–33

The God to whom we pray is a God who desires relationship. He created us for relationship, as is evident in Genesis 2, which depicts creation in the context of relationship.[1] In prayer we find proof that God seeks communion with His creation. As human relationships teach us, deeper relationships include deeper communication, including difficult conversations, brutal honesty, and a willingness to let the other see us at our worst. Although twenty-first century Western Christians do not frequently think of prayer in this way, it is abundantly evident in the Hebrew Scriptures, beginning with Abraham who dares to ask God a difficult question and boldly asks God to change His plans.

At first glance, this conversation might not strike the casual reader as a prayer. No formal prayer language is used and the scene is dialogue. It does, however, meet the basic definition of prayer (speaking to God[2]) and contains one of the most frequent forms of prayer (intercession).

---

[1] Relationship with flora (2.5–9), relationship with God (2.10–17), relationship with fauna (2.18–20), relationship with humankind (2.21–25).

[2] Though this scene does not meet the more precise definition used by Millar, *Calling on the Name of the Lord,* 19n1 including that God is "not immediately present." (I take Millar to mean *visibly* present, not to be denying God's omnipresence). By contrast, Miller, *They Cried to the Lord,* 267 says, "its character as intercession is unmistakable."

Context

The background of this prayer features three individuals: Abraham,[3] Lot, and God. Abraham has been called by God away from his homeland to inherit the great promises God has made for him. His "out of the blue" call is met with equally unexpected obedience. Though he has shown a tendency toward self-preservation (e.g., traveling to Egypt in the famine and concealing his marriage with Sarah) and self-will (attempting to fulfill God's promise by surrogate mother and suggesting to God that Ishmael would be an acceptable heir), he has largely shown himself to be a man of faith and obedience.

Lot, also unexpectedly, travels with Abraham. Since Abraham's chief servant is his heir after the departure of Lot and before the birth of Ishmael (Gen 15.2), it may be that the orphaned Lot (Gen 11.27–28) travels with the childless Abraham as an adopted heir.[4] Lot, however, chose to depart to the east and dwell among the cities of the Jordan Valley (Gen 13.10–13), first pitching his tent toward Sodom (Gen 13.12), being carried off with the Sodomites as a prisoner of war (Gen 14.12), and ultimately taking up residence in a house in Sodom (Gen 19.3).

God is the one character in all Genesis whose word can be trusted. Nearly everyone else is misleading, obfuscating, or outright lying at some point or other. This is particularly noteworthy, since God is the one who makes the most outrageous statements of anyone. And yet His statements are invariably true. On this occasion, God has come to Abraham's home along with two angels.[5] Their visit has two purposes: first, to relay the message of Sarah's impending pregnancy to her; second, to investigate the situation in Sodom. Although God does not need to investigate to acquire information, this action shows God's justice: He will not execute judgment on a capital case without the testimony of

---

[3] For simplicity, I will use "Abraham" and "Sarah" throughout, rather than reverting to the early forms of their name when referring to earlier texts.

[4] See Nathan Ward, *The Growth of the Seed*, 152–153 for more on this issue.

[5] Genesis 18.1 indicates that it was the LORD who appeared to Abraham. Add to this that the traveling party were three men (18.2), two of whom continued to Sodom (18.22; 19.1) while the LORD remained behind to talk to Abraham (18.17, 33).

two witnesses (cf. Num 35.30; Deut 17.6; 19.15). Finally, God's brief soliloquy indicates His desire for this conversation. He opens the door for Abraham's response by revealing His plans because of the covenant He established with Abraham.[6]

After the angels leave for Sodom to investigate, God remains behind to talk to Abraham. He tells Abraham that He intends to see if the inhabitants' actions match the accusation. Abraham knows at once what this must mean: judgment will soon follow. Because of the closeness of their relationship, Abraham boldly intercedes:

> So the men turned from there and went toward Sodom, but Abraham still stood before the LORD. Then Abraham drew near and said, "Will you indeed sweep away the righteous with the wicked? Suppose there are fifty righteous within the city. Will you then sweep away the place and not spare it for the fifty righteous who are in it? Far be it from you to do such a thing, to put the righteous to death with the wicked, so that the righteous fare as the wicked! Far be that from you! Shall not the Judge of all the earth do what is just?" And the LORD said, "If I find at Sodom fifty righteous in the city, I will spare the whole place for their sake."
>
> Abraham answered and said, "Behold, I have undertaken to speak to the Lord, I who am but dust and ashes. Suppose five of the fifty righteous are lacking. Will you destroy the whole city for lack of five?" And he said, "I will not *destroy* it if I find forty-five there." Again he spoke to him and said, "Suppose forty are found there." He answered, "For the sake of forty I will not do it." Then he said, "Oh let not the Lord be angry, and I will speak. Suppose thirty are found there." He answered, "I will not do it, if I find thirty there." He said, "Behold, I have undertaken to speak to the Lord. Suppose twenty are found there." He answered, "For the sake of twenty I will not destroy it." Then he said, "Oh let not the Lord be angry, and I will speak again but this once. Suppose ten are found there." He answered, "For the sake of ten I will not destroy it." And the LORD went his way, when he had finished speaking to Abraham, and Abraham returned to his place. (Gen 19.22–33)

---

[6] See MacKenzie, "The Divine Soliloquies in Genesis," 285. In addition to the covenant element, Duguid, *Living in the Gap Between Promise and Reality*, 89 points out that God frequently announces His plans in advance to His prophets.

Contents

Although God has not said anything explicit about the certainty of judgment, Abraham's knowledge of God and of the cities leads him to that inescapable conclusion. That same knowledge means his intercession cannot be rooted in their innocence or an appeal for God to simply ignore their transgression. Instead, he bases his appeal on God's justice and mercy. This does not necessarily mean Abraham thought God would do unjustly, although the implication may well be that if God destroys the righteous with the wicked He is (in Abraham's view) unjust.[7] Instead, Abraham argues that the fate of the city be determined by the righteous, not the wicked.[8]

And so begins one of the most famous scenes in the Bible: a man bargaining with God over how many righteous people it would take for Him to spare the city. Beginning at 50, Abraham moves down to 45, then to 40, to 30, to 20, and finally to 10. At each instance, God agrees not to destroy the city if He finds that many righteous people in it. The appeal Abraham makes is fluid, not simply appealing that their fate be determined by the righteous, but picking a number—and then changing it, and changing it again, and again, all the way down from 50 righteous to 10. This entire process raises at least three questions.

First, what motivated Abraham to bargain with God? Although some have suggested that this merely reflects the customary bargaining practices of the Near East, such a view must be rejected. Abraham will show that he is not beholden to such customs (Gen 23.10–16), and such a reading fails to understand the heart of intercession that Abraham exhibits in this scene. Perhaps Abraham was concerned God would do unjustly or he supposed himself to be more compassionate than God, but these views seem to stretch credulity as well.[9] (And even if Abraham did so suppose, neither was the case.) Likewise, the thought that Abraham was

---

[7] Camp, "Prayer in the Pentateuch," 28. Widmer, *Standing in the Breach*, 41 says, "Abraham seems to imply that there is greater injustice in the death of the innocent than in the life of the wicked."

[8] Roop, *Genesis*, 130. The idea that a life well lived can be a mode of rescue for others appears in other places in the Bible as well. In Jeremiah 5, it is as unsuccessful as it is here. On the cross, however, one righteous life does provide salvation. See Brueggemann, *Great Prayers*, 5.

[9] See Kaiser, *I Will Lift My Eyes unto the Hills*, 12.

only concerned with Lot cannot be sustained, as we will see in a moment. Instead, as Kidner says, "Abraham's spirit of love and justice derived from God as surely as it strove with him."[10] In other words, Abraham was made in God's image and as a righteous man he would seek to do the very things God would do. He thus sees the need for justice clearly but wants to show as much mercy as possible.

Second, how could God let Himself be so moved? Some readings of this conversation see God as, if you will forgive the analogy, little more than a bad used car salesman who cannot withstand a good haggler. This is also a poor reading of the text. God's position regarding Sodom is not being influenced by Abraham; Abraham is learning the truth of just how bad things are as God's justice is being proved. The righteousness of God does not change from the beginning of the discussion to the end, and God is not upset or annoyed by Abraham's continued appeal for mercy in the face of judgment.

Finally, why did Abraham stop at 10? This sort of reasoning could have continued until the number was down to one. Although the text does not give an answer to this question, some potential answers arise. Perhaps Abraham knew that a lower number reduced his plea from an intercession for the people to a request only for Lot and his family. Perhaps Abraham knew of the flood where eight were not enough to save the world. Perhaps he was sufficiently attuned to God's righteousness to know that anything fewer than 10 is no longer an act of mercy to those few righteous who remain. As it turns out, there was only one righteous person in the city (cf. 2 Pet 2.7), and even he tries to make a foolish, wicked bargain with the people, has to be dragged out of town, and begs God to go where He had expressly told him not to go. Again, God's position is not being changed; His justice is being confirmed as Abraham learns just how bad things in Sodom actually are.[11]

---

[10] Kidner, *Genesis*, 132.

[11] Miller, *They Cried to the Lord*, 269 suggests there is no literal meaning to stopping at ten (as if ten were good enough but nine would not be), but that the conversation as a whole "indicates that God will go as far as God can in behalf of the innocent even if that means pardon ... of the wicked."

Connections

Openness with God in prayer. Abraham's intercessory prayer for Sodom shows the modern reader what is sometimes called the free address of faith. Abraham takes daring initiative in making such an appeal and in humble boldness speaks his mind to God. He raises the question of God's justice and urges God to reconsider His plans. In all of this, God is not displeased with Abraham. God expects and desires His followers to be open and honest with Him in their prayer, for this is the very nature of relationship. In this instance, God takes the initiative of sharing His plans with Abraham (v 17), which opens the door for Abraham responding similarly: taking the initiative in sharing his reaction to God's plans. We should never feel that there are areas of our life that are off limits to God. As Chester says so simply and succinctly, "Friends share their thoughts with one another."[12] After all, He knows those matters anyway, so attempting to hide them in prayer—the very moment that we should be bringing them to the throne of God—is the height of folly.

Humility in prayer. As mentioned above, the boldness Abraham shows is a *humble* boldness. As his request progresses, Abraham refers to himself as dust and ashes (v 27), twice asks God not to be angry (vv 30, 32), and acknowledges the audacity of the appeal he makes (v 31). His humility before God does not prevent him from making the request, for God wants such openness in prayer; however, God's desire for bold prayer does not make Abraham entitled and arrogant in his approach. It is, indeed, "a profound mix of audacity and humility in his stance before God."[13] Such a balance should be constantly kept in mind when we approach the throne of God in prayer.

The character of God. Notice that the basis of Abraham's prayer is not what he thinks is best, but the character of God. His appeal to God is based on God's justice and God's mercy, not his own personal preferences. He trusts God to do what is right, so his appeal is not for his personal desire (that Lot be saved), but God's character (that God would show

---

[12] Chester, *The Message of Prayer*, 91.
[13] Miller, *They Cried to the Lord*, 268.

Himself to be just). As we will continue to see throughout this book, the character and promises of God are the grounds upon which most of the Bible's great prayers find their footing. No surer foundation to build upon exists than that which is unchanging.

Intercessory prayer. As already said, Abraham prays an intercessory prayer. God specially chose Abraham to be the one through whom all nations of the earth would be blessed and called him to be a blessing to those with whom he came into contact (Gen 12.3).[14] Here, he seeks to fulfill the latter and foreshadows, to some degree, that which his Offspring would do in a far greater way. Although we have not received the same promises as Abraham, we have been given great promises and a great commission—we too are to be a blessing to others and the means by which salvation will come to even the ends of the earth.

Some Christians so emphasize individual responsibility before God that they tend to shy away from intercessory prayers (except in matters like physical sickness or other, often trivial, physical concerns). Abraham's prayer—and others we will see as well—highlight the value of prayer directed away from self and toward others, including prayer for the wicked. If God takes no pleasure in the death of the wicked (Ezek 18.23; 33.11) and desires for all people to be saved (1 Tim 2.4), we should surely follow suit. To that end, what better place to express that desire than before the throne of God? And since we know we will be praying for the very things God Himself desires, we know we will be standing on sure footing in our prayer.

---

[14] Widmer, *Standing in the Breach*, 28.

Abraham's Servant

TWO

You Have Shown Steadfast Love

Genesis 24.12–14

The God to whom we pray is a God who makes great promises to the people with whom He is in relationship. Unlike the recipients of His promises, He is dependable and can be counted on to do what He said He will do, as He has shown time and again through the course of human history.

Context

Abraham's intercession for Sodom may technically qualify as a prayer, but it is certainly not the sort of prayer we are familiar with: one-way communication to God, making an appeal to Him and not receiving a verbal response. The first Biblical prayer of this sort is found on the lips of a minor character, an unnamed servant of Abraham,[1] who seeks guidance to complete an important task on behalf of his master.

Isaac has reached adulthood, and Abraham turns his focus to securing a wife for him, perhaps considering the promises God made concerning his offspring, which requires Isaac to have offspring as well. To do this, he will send his most trusted servant back to the homeland to find a wife for Isaac. Abraham is insistent that Isaac not leave the Promised Land to find a wife, perhaps learning from his own missteps (cf. 12.11–20), but he

---

[1] This servant may be Eliezar (cf. 15.1–2), but this is nearly 60 years after that scene and Eliezar may no longer be alive. (For the timeframe, see Genesis 16.16; 21.5; 25.20.)

also does not want Isaac to marry a wife from Canaan. This concern does not come from a desire that Isaac marry a worshipper of God,[2] because the family back in Mesopotamia did not worship God. Laban and Rachel will each prove to be idolatrous (31.19) as will the servants Jacob accumulates when he lives there (35.1–2). Most significantly, perhaps, Abraham's father Terah is explicitly said to have been an idolater (Josh 24.2). It is no wonder when God calls Abraham it is a call to get away from his country, kindred, and father's house (12.1).

If the homeland was as pagan as the new land, Abraham's concern must have been about something else. Although the text never clarifies his motives, a reasonable guess is his knowledge of the future of the Canaanites—namely that they would be removed by his own descendants when the time was right (15.13–16). To intermarry with the people they were to dispossess would indeed be problematic. In short, Abraham wanted Isaac to have a wife from the blessed Semites, not the cursed Canaanites.[3]

Whatever the case, Abraham's demand leads the servant to a reasonable question: "What if she won't come back with me? Should I take Isaac then?" Abraham's response is an unequivocal "no" (24.6–8), a point made clear by him introducing and concluding his response with "do not take my son back there." Between these prohibitions, Abraham's response is, in essence, God will provide—even as he had earlier told Isaac (22.8, 14)—and if He doesn't, you are free from your oath. This not only answers the question, but provides the servant with direction. Since God will be the source of his success, he will turn his focus to God to secure success. Upon arrival at Nahor, he goes to the well when the women went to draw water, seeking to complete his task, and prays,

> And he said, "O LORD, God of my master Abraham, please grant me success today and show steadfast love to my master Abraham. Behold, I am standing by the spring of water, and the daughters of the men of

---

[2] E.g., Leupold, *Exposition of Genesis*, 660 says that Abraham's "chief concern was to find a wife for Isaac who with him knew and believed in Yahweh and so would share with her husband a common faith and so allow for the deepest of all harmonies in the home, spiritual harmony."

[3] Waltke, *Genesis*, 327. Cf. Genesis 9.25.

the city are coming out to draw water. Let the young woman to whom I shall say, 'Please let down your jar that I may drink,' and who shall say, 'Drink, and I will water your camels'—let her be the one whom you have appointed for your servant Isaac. By this I shall know that you have shown steadfast love to my master." (Gen 24.12–14)

Contents

Abraham's servant's prayer is remarkable in a variety of ways. First, it is an entirely selfless prayer. Although he seeks success in his mission, it is not on his own behalf that he seeks it. The prayer is that God would bless him *on account of Abraham.* Even his suggestion about how he would know the right girl should not be seen as him prescribing to God what he thinks ought to happen, but expressing an earnest desire that it would please God to so bless Abraham (cf. v 27).

Second, it reflects a knowledge of God, which is more significant than it may seem at first blush. After all, when Jacob later returns to Canaan with his servants acquired in the home land, they do not know God. Abraham, however, has clearly taught his household about the God he follows. Not only does this servant pray—itself an indication that he knows God—he is confident God can act immediately and decisively and will do so because God has a special relationship with his master. He believes God can know who the right girl is, shape her behavior to conform to his request, and do so immediately ("today"). The servant models the kind of trust that should characterize all of God's people (cf. Prov 3.5–6).

Third, it shows knowledge of the covenant. It is one thing to know Abraham follows a particular God. This servant, however, is aware of the depth of the relationship God and Abraham share. He knows the promises God has made to Abraham, and why his own mission to find a wife for Isaac is so important in that context. He further shows this in his use of a term that frequently appears in the context of covenant relationships,[4]

---

[4] See, e.g., Mathews, *Genesis*, 332; Waltke, *Genesis*, 328; Block, *For the Glory of God*, 199. Throughout this book, I will try to capture as much of this word's potential meaning as possible by referring to it as God's "steadfast, merciful, covenant love and faithfulness." See TWOT, 305–307 for an argument that a covenant concept is not inherently denoted in its use.

translated "steadfast love" in the ESV quoted above. This is, then, an allusion to God's promises to Abraham; the servant asks that God would fulfill His stated will through the servant. The servant's prayer is focused on the fulfillment of God's covenant promises: "the God who gave Abraham this son of promise is now called upon to provide a wife for him, thereby ensuring that the covenant family continues."[5] His concluding prayer (vv 26–27) will reflect the same focus.

As to the specific request that the correct girl would be signified by her watering his camels, this would have indeed marked her out as unique. He traveled with ten camels (v 10), and each could drink as much as 25 gallons of water.[6] Not every girl would make such an offer and the one who did so would certainly show "kindness, hospitality, industry, and willingness to help a stranger."[7] Even so, his request is not for a miraculous sign, but "supernatural guidance in the way it so often comes, through the ordinary events of life."[8] When Rebekah arrives, she throws herself into a flurry of activity (vv 18–20), echoing Abraham's own earlier hospitality (18.2–8).

Finally, upon learning that the girl he met was of Abraham's extended family (cf. v 4), the servant understands his prayer has been answered and he returns to prayer yet again, showing faith that God had indeed answered, and gratitude for His covenant faithfulness to Abraham:

> The man bowed his head and worshiped the LORD and said, "Blessed be the LORD, the God of my master Abraham, who has not forsaken his steadfast love and his faithfulness toward my master. As for me, the LORD has led me in the way to the house of my master's kinsmen." (24.26–27)

Kidner summarizes this servant very well, saying,

> This chief steward is one of the most attractive minor characters in the Bible, with his good sense, his piety (vv 26f, 52) and faith, his devotion

---

[5] Millar, *Calling on the Name of the Lord*, 31–32.
[6] Walton, *Genesis*, 530.
[7] Waltke, *Genesis*, 328.
[8] Duguid, *Living the Gap Between Promise and Reality*, 152.

to his employer (vv 12b, 14b, 27) and his firmness in seeing the matter through (vv 33, 56). If he is the Eliezer of 15.2–3, his loyalty is all the finer in serving the heir who has displaced him, almost as John the Baptist to his master (cf. John 3.29–30).[9]

Connections

Covenant focus. Perhaps the most important thing about this prayer is how covenant-centered it is. It is thoroughly rooted in God's promises to Abraham, and everything in it is tied back to that fundamental starting point. The covenant is his driving concern and the motivation for his request: he wants what God has promised to come to pass. He does not come to God on the basis of what he wants, but on the basis of what God has said He will do.

That the servant is so aware of the relationship between God and Abraham is not to say that he does not have his own relationship with God. His opening, "O LORD, God of my master Abraham" is not intended to put distance between himself and God as if He is not also the servant's God, but to lean on the promises that were made to Abraham, because the prayer is about Abraham and the covenant. Instead, it seems that this man is a believer in and worshipper of God; God is his God, as well as being Abraham's God.

Faith that God acts. Abraham's servant knows he needs God's help, so he seeks God's help, receives God's help, and acknowledges it when he receives it—not just in giving thanks at the end, but in believing that God has responded to his prayer. Many Christians today tend toward an almost deistic understanding of God, reacting so strongly to those who claim God's intervention in their lives that they no longer seem to believe God does anything at all. Some do not even recognize and give thanks when God does the very thing they have been asking Him to do. Although the Bible never teaches that God is a cosmic micromanager of every detail in our lives, Christians should believe that God can and will respond to prayer, and we should have the circumspection to realize when He does.

---

[9] Kidner, *Genesis*, 146.

Finding God's will. Is the servant's prayer a model on how to determine the correct course of action? Should we seek to determine God's will in a similar way: asking God to show us a sign? Walton says, "As much as we might like to get direct and clear guidance on specific issues, we dare not come to this passage looking for a formula by which we can extract information from God, any more than we would come to it for a procedure on how to find a wife."[10] This is a nice turn of phrase, but is his assertion correct?

There are only two other cases of this sort of thing happening in the Bible:[11] Gideon's fleece (Jdg 6.36–40) and the Philistines' return of the Ark (1 Sam 6.1–9). Although God is willing on these occasions to use their methodology to accomplish His purpose—and might continue to do so on other occasions—it is safe to say that neither Gideon nor the Philistines are exemplars of character.[12] Abraham's servant seems to be more spiritually astute than either of them, but the precise depth of his knowledge of God cannot be known. Further, that he is seeking God's will where there is no Scripture or prophet to help him may well be relevant. As Walton says, "[M]echanistic oracles belonged to a particular time period when God's written revelation had barely begun. It is an antiquated and primitive approach and has been replaced by something that is far superior, God's written word."[13]

In addition to the dubious faith-status of the Old Testament characters to seek God's will by asking for a sign, there is no example of asking for signs in this way in the New Testament.[14] In addition to their obsolescence

---

[10] Walton, *Genesis*, 535. For a thorough discussion of this topic, see Waltke, *Finding the Will of God*.

[11] The casting of lots may be an exception. Lot casting, however, is frequently commanded by God (e.g., Lev 16.8–10; Num 26.55–56; Josh 7.14) and the Bible affirms God's control over this seemingly random act (Prov 16.33).

[12] Although Gideon is mentioned in Hebrews 11, that list speaks only to what they accomplished through faith, not an endorsement of everything done by the individual. Gideon was raised in a pagan household (Jdg 6.25) and led the people back into paganism by the end of his time, in a scene reminiscent of the golden calf incident (Jdg 8.22–28).

[13] Walton, *Genesis*, 536.

[14] Waltke, *Genesis*, 333.

due to the presence of God's written word,[15] Walton points out the flawed theology of this method:

> In the process of asking oracles, the inquirer assumes a position of control; deity is being summoned to be at his or her beck and call in ways far beyond normal prayer. An oracle requests (demands?) specific information in a specific way at a specific time. ... Anytime that we put ourselves in the position of trying to force God's hand by making him act in certain ways, according to our dictates, we are exercising an inclination that seeks to control God. ... In a nutshell, the problem with these oracular mechanisms is that they make demands on God. Unlike the bold prayers of the psalmists who call on God to be God, these are manipulative devices because they seek to oblige him to respond according to *our* specifications. ... The fact that sometimes oracles have worked is no excuse. That God does sometimes condescend and accommodate to our weaknesses and ignorance is a demonstration of his grace, not a license to repeat our presumptuous behavior.[16]

Finally, God never instructs His people to seek information or direction in this way, nor has He given any assurance that He will regularly respond to such inquiries. If anything, such mechanistic methods for determining God's will minimizes Him to, say, the toss of a coin. God is far greater and His providence is far more sovereign than how a coin lands. Rather than seeking *the* answer to our question, Christians would be far better seeking guidance in prayer and trusting that God will provide that guidance, whether or not we ever see overt evidence of it.

---

[15] See Ibid., 59–85.
[16] Walton, *Genesis*, 536–537. Emphasis in original.

THREE

Please Deliver Me

Genesis 32.9–12

The God to whom we pray is a God who can be trusted to keep covenant. If God has made promises, we can be certain that those things will happen, regardless of how outlandish they may seem or what seemingly insurmountable obstacles stand in the way. In the case of Jacob's prayer, the promise may seem less outlandish than God's promise to his century-old grandfather several decades earlier, but the obstacle—a murder-bent Esau and his 400-man militia—would surely prevent Jacob from becoming a great nation.

Context

Jacob's prayer for deliverance is situated in two contexts: first, the life of Jacob; second, the relationship between Jacob and Esau.

Jacob has frequently sought to go about things his own way. Before he was born, God had promised to bless him above his brother (Gen 25.23), yet when Rebekah learns of Isaac's plans to secretly bless Esau instead, Jacob goes along with Rebekah's plan to steal it through deception (Gen 27). When he enters a contract with Laban about which sheep will be counted as whose, he attempts to genetically engineer the results to his own benefit (Gen 30.37–43).[1] When he departs from Laban, he does so

---

[1] The practice here described, though odd to us, was apparently believed to be successful in the ancient world.

surreptitiously, calling his wives into the field for a secret meeting (Gen 31.4–16) and departing while Laban was a three days' journey away (Gen 30.36; 31.22), shearing his sheep (Gen 31.19). The text's declaration that he tricked Laban (Gen 31.20) implies deceit.[2] Perhaps Jacob believed an open, honest departure to be impossible, but since God had instructed him to leave (Gen 31.11–13), Jacob should have trusted God to provide a way to accomplish this without the need to lie. As a result of this, Laban hotly pursued Jacob (Gen 31.22–24). Indeed, Jacob has been on the run since his deceit of Isaac. Back in Palestine, Jacob had deceived Isaac and fled from Esau; now, in Haran, he deceives Laban and flees from him. In sum, his entire journey in Paddan Aram is marked by deceit and flight.[3]

The second important context is Jacob's relationship with Esau. Jacob takes advantage of Esau's hunger and impulsiveness and bargains away the birthright for a bowl of stew (Gen 25.29–34). Unlike the birthright, however, Esau cared deeply about receiving the blessing.[4] Although it was promised to Jacob, Isaac seeks to bless Esau secretly. Rebekah, however, seeks to deceive Isaac and Jacob participates in the lie to receive the blessing. Esau, upon returning, learns that Jacob has received the blessing and begs for one of his own. Isaac, finally humbled to allow God's purposes to stand, blesses Esau with a far more negative prophecy than he cared to hear, and Esau determines to kill Jacob as soon as Isaac has died. Rebekah

---

[2] Literally, "stole the heart of." As the ancients saw the heart as the seat of understanding rather than emotion, to steal one's understanding is an idiom for deception.

[3] Though certainly flawed and still in need of much growth, Jacob's faith is more complex than some expositors seem to suggest. Esau is consistently blamed for the theft of the birthright, both in the Old and New Testaments. In context, the narrator tells us the story in a way to exhibit Esau despising his birthright, not Jacob stealing it (Gen 25.34), and the author of Hebrews points to it as a prime example of the faithlessness that Christians should avoid (Heb 12.16). As to the theft of the blessing, there was no theft involved, as the blessing was already his, earmarked to him by God (Gen 25.23). He was morally culpable in *how* he secured it, but not *that* he secured what was his. Finally, in spite of his attempted genetic engineering, he ultimately acknowledges it was God who had changed the flocks (Gen 31.5–9), and his return to Palestine is in response to God's call (Gen 31.11–13). See Balentine, *Prayer in the Hebrew Bible*, 64–71 for a reading of this prayer that sees it as an attempt "to control his own destiny through a shrewd combination of cunning and piety" (64).

[4] I see the birthright and blessing as distinct: the former being the double portion of the physical inheritance and the latter (in the context of Abraham's family) being the messianic line. This is most clear in the case of Jacob's sons, where Joseph receives the birthright and Judah the blessing (cf. Gen 49.8–12; 1 Chron 5.1–2).

learns of Esau's intent and plans to send Jacob to safety with Laban, telling Jacob that she would let him know when Esau's fury had abated and shrewdly allowing Isaac to think that Jacob's journey is his own idea.

Now, twenty years later, Rebekah has still not called for him, but his departure from Haran has been problematic. If fleeing with his wives without their father's knowledge was burning all the bridges behind him to the ground, then the angry upbraiding he gives Laban may well have come across as spitting on the ashes. He can have no certainty that Esau will not kill him on sight, but he has nowhere else to go. He sends word ahead to Esau begging for his favor (Gen 32.3–5) and only receives word back that Esau is coming to meet him with four hundred soldiers in tow (Gen 32.6).[5]

Although Rebekah had not called Jacob back, God had. And the God who Jacob learned could protect him against Laban's scheming, he must now also trust to protect him from Esau's anger.

> And Jacob said, "O God of my father Abraham and God of my father Isaac, O LORD who said to me, 'Return to your country and to your kindred, that I may do you good,' I am not worthy of the least of all the deeds of steadfast love and all the faithfulness that you have shown to your servant, for with only my staff I crossed this Jordan, and now I have become two camps. Please deliver me from the hand of my brother, from the hand of Esau, for I fear him, that he may come and attack me, the mothers with the children. But you said, 'I will surely do you good, and make your offspring as the sand of the sea, which cannot be numbered for multitude.'" (Gen 32.9–12)

Contents

This prayer breaks down into a basic A-B-B-A pattern:

    A   Appeal to covenant (v 9)
        B   Humility and dependence (v 10)
        B'   Humble petition (v 11)
    A'   Appeal to covenant (v 12)

---

[5] Although no special word indicating "soldier" is used here, Waltke, *Genesis*, 442 says it is the standard number for a militia.

The first and last elements are clearly connected. In both there are quotations from God: His command to return to Palestine and His promise as Jacob departed. Further, the reference to Abraham and Isaac at the outset of the prayer parallels the promise of a great nation that Jacob receives at the end. Although not strictly part of the *A* element, the reference to steadfast love and faithfulness (v 10) is worth noting here as well, as they are covenant terminology and show just how thoroughly the idea of covenant permeates this prayer. The "faithfulness" Jacob speaks of is a reference to God protecting and providing for Jacob as He had promised he would. "Steadfast love" is from a Hebrew word that has many different English translations among the versions, as there is no good single English word that encompasses all that it means. When used of God it frequently carries with it the implication of covenant loyalty as well as the translations' mercy, loving-kindness, and the like.[6] Even as he acknowledges his dependence upon God, Jacob appeals to God's keeping of His covenant.

This humility before God and dependence upon Him is also parallel to the request Jacob will make to God. Jacob knows he cannot deliver himself just as he knows he has not accomplished the growth in wealth and numbers that have happened while he was sojourning in Paddan Aram. Since God "is known as one who responds to the plight of the small, the weak, the insignificant in the world,"[7] Jacob—the one who is "not worthy of the least of all the deeds of steadfast love and all the faithfulness that you have shown to your servant"—can count on being heard in his distress. So he pleads with the God who granted him this growth to deliver him and his wives and children from Esau.

Connections

There is much to commend about this prayer as a model for us to follow. Its confidence rests securely on the foundation of God's covenant. It shows a true spirit of worship in wonder at God's mercy. Even in the face

---

[6] See page 10, note 4 for a further discussion of this word.
[7] Miller, *They Cried to the Lord*, 116.

of great danger, Jacob's petition is withheld until he has properly positioned himself before God as an undeserving supplicant.

Covenant foundation in prayer. Consider again that Jacob's prayers are rooted in promise and covenant. Far too frequently "your will be done" enters our prayers as a quasi-apology for what we just asked for—something along the lines of, "This is what I want, but not really (unless you're okay with it, in which case I do want it)." Although we should certainly submit our wills to God's, there are times where we can pray confidently for God's will *because He has already told us what His will is.* As we have already said (and will continue to say), God's promises are not given so that we can know what to take for granted, but so we can know where to take our stand in prayer. As Duguid says, this is always the best approach to prayer in difficult circumstances: "You lay out all of your fears before the Lord, ask him to do what he has committed himself to do in his Word, and then press on in faith."[8]

Humility in prayer. God's promises, however, should not lead to an attitude of entitlement. The privilege of praying in confidence when praying in covenant does not give us a right to an entitled attitude; boldness must not become arrogance. Just because God has promised does not mean that we deserve what He is giving. Perhaps this is why Biblical prayer frequently shows abasement of self and praise of God before petition. Although there are not sufficient data to prescribe an order to our prayers, there certainly is wisdom in properly aligning self before bringing our requests to Him as it helps us fight against this temptation to entitlement.

Action after prayer. Finally, the blessing of prayer should not create inaction in the one who prays. Jacob is frequently seen as faithless in two regards in Genesis 32—first in acting before praying (v 7) and second in acting after praying (vv 13–21). As a Floridian, I tend to understand Jacob's action. Although we pray for safety as a hurricane approaches, we still take precautions against the storm—boarding windows, securing loose objects, and even evacuating if needed. There is a vast difference

---

[8] Duguid, *Living in the Grip of Relentless Grace*, 111.

between faithlessly helping oneself and using prudent judgment and acting with wisdom.

What about Jacob's action before prayer? First, this mistakenly equates temporal sequence with rank of importance. Although these two things are sometimes the same, they do not necessarily correspond. Second, there are certain situations that may pragmatically require action first and prayer second. If a known murderer were standing on your lawn, you might find yourself locking the door and calling the police before kneeling to pray.

Or, to be more Biblical, perhaps an executioner is at the door to kill you and your friends and you suppose that your gift from God can save all of you. Is it faithless to do what you can to stay the sword before pleading with God to reveal the King's dream? Those who indict Jacob for faithlessness in acting before prayer never seem to have a problem when Daniel does the same thing (Dan 2.13–18).

Again, such actions do not indicate faithlessness, but prudence. It is easy to call Jacob faithless from the security in which we stand. Yet if there were someone nearby who, last we knew, wanted to kill us, we would find ourselves acting in very much the same way. And this is okay, because proper faith and prayer do not produce inaction.

FOUR

Please Bless Me

Genesis 32.26–30

The God to whom we pray is a God who lets us fight with Him, but will ultimately defeat us for our own good. God is the one who can bless us or prevent us from achieving our aims, not human benefactors or opponents. And so it is God whom we must fear and with whom we must wrestle. Interestingly many early interpreters thought of this scene as an allegory for either a spiritual conflict (Philo, Clement of Alexandria) or long, earnest prayer (Jerome). Even without such an interpretation of the fight, the dialogue that follows fits the basic definition of prayer as a conversation with God.

Context

Because this follows closely on the heels of Jacob's prayer for deliverance from Esau, the context discussed in the previous chapter applies here as well. In particular, Jacob's self-sufficient streak plays a key role.

The immediate context of the prayer is the fight itself, which raises its own set of questions. First, with whom is Jacob fighting? The text simply identifies Jacob's opponent as "a man," but Jacob understands it to be God (v 30). Hosea's reference to it being an angel (Hos 12.4) should be interpreted in the context of it being coupled with "God" in parallelism. The Angel of the LORD is a recurring Old Testament character who bears God's name and authority, a *representation* of God rather than a *representative* of Him.[1] It seems that He attacked at night to conceal His identity (v 26).

Second, if this is some physical manifestation of God, how is Jacob able to contend with Him all night long? The answer to this must be that God allowed it to suit His purposes, which is ultimately the prayer with which the scene concludes. Surely Jacob could not have competitively fought with God unless God permitted it to happen.

Third, who won the fight? Although we do not want to become so focused on the fight that we miss the real point (the dialogue),[2] the text itself raises this question. On the one hand, the man did not prevail against Jacob (v 25) and Jacob has prevailed with God (v 28). On the other hand, Jacob, at best, fought to a draw, had *his* hip dislocated, and limped away. The answer to this final question is found in understanding the conversation that follows:

> Then he said, "Let me go, for the day has broken." But Jacob said, "I will not let you go unless you bless me." And he said to him, "What is your name?" And he said, "Jacob." Then he said, "Your name shall no longer be called Jacob, but Israel, for you have striven with God and with men, and have prevailed." Then Jacob asked him, "Please tell me your name." But he said, "Why is it that you ask my name?" And there he blessed him. So Jacob called the name of the place Peniel, saying, "For I have seen God face to face, and yet my life has been delivered." (Gen 32.26–30)

Contents

Jacob, having been injured and incapacitated from further fighting, refuses to let go. Even when urged to do so, he stubbornly clings to his assailant, demanding a blessing. Jacob now fights with words—with prayer—not with strength.[3] This also, however, shows the inferiority of Jacob. Not only is he the injured one, but he is the one who begs for a blessing (cf. Heb 7.7), and he gives up his name and has it changed.

---

[1] See Ward, *The Growth of the Seed*, 185–187 for a brief discussion of the Angel of the LORD.
[2] Ross, "Studies in the Life of Jacob, Part 2," 343.
[3] Waltke, *Genesis*, 446.

Despite this undeniable inferiority, God says that *Jacob* has prevailed (v 28). This is best explained by Jacob ceasing to fight against God, for God cannot prevail over the one who does not fight against Him. God will indeed prevail over the one who refuses to submit to His will, but as our will "learns ever more to perfectly submit to God's will, God can no longer 'prevail'" over us.[4] Jacob "wins" because he has finally realized his dependence upon God for blessing, rather than going about it his own way.[5] Even as Paul must learn to rely on God's strength in his own weakness (2 Cor 12.7–10), so also Jacob must stop relying on his own cunning and begin to rely on God.

This same idea stands behind Jacob's giving of his name and receipt of a new name. As Ross says,

> The object was to contrast the old name with the new. When one remembers the significance of names, the point becomes clear: a well-established nature, a fixed pattern of life must be turned back radically! In giving his name, Jacob had to reveal his nature. This name, at least for the narratives, designated its owner as a crafty overreacher. Here, the "heel-catcher" was caught and had to identify his true nature before he could be blessed.[6]

He had exited Canaan as Jacob, self-sufficient and crafty enough to make his own way. Through twenty long years, that person had slowly changed. Now, he must be completely done away with. Instead, Israel, the man who had striven with God and prevailed, is the one who must return to Canaan.

Shortly after the truth of his need to rely on God dawns on him, the morning does as well. The narrator's reference to the sunrise (v 31) is either a random time reference that shows up for no real reason or it has a deeper meaning. In addition to being the first such reference since Genesis 28.11 when the sun set as he departed the Promised Land (thus narratively characterizing his time away as a period of darkness), it represents

---

[4] Leupold, *Genesis*, 877.
[5] Curtis, "Structure, Style and Context," 135. Walton, *Genesis*, 606 also sees Jacob's clinging for a blessing as an indication of "Jacob's willingness to submit himself to God's demands on him."
[6] Ross, "Studies in the Life of Jacob, Part 2," 345.

a new day dawning for Jacob. This is Jacob's spiritual awakening; the long night of self-sufficiency and deceit has passed.

Finally, this scene serves as an answer to Jacob's previous prayer. Jacob's statement that his life has been delivered (v 30) uses the same word as in his petition to God to deliver him from Esau (32.11). God stands before Jacob and blesses him; God has delivered him from God's very own presence. Surely, if this is so, he will be delivered from Esau as well.[7]

Connections

Cling for a blessing. In Jacob we see the need to cling for a blessing. Even one who struggled so mightily against God to go his own way and do his own thing can be, in a moment, turned to rely on Him for a blessing. Such a change is not an easy thing and can only be found in humbling oneself, giving in, and confessing. Jacob fought only when he thought that he could win. With the crippling touch, he turns his efforts in a new direction and with the same persistence he clings to God for a blessing. Crippled in his natural strength, Jacob finally becomes bold in faith. As a result, he is given a new name—a new character—and finds a new life as this new day dawns.

The same can be true for any believer. We can sometimes think of the struggle of prayer only in terms of Jesus' parable of the persistent widow (Luke 18.1–8); if we pray enough, we'll eventually badger God into giving us what we want just to get us off His back. Aside from that hardly being the point of Jesus' story, it misses what is the bigger struggle of prayer: the battle with self. Much of the point of prayer is learning to conform our will to God's, learning to recognize who He is and who we are by comparison, and learning to trust that He will do what is best. This simply cannot happen until we stop fighting with Him and cling to Him for a blessing.

The Struggle of Faith. Any depiction of Christian life that doesn't deal with the reality of a struggle is peddling a false Christianity. In addition to struggling with trials and temptations, struggling with the circumstances

---

[7] Hamilton, *Genesis*, 337.

of life, and struggling to get out of our own way, all Christians at some point or other struggle with God. This should not be surprising, because the faithful through the ages have struggled with God, too. In addition to this scene (and the larger life of Jacob), Job struggles with God,[8] Jeremiah struggles with God, multiple psalmists struggle with God, Epaphras struggled in prayer (Col 4.12), and even Jesus "learned obedience through what he suffered" (Heb 5.8), as seen in Gethsemane where Jesus' struggle between His desire not to go to the cross and His desire to do God's will is clearly revealed.[9]

Although most Christians are quick to reject the Health and Wealth Gospel for the fraud it is, we are tempted to replace it with an equally false Happiness and Perfect Trust Gospel, where Christians pretend their lives are flowing smoothly in every way. We don't want to talk about our struggles, sins, and doubts, resulting in Christians who pretend their faith is perfect even as it daily teeters on the brink of collapse.[10] This prayer—like so much else in Scripture—reminds us that the faithful wrestle not only with life, but with God Himself.

---

[8] See Duguid, *Living in the Grip of Relentless Grace,* 114 for a paralleling of Jacob's experience with Job's.

[9] Chester, *The Message of Prayer,* 98.

[10] For a podcast discussion of the issue of doubt, see https://tinyurl.com/ward-doubt (accessed October 22, 2022).

FIVE

Please Pardon This People

Numbers 14.13–19

The God to whom we pray is a God who is true to Himself. I don't mean "true to Himself" in the modern sense of self-indulgence, but that God will always be who He is. There is no variance in God and His most core character traits and identity are unchanging. We see among these traits the paradoxical joining of perfect love and mercy and perfect judgment. Because God can be trusted to be who He is, Biblical prayer is often built upon that character.

In Genesis 19, we encountered Abraham's prayer of intercession for the city of Sodom. Here, we encounter Moses' intercessory prayer for Israel. It is striking that two of the most significant Old Testament figures offer prayers of intercession, and do so in different, important ways. Abraham, the one through whom all nations will be blessed and the father of the faithful—not merely the Israelite faithful, but all the faithful (cf. Rom 5.11–12, 16–17; Gal 3.28–29)—intercedes for a group of outsiders, who were not then a part of the community of God. Moses, the first great leader of the nation of Israel and the lawgiver, intercedes for the insiders, the very covenant community of God.

Context

This prayer has a variety of important contexts. First, Moses' early life seems to have been an exercise in learning how to be a middleman. In deciding to identify with his people rather than the Egyptians who raised him, Moses is soon caught in the middle when he sees an Egyptian beating a Hebrew (Exod 2.11–12). He then inserts himself into an argument between two Hebrews (Exod 2.13–14). After his flight to and return from Midian, God appoints Moses as the middleman between Himself and Pharaoh (Exod 3.10), a role that will dominate Moses' life until the Exodus. Finally, after escaping into the wilderness, Moses finds himself standing between God and the nation of Israel as they constantly complain about their circumstances, their leader, and their God.[1]

Moses will spend the remainder of his life in this final role. He himself is regularly at odds with Israel (e.g., Exod 14.11–13; 17.2–3). More significant, however, are the times the people are at odds with God—or, to be more precise, they create a situation where God is at odds with them. In these moments, Moses must stand in the breach and repair the damage. An earlier example of the same sort of intercession happens after the Golden Calf incident at Mount Sinai. The Golden Calf incident is sometimes likened to a wife cheating on her husband on the wedding night. Although this is a reasonable analogy both in terms of idolatry as adultery (a common biblical metaphor) and temporal significance, as the relationship has only begun, the truth may be even worse. Moses and God are away from the people because the covenant itself is being given.[2] It is not on the wedding night that Israel is cheating on her God, but *during the wedding ceremony!* It is no wonder that both God and Moses are furious about this. Even so, Moses pleads for the people:

> But Moses implored the Lord his God and said, "O Lord, why does your wrath burn hot against your people, whom you have brought out of the land of Egypt with great power and with a mighty hand? Why should the Egyptians say, 'With evil intent did he bring them out, to kill them in the mountains and to consume them from the face of the earth'? Turn from your burning anger and relent from this disaster against your

---

[1] Brueggemann, *Great Prayers*, 11–12.
[2] God being "away from the people" is said accommodatively. I am aware that God is not, technically speaking, away from them.

people. Remember Abraham, Isaac, and Israel, your servants, to whom you swore by your own self, and said to them, 'I will multiply your offspring as the stars of heaven, and all this land that I have promised I will give to your offspring, and they shall inherit it forever.'" ... So Moses returned to the Lord and said, "Alas, this people has sinned a great sin. They have made for themselves gods of gold. But now, if you will forgive their sin—but if not, please blot me out of your book that you have written." (Exod 32.11–13; 31–32)

Given the similarity of this prayer with the prayer in Numbers 14, we will not consider it separately, except to note Moses' concern for God's glory and God's covenant with Israel as he pleads for the people.[3]

A second context is Moses' appeal that God would reveal Himself to Moses, and God's response (Exod 33.12–23; 34.6–10). In short, Moses seeks to see God's glory, but cannot do so and survive the experience. Instead, God shows Moses the glory of His name and His character.[4] This truth—that He is a God who is slow to anger and abounding in steadfast, merciful, covenant love and faithfulness—becomes the refrain of the Old Testament (Exod 34.6; Num 14.18; Neh 9.17; Pss 86.15; 103.8; 145.8; Jer 15.15; Joel 2.13; Jon 4.2; Nah 1.3). Immediately after this self-revelation, Moses seeks God's pardon for the people and God renews the covenant with them.

Not too long after this, the people reach the entrance to the Promised Land and are, yet again, grumbling. They repudiate the leadership of Moses and refuse to go where God instructed them (Num 14.1–4), essentially rejecting all the promises God has made since first calling Abraham to go to Canaan.[5] God's response shows His intense frustration and the exhaustion of His patience: the double "how long" question and His

---

[3] See Widmer, *Standing in the Breach*, 82–94 for a discussion of Exodus 32–34 in the context of intercession and Block, *For the Glory of God*, 201 for a helpful chart comparing Moses' prayers.

[4] Carson, *Praying with Paul*, 151 paraphrases the ESV's "You shall see my back" (33.23) as Moses seeing "the trailing edge of [God's] glory."

[5] Olson, *Numbers*, 79. Olson goes on to point out that successive rebellion stories show a progression of rebellion from the fringe of the camp (11.1–3) to the people as a whole (11.4–35) to the leaders, Aaron and Miriam (12.1–16), culminating in this quintessential rebellion against God's intention for His people.

stated purpose of disinheriting Israel and replacing them with a new line from Moses surely indicate just how close to disaster they truly are.[6] In response, Moses prays:

> Then the Egyptians will hear of it, for you brought up this people in your might from among them, and they will tell the inhabitants of this land. They have heard that you, O Lord, are in the midst of this people. For you, O Lord, are seen face to face, and your cloud stands over them and you go before them, in a pillar of cloud by day and in a pillar of fire by night. Now if you kill this people as one man, then the nations who have heard your fame will say, "It is because the Lord was not able to bring this people into the land that he swore to give to them that he has killed them in the wilderness." And now, please let the power of the Lord be great as you have promised, saying, "The Lord is slow to anger and abounding in steadfast love, forgiving iniquity and transgression, but he will by no means clear the guilty, visiting the iniquity of the fathers on the children, to the third and the fourth generation." Please pardon the iniquity of this people, according to the greatness of your steadfast love, just as you have forgiven this people, from Egypt until now. (Num 14.13–19)

Contents

Moses' prayer of intercession speaks volumes about the concern a person of God should have in the face of divine judgment for sin. Although Moses is clearly worried about the fate of the people, his focus is entirely on God. Of course, such a focus must dominate, because no defense can be made for the sin itself;[7] forgiveness can only come from God.

God's Glory. Moses is jealous for the reputation of God.[8] If God does this, Egypt will hear of it and misconstrue it as failure on God's part—and tell others the same. Moreover, others who have heard of God will

---

[6] Brueggemann, *Great Prayers*, 15. The greater theological questions of what such action would mean regarding God's earlier promises, God's foreknowledge, and the like are far beyond the scope of this present book. For a discussion that shows the range of perspectives on these issues, see Dennis Jowers (ed.), *Four Views on Divine Providence* or Bielby and Boyd (eds.), *Divine Foreknowledge: Four Views*.

[7] Widmer, *Standing in the Breach*, 96.

[8] Kaiser, *I Will Lift My Eyes Unto the Hills*, 27.

think the same: this God of Israel is unable to do what He has promised![9] Surely, they could not be expected to understand that God deals in covenants that demand responsiveness. In their minds, this God operates as all gods did: strictly in terms of power; God has failed, so He must have no power.[10]

Notice in all of this, Moses' concern is for God's reputation among non-Israelites. Moses presumes they are watching and waiting to see whether God can fulfill His promise of deliverance or if His power would fail.[11] His concern is that God be glorified not only among His own people, but among the nations (cf. Isa 42.6; 45.23; 49.6). Further, notice Moses' concern is for God's glory, not his own. Faced with an opportunity to become the head of his own new nation, a nation greater and more glorious than these rebellious Israelites have ever been or could be (v 12), Moses' only thought is of what such a scenario would do to God's glory.

God's Character. Moses appeals to the greatness of God's power (v 17)—not to His great destructive power to wipe Israel off the earth, but His great positive power: His ability to forgive (cf. Isa 55.6–9). This power is inherent to His character, as revealed to Moses at Sinai: Moses takes his stand on God's own self-revelation. His character manifests itself in His promises and covenant, which itself rests solely on God's characteristic patience and mercy. In short, Moses summons God to His own self-resolve—it is an appeal to God's grace based solely on God's claim to be gracious. This is the only place Moses can stand, because there is nowhere else to stand: Israel deserves nothing but God's wrath; we see no repentance or confession of the people on which to base his plea. So Moses' plea that God pardon them does not have even the slightest implication that they deserve pardon or that God is even remotely obligated to forgive. Instead, it is God's steadfast, merciful, covenant love and faithfulness—His

---

[9] As Cole, *Numbers*, 231n152 indicates, the concern that others would know of God's dealing with His people is not merely hypothetical. See Numbers 21.1; 22.2–6; Joshua 2.8–14; 9.1–15.

[10] Brueggemann, *Great Prayers*, 16.

[11] Ibid.

core identity as He revealed Himself—that binds Him to Israel in spite of her constant sinfulness.[12]

God's Grace. Although it is beyond the text of the prayer, God's response to Moses (vv 20–23) is important to consider briefly. He indicates that He will forgive and Caleb will survive as a model of obedience for the next generation. God's glory, however, requires justice and their pardon does not exempt them from all punishment.[13] Thus, while the people will not be destroyed and disinherited, they will not enter into the Promised Land. In short, the people receive the death in the wilderness they asked for (14.2), while simultaneously receiving far more than they deserved: forgiveness and a second chance with a new generation.[14]

Connections

Moses' prayer of intercession is a remarkable moment both in the history of Israel and in the history of prayer. He successfully pleads on behalf of the people that they would not be destroyed, in spite of God's stated plan to do just that, taking a bold stand against God's stated will in the matter. In light of this prayer, there are a variety of important lessons to consider.[15]

The believer's love for community. The ambiguity of "community" here potentially opens the door for wider application than just that which we see in Moses' prayer. Our own communities can be as small as our immediate family or as large as the human race, though we might primarily think in terms of our congregation, our local community, and our nation. When the group, whichever group it might be, is sinful, it brings a confrontation with God. We should love our community enough to want to do something about it.

The believer as intercessor. The believer should stand in, and repair, the breach. As stated in chapter 1, the prominence of intercessory prayer in the

---

[12] Ibid., 17–19; Balentine, *Prayer in the Hebrew Bible*, 134. Duguid, *Numbers*, 174 rightly notes that Moses "does not falsify the Scriptural record by only quoting the first half of God's self-description," but that he appeals both to God's mercy and His justice.

[13] Wenham, *Numbers*, 122.

[14] Olson, *Numbers*, 85.

[15] As much of the rest of this chapter is, so these applications draw heavily from Brueggemann, *Great Prayers*, 21–22.

Bible should encourage us to pray likewise. Although none of us has the role Moses did in Israel—and it is certain that Jesus fills the role of intercessor in a way that none of us can—God has not given us so many examples of intercession for us to write it off as something not applicable to us. Instead, the Bible indicates that God hears and is impacted by such prayer.[16]

Asking against God's will. The believer should be willing to ask God for something that is not His will. This, of course, needs to be delicately unpacked. The point is not that we should constantly seek to undermine God's will or stand against Him. But in this case, Moses took a step in the opposite direction from that which God had told him. God's stated will was to destroy the people; Moses pleaded that He would not do so, taking bold initiative founded on his faith that prayer is effective.

A real relationship with God. Moses was able to do this because he had a well-established relationship with God. He was no stranger with a bizarre, new idea being presented before the Almighty. His prayer is rooted in a well-established relationship with God that included his constantly being a mediator between God and the people.

God's character and covenant. As said before (and will be said again), prayer of this sort is built firmly on the foundation of God's character (Num 14.17–19) and covenant (Exod 32.13). Moses' prayer is not based on a spur-of-the-moment thought or a fleeting emotional need. Moses appeals to God's revealed character, which is itself expressed in a renewal of His covenant with Israel. He goes so far as to quote God to Himself! Moses' success, then, is not due to his skill as an intercessor or negotiator, but to God's own character and commitments.[17]

Prayer rooted in God's glory. Moses' foremost concern is not for Israel's need and certainly not for his own esteem, but for God's glory among unbelievers. As we saw with Abraham, it is not because the intercessor

---

[16] The exact nature of how an eternal, sovereign God can listen and respond to the prayers of finite, temporal humans is a mystery that has been debated for centuries. But as Duguid, *Numbers*, 173 says, "[T]he reality and effectiveness of intercession on behalf of others is a constant Biblical theme, albeit one we are far more likely to confess with our mouths than act on consistently." See Widmer, *Standing in the Breach*, 99–101 for a helpful discussion of the relationship between the Old Testament passages about God changing His mind and His disclosure of His name (Exod 34.6–7).

[17] Millar, *Calling on the Name of the Lord*, 40.

thinks he is more compassionate than God that he prays, but because of his deep concern for his fellow man and God's reputation. He calls for the vindication of God's power and purpose.[18] In this case, Moses understands that God has called him to lead this stiff-necked people and prepared him to be just such an intercessor.[19] Such a focus on God's glory and such a realization of one's role requires deep reflection. As Brueggemann says, "[P]rayer requires us to be knowingly and intentionally *theological*, because it is to *God* that we pray."[20] In the end, praying for God's glory will "dramatically reshape what we pray for and the way we pray for ourselves and those around us."[21]

As the rest of Numbers will show, the need to mediate does not end here. The people will continue to rebel and continue to be punished. Although God will not again threaten to wipe them all out, Moses must continue to stand in the breach and seek to repair it. This, perhaps, is the greatest difference between him and Christ. Jesus' intercession is far greater, as He always lives to make intercession (Heb 7.25) and His blood is continually available to cleanse from sin (1 John 1.7–9). As we read through the wilderness journey, we cannot help but wonder whether Moses' intercession will be successful *this* time—has God's patience finally worn out? But the New Testament affirmation is that such a question should never darken the minds of Christians: Jesus can always intercede successfully.

---

[18] Miller, *They Cried to the Lord*, 272.
[19] Kaiser, *Unto the Hills*, 26.
[20] Brueggemann, *Great Prayers*, 22, emphasis in original.
[21] Duguid, *Numbers*, 174.

SIX

I've Poured Out My Soul

1 Samuel 1.10–11; 2.1–10

The God to whom we pray is a God who delivers the needy, because He is a God of reversals. Throughout the Bible, God gives children to the barren, delivers the weak, enriches the poor, raises the dead, humbles the proud, and exalts the humble. He brings everything into existence out of nothing, producing order where there was once chaos (Gen 1). He takes a people who want to make a great name for themselves and scatters them and then finds a nobody and promises to make a great name for him (Gen 11–12). He chooses a nation that is small and wicked (Deut 7.7; 9.4–5) and makes them the most significant nation in the history of humanity. Throughout all of this, He repeatedly delivers through great reversal.

Context

The period of the Judges ends with multiple references to there being no king in Israel. It serves as a framework around the entire final section of the book (Jdg 17.6; 21.25), with reminders of this fact as opening lines to two specific accounts (Jdg 18.1; 19.1). With this refrain, Judges asserts the lack of a king led to this period of gross immorality.[1] Further, kingship had been promised as far back as Abraham (Gen 17.6; cf. 35.11; 49.10) and legislated in the covenant with the conquest generation of Israelites (Deut 17.14–20).

---

[1] This is not to suggest that they fared much better when there was a king or that the people's choice of a king based on the standards they thought best was a good one.

In this context—the desperate need for a king—the book of Samuel begins.[2] Elkanah, a man who cannot control his own family (1 Sam 1.6–7), was clearly not the man for the job. Nor was the priest Eli, who failed to control his sons (3.11–13) and had so little spiritual discernment he could not tell the difference between prayer and drunkenness (1.12–13).

The prayers of Hannah occur in the midst of this setting, surrounded by these two men. She is one of two wives of Elkanah—a barren wife who is provoked by her rival about this matter (1.1–9). Hannah's barrenness is the first sign to the reader that she will be significant, as she joins Sarah, Rebekah, and Rachel as a significant biblical woman with this problem. Indeed, barren women are repeatedly instruments to raise up key figures in Redemption History, which is perhaps another way God shows us that His plan works neither through coincidence nor achievement, but according to His initiative and work.[3]

Hannah did not have the benefit of this larger perspective and because of her inability to have children and her rival's provocation, she wept, would not eat, and was deeply distressed. It is important to note here that barrenness was not merely an unfortunate reality of the ancient world, but was virtually the dehumanizing of a woman. For an ancient woman, having a child was not merely a nice feature of life, but it was the singular, definitive purpose of her life. Hannah's plight of barrenness was "in a world where blessing is rooted in posterity and a woman's place in the eyes of the world is determined by her ability to bear children and especially sons" and her suffering in such a state was "not at all unequal" to the suffering of the psalmists "of isolation and being cut off from the community, of being shamed before others, of enemies who taunt and insult the one who prays in pain."[4] Say what we will about how insensitive Elkanah sounds as he tries to comfort her (1.8), the fact he tries at all and loves her in spite of her barrenness shows he loves her far more deeply than his society might expect.

---

[2] In the Hebrew Scriptures, Ruth is not interposed between Judges and Samuel.
[3] Kaiser, *I Will Lift My Eyes unto the Hills*, 36.
[4] Miller, *They Cried to the Lord*, 237.

Hannah, however, is not comforted by Elkanah's words and takes her concern to God:

> She was deeply distressed and prayed to the LORD and wept bitterly. And she vowed a vow and said, "O LORD of hosts, if you will indeed look on the affliction of your servant and remember me and not forget your servant, but will give to your servant a son, then I will give him to the LORD all the days of his life, and no razor shall touch his head." (1 Sam 1.10–11)

Following this prayer she leaves satisfied—her face no longer sad and eating once again (1.18). God hears her prayer, she conceives, and gives birth to Samuel. After he is weaned, she fulfills her vow, returning Samuel to the LORD who gave him (1.19–28), praying yet again:

> My heart exults in the LORD;
>   my horn is exalted in the LORD.
> My mouth derides my enemies,
>   because I rejoice in your salvation.
> There is none holy like the LORD:
>   for there is none besides you;
>   there is no rock like our God.
> Talk no more so very proudly,
>   let not arrogance come from your mouth;
> for the LORD is a God of knowledge,
>   and by him actions are weighed.
> The bows of the mighty are broken,
>   but the feeble bind on strength.
> Those who were full have hired themselves out for bread,
>   but those who were hungry have ceased to hunger.
> The barren has borne seven,
>   but she who has many children is forlorn.
> The LORD kills and brings to life;
>   he brings down to Sheol and raises up.
> The LORD makes poor and makes rich;
>   he brings low and he exalts.

He raises up the poor from the dust;
    he lifts the needy from the ash heap
to make them sit with princes
    and inherit a seat of honor.
For the pillars of the earth are the LORD's,
    and on them he has set the world.
He will guard the feet of his faithful ones,
    but the wicked shall be cut off in darkness,
    for not by might shall a man prevail.
The adversaries of the LORD shall be broken to pieces;
    against them he will thunder in heaven.
The LORD will judge the ends of the earth;
    he will give strength to his king
    and exalt the horn of his anointed. (1 Sam 2.1–10)

Contents

Hannah's first prayer is brief and to the point. This does not seem to be just a rehearsal of detail or practiced ritual phrases; instead, she prays out of her distress, pouring her heart out before God. She begs God to *remember* her, a word that, when used of God, connotes not mere recollection, but action toward a covenant partner (cf. Gen 8.1; 30.22; Exod 2.24; Pss 25.6–7; 74.2; 105.8; 106.4; etc.) and promises she will return any child she is given to God for service to Him. Her humility is evident; in a prayer of just one sentence, she refers to herself as "your servant" three times.[5] Hannah understands that God's concern for His people is not merely national but personal, not restricted to military exploits but knowledge and care for her—and to that end, she knew any son she had would be an answer to her prayer.[6]

The second prayer is much longer and follows a poetic form and logical progression. It is frequently called "Hannah's Song" and there is debate as to whether she composed it herself or whether she took ownership of an existing psalm, much as, in a moment of suffering, a Christian today

---

[5] Willis, "Prayer in the Deuteronomistic History," 47.
[6] Baldwin, *1 and 2 Samuel*, 17.

might make "Abide with Me" his or her own prayer. In either case, this is not spontaneous, but a carefully crafted psalm of thanksgiving.[7]

The prayer begins with thanksgiving for deliverance (vv 1–3), before speaking of God as the one *who* delivers and *how* He delivers (vv 4–8), and concluding with a note of the continued deliverance God will bring in the future (vv 9–10).

God gives power and protection (vv 1–2, 10),[8] and is the one who can correct the injustices of life. Those who are rich, full, and powerful—those rivals who provoke the righteous by gloating in their temporal success—fail to realize they stand before an all-knowing judge (vv 2–3). At the heart of the prayer is a series of seven contrasts, focused on God reversing the fortune of the desolate. The weak He makes strong, the hungry He fills, and the barren He makes fertile (v 5). He brings life where there is death and health where there is sickness (v 6). And the impoverished are made rich, because, in all cases, God exalts the humble (v 7).[9] They are indeed helpless in the world now, but they will not remain so for long, because God sees. However long it may seem for God to rectify things, it is but a drop in the bucket of eternity, and the world cannot stay as it is now, because it is not the world God intended. What the world accepts as the status quo will not stand, because God sees, knows, and wills otherwise. And He will act to bring life, make rich, and raise up.

The prayer concludes with the statement that God will continue to guard the faithful and destroy His enemies (vv 9–10), and this will be done through His king, His anointed one. The statement at the end of verse 9 is the explicit stating of the theme that runs through the entire prayer: man does not prevail by his own might, but by the Lord's presence.[10] But God's presence occurs in different ways at different times. Sometimes God di-

---

[7] Miller, *They Cried to the Lord*, 184–198 compares this, Hezekiah's praise (Isa 38.10–20), and Jonah's prayer (Jon 2.2–9; see ch 13) to psalms of thanksgiving in some detail.

[8] The horn referred to is an animal's horn and source of strength (note that it appears at the beginning and end of this prayer), the usual use of this metaphor in the Bible. Chisholm, *1 & 2 Samuel*, 11 suggests the reference to God being a rock refers to an inaccessible rocky cliff, providing protection from enemies, thereby depicting God as a place of refuge and safety.

[9] Kaiser, *I Will Lift My Eyes unto the Hills*, 41.

[10] Firth, *1 & 2 Samuel*, 61.

rectly intervenes and sometimes He acts through human agency. In this moment, Hannah speaks of a coming king who will carry out His justice. Samuel, it turns out, will not be the long-anticipated king either. He will, however, be the king-maker.

Just as the book of Samuel is introduced with the concern about a king, so it concludes with that same concern.[11] The Song of Hannah that introduces the book of Samuel is balanced by the song of David that concludes it (2 Sam 22). Each speak of the metaphoric horn of strength, each refers to God as a rock, but most significantly, each refers to God's king and anointed one.[12] In the end, then, the climactic moment of these prayers is not the birth of Samuel, but the promise of a coming anointed king.[13] Even as Hannah celebrates her own blessing, she keeps in mind that God and His promises extend beyond just her.

Finally, this second prayer is thoroughly inundated with biblical language. Millar says that it "breathes in the world of Deuteronomy 32 and Psalm 2," and adds in a footnote that "practically every second line of Hannah's prayer is echoed somewhere in the Psalms," adding several references to Job as well.[14] As Chester says,

> Hannah has a developed doctrine of God. She can draw on biblical language and biblical truths to express her praise. The more we know of God, the more our hearts are tuned to praise him. The route to true heart-felt praise is not evocative music or emotional atmospheres but the truth of God's character and ways.[15]

Connections

Much as Hannah's second prayer contains a series of contrasts, so also the applications of Hannah's prayer can be seen in this light.

---

[11] Samuel, Kings, and Chronicles were not intended to be two separate books (as the New Testament 1 and 2 books are), but were single books too long for a single scroll and were divided onto two for pragmatic reasons.

[12] Many authors make these connections. Among those I consulted were Chester, *The Message of Prayer*, 131–135 and Kaiser, *I Will Lift My Eyes unto the Hills*, 39–40.

[13] Millar, *Calling on the Name of the Lord*, 54.

[14] Ibid. Cf. Firth, *1 & 2 Samuel*, 59–63, who also makes several connections.

[15] Chester, *The Message of Prayer*, 127.

God hears everyone. Hannah's prayer shows God will listen to anyone. A barren woman would be near the bottom of the social ladder in ancient Israel. And yet, Hannah's prayer exhibits theological depth of understanding. She knows God hears her—a barren woman with no relationship to the priesthood—and so she calls on the God of the covenant by His covenant name to deliver on His covenant promises.[16] And He hears and responds. Sometimes Christians read Hebrews 9.7 to indicate that our access to God *in prayer* is somehow greater now than in the Old Testament. Whatever it might mean, it cannot be this, because the Old Testament itself constantly shows us faithful people of all social strata who have full access to God in prayer.

Prayer appropriate to the occasion. Hannah's two prayers differ greatly in their form. Although great thought has been given to Hannah's first prayer—i.e., it's not merely an extemporaneous burst of words—it is what she says in the moment of emotional turmoil. Her second prayer, however, is in a poetic form that resembles psalms that would have required even more thought and effort to craft. Both ways of praying are appropriate. There are religious traditions that miss on both ends: some are so beholden to religious formula, prayer books, and liturgy, that spontaneous prayer is frowned upon; others are so against all things liturgical that a written-down prayer is seen as somehow substandard. Hannah, however, is one among many who shows us both methods of prayer.[17]

Submissive yet bold. Hannah is submissive to God, yet challenging of His apparent will. There is clear humility in her voice in chapter 1, and acknowledgement of being one who had desperately needed His ability to lift her in chapter 2, but she does not accept the status quo of her barrenness—something the text makes plain is God's doing (1.5–6). In spite of her ongoing barrenness, "she does not turn her back on a God who would seem to have turned His back on her," instead trusting and making "the

---

[16] Millar, *Calling on the Name of the Lord*, 54. See also Peskett, "Prayer in the Old Testament," 22.

[17] See Greenberg, *Biblical Prose Prayer*, 38–57 for more on spontaneity vs. prescription in prayer. To be precise, given her place on the lower end of the social ladder and ancient literacy rates in general, it is unlikely that Hannah herself ever wrote down this prayer.

response of faith, which is to pray."[18] She implores God to change the state of affairs that He had arranged. While prayer remains a means by which we submit our will to God, it seems there are times God's will is for us to challenge what *appears to be* His will. Perhaps prayer that is merely submissive resignation is an obstacle to deepening our spiritual lives, and a too-quick acquiescence to "thy will be done" may be feebleness or sloth, rather than the wrestling and triumph it ought to be.[19]

The immediate impact of prayer. Hannah's prayers show what prayer should do for the believer: the move from despondent to content, from lowly to exalted. From vexation to face no longer sad and from fasting to eating—and ultimately to her song of exuberant joy and celebration—Hannah serves as a model of the impact prayer should have. It is noteworthy that Hannah's contentment comes before she conceives, even if her celebration does not. Her prayer alone brings her peace and resituates her life. As to the celebration, we have even greater promises and revelation than she did. In this light, Chester is correct:

> We may not enjoy the comfort she received in this life but her redemption is a picture of what is to come for all who trust in God. If we only sing of our happiness on earth we shall not have the resources to cope in times of anguish. Sometimes congregational praise can have an element of unreality about it—we sing as if all is good when many in the congregation are hurting. However, we *can* sing with joy not by denying the pain of the present but surmounting it through the gospel with the songs of heaven. We do not deny reality, but we can counter it with the promise of a new reality.[20]

The value of all kinds of praying. Although not quite as contrasting as the other points are, notice that Hannah's prayers feature both petition and thanksgiving. It is easy to say from a position of comfort that petitionary prayers are of a lower class than prayers of praise or thanksgiving.

---

[18] Chester, *The Message of Payer*, 122.
[19] Forsyth, cited in Chester, *The Message of Prayer*, 122.
[20] Chester, *The Message of Prayer*, 130. Emphasis in original.

Such a position, of course, is not merely one of comfort but of biblical illiteracy, for the Bible never frowns on such prayer and constantly gives us examples of God's people expressing such petition. For Hannah, her prayers are laser-focused. She prays not for everything—or even for a broad sampling of things. She prays for a son when her concern is having a son. She prays in exaltation of God when her concern is to exalt God. Every prayer need not say everything, and situational praying of what is foremost on our minds is the constant pattern of biblical prayer.

Intentional imprecision. Hannah's second prayer is particularly remarkable because of how general it might seem to be. Rather than a specific song of thanksgiving for the specific blessing of her specific son, she speaks in generalities of God as one who acts in a particular way. She "sees what has happened to her against a bigger canvas,"[21] understanding that God has not just done this thing for her, but this is how He characteristically acts. The importance of this cannot be overstated, because, "we, too, are part of the same story."[22] We, too, look to the same God who acts in the same way and who still rules in justice through His anointed one.

Selflessness in prayer. Notice also how this reflects a selflessness in her prayer, as it later will in Mary's prayer which seems to be modeled on this one. As Wordsworth says,

> Sacred Poetry ... is not egotistical. ... It looks forward from the special occasion which prompts the utterance of thanksgiving, and extends and expands itself, with a loving power and holy energy, into a large and sympathetic outburst of praise to God for His love to all mankind in Christ. Like a pebble cast into a clear and calm lake, it sends forth concentric rings of waves, ever enlarging toward the margin.[23]

Unlike the Pharisee who thanks God for what was done for *him* (Luke 18.11–12), Hannah and Mary give thanks without seeming to

---

[21] Ibid., 129.
[22] Ibid., 137.
[23] Wordsworth, *The Books of Samuel*, 3.

think of themselves at all. Their eyes are too busy looking toward the most distant imaginable horizons, in time as well as space, to pay any significant attention to self.[24]

---

[24] Thanks to Evan Blackmore for this final point, including the Wordsworth quote and the precise wording of the final sentence.

SEVEN

Who Am I?

2 Samuel 7.18–29; 1 Chronicles 17.16–27

The God to whom we pray is a God who makes great promises. Even more, the promises He makes are invariably fulfilled. Unlike most other Biblical characters, who tend to be untrustworthy to varying degrees at some point in their lives, God can be trusted to do what He says, even when His promises seem outlandish. Whether telling a nobody that his name will be great, telling an 89-year-old woman that she will conceive, or telling people that death can be reversed, God can be taken at his word. In this case, God chose a forgotten-about shepherd, made him king over His own people, and promised him an eternal dynasty.

Context

The next several chapters will consider a variety of prayers through the history of monarchical Israel. An important context to each of these is the time in which Samuel-Kings and Chronicles were written. Samuel-Kings is frequently thought of as a single history of Israel, written by the same author or around the same general time. Chronicles is by a different author, written later.[1] One clue to this time distinction is that the end of Kings mentions the fall and exile of Judah, but not the return (2 Kgs 25), while Chronicles continues through the return from captivity (2 Chron

---

[1] See Dillard and Longman, *An Introduction to the Old Testament*, 136–140, 152–156, 170–172 for further discussion.

36.22–23). Although precise information about the time of composition and circumstances of the original audiences cannot be known, it seems Samuel-Kings is exilic and Chronicles is post-exilic. The same accounts would surely have different points of emphasis and teach different lessons to these different groups in their own historical contexts.

As mentioned in the previous chapter, kingship in Israel was no surprise to God. He had spoken of this very thing since His covenant with Abraham and his descendants, including legislation about kingship in Deuteronomy. Further, the failures at the end of Judges were connected to there being no king, and Hannah foresees a king on the horizon (1 Sam 2.10). The people, however, chose a king to be like the other nations, according to external, physical standards (1 Sam 8–9). Saul's kingship had a few successes, but was largely a failure, as is evidenced by his repeated refusal to listen to God and God's removing the kingship from his family line (1 Sam 13.13–14; 15.17–29).[2]

In Saul's place, God sought a man after His own heart (1 Sam 13.14) who would be better than Saul (1 Sam 15.28) and found that person in David, a youth who even his family had no regard for (1 Sam 16.6–12; 17.12–30). God's standards, however, are not human standards and David was chosen. Throughout much of 1 Samuel, the conflict between Saul and David escalates, but it is clear that David will come out on top, for God has taken the kingship from Saul and given it to David—a matter even Abigail recognizes (1 Sam 25.28). Even though Saul still occupies the throne and Abner and Ishbosheth will yet stand in the way (2 Sam 3–4), God is working behind the scenes to ensure David's rise to the throne.[3]

Throughout all of this and into his early years as king, David continues to pursue God's ways and ultimately decides he will build a house for God. It was not right, he thought, that he should be living in a fine

---

[2] A further indication of Saul's failings is his repetition of many of the weaker moments of the judges, whether his fear of going into battle (1 Sam 17.10–11; Jdg 4.8; 6.11), his foolish vow that endangered the life of his son (1 Sam 14.24–46; Jdg 11.29–40), a variety of subtle echoes of the Levite and his concubine, or the similarity of his and Abimelech's deaths (1 Sam 31.3–5; Jdg 9.50–55).

[3] Brueggemann, *Great Prayers*, 36.

palace while God dwelt in a tent.[4] He informs the prophet Nathan of his plan to build a house for God, which Nathan initially commends, before receiving a different message from God: No, David will not build a house for God; God will build a house for David—a prophecy among the most significant in the entire Bible (2 Sam 7.4–16).[5] God assures David that He has been working for him in the past (vv 8–9) and will continue to work for him in the future (vv 11–16), making an everlasting dynasty for him so that David's kingship will long outlive him. David's son will build God's house (vv 12–14) and will have a privileged relationship with God (vv 12–14) so that God will never, under any circumstance, remove His covenant faithfulness from David's line—forever (vv 15–16).

It is in response to this incredible promise that David prays:

> Then King David went in and sat before the LORD and said, "Who am I, O Lord GOD, and what is my house, that you have brought me thus far? And yet this was a small thing in your eyes, O Lord GOD. You have spoken also of your servant's house for a great while to come, and this is instruction for mankind, O Lord GOD! And what more can David say to you? For you know your servant, O Lord GOD! Because of your promise, and according to your own heart, you have brought about all this greatness, to make your servant know it. Therefore you are great, O LORD God. For there is none like you, and there is no God besides you, according to all that we have heard with our ears. And who is like your people Israel, the one nation on earth whom God went to redeem to be his people, making himself a name and doing for them great and awesome things by driving out before your people, whom you redeemed for yourself from Egypt, a nation and its gods? And you established for yourself your people Israel to be your people forever. And you, O LORD, became their God. And now, O LORD God, confirm forever the word that you have spoken concerning your servant and concerning his house, and do as you

---

[4] This should not be understood as a misconception about God on David's part, as if God were limited to the Tabernacle in any real sense. Rather, David is reflecting the devotion to God and His glory the people of Haggai's day were chastised for not having (Hag 1.2–11).

[5] A full discussion of the significance of this prophecy cannot be traced in this book, but language from it echoes through the Psalms and into the New Testament.

have spoken. And your name will be magnified forever, saying, 'The LORD of hosts is God over Israel,' and the house of your servant David will be established before you. For you, O LORD of hosts, the God of Israel, have made this revelation to your servant, saying, 'I will build you a house.' Therefore your servant has found courage to pray this prayer to you. And now, O Lord GOD, you are God, and your words are true, and you have promised this good thing to your servant. Now therefore may it please you to bless the house of your servant, so that it may continue forever before you. For you, O Lord GOD, have spoken, and with your blessing shall the house of your servant be blessed forever." (2 Sam 7.18–29)

Contents

Fully understanding a prayer is more than just noting repeated words, but high-frequency repetition can clue us in to major themes. In this case, the twin themes of doxology and deference are made prominent by the tenfold repetition of "your servant" and the sevenfold repetition of "Lord Yahweh," the latter being a phrase that appears nowhere else in Samuel.[6] In short, this prayer is all about the Lord, His actions and faithfulness, and His uncommon generosity toward David. David acknowledges the enormous difference there is between God and the one who prays to him: God is described in wonder and majesty;[7] David is humble and insignificant. David, the eighth son, once a little kid with no claim of any kind to anything, is now promised an eternal dynasty over God's chosen people. For David, this is a marvelous and wondrous thing to have happened; for God, it is nothing at all.[8]

Similar to David's own humility is his humble perspective about the people he reigns. The incomparability of God (v 22) is followed by the incomparability of Israel (v 23), but notice her incomparability is derivative: she is only remarkable because of the God who redeemed her, established

---

[6] Kaiser, *I Will Lift My Eyes*, 55 sees further covenant-connection significance in the fact that this is the title used by Abraham (Gen 15.2, 8) and in other prayers (see Deut 3.24; 9.26; Josh 7.7; Jdg 6.22; 16.28).

[7] Miller, *They Cried to the Lord*, 63 says this is the most extensive declaration of praise in the context of address to God in a prose prayer.

[8] Brueggemann, *Great Prayers*, 40.

her, and became her God (cf. Deut 4.7–8).[9] By connecting all of this to the promise, David realizes his unfolding story is another chapter in God's developing purpose for Israel and human history.[10]

David's perspective is guided by his position "before the LORD" (v 18), a place one cannot be without humility. Awareness of being in God's presence cannot but impact one's attitude in prayer.[11] This theme is repeated in David's petitions that his house "will be established before you" (v 26) and that God would bless his house "that it may continue forever before you." David has taken a physical position "before the LORD" and this idea drives the petitions, and the prayer is that God would continue His approval and support of David's house.[12]

Another key to this prayer is the sevenfold repetition of "house," the very topic of this entire chapter. David desired to build a house for God and his plans were rejected in favor of God building a house for him. Now, David's prayer continues this focus: his house is nothing (v 18), but God has spoken about it (v 25) and will thus build (v 27), establish (v 26), and bless it (v 29). And this blessing will endure "forever," a word appearing five times in this prayer. The Hebrew word does not always indicate eternity, and can sometimes only refer to a distant unknown future.[13] At the very least then, David's prayer is that God's promise will continue to his descendants for a very long time to come—a message intended for generations long beyond David—a point that finds fulfillment in the 400 years of the rule of David's house until the exile[14] and is particularly noteworthy given its repetition in 1 Chronicles 17, written when there is no Davidic king on the throne.[15]

As we have seen in previous prayers, this prayer has a strong covenant focus. This is most clearly apparent in the prayer being in response to a

---

[9] Ibid., 39–40.
[10] Baldwin, *1 and 2 Samuel*, 233.
[11] Willis, "Prayer in the Deuteronomic History," 43.
[12] Ibid.
[13] See BDB 761–763; HALOT 798–799. In the larger Biblical context, the New Testament's application of this promise to Jesus makes it clear the promise does, in its fullest sense, mean eternal.
[14] Anderson, *2 Samuel*, 128.
[15] Hill, *1 & 2 Chronicles*, 245.

covenant God is making with David. Second, the repeated use of God's covenant name Yahweh (LORD) marks this out as a covenant-focused prayer. Third, David recounts the history of Israel in context of God redeeming them and making them His own covenant people (vv 23–24). Fourth, verse 24 is a paraphrase of God's statement to Israel, "I will be your God and you will be my people" (Exod 6.7; et al.). This simple statement is at the very heart of the covenant; indeed, everything else is a practical working out of its meaning. Finally, as David enters into the petitions of the prayer, he quotes the very promises that God has just made (vv 26–28). David goes to the covenant God who has made a covenant with the nation he rules and has just extended a special covenant to him and, in full view of all of this, prays that God will indeed keep His covenant.

And that is the upshot of David's prayer: that God will do what He has promised. The petitions are found in the threefold "and now" (vv 25, 28–29; cf. vv 13, 16), a phrase that frequently marks out the petitions of Old Testament narrative prayers. The two petitions surround the middle "and now," which is an acknowledgment of the promise. It is almost as if David—who even here cannot but speak of himself as God's servant—must remind himself it is not too bold to make such requests when God has promised this very thing. Around the statement of God's promise (v 28) are the twin pleas for God to confirm forever what He had spoken about David's house (v 25) and bless the house that it may continue forever (v 29). The very next chapter details the victories of David, indicating that God begins doing this very thing.

Connections

The place of praise. David's prayer in response to God's promise recalls a few lessons we have already considered—and that we will see many times again. First among these is the place of praise in prayer and the place of humility in the one who prays, two ideas that always occur together. Even David, the king hand-selected by God to manifest the character God wants His leaders to have was not so bold as to presume upon God's graciousness. David knew he did not deserve the palace he lived in or the throne he sat on, nor could he ever be so devoted to God to earn a promise that would endure far beyond his own life. He, the hand-picked king of God's chosen people, was nothing but a lowly slave before the God who gave him all these things. So also it is with our place before God. The one who understands (as well as is possible) the God to whom we pray cannot be haughty before Him; the one who is properly humble before God will naturally turn to praise.

Praying the promises. David is among those who pray the promises. He does not merely hint at the covenant by mentioning God's covenant name or recalling God's past dealings with His covenant people. Rather, he quotes God's very promise back to him directly (v 27) and indirectly (vv 28–29). Millar says of this prayer what we have already seen multiple times and will continue to see throughout this study: David asks of the Lord what He has already promised, which "takes us right to the heart of Biblical prayer. Prayer is, in essence, calling on Yahweh to do what He has said."[16]

A confident approach. David comes to God not only in humility but in confidence. An early, speaking-outline form of this material engaged in alliteration in the "Content" part of the study: I had divided it into doxology, deference, and demand,[17] the final part being a discussion of the petitions. I indicated in the outline that I hesitated to use that term, but that (in addition to the alliteration) the petitions felt stronger than mere pleas: "And now, confirm forever the word that you have spoken concerning your servant and concerning his house, and do as you have spoken" (v 25). Although humble, David is yet bold in his approach to the Lord. He stands on the unshakable ground of God's promises and unflinchingly asks God to make his dynasty last forever. Again, the one who pleads with God for what God has promised has no need to fear whether God will not give it; it may or may not be on our timeline or as we expect, but God will do what God has said.

---

[16] Millar, *Calling on the Name of the Lord*, 58.
[17] Borrowed from Brueggemann, *Great Prayers*, 42.

The rationale of prayer. If God will do what God has said, why bother praying? I have, and will continue, to address this question in various ways at various points throughout, but for this chapter I will simply indicate that such prayer is an expression of trust. God's promises are not to be received casually and in an entitled spirit, but with submissive thanksgiving.[18] God is a relational being who wants relationships with His creation. One key element in all relationships is trust, particularly when one party is stronger than the other. How much more, then, is this the case when the one party is not merely stronger, but is God! Our expression of God's promises to God himself is a way we remind ourselves of the one we trust in as we seek to align ourselves more to His will and less to our own.

Changing perspective, not circumstances. Notice the appeal to God to do what He said is an example of how prayer sometimes changes not the circumstances but the perspective of the one who prays. At the beginning of the chapter, Nathan tells David to do what he has said. Now, David forfeits all such plans and tells God to do what He has said.[19] This is in direct contrast to Saul, who could never admit to being wrong and constantly argued with Samuel's condemnations of his behavior and thus, had his kingdom taken away.[20] David, rather, was more concerned about honoring the Lord than guarding his own reputation, and had his kingdom established forever.[21] Although our own kingdom is not at stake as it was for Saul and David, we are citizens of a kingdom where our choice to honor God or self, whether we can admit to being wrong or selfishly seek to blame others matters greatly. David's ability to admit wrong will be the key to his reign, as he will make mistakes and must plead for forgiveness, as we will see in the next chapter.

---

[18] Selman, *1 Chronicles*, 181.
[19] Ibid., 183.
[20] Firth, *1 and 2 Samuel*, 392.
[21] Baldwin, *1 and 2 Samuel*, 234.

EIGHT

I Have Sinned Greatly

2 Samuel 24.10–14; 1 Chronicles 21.8–13

The God to whom we pray is a God who forgives, even in the midst of judgment.[1] A common message of the Old Testament prophets is that, despite the late hour, the opportunity for repentance and pardon has not passed. This prophetic preaching is prefigured in David's sin with the census, God's judgment as a result, David's recognition that in God's hand remains the safest place to be, and God's ultimate relenting of the complete disaster that could have come.

Context

David was hand-picked by God to be king, not because he met any particular human standards for kingship, but because he was a man after God's own heart. After facing various difficulties in securing the throne, God promised David he would never lose it. Shortly after this promise, however, David committed adultery with the wife of one of his most valiant soldiers and had him killed to cover the sin (2 Sam 11; cf. 23.8–39).

Although David's penitence (2 Sam 12.13; Ps 51) shows he has not rejected God, his reign is not what it could have been; instead many of his years as king are consumed with violence that rose up even from his

---

[1] Of the prayers covered in this book, this prayer is the shortest. Given its brevity and some of the difficulties with interpreting the events around the prayer, I strongly considered omitting it. There are, however, important lessons here.

own household (2 Sam 13–21). David's son Amnon rapes his half-sister, David's daughter Tamar, which leads to Amnon's murder by her full brother Absalom (cf. Deut 22.25–27). Absalom fled from Jerusalem for three years before returning, only to rebel against David and seek the throne. Shimei curses David, hurling stones at him. Sheba leads a rebellion. A famine strikes the land because of sin that had been committed by Saul. In short, what begins as God's man leading God's people in its greatest period of history up to this point turns into a nightmarish conclusion to David's reign because of his sin.

With this period of violence having come to a close, David praises God for His deliverance (2 Sam 22). All is not well, however. This epilogue to David's reign (2 Sam 21–24) begins and ends with God's anger (chs 21, 24),[2] and the list of David's mighty men in chapter 23 ends with Uriah, standing "as a reminder of one of David's worst offenses against God and fellow humans."[3] In the very next verse, something again happens that angers God (2 Sam 24.1). Notice that the anger of God precedes David's action in this case, so some behavior leads to God inciting David, which leads to their greater sin, which leads to the punishment that will fall on them.

Contents

Although there are minor differences, the bulk of the narrative in 2 Samuel 24 is the same as its retelling in 1 Chronicles 21. The biggest difference is who incites David to number the people. In 2 Samuel 24, God incites David; in 1 Chronicles 21, Satan incites David—a striking difference, to say the least.[4]

Students of the Bible have handled this difference in a variety of ways. One way of approaching it sees Satan not as the personal name of the devil, but as some other sort of enemy of David. This draws from the fact that the Hebrew word *satan* simply means adversary and is used of other

---

[2] See Youngblood, "1 & 2 Samuel," 1051 for a proposed chiastic structure of this section of text.
[3] Widmer, *Standing in the Breach*, 228.
[4] See Hill, *1 & 2 Chronicles*, 292 for a listing of differences.

adversaries in other contexts.[5] It always includes the definite article when referring to Satan and does not in this case, so that may be a clue to this understanding. In this view, the adversary is perhaps a human enemy of some kind (such as an attack from an enemy prompting David to want to number the people)[6] or maybe even God Himself.[7] God is judging Israel for some unspecified sin by allowing an adversary to lead them further astray in order to bring judgment. Although this might seem odd, it may be comparable to God sending a lying spirit to mislead the false prophets of King Ahab in order to bring about his demise (1 Kgs 22.19–23; cf. 1 Cor 5.5; 1 Tim 1.20).

On the other hand, others understand this to be Satan. The article not appearing with the word is not a guarantee that it is not Satan, since the word is only used of him two other times, too small a sample size to provide definite answers. Perhaps the article not being used is evidence that "the adversary" is evolving from a description of the devil to a proper name for him.[8] Although some struggle with equating the work of God and the work of Satan, there is certainly an analogy for seeing it this way. In Job, God grants permission for Satan to tempt Job. Satan presented the idea of tempting Job and, presumably, is the one who follows through. In spite of this, God will say, "He still holds fast his integrity, although you incited me against him to destroy him without reason" (Job 2.3). God takes the blame for what Satan has done, perhaps because God is sovereign and Satan's malice does not happen outside of that sovereignty. Thus, Satan would not have been allowed to do anything to Job apart from God's consent and Satan could not tempt David unless God allowed it.[9]

However we might reconcile the difference between Samuel and Chronicles on who incited David, the result was that David decided to

---

[5] HALOT, 1317.

[6] Leithart, *1 & 2 Chronicles*, 71.

[7] Chisholm, *1 & 2 Samuel*, 306–307. As surprising as it might be to use the word *satan* to describe God, this is the word used of the Angel of Yahweh when he stands in Balaam's path (Num 22.22).

[8] Payne, "1 & 2 Chronicles," 407.

[9] Firth, *1 and 2 Samuel*, 542–543; Widmer, *Standing in the Breach*, 231.

number the people. This seems harmless enough, since a census is not an inherently evil act (cf. Exod 38.21–31; Num 1.1–3; 26.2), but David, upon completing it, prays,

> I have sinned greatly in what I have done. But now, O LORD, please take away the iniquity of your servant, for I have done very foolishly.
> (2 Sam 24.10)

What did David do that was so wrong? Unfortunately, the text never clarifies for us the answer to that question. Most have seen it either in the light of trusting in his military forces rather than God (cf. 1 Sam 14.6; Isa 31.1),[10] which was a sort of self-sufficient pride,[11] or in the context of Exodus 30.12, which indicates that a ransom payment is necessary when a census is taken.[12] Although the precise failure of David cannot be known with certainty, since the text is silent on the matter, the connection to Exodus 30 is striking, given other failings in the life of David. Just as David did not prepare properly for moving the Ark of the Covenant (2 Sam 6.1–7), so he now does not prepare properly for a census.[13] Although it is not directly parallel, it is also noteworthy that his sin with Bathsheba comes because he remains in the comfort of his palace rather than on the battlefield with his people, which itself can be seen as a kind of laziness in leadership.

There are also similarities with other Biblical stories and characters, which may be instructive for recognizing the sin here. Leithart sees David as "seizing forbidden fruit, God's host" and "treating it as if it were his own," comparing this both with Adam's sin in the garden and David's own sin with Bathsheba. He also sees the reappearance of the angel of destruction (1 Chron 21.15) as an echo of the last time this figure appeared, in judgment of the Egyptians (Exod 12.23): in this view, David has be-

---

[10] Anderson, *2 Samuel*, 284; Hill, *1 & 2 Chronicles*, 294.

[11] Baldwin, *1 and 2 Samuel*, 315.

[12] Chisholm, *1 & 2 Samuel*, 307; Leithart, *1 & 2 Chronicles*, 72–73. The nature of the ransom payment itself is a further question. Widmer, *Standing in the Breach*, 237 raises the possibilities that it may be "propitiatory (pacifying divine wrath), expiatory (a favorable reminder before God; cf. Exod 30.16; Num 31.54), or rather ransom money (a recompense or God's exclusive ownership of a person; cf. Exod 13.12–13; Num 18.16)."

[13] Leithart, *1 & 2 Chronicles*, 73.

come Pharaoh, seizing God's people for his own purposes.[14] Finally, this scene likens David to and distinguishes him from King Saul. The "foolishness" of David (2 Sam 24.10) is a word used twice of Saul in his failings, both in his burnt offering (1 Sam 13.13) and his pursuit of David (1 Sam 26.21), which puts David in the category of behaving like Saul.[15] On the other hand, his repentance without any attempt to justify his actions or deny wrongdoing sets him apart from Saul's behavior.

Whatever the case, David sees his guilt and pleads for forgiveness. God, in response, offers him three choices, which decrease in length as they increase in severity: three years of famine; three months of devastation by his enemies; three days of pestilence on the land (2 Sam 24.12–13). David's response to the prophet who brought him the message is remarkable: "I am in great distress. Let us fall into the hand of the LORD, for his mercy is great; but let me not fall into the hand of man" (2 Sam 24.14). He rejects the second option and leaves it in God's hands whether He would choose the first or the third.

The pestilence comes and people begin to die, leaving David with 70 fewer contingents of soldiers than he had at the beginning (2 Sam 24.15).[16] As the angel of the Lord approaches Jerusalem, David prays again:

> Behold, I have sinned, and I have done wickedly. But these sheep, what have they done? Please let your hand be against me and against my father's house. (2 Sam 24.17)

David's second prayer seeks to spare the people from further disaster, instead desiring to take the full brunt of God's punishment on himself and his family. David knows what it means to be a shepherd, namely that it is entails self-sacrificial responsibility not self-exalting privilege.[17]

---

[14] Ibid.

[15] Chisholm, *1 & 2 Samuel*, 308.

[16] Firth, *1 and 2 Samuel*, 546. The word for "thousand" is notoriously difficult, sometimes meaning a literal thousand and sometimes referring to a group of soldiers of a significantly smaller (but indefinite) number. Since this is a military census—and the numbers are so astronomically large: 1.3 million *soldiers* (2 Sam 24.9), it is probably the latter usage throughout this chapter. See NIDOTTE 1:416–417; TWOT 1:48.

[17] Baldwin, *1 and 2 Samuel*, 318. Interestingly, the intertestamental work 2 Esdras sees David as one of Israel's great intercessors because of this event (2 Esd 7.106–111).

This second prayer either precedes or is concurrent with God's relenting, which seems to come before the three-day period is up: He has indeed been merciful.

Connections

Brevity in prayer. One of the reasons I chose to include this short prayer is specifically for that reason: it is short. A mistake we sometimes make in prayer is presuming God should be talked to as people are. That is, we must reason with Him, convince Him, overwhelm Him with the number of petitions we can raise, and other such things. This is a fine line to balance, because the behavior can look identical regardless of the motive. For example, one person may think that God needs to be convinced of his penitence and prays long, heaping up proofs of his sorrow. At the same time, a true godly sorrow can produce long, *sincere* prayers of confession. Although we surely do not want to take God's mercy for granted in cases of sin—and there is surely nothing wrong with long, sincere prayers—the notion that we must spend hours proving our sincerity to Him or that we must make a compelling case of some kind to convince God is clearly not what the Bible shows at any point. The brevity of David's prayer of penitence is just one example of such prayer.[18]

Multiplying prayers. A similar issue arises when it comes to asking people to pray petitionary prayers on our behalf, or on the behalf of a loved one. On the one hand, a person of faith will surely ask for the prayers of others, because of his or her faith. Belief in God and belief in prayer will naturally result in requests for prayer. However, it is easy to fall into a "power in numbers" trap where we (subconsciously?) think that if we can just muster up enough numbers to overwhelm God, then He will *have to* do what we want—as if God can be so manipulated. Or that God must be convinced to do what (we think) is best for us. Or that God is unaware of our needs and we must gather up enough "prayer warriors" in order to catch His attention.

---

[18] Although it is clearly not formulaic Greenberg, *Biblical Prose Prayer*, 28 sees this as an example of a penitential prayer that has three basic elements: confession, petition, acknowledgement of folly.

If we give this any thought at all, we know that it is flatly anti-Biblical and, frankly, a bit pagan—a little reminiscent of the priests of Baal at Mt. Carmel (1 Kgs 18.25–29). God is not impressed by our numbers and we don't need at least a thousand signatures on our petition before He will act. And we will certainly never compel Him to respond by our Organized Action for whatever purpose we are seeking. But, at the same time, it is not wrong to ask for prayers—and for the prayers of many. Notice, however, that when Paul does this very thing it is for the sake of the many, not for the sake of God: "You also must help us by prayer, so that many will give thanks on our behalf for the blessing granted us through the prayers of many" (2 Cor 1.11). The point in all of this is to consider both our motives and the nature of God. Why are we asking for prayer? Why are we praying long in our confession? If it is because we think God needs to be informed or God needs to be convinced, our understanding of God is faulty, to say the least. God does not need to be informed, because He already knows. God does not need to be convinced, because He is merciful by nature. God hears and is moved by the prayer of the individual.[19]

While God is indeed merciful by nature, He is also just and His judgment is real. While God takes no delight in the death of the wicked (Ezek 33.11) and desires all people to be saved (1 Tim 2.4), the wrath of God will be poured out on the disobedient (Col 3.6). It is this meeting point of justice and mercy that so many prayers of this sort wrestle with. In the Bible, guilt is never just taken away without some sort of payment.

---

[19] Some have argued that if a righteous person's prayer is effective (Jas 5.16), then two righteous people's prayers will be even more effective. This application of mathematics to prayer fails because it cannot be traced out to a logical conclusion. If it is true then we could, in fact, accumulate enough righteous prayers to strong-arm God into doing our will. Or, if not, it would either be because the incremental effectiveness of added prayer is so insignificant that we could never mathematically reach such a point (meaning that each individual's prayer is essentially useless on its own) or there are diminishing returns in efficacy of adding righteous prayers (meaning that some righteous people's prayers are less effective than others and eventually some are not effective at all). If this entire footnote seems absurd, that's because it is. Strong-arming God is impossible. Suggesting that the prayers of the righteous are only minutely effective or that the efficacy drops off as prayers are added—the very notion of charting the diminishing returns of prayer efficacy!—all flies in the face of the point of James 5.16. The solution to all this absurdity is simple and straightforward: James 5 is not about the mathematics of prayer; it is about the efficacy of *a* righteous person's prayer. Or, as I said, God hears and is moved by the prayer of the individual.

David's prayer for forgiveness is not a request for the sin to vanish and him to feel no ill effects, but for God to deal graciously as He administers His justice,[20] as Habakkuk will also plead (Hab 3.2). Similarly, the Bible never guarantees God's children will be sinless or avoid all punishment. Rather, God's covenant with David indicated his descendants would sin and be punished (2 Sam 7.14), but God would forgive and continue His covenant (2 Sam 7.15–16). This scene is an outworking of those promises and a model for later generations of how deliverance can be found in the mercy of God.[21] Or, as Millar says, "Hope remains both for the house of David and for Yahweh's people who cry to him for mercy."[22]

God delights in forgiveness. It may be surprising to learn this story is about God's forgiving grace, but this is evident not only in David's prayers of penitence and his confident assertion, but also in God stopping short of the disaster He could have brought. Chisholm suggests passages like this are further informed by others like Hosea 11, "where God pulls back the curtain that covers his heart and gives us a glimpse of the emotional conflict he experiences when he is forced to punish his people."[23] He does not delight in punishment, but in doing good. His wrath is temporary, but His steadfast, merciful, covenant love and faithfulness endures forever.[24]

This scene ends at the threshing floor of Araunah the Jebusite (2 Sam 24.16). There, David will build an altar (2 Sam 24.18–25) and there, Solomon will build the Temple (1 Chron 22.1). The mercy and forgiveness this story is about will soon find a permanent home in the Temple at this very location, for the Temple "was above all a place of forgiveness, where sin and all its consequences could be removed."[25]

---

[20] Anderson, *2 Samuel*, 285.
[21] Ibid., 287.
[22] Millar, *Calling on the Name of the Lord*, 130.
[23] Chisholm, *1 & 2 Samuel*, 311.
[24] Abraham J. Heschel, *The Prophets* vol. 2, 59–78 provides an outstanding discussion of God's wrath.
[25] Selman, *1 Chronicles*, 201.

NINE

Direct Their Hearts Toward You
1 Chronicles 29.10–19

The God to whom we pray is a God who gives of Himself. This might initially seem like an odd starting place for a prayer that is set in context of people giving gifts to God, but further reflection should bring the believer to the obvious truth: we have no possessions that are not from God and that we should not return to Him for His glory, a truth sometimes called the doctrine of stewardship.[1] In this prayer, David explicitly recognizes this.

Context

David wanted to build a house for God, but God refused him that privilege. Instead, God said, He would build a house for David and David's son would build the Temple (2 Sam 7.1–17).[2] Now, at the end of David's life, just as he is preparing to pass the baton of kingship to Solomon, the question of the Temple comes around again (1 Chron 29.1–9).

David acknowledges the grand scope of building a house for God. He indicates he has already prepared, as much as he has been able to, the accumulation of materials for Solomon to use: gold, silver, bronze, wood, jewels, and the like. And yet he knows that this will not be enough, and

---

[1] See Blomberg, *Christians in an Age of Wealth*, 173–193 for a practical discussion of individual stewardship in contemporary life.
[2] See chapter 7.

so he appeals to the people to make their own freewill offerings to the cause of building the Lord's Temple. The people's gift is astounding to say the least: the 5,000 talents of gold translate to something like 375,000 pounds, not including the 10,000 darics;[3] add to that 750,000 pounds of silver, 1.35 million pounds of bronze, 7.5 million pounds of iron, and an unquantified amount of precious stones.

These numbers are astonishing and reflect a generosity that speaks both to the character of the people and their understanding of the importance of their task. If either of these traits were not present, no such gift could be marshaled. That they rejoice upon giving so freely to God (v 9) speaks further to their character and to the kind of nation that David had led them to be. In response to this gift and their joy, David prays:

> Therefore David blessed the LORD in the presence of all the assembly. And David said: "Blessed are you, O LORD, the God of Israel our father, forever and ever. Yours, O LORD, is the greatness and the power and the glory and the victory and the majesty, for all that is in the heavens and in the earth is yours. Yours is the kingdom, O LORD, and you are exalted as head above all. Both riches and honor come from you, and you rule over all. In your hand are power and might, and in your hand it is to make great and to give strength to all. And now we thank you, our God, and praise your glorious name.
>
> But who am I, and what is my people, that we should be able thus to offer willingly? For all things come from you, and of your own have we given you. For we are strangers before you and sojourners, as all our fathers were. Our days on the earth are like a shadow, and there is no abiding. O LORD our God, all this abundance that we have provided for building you a house for your holy name comes from your hand and is all your own. I know, my God, that you test the heart and have pleasure in uprightness. In the uprightness of my heart I have freely offered all these things, and now I have seen your people, who are present here, offering freely and joyously to you. O LORD, the God of Abraham, Isaac, and Israel, our fathers, keep

---

[3] A talent is a unit of weight, approximately 75 pounds. A daric was a coin weighing about a quarter ounce.

forever such purposes and thoughts in the hearts of your people, and direct their hearts toward you. Grant to Solomon my son a whole heart that he may keep your commandments, your testimonies, and your statutes, performing all, and that he may build the palace for which I have made provision." (1 Chron 29.10–19)

Contents

This prayer divides neatly up into three parts: *doxology:* praise of God and His sovereignty (vv 10–13); *thanksgiving:* God as the source of the people's wealth to give (vv 14–16); *supplication:* David's petition that future generations would maintain the attitude of the present people (vv 17–19).[4] Throughout the prayer, the dominant focus is on God, with six occurrences of "LORD" and five of "God," including a reference to God at the opening of each section and attributions of praise that run throughout it. Balentine points out that "in the whole prayer invocations of the name or ascriptions of grandeur and sovereignty" are lacking only in three verses (vv 14–15, 19), each of which uses the second person pronoun to address God directly, concluding it all combines "to give the impression that hardly a word may be spoken without first pausing to acknowledge the true object of the prayer's focus."[5]

The opening stanza of praise is written in an inverse parallelism: it opens and closes with praise (vv 10b, 13), moves inward to speak of the greatness, power, and might that belong to God (vv 11a, 12b), and finds God's kingdom and rule at the center of the praise (vv 11b, 12a): "It is a great encouragement to every reader that the God who possesses everything also gives freely to everyone."[6] Since the kingdom of God is at the center of this chiasm, it is at least something of a focal point,[7] a point that also finds a place for praise in Psalm 145. And at this center point we find that God does not selfishly keep His greatness, power, and glory to Himself, but shares all three attributes with His people: riches and

---

[4] Selman, *1 Chronicles*, 259; Hill, *1 & 2 Chronicles*, 348–350.
[5] Balentine, *Prayer in the Hebrew Bible*, 101–102.
[6] Selman, *1 Chronicles*, 260.
[7] Dorsey, *Literary Structure of the Old Testament*, 40–41.

honor come from God and He makes great and gives strength. Leithart says, "God is great, but he does not reserve greatness to himself. He is great by 'greatening' all. He is powerful, but he does not reserve power to himself but strengthens all. Everything in heaven and earth comes from him, yet he gives riches and honor. He is great by greatening, strong in his strengthening, rich in enriching."[8]

The middle stanza is David's thanksgiving to God. Hill sees this as being parallel to Thanksgiving Psalms, which include statements of the worshipper's gratitude (v 13), a narration of an experience of God's gracious help in need (vv 14–15), and a confession of God's graciousness and goodness (v 16).[9] The opening line of "who am I, and what is my people…?" is strongly reminiscent of David's first prayer, after God makes the covenant with him (cf. 1 Chron 17.16, 21), and reminds the reader that a true awareness of God's greatness, presence, and help in life will inevitably impact the one who is praying. In particular, David has come to understand—and doubly emphasizes—that they have only given God what is His own, for all things are already His (vv 13, 16). In addition, David connects the people of his day with their forefathers—strangers and sojourners (v 15). Abraham, his son, and his grandson were sojourners because the land did not belong to them. David, in possession of the land, realizes that life itself is a sojourn (cf. Heb 11.13–16). In all this, the contrast between the power of God and the powerlessness of David is manifest, indicating his full awareness that they completely depend on the God from whose hand all blessing comes.[10]

Finally, David turns to his request: "keep forever such purposes and thoughts in the hearts of your people, and direct their hearts toward you" (v 18). For David, the man after God's own heart, there is nothing more vital than that the hearts of the people would also be after God, from generation to generation. More specifically, he pleads that Solomon would chase after God as well, obeying Him fully—having "a whole

---

[8] Leithart, *1 & 2 Chronicles*, 94–95.
[9] Hill, *1 & 2 Chronicles*, 349.
[10] Balentine, *Prayer in the Hebrew Bible*, 102.

heart" that would keep God's Law.[11] Even as David makes his petition, he appeals back to the covenant with Abraham, Isaac, and Jacob and the covenant God has made with him. The former is obvious in his opening to the appeal. The latter is hinted at in the echoes of the earlier prayer and, even more, in his reference to Solomon, his son who God assured him would build God's house in his stead, which David refers to as the prayer ends.

In conclusion, David tells the assembly to bless God and they all bow and worship (v 20).

Connections

Praise in prayer. As so many Biblical prayers remind us, so also this prayer points to the place of praise in prayer. This "place" is not only the fact that it so frequently opens the prayer, helping to situate the one who prays properly before the God to whom he prays, but that it is continually present. Whether first, last, or somewhere else, praise so frequently finds its place in these prayers that we cannot help but be shaped by its presence. Although we could not contend that all prayer *must* include praise or that any prayer without praise is somehow deficient or inferior, it is also manifest that a large percentage of our prayers should make room for acknowledging who God is and how He impacts our lives for the better.

The role of a steward of God's possessions. Although stewardship is not necessarily a regular part of prayer, the attitude of David regarding possessions is remarkable and the doctrine of stewardship comes from passages like this. All things come from God and belong to God—"It is as if nothing ever leaves the hand of God, and yet the things that we receive become genuinely ours, subject always to a double possessive (*his* things and *mine*). For creatures there *is* no possession but double possession."[12] Additionally, life is a sojourn, and we will retain nothing of what we have.

---

[11] The "whole" heart is from the same *s-l-m* root that "Solomon" and the more familiar *"shalom"* also come from.

[12] Leithart, *1 & 2 Chronicles*, 96. Emphasis in original.

In short, our property is His and it is only ours temporarily and in trust. Therefore, it should be used to serve and glorify Him.[13]

The source of all blessing. Similarly, God's great gifts come out of His own great character. In a sense, this is similar to our recurring theme of making appeal based on God's promises and character. Here it is seen in how God blesses His people: with His own greatness, strength, and riches. David is grateful, not that they have things, but that God has shared, in some small measure, out of His very own bounty. We should hone our perception more to recognize this and be more regularly amazed at the great truth of it.

The need for God's help. Finally, this prayer speaks to the need for divine assistance in life—not merely for basic provisions of life, but especially to stay on the correct spiritual path. By the time of the postexilic generation who is first reading Chronicles, it is abundantly clear, proven time and again, that no generation of the Israelite people had the spiritual wherewithal to keep the covenant, and that all of God's people need His spiritual support. Millar says, "This prayer captures that beautifully, and in doing so offers powerful testimony that hope for the post-exilic generation can be found only in throwing themselves on God and calling on his name, asking him in mercy to fulfill his promises."[14] As Paul will later say in Ephesians 1 and 2, every spiritual blessing that can be found comes from God and salvation is no human achievement or meritorious reward. So also it was in David's day and so it is in ours: we cannot work out our own salvation apart from God being at work within us (Phil 2.12–13).

---

[13] Payne, "1 & 2 Chronicles," 438.
[14] Millar, *Calling on the Name of the Lord,* 129.

TEN

Give Me an Understanding Mind
1 Kings 3.3–14; 2 Chronicles 1.7–12

The God to whom we pray is a God who created the rational mind and desires His followers to be rational individuals. Wisdom is prized in the Old and New Testaments alike, and the call to believers is to reject folly and simple-mindedness in favor of the pursuit of wisdom. Biblical wisdom is not merely an intellectual pursuit, to be sure, but the praise of wisdom, knowledge, understanding, and insight that runs throughout the Bible makes it clear that God's people are to pursue rationality that is undergirded by the fear of the Lord. As Solomon begins his reign, he perceives a deficiency in this very regard.

Context

Solomon is the king of Israel. He has not, however, come to the throne easily. In addition to Absalom standing in his way during the reign of David (2 Sam 15–18), Adonijah tries to take the kingship as David nears death (1 Kgs 1.5–10). David gives final instructions to Solomon about dealing with those who would be enemies of the throne, and the blood flows liberally: Solomon kills Adonijah (2.19–25), Joab (2.25–35), and Shimei (2.36–46). Abiathar the priest was told he deserved death as well, but, although he was expelled from the priesthood, he was allowed to live (2.26–27).

In summation of Solomon establishing his reign, Walter Brueggemann says, "Solomon's ascent to power is orchestrated in a series of killings that parallel the violent choreography of *The Godfather*."[1] Although there is certainly some hyperbole in Brueggemann's assessment of Solomon's ascendency to the throne, it may be accurate enough to shake the average Christian into moving from the sanitized Sunday school version of the Biblical stories to a more accurate understanding of the ugly realities that were sometimes a part of the ancient world. Solomon's rise to power was neither easy nor peaceful.

A second important context to Solomon's prayer is his worship of God at the high places (3.3). Usually, the high places were local places of worship, as opposed to worship at the Temple (or Tabernacle before it) and in the broader context of Kings, it is always wrong to worship there.[2] The Chronicler, however, makes it clear that the Tabernacle was at the high place at Gibeon (1 Chron 16.39–40; 21.29; 2 Chron 1.3–6), which raises the question of why the author of Kings would leave the reference so ambiguous and implicitly negative instead of specifying that Solomon went to the Tabernacle, a matter to which we will return shortly.

Finally, the prayer is in the context of a dream (v 5). This is not to say it was not a real occurrence, created merely by Solomon's subconscious as he slept, but it was a revelation from God as he slept.[3] In this dream, God told Solomon to name his request, giving him a virtual divinely-signed blank check he could cash in on whatever he chose as his reign began. Solomon replied,

> You have shown great and steadfast love to your servant David my father, because he walked before you in faithfulness, in righteousness, and in uprightness of heart toward you. And you have kept for him this great and steadfast love and have given him a son to sit on his throne this day. And now, O LORD my God, you have made your servant king in place of David my father, although I am but a little child. I do not know how to go out or come in. And your servant is in the midst of your people whom

---

[1] Brueggemann, *Great Prayers*, 48.
[2] Provan, *1 and 2 Kings*, 48. But see 1 Chronicles 16.39–40; 21.29.
[3] Wiseman, *1 & 2 Kings*, 84 says that Hebrew does not differentiate between dreams and visions, adding revelation from God by dream is well attested in the Hebrew scriptures (Gen 26.24; 28.10–17; Jdg 7.13; 1 Sam 3; 28.6; Dan 2.4; 7.1) and the New Testament (Matt 1.20; 2.13, 22).

you have chosen, a great people, too many to be numbered or counted for multitude. Give your servant therefore an understanding mind to govern your people, that I may discern between good and evil, for who is able to govern this your great people? (1 Kgs 3.6–9)

Contents

When presented with an opportunity to receive whatever one wants, most people would take one of two paths: either we have already thought long and hard about what we most desire, know exactly what we want, and respond promptly or we would want some time to give serious thought to such an important matter. Solomon seems closer to the former, as he responds in this conversation, but it is significant that he delays his request. Rather than immediately jumping on the opportunity of a lifetime, Solomon pauses to praise God and humble himself before Him. Just as we saw doxology and deference in David's prayer at the beginning of his reign (2 Sam 7.18–29), so also young Solomon postpones his petition to deliver doxology and deference.[4]

Solomon's praise of God celebrates God's covenant faithfulness to David (v 6), not unlike the way others prayers do the same (e.g., Gen 24.12–14). In this case, God's faithfulness is rooted in His fulfillment of the 2 Samuel 7 promise and David's obedience to God, seeing his own kingship as proof of God's faithfulness. Solomon twice uses the covenant-loaded term that acknowledges God's steadfast, merciful, covenant love and faithfulness and places David's obedience between the two uses.[5] The modern theological debate about God's faithfulness and human obedience fails to recognize how inextricably intertwined the two are, a point Solomon seems to grasp in this prayer. Though perhaps more subtle, Solomon also indicates God has been faithful to His promises to Abraham as well (v 8), by creating in Israel a multitude too great to be numbered (cf. 2 Chron 1.9).

As Solomon prepares to make his request, he characterizes himself as a child—that is, he lacks the understanding and maturity properly

---

[4] Brueggemann, *Great Prayers*, 50.
[5] Ibid.

belonging to kingship, and thus lacks the competence to do the things kings are supposed to do.[6] In particular, Solomon's "I do not know how to go out or come in" (v 7) is an idiom referring to the skills of leadership (cf. Num 27.17; Deut 31.2–3; Josh 14.11; 1 Sam 18.13, 16; 29.6; 2 Kgs 11.8).[7] In addition to these deficiencies, the complexity of leading Israel is a monumental task. As a result, Solomon is in a position of dependence and need. Fortunately, Solomon understands God will be the cause of any success he may have. Since God has been exceedingly generous in His offering and Solomon is exceedingly lacking, the only question is what he will ask for. He is in a position to name his greatest desire and in his self-confessed immaturity and ignorance, he may well ask for extravagant frivolities.

Although God has given Solomon an open invitation to ask for whatever he wants, Solomon only wants one thing. His request is not for his own comfort, pleasure, or glorification, but to enable him to better serve the people he will lead. Further, his request is made in relation to God: he speaks of himself as "your servant" and Israel as "your great people." He realizes his kingship does not exist in a vacuum, and so his request—even as he asks for himself—brings nothing of *I* or *me* to God.[8] The request itself is simple: an understanding mind.

The word translated "understanding" is more literally "hearing," the same word that begins the fundamental command to all of God's people of all time (Deut 6.4–5),[9] the word that is, to this day, the Jewish title of that text. Solomon wants to hear God, in order to discern good and evil and thereby govern God's people. Further, in the Old Testament, to hear is to obey, as both English words come from the same Hebrew, "a linguistic trait with practical implications. Only those who obey authority figures have really *heard* them."[10]

---

[6] Dillard, *2 Chronicles*, 12 estimates Solomon's age at the time of his accession to be 20.
[7] House, *1, 2 Kings*, 110.
[8] Brueggemann, *Great Prayers*, 52.
[9] Ibid.
[10] House, *1, 2 Kings*, 110.

The word translated "mind" is more literally "heart," though it does not signify the seat of emotions in ancient thought. Its significance here is that it frames the prayer: David had a heart for God (v 6) and Solomon prays for one as well.[11] In short, at this stage in his life, Solomon recognizes his hopes for success reside in the same place David found it: an ongoing relationship with the God of Israel.[12] Further, it seems Solomon is already on the path David had blazed, for this is the very thing David wanted for him (1 Chron 22.12; 29.19).[13]

What follows this prayer is significant in two ways. First, God responds to Solomon's request by granting him the understanding he seeks and blessings beyond his request (vv 10–14). His request itself is commended and, because he seeks first God's kingdom, God grants not only the kingdom but even more (cf. Matt 6.33). There is, however, a stipulation added: Solomon must continue to walk in God's ways, following His laws. Second, Solomon does not do so. The wise Solomon eventually becomes a fool. Led astray by his pagan wives, he turns to idolatry—raising the possibility that the high places this story begins with is a foreshadowing of the path Solomon will ultimately follow (cf. 1 Kgs 11.7–8). He has moved from loving God (v 3) to loving his wives (11.1).[14] His heart is turned after other gods, unlike David whose heart was for God (11.4). It seems Solomon has seized upon the extras, the riches and honor—and the women that came with kingship—rather than the clinging to that fundamental request of a heart that hears God.[15]

Connections

Praise, Humility, and Covenant. By this point in the book, I should be brief on two points present in this prayer we are already very familiar with: first, the place of praise and humility; second, the presence of a covenant focus. Briefly, I will add that the former is particularly significant as it

---

[11] Leithart, *1 & 2 Kings*, 44.
[12] House, *1, 2 Kings*, 111.
[13] Payne, "1 & 2 Chronicles," 441. See chapter 9.
[14] Leithart, *1 & 2 Kings*, 43.
[15] Brueggemann, *Great Prayers*, 55.

relates to Solomon's request. If we truly enthrone God in our hearts and recognize who we are by comparison, it will be impossible to selfishly pray for our own transient, superficial yearnings. Instead, we will desire His will to be ours and our lives to serve His people and purposes.

The utter generosity of God. For the one who seeks first God's kingdom, He gives all that we will need. And our focus should be on the most basic needs, not the extras God may generously give. That which is most basic is not what is needed for our physical survival, but what is needed for our spiritual survival. To seek God's kingdom is not merely to seek for the growth of the church, but, on an individual level, to seek His sovereignty and reign over our lives. We must focus on this most basic need, not any extras that God may or may not give, for the extras are not essential to our spiritual growth and survival. Solomon begins in the right place, but turns from God (1 Kgs 11.1–8). He starts by seeking God's sovereignty and ends by pursuing his own paths. Perhaps he was too enamored with his own wisdom, wealth, and kingship—the extras God gave. In this light, it is striking that when Jesus speaks about the things that we most need He contrasts those who simply live by God's good gifts with Solomon in all his glory (Matt 6.28–29). Solomon in all his glory lost his focus, strayed from God, and was not as well off as those who simply live by God's gifts.[16]

Asking for wisdom. Solomon teaches us to ask for an understanding mind—to be people who listen to God, to have discernment in order to properly accomplish our God-given responsibilities.[17] Solomon's request is reminiscent of several of Paul's prayers. Paul prays that the Ephesians would be given a "spirit of wisdom and of revelation in the knowledge of him" (Eph 1.17), that the Philippians love would abound "with knowledge and all discernment" (Phil 1.9), and that the Colossians would be "filled with the knowledge of his will in all spiritual wisdom and understanding" (Col 1.9).[18] Clearly, wisdom is a thing we should seek. But wisdom and

---

[16] Ibid., 56.
[17] Balentine, *Prayer in the Hebrew Bible*, 60.
[18] See chapters 32, 34–35 for more discussion.

understanding will not come to the complacent and self-satisfied. Solomon is only able to grow in these ways because he realizes how far he has to go. The one who recognizes his immaturity and ignorance is the only one who can hope to grow past it.

God's faithfulness and our faith. God's historic faithfulness to His covenants is directly related to His ongoing relationships with His people. This is understood by those who pray in the Bible and should be at the forefront of our minds as well. God's past faithfulness should inform and strengthen our present faith, and direct us to pray with wisdom and confidence. As Kaiser says, "Herein lies the true foundation for all prayer: the history of God's past gracious work on our behalf should inspire us to ask for even greater trust and dependence on him for the present and the future."[19]

---

[19] Kaiser, *I Will Lift My Eyes*, 65.

ELEVEN

Open Your Eyes Toward This House
1 Kings 8.23–53; 2 Chronicles 6.14–42

The God to whom we pray is a God who is accessible. Far from the imagined gods of deism, He is concerned with His creation, though it is not mere concern; rather, He has made it His purpose to dwell with His people. This idea runs from cover to cover of the Bible, starting with Eden, continuing through the tabernacle and temple, imagery that continues on in the New Testament, before findings its culmination in Revelation's depiction of eternal dwelling with God. It is not surprising, then, that the God who so desires dwelling with His people is a God who desires prayer to be made to Him. Solomon's prayer at the dedication of the Temple emphasizes this fundamental truth: God will hear those who call to Him.

Context

Since the time of Moses, God's presence among the camp of Israel was found at the Tabernacle. Although it is self-evident that God could not be contained in the Tabernacle, we would be wrong to say that God did not, in some sense, dwell among His people. The very essence of the covenant was that He was their God, they were His people, and He dwelt with them (e.g., Lev 26.12). The visible manifestation of God at the tabernacle, and later the Temple, further emphasized that God wanted it to be understood He dwelt with them (Exod 40.33–35; 2 Chron 5.13–14). Indeed,

God told them to build the Tabernacle *so that* He could dwell with them (Exod 25.8) and that He brought them out of Egypt *so that* He might dwell with them (Exod 29.45–46).

The Tabernacle, however, was merely a tent. It was designed to be portable for their wilderness wanderings and had continued to be the place of worship for the first several generations of Israelite life in Canaan. David was unhappy with God dwelling in a tent while he lived in a palace (2 Sam 7.1–2), and desired to build God a house. God declared that Solomon would do this job, and Solomon built the most splendid Temple for God he possibly could.[1] This move from transience to permanence seems like a good thing, and God was surely not opposed to it being done (cf. Hag 1), but it brings its own set of temptations. The Tabernacle's "very structure and potential for easy removal should have reminded the Israelites of the conditional nature of God's presence among them, and the ease with which it could be removed." Meanwhile, the permanence of the Temple could easily be "transformed into a sinful overconfidence in the permanence of God's presence, which Jeremiah tells us is exactly what did take place (Jer 7.1–15)."[2]

Even so, the completion of the Temple and its dedication is a high point in the history of Israel. Further, this prayer is at a center point in the literary structures of both the Kings and Chronicles narratives. In Kings, it is the center point of a chiasm that makes up 1 Kings 8, making it the key element in the entire temple dedication.[3] In Chronicles, the entire temple dedication is the center of the even larger narrative of Solomon's reign.[4] In both cases, its central location highlights its importance, both in the dedication of the Temple and the entire reign of Solomon.

After the Temple is completed and furnished (1 Kgs 6–7), the Ark of the Covenant is brought and God's glory fills the Temple (1 Kgs 8.1–11).

---

[1] See pages 60–61 for some details of the materials prepared at the end of David's life.
[2] Phil Roberts, "The Story of the Tabernacle," 57–58.
[3] Dorsey, *Literary Structure*, 138.
[4] Ibid., 148; Dillard, *2 Chronicles*, 5–6, 52. In Chronicles, the prayer is longer than the account of the construction of the temple, which may also be a statement about the centrality of this prayer (Hill, *1 & 2 Chronicles*, 393).

In response, Solomon praises God for His faithfulness to His covenant with David (1 Kgs 8.12–21), and then prays:

> O LORD, God of Israel, there is no God like you, in heaven above or on earth beneath, keeping covenant and showing steadfast love to your servants who walk before you with all their heart; you have kept with your servant David my father what you declared to him. You spoke with your mouth, and with your hand have fulfilled it this day. Now therefore, O LORD, God of Israel, keep for your servant David my father what you have promised him, saying, "You shall not lack a man to sit before me on the throne of Israel, if only your sons pay close attention to their way, to walk before me as you have walked before me." Now therefore, O God of Israel, let your word be confirmed, which you have spoken to your servant David my father.
>
> But will God indeed dwell on the earth? Behold, heaven and the highest heaven cannot contain you; how much less this house that I have built! Yet have regard to the prayer of your servant and to his plea, O LORD my God, listening to the cry and to the prayer that your servant prays before you this day, that your eyes may be open night and day toward this house, the place of which you have said, "My name shall be there," that you may listen to the prayer that your servant offers toward this place. And listen to the plea of your servant and of your people Israel, when they pray toward this place. And listen in heaven your dwelling place, and when you hear, forgive.
>
> If a man sins against his neighbor and is made to take an oath and comes and swears his oath before your altar in this house, then hear in heaven and act and judge your servants, condemning the guilty by bringing his conduct on his own head, and vindicating the righteous by rewarding him according to his righteousness.
>
> When your people Israel are defeated before the enemy because they have sinned against you, and if they turn again to you and acknowledge your name and pray and plead with you in this house, then hear in heaven and forgive the sin of your people Israel and bring them again to the land that you gave to their fathers.
>
> When heaven is shut up and there is no rain because they have sinned against you, if they pray toward this place and acknowledge your name

and turn from their sin, when you afflict them, then hear in heaven and forgive the sin of your servants, your people Israel, when you teach them the good way in which they should walk, and grant rain upon your land, which you have given to your people as an inheritance.

If there is famine in the land, if there is pestilence or blight or mildew or locust or caterpillar, if their enemy besieges them in the land at their gates, whatever plague, whatever sickness there is, whatever prayer, whatever plea is made by any man or by all your people Israel, each knowing the affliction of his own heart and stretching out his hands toward this house, then hear in heaven your dwelling place and forgive and act and render to each whose heart you know, according to all his ways (for you, you only, know the hearts of all the children of mankind), that they may fear you all the days that they live in the land that you gave to our fathers.

Likewise, when a foreigner, who is not of your people Israel, comes from a far country for your name's sake (for they shall hear of your great name and your mighty hand, and of your outstretched arm), when he comes and prays toward this house, hear in heaven your dwelling place and do according to all for which the foreigner calls to you, in order that all the peoples of the earth may know your name and fear you, as do your people Israel, and that they may know that this house that I have built is called by your name.

If your people go out to battle against their enemy, by whatever way you shall send them, and they pray to the LORD toward the city that you have chosen and the house that I have built for your name, then hear in heaven their prayer and their plea, and maintain their cause.

If they sin against you—for there is no one who does not sin—and you are angry with them and give them to an enemy, so that they are carried away captive to the land of the enemy, far off or near, yet if they turn their heart in the land to which they have been carried captive, and repent and plead with you in the land of their captors, saying, "We have sinned and have acted perversely and wickedly," if they repent with all their heart and with all their soul in the land of their enemies, who carried them captive, and pray to you toward their land, which you gave to their fathers, the city that you have chosen, and the house that I have built for your name, then hear in heaven your dwelling place their prayer and their plea, and maintain their cause and forgive your people who have sinned against you, and all their transgressions that they have committed against you, and grant them compassion in the sight of those who carried them captive, that they may have compassion on them (for they are your people, and your heritage, which you brought out of Egypt, from the midst of the iron furnace). Let your eyes be open to the plea of your servant and to the plea of your people Israel, giving ear to them whenever they call to you. For you separated them from among all the peoples of the earth to be your heritage, as you declared through Moses your servant, when you brought our fathers out of Egypt, O LORD God. (1 Kgs 8.23–53)

Contents

Solomon's prayer divides up into a few basic parts, most of it being a series of seven petitions.[5] The basic outline is as follows:

God's covenant faithfulness (vv 22–30)
    To David (22–26)
    To the people (27–30)
Seven petitions (vv 31–52)
    Wronging a neighbor (31–32)
    The nation defeated (33–34)
    Disaster from drought (35–36)
    Other natural disasters (37–40)
    The prayer of foreigners (41–43)
    Success at war (44–45)
    Defeat and exile (46–52)
God's covenant with Moses (v 53)

A thorough study is impossible given the scope of this book, but a few observations about this prayer are important to consider. First, for a prayer that is the high point of the dedication ceremonies for the new Temple, strikingly little is said about the Temple. The Temple is in the

---

[5] Given the length of this prayer and the nature of this book, we will need to be even more abbreviated than usual. See Widmer, *Standing in the Breach*, 257–276 for a discussion of this prayer in the context of intercession.

prayer, to be sure, but it is in background role, as the Covenant comes to the foreground:

> That fact is everywhere in 1 Kings 8. The prominence of the *Ark of the Covenant* in the opening section sets the tone for all that follows. The emphasis is on God's people *assembling*, just as they did on Mount Sinai when they became a nation proper. The word "Israel" is used thirty-five times. There are constant references to God's *keeping the promises He made to David* (8.15, 20, 24–25, 66) and the covenant promises *made at Sinai* (8.40, 48), and the characterization of God as a covenant keeping God in 8.23.[6]

God's covenant faithfulness or "steadfast love" appears at the beginning of this prayer (v 23) and, in Chronicles, concludes it as well (2 Chron 6.42). Further, most of the potential disasters featured in Solomon's prayer are drawn from the covenant curses in Leviticus 26 and Deuteronomy 28.[7] Solomon is not creating calamity out of whole cloth, but speaking to the very real possibility of punishment, "for there is no one who does not sin" (v 46).

Second, God's hearing prayer and the people's need for forgiveness is a constant theme in the petitions of this prayer. The second, third, fourth, and seventh petitions all deal with the problem of sin, where the chief need in every case is forgiveness.[8] Rather than a self-congratulatory prayer about the magnificence of the temple (cloaked in a veneer of pseudo-thanksgiving), Solomon focuses on the hard fact of sin and the people's ongoing need for God in the midst of their failure.[9] Given this covenant context, particularly as it relates to the covenant curses, this prayer should teach the Israelites who follow Solomon how to respond when there is sin in the community. Instead of being instructive to the kings who followed Solomon—or even Solomon himself—there is very little penitential prayer in the rest of the book of Kings, in spite of the sin that plagued the land and subsequent covenant curses. Instead, this prayer, recorded in exilic Kings

---

[6] Millar, *Calling on the Name of the Lord*, 61.
[7] Leithart, *1 & 2 Kings*, 68–69; House, *1, 2 Kings*, 143.
[8] Provan, *1 and 2 Kings*, 79–80; Selman, *2 Chronicles*, 328.
[9] Kaiser, *I Will Look unto the Hills*, 80.

and postexilic Chronicles teaches the surviving remnant what they must do to return to the land and continue in it as they rebuild, respectively.

Third, this prayer, and the Temple itself, is a reminder of the immanence and transcendence of God. God cannot possibly be contained in even the grandest structure. Yet God is not so great that He does not dwell with His people. He is lofty, holy, and mysterious—and yet approachable. In the Temple, "the unapproachable Lord becomes approachable and ready to help those who worship, sacrifice, and pray."[10] Solomon is clear that God dwells in heaven and cannot be contained in His Temple. And yet although He hears their prayers in heaven (vv 32, 34, 36, 39, 43, 45, 49), His temple is the place from which He hears (vv 27–30).[11] However difficult it might be to understand the paradox of God's immanence and transcendence, it is only by embracing both that we can do justice to the full biblical teaching about God.[12]

Regarding these last two points of forgiveness and God's transcendence, Provan says,

> The temple is an important building, to be sure. … But God, who is not confined by a building and who is certainly not dependent upon it, will survive even its destruction and hear the people's prayers in exile. Likewise, obedience to the law is very important. … Yet Solomon holds out hope for restoration beyond failure, for he holds out hope that grace will have the last word.[13]

That God cannot be contained in the Temple has significant implications for the exilic community. In their world, the Temple had been destroyed. Of course, God's glory had already departed from it (Ezek 8–11), but the people still trusted in the presence of the building itself, as mentioned above. Their misplaced trust could not possibly save them,

---

[10] House, *1, 2 Kings*, 144.

[11] Provan, *1 and 2 Kings*, 79. Balentine, *Prayer in the Hebrew Bible*, 80–81 points out the uniqueness of this prayer, in that it is not a petition about a particular problem, an expression of thanksgiving or praise for deliverance, or repentance and confession in the context of sin, but instead a prayer about prayer. Or, to be more precise, "[I]t is a prayer about the temple as the preeminent *place* of prayer."

[12] Kaiser, *I Will Look unto the Hills*, 79.

[13] Provan, *1 and 2 Kings*, 81.

and their city was destroyed along with God's temple (2 Kgs 25.1–21). And yet the story of Israel does not end here, for God's grace always has power over human sin.[14]

Connections

The role of covenant. God's promises play a significant role in a Biblical prayer yet again. This time, they serve as a framework around the entire prayer, give the theological foundation for God's dwelling among the people, and provide the key points on which the petitions are built. Again, Biblical prayer is not built out of a random whims or a poorly thought out wish list, but the very promises of God Himself.

The prayers of individuals matter. In emphasizing the superiority of the New Covenant, Christians often (rightly) argue that Jesus supersedes the Old Testament priestly system by providing constant access to God, whereas only the Aaronic High Priest had access to God only once each year. The truth of this cannot be argued and is even a point made by the author of Hebrews as he builds his case for Christ's supremacy (Heb 7–9). Even so, we should never get the impression from this that God did not hear the Israelites when they called to Him. God has always heard the individual who acknowledges Him as God—whether a king like Solomon or a despondent, barren mother like Hannah. So also now, we need not be experts in theology or leaders in the church or a head of state to catch God's attention. He will hear us when we call.

Everyone needs the Lord. Although it did not feature in our discussion above, a surprising element of this prayer is the sudden concern for the foreigner (vv 41–43). God's particular choosing of Israel did not mean that He desired the nations to be condemned.[15] Rather, those Gentiles who heard of Him and came to Him could be saved (e.g., Josh 2.11; Ruth 1.16). Indeed, God's placement of His people on the single land bridge connecting Europe, Asia, and Africa may well have been designed to facilitate their role to "be a light to the nations" (Isa 49.6; cf. Gen 12.3; Isa

---

[14] See chapter 19.
[15] See Peskett, "Prayer in the Old Testament," 23.

56.6–8; 60.3). How much more is this the case in a covenant where God's particular election of Christians includes an explicit command to evangelize the nations (Matt 28.18–20).[16]

Forgiveness is always available. Solomon's prayer clearly emphasizes that sin is universal and all need forgiveness and grace. The recurring request is that God will hear and, in hearing, forgive. Even in exile, the ultimate covenant curse for Israel's failings, they can still pray toward the temple and find forgiveness. Leithart says, "Prayer is the solution to all Israel's ills, but it is not *pro forma*. It must be accompanied by full-scale repentance, involving thought, verbal confession, supplication, and a 'return' of heart and soul."[17] That is, forgiveness can always be found, but it is found both in seeking grace and in seeking reform in our own lives.

---

[16] Most English translations obscure the fact that the main verb of this sentence is not "go," but "preach the gospel." This basic instruction is further explained by three participles indicating how this evangelism is done: going, baptizing, teaching.

[17] Leithart, *1 & 2 Chronicles*, 113.

TWELVE

Our Eyes Are On You

2 Chronicles 20.6–12

The God to whom we pray is a God who is there in times of trial. He is a God who hears the downtrodden and overcome, lifting them up and making them victorious. He is a God who specializes in turning weakness into strength for the humble who trust in Him. Jehoshaphat finds himself in just such a situation and makes just such an appeal.

Context

By this point in the history of the kings in Israel and Judah, the reader is not accustomed to meeting one who prays to God. After all, most of their reigns are summarized as idolatrous, wicked, and filled with injustice. Jehoshaphat, however, is one of the few good kings. Although he is far from perfect—"intrinsically naïve and foolish"[1] is perhaps a good way of describing his marriage alliance with Ahab (2 Chron 18)—Jehoshaphat's wise reliance upon God in this chapter stands in contrast with that sinful alliance with Ahab (cf. 2 Chron 19.2).

In this particular story, Jehoshaphat is surrounded by enemies: the Moabites, the Meunites (who are linked with Arabs in 17.11; 26.7), and the Edomites (v 1). This group came from "beyond the sea," which, given the location of these groups, likely refers to the Dead Sea, and together formed "a great multitude" (v 2). In short, multiple nations are gather-

---

[1] Millar, *Calling on the Name of the Lord*, 133, using this phrase to describe him in 2 Kings 3.

ing together and have formed a coalition that seems to outnumber the armies of Judah.

Strikingly, this assault upon them happens "after this," which must refer to Jehoshaphat's religious reforms. Although this could be read as punishment for failing to reform correctly or thoroughly, it is worth noting that the same thing happens to Hezekiah in chapters 29–32. Hezekiah cleanses the Temple, restores worship, celebrates Passover, organizes the priesthood for service, and "After these things and these acts of faithfulness, Sennacherib king of Assyria came and invaded Judah" (32.1). Rather than seeing God as punishing these kings for some perceived failure in their reforms, the Chronicler is highlighting how God rewards them. The invasion is, indeed, a terrifying ordeal, but in both cases, the end result is God's presence and victory: a righteous king enjoys victory in warfare and rest from his enemies.[2]

Rather than accusing God of betraying him, Jehoshaphat turns to God and encourages the people to as well. He proclaims a fast throughout "all Judah" (v 3) and "all the cities" will gather to seek the Lord (v 3) so that "all Judah" will come and stand before Him as Jehoshaphat prays (v 13). Their seeking of God mirrors their king, who also "set his face to seek the LORD" (v 3), something that has been characteristic of his reign (17.3–4; 18.4; 19.3).[3] Jehoshaphat, and now his people, are turning toward God in worship, dependence, and an effort to discern His will. To the point, Jehoshaphat has a higher degree of trust in God than in military resources, and rightly sees the temple as the place to seek God. He prays,

> O LORD, God of our fathers, are you not God in heaven? You rule over all the kingdoms of the nations. In your hand are power and might, so that none is able to withstand you. Did you not, our God, drive out the inhabitants of this land before your people Israel, and give it forever to the descendants of Abraham your friend? And they have lived in it and have built for you in it a sanctuary for your name, saying, "If disaster comes upon us, the sword, judgment, or pestilence, or famine, we will stand be-

---

[2] Dillard, *2 Chronicles*, 256.
[3] The ESV's "inquire" in 18.4 is the same Hebrew as "seek" or "sought" in the other passages.

fore this house and before you—for your name is in this house—and cry out to you in our affliction, and you will hear and save." And now behold, the men of Ammon and Moab and Mount Seir, whom you would not let Israel invade when they came from the land of Egypt, and whom they avoided and did not destroy—behold, they reward us by coming to drive us out of your possession, which you have given us to inherit. O our God, will you not execute judgment on them? For we are powerless against this great horde that is coming against us. We do not know what to do, but our eyes are on you. (2 Chron 20.6–12)

Content

As we have seen time and again in other prayers, Jehoshaphat's prayer also begins with praise for God's sovereign power (v 6), including His power over all kingdoms and nations (cf. 1 Chron 29.30; 2 Chron 17.10; 20.29), a particularly relevant topic given the circumstances: a powerless Judah surrounded by an alliance of three enemy nations. This praise, formed in a series of questions, also serves as the primary complaint of the prayer. Asking such questions to God—in essence, saying, "If these things are true, why is this happening?"—is a common form of complaint.[4]

From this beginning point of prayer, Jehoshaphat engages in a brief historical retrospective (vv 7–10). The rhetorical question with which this section begins speaks to Jehoshaphat's absolute certainty of this point: God did indeed drive out the inhabitants of the land and gave it to His people in fulfillment of His promise to Abraham. Further, Jehoshaphat knows the purpose of the Temple, the place where God dwells among His own and hears their pleas. Here, Jehoshaphat clearly refers back to Solomon's prayer of dedication—standing before God at the Temple and crying out to Him in their affliction in time of disaster (2 Chron 6.24–39). The final line of the summary, "you will hear and save," is an alliterative wordplay, "a punning poetic hint that, for Yahweh, to hear is to save, that he is the saving God because he is the hearing God."[5] Furthermore, it is

---

[4] Miller, *They Cried to the Lord*, 65.
[5] Leithart, *1 & 2 Chronicles*, 172–173.

entirely appropriate to refer to Solomon's prayer in this context because God had explicitly confirmed He had heard Solomon's prayer and would continue to hear prayers like this one (2 Chron 7.10–12).

Verse 10 is a pivot between the historical retrospective and the current plea, and with verse 11 forms the complaint against their enemies. In Moses' day, God had not allowed Israel to go to war with Moab and Ammon (Deut 2.9, 19). They had followed God's will in not invading these people and *this* is how their kindness is repaid—a point that could indicate frustration with the enemies, with God, or both. Jehoshaphat's point is they are innocent of anything that should lead to this moment and do not deserve what is presently happening to them.

On the basis of God's sovereignty, God's promises, and Israel's obedience in relation to these nations, Jehoshaphat turns to his plea (v 12). In this case, he makes no specific request beyond the rhetorical question indicating God would surely execute judgment, nor does he ask for a specific answer. The hope is that God would come in judgment against those who have so clearly challenged His purposes.[6] But Jehoshaphat's final statement of faith is simple. It does not seek to convince God and certainly does not try to manipulate His hand. Instead, Jehoshaphat confesses their helplessness: they are overwhelmed—both in number and regarding knowledge of what to do next—and leaves the matter entirely in the hands of God: "We do not know what to do, but our eyes are on you."

Connections

Praying the promises. Although referring to God's promises, character, and history with His people seems to be stock language in Biblical prayer, we are hard pressed to find an example filled any more densely than this short prayer. In it, Jehoshaphat quotes or paraphrases both David (20.6; 1 Chron 29.11) and Solomon (20.9; 2 Chron 6.28, 34–35). He refers to "Abraham your friend" (20.7; cf. Isa 41.8; Jas 2.23) and the time of Moses (20.10; Deut 2.9, 19) and Joshua (20.7; Deut 28.7), some 400 years

---

[6] Selman, *2 Chronicles*, 426–426.

earlier. In this, he makes allusion to the Abrahamic, Mosaic, and Davidic covenants,[7] convinced that "our God" and "the God of our Fathers" is one and the same. In Jehoshaphat's mind, God's reported words and deeds of the past are true, which means he could expect to see God's good deeds repeated in his own time of need. For Jehoshaphat, and for us, the facts of the past and present merge together in prayer: who God is remains who He will be. His promises are certain and His character unchangeable. Balentine correctly says that who God is and what God has promised are the only resources available to Jehoshaphat and his people.[8] I would add that such resources are not only all that a believer needs, but the only certain resources that exist.

Thoughtful prayer. It seems unlikely that this prayer is "off the cuff," not just because it is so thought out, but because it is preceded by a fast and all of Judah coming together to seek God (v 4). Jehoshaphat had likely been praying this and similar prayers for several days leading up to this point. Here, however, the nation has gathered and the king stands in the midst of them to lead them all before the throne of God and his prayer does not disappoint. It is not only rooted in God's promises and His history with His people, but shows his understanding of the very nature of His relationship with them, both through the Temple and in battle, where He has frequently led them to victory over much larger and stronger forces. The praise that Jehoshaphat gives at the outset is appropriate, given the circumstances. The promises and history cited are appropriate for the moment. The call for judgment and humble acknowledgment that God's power is what must save the day is precisely what a faithful person should say. Jehoshaphat, it would seem, has given much thought to just how he would lead his nation in a public appeal to their God. Such careful thought, particularly, but not exclusively, in times of crisis, should characterize leaders in the kingdom today as they direct God's people collectively to pray before Him.

The nature of God. Notice the depiction of God in the opening of Jehoshaphat's prayer. God is personal and present, ancestral and faithful,

---

[7] Ibid., 425; Hill, *1 & 2 Chronicles*, 490.
[8] Balentine, *Prayer in the Hebrew Bible*, 100.

transcendent and present, universal and local, omnipresent and omnipotent. The God Jehoshaphat serves is one who is not so far away He cannot hear, but not so nearby His reach cannot extend over other nations. He is trustworthy now because He has shown Himself to be trustworthy in the past; His promises have all been fulfilled. His power and presence are not limited in any way whatsoever and His nature as the creator of the universe means there is no nation, whether ally or foe, who is outside of His realm of control.

God's power in dire distress. Regardless of any doubts a believer may have at certain points of life, one thing the Bible never calls into question is God's power and presence. When there is nowhere else to go, God is a constant. He is there. He hears. He acts, and does so decisively. Although this is similar to the above point, this fundamental truth drives home a lesson that is far too easy to forget: the one to whom you can turn when there is nowhere else to go is the one to whom you should *first* turn on every occasion.

Strength is found in weakness. Far too often we would rather turn first to our own strength and trust in our own abilities. We do not, in fact, turn to God first on every occasion and God sometimes allows situations to arise to press home that point. Paul's experience with this matter is an obvious illustration, and for good reason. Paul needed to learn humility and so God allowed an enduring difficulty to plague him, teaching him beyond all doubt that he must rely on Christ's power in him rather than any power of his own. It is in his weakness that Paul would boast, because that is when he allowed Christ's power to rest upon him; only in his own weakness could he be strong (2 Cor 12.7–10). So also it was with Jehoshaphat. His army could not deliver and his trust must be in God: "we are powerless against this great horde … but our eyes are on you" (v 12). And so also it must be with us. We cannot trust in ourselves and our own strengths or abilities. Such is the very essence of foolishness and the certain path to loss and destruction. It is in our weakness and dependence that we find God's strength and victory, for apart from God's power, we can do nothing (John 15.5).

Confidence in God's response. Jehoshaphat rose early the following morning, a phrase that frequently appears in contexts where someone faces a hard task resolutely,[9] and the people began their journey to the battlefield. Far from being overwhelmed with continuing fear, Jehoshaphat is now ready to lead his people into battle, confident God will be victorious: "Believe in the LORD your God, and you will be established; believe his prophets, and you will succeed" (v 20). He appoints singers to lead the army, urging thanksgiving to God because of His steadfast, merciful, covenant love and faithfulness. Jehoshaphat's prayer produces trust and his trust produces action. Prayer should bring comfort (Phil 4.6–7; 1 Pet 5.7) and faith should result in works (Jas 2.14–26). This is not to say that all concerns are miraculously and immediately removed or that our trust should shift from our God to our deeds, but the Bible is abundantly clear on both matters. We can be confident in God's response, because we trust Him. And because we trust Him, we act in the way He would have us act.

The difficulty of seeing the blessing during the trial. As we said above, the connection between Jehoshaphat's reforms and the invasion of his enemies raises a difficult question in the moment itself: "Why is God punishing me for obedience?" At the end of the story, however, we find a king who has experienced victory and rest from his enemies, two great blessings to any ancient king. This broader perspective—whether seen here or other places, such as Joseph's evaluation of his trials (Gen 45.5; 50.20)—reminds us that it is impossible to see the full picture from the middle of the storm. While we may be asking God where He is in our trials, He is the same place He always is: reigning on His throne. The real question is where *we* are in the trial and what blessings God will bring the faithful on the other side of it.

---

[9] Nathan Ward, *The Growth of the Seed,* 229. cf. Genesis 19.27; 20.8; 22.3; 26.31.

THIRTEEN

Out of My Distress

Jonah 2.1–9

The God to whom we pray is a God who sometimes pins us into an unpleasant corner for our own good. Whether from pseudo-pious self-reliance or outright rebellion, we may find ourselves in need of humbling and God knows just how to humble us. The question in all such situations is how we will respond. Jonah provides a good example of such a situation and the ambiguity of his prayer allows the reader to reflect on it in a variety of ways.

Context

Jonah's prophecy is associated with the time of Jeroboam II (eighth century BC) in the Northern Kingdom of Israel (2 Kgs 14.25), a time of relative prosperity and strength for Israel.[1] Assyria, meanwhile, found itself in a particularly rough time of its history. The late 800s had seen nearly a decade of internal strife followed by several decades of decline, including the time of Jonah himself.[2] The notion that Jonah did not want to preach to Nineveh because they were a superpower certain to overthrow Israel any day is simply not correct. Perhaps he knew of their past strength and anticipated an eventual return and this motivation did play some role in his disobedience, but Assyria was not an imminent threat.

---

[1] The text only says that his prophecy was *fulfilled* at that time, though most commentators take it to be the same time that Jonah was working.

[2] Alexander, "Jonah," 77–81.

Jonah was an Israelite and a worshipper of Yahweh, the God of Israel (1.9). In this, he understands that God is not merely a regional deity, as pagans believed about their gods, but the true creator—and, thus, sovereign—of sea and land. But Jonah is a *disobedient* Israelite and worshipper of Yahweh (1.2–3). He has been called to prophesy in Nineveh, but instead flees to Tarshish, the farthest point in the opposite direction. Jonah goes down to Joppa, then down into the ship, and then down into the inner part of the ship. Jonah's downward trajectory matches his spiritual fall and foreshadows his ultimate journey toward the very gates of death. Jonah *knows* but does not *do*, setting up the account of divine wrath and human disaster, and he understands that his disobedience has provoked divine punishment.

To be brief, God hurls a storm upon the sea, the mariners hurl their cargo into the sea to lighten the load, and they ultimately will hurl Jonah himself into the sea. Jonah's journey is not merely downward from the Promised Land to the edge of death, but from land to ship to sea to fish to land. At all points, the God "who made the sea and the dry land" (1.9) was in control of what was happening to Jonah; Jonah was never outside of God's rule.[3]

Jonah's prayer from the belly of the fish[4] is bracketed by divine actions related to the two realms Jonah has confessed God controls (1.17; 2.10). The prayer itself speaks of Jonah's dire circumstances and God's rescue. Jonah is not yet rescued fully, but anticipates that God will indeed deliver him in a complete sense. He prays,

> I called out to the LORD, out of my distress,
>   and he answered me;
> out of the belly of Sheol I cried,
>   and you heard my voice.

---

[3] Brueggemann, *Great Prayers*, 60.

[4] We should be careful not to envision Jonah's three-day journey in light of the whale scene in Disney's *Pinocchio*, which is probably the first image that subconsciously comes to mind as we imagine what it would have been like. For example, Limburg, *Hosea–Micah*, 146 says, "We have to imagine Jonah safe and sound, sitting inside that huge creature of the sea, singing praises to the Lord." This view is surely incorrect, both in its conflation with Disney and its attributing a Paul-and-Silas like attitude (Acts 16.25) to Jonah.

> For you cast me into the deep,
>> into the heart of the seas,
>> and the flood surrounded me;
> all your waves and your billows
>> passed over me.
> Then I said, "I am driven away
>> from your sight;
> yet I shall again look
>> upon your holy temple."
> The waters closed in over me to take my life;
>> the deep surrounded me;
> weeds were wrapped about my head
> at the roots of the mountains.
> I went down to the land
>> whose bars closed upon me forever;
> yet you brought up my life from the pit,
>> O LORD my God.
> When my life was fainting away,
>> I remembered the LORD,
> and my prayer came to you,
>> into your holy temple.
> Those who pay regard to vain idols
>> forsake their hope of steadfast love.
> But I with the voice of thanksgiving
>> will sacrifice to you;
> what I have vowed I will pay.
>> Salvation belongs to the LORD!" (Jon 2.2–9)

Contents

Jonah's prayer is similar to psalms of thanksgiving. In addition to having the poetic form of a psalm, it contains all the elements of this type of psalm: summary of answered prayer, reports of personal crisis and divine rescue, and a vow to praise. Psalms of thanksgiving are closely related to laments: they focus on a particular crisis in the psalmist's life, though the perspective is from the one who has been delivered rather than the one who is experiencing the difficulty.[5]

Perhaps the greatest difficulty of Jonah's prayer is determining what to do with it in the broader context of the narrative. Views range from true repentance[6] to a deficient repentance that focuses too much on self[7] to a completely self-deluded fiction.[8] This book cannot engage in a thorough discussion of these matters, but we will return to it at relevant points throughout our discussion.

As to the content of the prayer, it is an extended description of Jonah's journey to the very doors of death only to be rescued at the last moment. His call to God was "out of the belly of Sheol" (v 2). The description in verses 5 and 6 are particularly evocative: surrounded by water, which closed in on him to take his life with weeds wrapped around him. The image is almost one of Jonah being wrapped in grave clothes and buried in a tomb.[9] The bases of the mountains may refer to the ancient concept of two subterranean mountains that flank the gates of Sheol, which are essentially the doorway to the underworld.[10] This is the key point of Jonah's prayer: he was near death, he cried out to God, God heard him and responded. At his lowest point, the bars of the underworld threatened to close upon him forever—until God snatched him up from the pit.[11]

---

[5] Commentators take different approaches to the structure of Jonah's prayer. For a detailed discussion of the poetic structure of Jonah 2, see Youngblood, *Jonah*, 99–106.

[6] Allen, *Joel, Obadiah, Jonah, and Micah*, 215–219 seems to approximate this view. Cf. Kaiser, *I Will Lift My Eyes*, 89–98.

[7] Youngblood, *Jonah*, 118 says, "The experience convinced Jonah for a while that divine judgment is not preferable to the divine commission," but his actions in chapter 4 indicate "that he was not fully prepared to accept the implications of this bold confession."

[8] Millar, *Calling on the Name of the Lord*, 99 reads Jonah's prayer in a particularly negative light referring to some of its claims as "poetic license" and saying that the "poetic license seems to turn into something resembling post-apocalyptic dystopian teenage fiction." I'm not sure how accurate that analogy is, but my guess is Millar was engaging more in rhetoric than precision.

[9] Youngblood, *Jonah*, 112.

[10] Ibid., 113. Youngblood also points to other terms which are images of death and Sheol: the deep, the heart of the sea, the river (110).

[11] "Pit" is a common Old Testament word for the grave. Stuart, *Hosea–Jonah*, 477. says that the "bars of the underworld" is an expression that has an Ancient Near Eastern background referring to death and is the precursor to the New Testament's "gates of Hades."

Jonah's prayer features God at the beginning, middle, and end (vv 1, 6–7, 9). It is clear Jonah understands he is never outside the realm of God, even in the fish's belly. He understands God is "the decisive player in the dramatic transformation from trouble to restoration, from pit to temple."[12] Likewise, he understands his plight is God's doing (v 3), which, with 1.12, indicates he knows it is because of his sin. Even so, it is surprising to find no real confession of sin in this prayer, which may be a hint that Jonah is not as penitent as he should be.

What might be surprising is the prayer's focus on the Temple (vv 4, 7), although this may be less unexpected after studying Solomon's prayer of dedication and seeing Jehoshaphat's references to it. Jonah also seems to know this prayer and, at least in spirit, prays toward the Temple where God will hear him. Jonah is a bit like the prodigal. He has wandered away from God and found estrangement not to his liking.[13]

Abruptly, Jonah contrasts himself with idolaters: I remembered the Lord, those who pay regard to idols forsake their steadfast love, but I will pay my vows. In general, there is much truth in Jonah's brief polemic about idolatry, but in the larger context of Jonah, it is highly ironic. We know of two groups of idolaters in the book, the first of whom Jonah had just been with. God had shown His steadfast love to them in calming the storm when they fulfilled His will of throwing Jonah overboard. Far from forsaking that steadfast love, however, they made their sacrifices and vows (1.16), while Jonah uses the Old Testament refrain about God's steadfast love as an indictment of Him (4.2). Indeed, in the narrative, they pray to Jonah's God, sacrifice to Jonah's God, and vow to Jonah's God before Jonah does.[14]

---

[12] Brueggemann, *Great Prayers*, 63.

[13] Kaiser, *I Will Lift My Eyes*, 91. This is admittedly in tension with the earlier "hint that Jonah is not as penitent as he should be" and the generally negative reading of Jonah I take. There are admittedly different ways to read Jonah: either he repents and relapses in chapter 4 or his repentance is coerced by his situation and not terribly sincere (as is proved by chapter 4).

[14] Balentine, *Prayer in the Hebrew Bible*, 75 points out that this "intent on heading for Jerusalem to offer sacrifices and vows in the temple" stands in contrast with his still-existing mission to Nineveh and may reflect that Jonah has not repented. Such a trip would be required to offer sacrifices, because of the Temple's location in Jerusalem; perhaps he only intended it as a short stop on the way to Nineveh.

The irony of Jonah's contrasting his own righteousness with idolaters, when they have proven themselves to be more righteous than he, is only magnified with his closing declaration, "Salvation belongs to the LORD." Jonah is, of course, right. He could not deliver himself, nor could he count on any other god to deliver him. This truth has been known by Israel since the Exodus, and countless other deliverance stories since have only reinforced it. God is sovereign over salvation, and it is His—and only His—prerogative. The irony comes in chapter 4 when, despite what he says here, Jonah wants to be sovereign over salvation. God delivers Nineveh—the second group of pagans who also seem more ready to call upon the Lord than Jonah—from the destruction He had previously announced through Jonah. Jonah not only becomes angry about this to the point of despair, but quotes God's glorious covenant character back to Him as an accusation (4.2; cf. Exod 34.6).[15] The very refrain of hope throughout the Old Testament has become the indictment that has led Jonah to a place of sullen, selfish despondency. What should be a climactic exultation of Jonah's prayer is instead nothing but orthodox talk not backed up by Jonah's actual beliefs or practices.

Connections

Scripture informs the language of prayer. One of the remarkable things about Jonah's prayer is that it is thoroughly informed by the language of the Psalter. Jonah quotes or alludes to canonical psalms seven times during his prayer (2.2=Ps 120.1; 2.3=Ps 42.7b; 2.4=Ps 31.22; 2.5=Ps 69.1b; 2.7=Ps 142.3; 2.8=Ps 31.6; 2.9=Ps 3.8). Jonah thoroughly knew Israel's inspired hymnal and leans heavily on it as he prays. In spite of his disobedience, he is indeed a Yahweh worshipper who is well versed in Scripture. We will return to Jonah's orthodoxy shortly, but for now there is a valuable lesson to be learned here. As Kaiser says,

> [T]he best way to give voice to our own calls for help when we pray is to meditate and to memorize the language of the saints who called out

---

[15] Millar, *Calling on the Name of the Lord*, 100.

to God in the Psalms. The language of the Psalms will teach us how to pray both in private and in public. In fact, this is one great reason why we should memorize portions of the Psalms; this will supply the language our hearts search for in times of major distress.[16]

Sinners have every right to go to God. Jonah was completely, willfully rebellious against the will of God. God had given Jonah a task and he did not merely ignore it or forget it through negligence. He blatantly disobeyed it to the point of trying to do the exact opposite. When roused by the sailors and urged to pray to his god, the text gives no indication that he did (1.6). He must have known the storm was his fault, but he seems to remain silent until the lot falls upon him, at which point he confesses to them his wrong, and instructs them to throw him overboard. At some point, as he neared death in the sea, he prays. God heard him and delivered him (1.17). In spite of Jonah's blatant disobedience, he was heard. In spite of his horrific attitude in chapter 4, God will continue to work with him. Whether Jonah ever learns anything in this book where the titular character, God's prophet, is the antagonist is left unanswered. But throughout, God continues to hear Jonah. He continues to correct Jonah. Because God does not ever want to give up on His people.[17]

Turning to God as a last resort. Sometimes, we find ourselves pinned into a corner with no ready solution to our problems. Though we have surely never been fish-belly pinned in, we may well have felt that way. People of faith naturally turn to God in those moments. People who are drifting, not as firm as they should be, also turn to God in those moments. For that matter, in particularly dire moments, people who have never wanted to have anything to do with God will sometimes turn to God in those moments! It is easy to look down on so-called "foxhole religion" as something

---

[16] Kaiser, *I Will Lift My Eyes*, 93. See Magonet, *Form and Meaning*, 44–49 for a thorough discussion of the parallels.

[17] In addition to Jonah's being heard despite his disobedience, the Ninevites' later repentance proves this as well. Further, Greenberg, *Biblical Prose Prayer*, 15 points to the sailors in chapter 1 as "evidence of the Scriptural assumption of the universal capacity for prayer and its unlimited efficacy." That Jonah's own story is left open suggests that we should be cautious before condemning him too heartily. We do not know what the text does not say, including all that happens after this particular story is over.

inferior. But it is surely axiomatic that the one thing worse than turning to God only when there is nowhere else to turn is *not* turning to God when there is nowhere else to turn. Indeed, God may well have driven us into the foxhole to get our attention. He regularly rescues those who turn to Him in crisis. In those moments, Duguid says, God has us exactly where He wants us: "at the place where nothing and no one but him can possibly help you. ... He will not turn your cry away because you are a sinner or because you are utterly lost. After all, Jesus Christ came to rescue sinners and to seek and to save that which was lost (Luke 19.10)."[18] We all must learn to reject self-reliance and trust entirely in God.

The Possibility of Self-Delusion. The rest of the book of Jonah—both his disobedience before the prayer and his attitude about God and forgiveness after—raises serious questions about what he means while he prays. The lack of confession in this prayer is particularly striking.[19] Jonah knows the right things. He knows Scripture, both Solomon's temple prayer and the book of Psalms. He knows of the futility of idolatry. He knows salvation belongs to the Lord. And yet he cannot seem to apply any of it beyond the mere words. As Youngblood says, "Jonah was readily able to quote beautiful truths from the psalms, [but] he appears not to have grasped their implications."[20] Jonah is a reminder that it is possible to say all the right things and still be in the wrong. And it is possible to learn a hard lesson—only to forget it a few days later. As Duguid says,

> Jonah may have been redeemed and delivered from death, but he hasn't yet been deeply changed by his experience of grace. Like the unmerciful servant in the parable that Jesus told, he is joyful because all his debts have been forgiven and he has been set free, but he doesn't yet grasp the enormity of that debt and therefore lacks love and compassion toward other sinners. He thinks of them as merely idol worshippers who don't deserve

---

[18] Duguid, *The Rebel Prophet*, 26. But cf. Proverbs 1.24–31; 28.9.

[19] A more sympathetic reading of Jonah would include the likelihood that his days in the fish included far more prayer than this recorded one and we do not know what he did (or didn't) pray about then. Of course, we can neither import more confession into those silences with certainty nor demand that they were not there. They at least open the possibility of penitence beyond chapter 2.

[20] Youngblood, *Jonah*, 109.

anything from the Lord, unlike upstanding prophets like him who deserve God's grace when they mess up. ... [T]he message of this chapter is not that we should repent as Jonah did and learn to be like him: it is that we should repent as Jonah didn't. Jonah is not so much an example of how we *should* behave as a picture of how we often *do* behave.[21]

Salvation belongs to the Lord. Jonah knows the truth of this great statement, even if he doesn't want to let it be true when he dislikes the implications. Even so, its fundamental truth must guide our own lives. Salvation is far outside the reach of any one of us. In addition to our inability to save ourselves, we have no say about who else God offers it to. It is difficult to fathom how someone who has been forgiven so much could ever begrudge forgiveness being offered to another, but Jonah shows an example of someone doing that very thing. Further, Jesus' parable emphasizing the truth of it even more (Matt 18.21–35) proves the problem remains. And if we honestly search our hearts, we may well find that we have been guilty of the same thing. Perhaps, then, it is not so difficult to fathom after all.

"Salvation belongs to the Lord" is one of the most amazing truths in the universe, particularly when it is coupled with the Lord being a God of grace and mercy far exceeding our capacity to comprehend. It should be the pinnacle of our praise to God for what He has done for us. We must never allow it to turn into merely orthodox talk that isn't backed up by our actual beliefs or practices.

---

[21] Duguid, *The Rebel Prophet*, 27–28. Emphasis in original. Again, it is possible to read Jonah in a more sympathetic light. Consider: he confesses his sins to the sailors, he volunteers to be thrown overboard to save their lives, he believed against all odds that God would deliver him, and he goes to Nineveh immediately upon his return to the shore. Perhaps, as is often the case, the truth lies somewhere between the most optimistic and pessimistic readings of Jonah. Duguid has a particularly harsh reading of Jonah. I have included this point including some of the rhetorically-loaded language (e.g., "unlike upstanding prophets like him who deserve God's grace") for two primary reasons: first, I tend to take a more negative (though perhaps more nuanced) view of Jonah; second, the in-your-face nature of the point is what many religious people need to hear. Even if is too harsh a reading of Jonah, it may not be too harsh a reading of me.

FOURTEEN

You Alone Are God

2 Kings 19.15–19; Isaiah 37.16–20

The God to whom we pray is a God unlike any other. The other gods known to humankind are human inventions, products of human imagination and ingenuity. In addition to the clear Biblical assertions of God's unique nature, the manmade nature of idols is manifest in a variety of ways, such as the humanlike behavior and motives of these gods in their various stories, to say nothing of their complete impotence to do anything.[1] These are clearly gods made in man's image, the exact opposite of the Biblical claim concerning Yahweh, the creator of heaven and earth, a God who can indeed intervene and deliver His people.

Context

Hezekiah was, like Jehoshaphat, one of the few good kings after the division of Israel. His reign is spoken of even more positively than Jehoshaphat's, and his moral leadership of the nation may have been second only to David. Although he had his failings, the general summation of his reign is glowing, to say the least (2 Kgs 18.3–7).

In response to Hezekiah's obedience, God allows a situation to unfold that will show just how powerfully present He is.[2] In this case, Sennacherib, the king of Assyria, invades. The Northern Kingdom had already

---

[1] See Ward, "The Reign of Ahab," 95–99 for a discussion of this in the context of Baal.
[2] See comments about the similar situation with Jehoshaphat on page 83.

fallen to Assyria. Now, Assyria has its sights set on Judah, and all the fortified cities, save Jerusalem, have fallen (18.13). With the Assyrian army surrounding Jerusalem, the psychological warfare begins: the Rabshakeh[3] brings messages to dispirit the people of Jerusalem and urge them to surrender without a battle.[4] This leads to three exchanges, all of which include an Assyrian speech and Judahite response.

The first Assyrian speech (18.19–25) begins with a series of questions revolving around the word "trust" and builds to Judah's military vulnerability. The Rabshakeh says Judah has no basis for trust, either in Egypt or in their own God—and certainly not in themselves, for they could not man an army upon a gift of 2,000 horses! The point is that Hezekiah has nothing reliable at all in the face of Assyrian power and, therefore, must surrender. In response (18.26–27), the Judean delegation that had been sent out to speak with him requested that they speak in Aramaic, the imperial language not known by the common Judean. This, of course, is no response at all, just an attempt to hide the humiliation and vulnerability of the city.

The Assyrian response that begins the second exchange (18.28–35) is a clear rejection of the Judean request, as he stands and calls out in a loud voice in Hebrew. This time, the focus has shifted from "trust" to "deliverance," and the message is that there is none. Twice, he repeats the imperative that they must not allow Hezekiah to make them trust God (vv 30, 32). Just as they have no reason to trust and no place in which to put their trust, so also there will be no deliverance from the hand of Assyria. Three times, the people are urged not to listen to Hezekiah, who, he says, misleads them. No other god had delivered its people—including Judah's own sister nation to their north; likewise, there is no reason to believe that the Lord would deliver Jerusalem. The statement about being taken away sounds assuring, but, considering how the Assyrians

---

[3] This word means "chief cupbearer"—in Akkadian and Hebrew, *šqh* means "to give drink"—and it is always used in reference to a high-ranking Assyrian officer. In the context of 2 Kings 19, it could be translated "chief officer" (REB). See CAD, 17.2.28–30; DCH, 7.389.

[4] Kaiser, *I Will Lift My Eyes*, 103.

treated their captives, constitutes a threat that makes this speech more ominous than the first.[5] In response (18.36–19.7), the Jews say nothing. At least, that is their first response, for Hezekiah had instructed them not to respond. Instead, they return to Hezekiah with the message, who then sends for Isaiah.[6] In response, God says not to be afraid and that He Himself would act on their behalf. Although the king and his men remain silent, God replies with a prophetic promise.[7]

The final Assyrian speech (19.10–13) is sent by letter, as a skirmish with Cush had broken out that required their attention. It is a summation of the first two, returning to the themes of trust and deliverance and trying to drive home the point that Yahweh their God will be as inept and inconsequential as every other god they had previously faced.[8] Your only sane option, he seems to be saying, is surrender. Hezekiah takes the letter to the Temple—indicating his awareness that God is his only hope[9]—and spreads it out before God to see, an act not to inform God but to provoke a response. And Hezekiah prays:

> O LORD, the God of Israel, enthroned above the cherubim, you are the God, you alone, of all the kingdoms of the earth; you have made heaven and earth. Incline your ear, O LORD, and hear; open your eyes, O LORD, and see; and hear the words of Sennacherib, which he has sent to mock the living God. Truly, O LORD, the kings of Assyria have laid waste the nations and their lands and have cast their gods into the fire, for they were not gods, but the work of men's hands, wood and stone. Therefore they were destroyed. So now, O LORD our God, save us, please, from his hand, that all the kingdoms of the earth may know that you, O LORD, are God alone. (2 Kgs 19.15–19)

---

[5] Brueggemann, *Great Prayers*, 81.

[6] Note that Hezekiah says "it may be" that God heard what was going on (19.4). This does not indicate a lack of trust in God's omniscience, but is a standard Old Testament way of indicating God's sovereignty while protecting the fact that it is *His* right to be sovereign, not theirs to presume upon it. See Ward, *God Unseen*, 125–134 for more on this idea.

[7] Brueggemann, *Great Prayers*, 82.

[8] Ibid.

[9] Oswalt, *The Book of Isaiah*, 653. Balentine, *Prayer in the Hebrew Bible*, 95 says this scene shows "prayer as the effective and paradigmatic response of a faithful servant."

Contents

Hezekiah's prayer, like so many others, begins with doxology. He speaks to the identity of God, which replaces—but is, in essence, identical to—the promises of God that fill so many other prayers. This God is the God of Israel, committed to Israel's well-being. He is the resident of the Temple in Jerusalem (cf. 1 Kgs 6.23–28),[10] which stands as evidence of His abiding presence with His people. He is the only true God in the entire international arena. He is the creator of all, who is responsible for and capable of the right ordering of all reality. In this doxology, "The *God of all* is summoned to *the need of Israel*."[11]

Any of those individual points could be worth a paragraph (or an entire book!). In direct opposition to the taunts of the Rabshakeh, Hezekiah affirms that Yahweh is "the living God" and the corresponding contrast with the idols Assyria had previously defeated. This is, after all, the essence of the issue. Assyria is confident that Judah's God cannot stop them because no other God had; indeed, their defeat of Judah's other fortified cities seems to have provided conclusive proof about the matter. Hezekiah, however, continues to trust that their God is fundamentally different from the idols of the nations around them, asking God to see and hear, which is itself an echo of Solomon's Temple prayer (1 Kgs 8.27–30).[12] As Oswalt says,

> In contrast to the idols, which have eyes but cannot see and ears but cannot hear ([Isa] 43.8), Hezekiah appeals to the living God, who sees without eyes and hears without ears. The term *living God* appears largely in the context of the Israelite conflict with idols (see Deut 5.26; Josh 3.10; 1 Sam 17.26, 36; Pss 42.2; 84.2; Jer 10.10; 23.36; Dan 6.20, 26; Hos 1.10). As such it expresses the conviction that the gods are indeed lifeless, for their only power is that derived from their makers. The living God is not dependent upon his creatures. They, in fact, derive their life from him. Thus,

---

[10] In particular, the phrase "enthroned between the cherubim" is a clear reference to the Ark of the Covenant in the Temple, which indicates God's presence among His people.

[11] Brueggemann, *Great Prayers*, 83. Emphasis in original.

[12] Leithart, *1 & 2 Kings*, 258.

when God's true greatness is unfolded, his creatures can be delivered. If the creature is exalted, salvation is impossible.[13]

Balentine enumerates a series of contrasts appearing in Hezekiah's prayer between God and the gods, concluding, "By stating the contrast between God and the 'not gods' so clearly, and from a verity of perspectives, Hezekiah's declaration effectively seeks to petition God to act now in a manner consistent with the divine character. In other words, the Lord's reputation as a living God is at stake."[14]

Hezekiah's continues his prayer with a description of the cynical Sennacherib, whom God is urged to see and hear. He is characterized as the ultimate opponent of God, who sets himself against the living God by his scorn and destroying the people and their lands God created. The living God is the creator of the heavens and the earth; Sennacherib is "a devastator of *the earth* and a mocker of *heaven* ... an autonomous king that is in defiance of the ordering of the world for which YHWH is responsible."[15]

As usual, "and now" introduces the petition, tying it to the previous doxology and description of the situation. He appeals to their existing relationship ("our God") and prays God will do the very thing Assyria said He could not ("save us, please"). Hezekiah has rejected Sennacherib's logic and insists Yahweh is unlike the other gods; He can, in fact, deliver—even from the great power of Assyria.[16] In a sense, this has become another Mt. Carmel (1 Kgs 18.17–40). The real contest is not between Assyria and Jerusalem or between Sennacherib and God, although it might look that way to the physical eye. Instead, the contest is between Yahweh and the pagan deities.[17] Can He or can He not deliver in a way that no other god could?

---

[13] Oswalt, *The Book of Isaiah*, 654. Emphasis in original. Two minor changes in my quotation should be noted: the parenthetical citations appear as a footnote in the original and the Psalms citations have been adjusted to indicate only the English versions versification rather than both the Hebrew and English numbering.

[14] Balentine, *Prayer in the Hebrew Bible*, 94.

[15] Brueggemann, *Great Prayers*, 84. Emphasis in original.

[16] Ibid.

[17] Hailey, *A Commentary on Isaiah*, 308.

Finally, Hezekiah lays out the motivation for his entire request: the glory of God. That the world may come to know what Hezekiah already does: Yahweh alone is God (19.15, 19).

God responds decisively. He indicates He is aware of their challenge and mockery (19.22–24), but the Assyrian success was not of their own strength but from His hand—and He will now bring it to an end (19.24–28). Judah will survive and Assyria will be defeated (19.29–34). God sends His angel, who slaughters the Assyrian army, forcing Sennacherib to retreat to Nineveh, where he is eventually assassinated by two of his sons (19.35–37).[18] Ironically, Sennacherib will die in the temple of his god, a final twist in the story that shows who truly is God. Hezekiah, helpless and hopeless, is saved by his God who Sennacherib said could not save; Sennacherib's god, however, is truly powerless and unable to deliver him.

Connections

Prayer rooted in God's character. Hezekiah understands there is no hope for Judah on the basis of their righteousness and instead bases his appeal solely on God's character and identity. Sennacherib had called God's identity into question. He has tried to define who God is, although the God who made the heavens and the earth is the one who defines all things.[19] Hezekiah, in effect, asks God to reveal who He really is to the posturing Assyrian.

As indicated above, God's character and His promises are closely aligned, for His promises derive from who He is. Although Hezekiah does not appeal to God on the basis of His promises, God responds on that basis: "For I will defend this city to save it, for my own sake and for the sake of my servant David" (19.34). As Chester says, "In the midst of the turmoil of history we can pray confidently to the God who keeps his promises. Without this confidence, prayer is reduced to wishful think-

---

[18] Sennacherib's annals (found on three clay prisms now held in various museums) detail the Assyrian campaign against Judah, including reference to the defeat of various cities, including Lachish. Regarding Jerusalem, Sennacherib claims to have had Hezekiah trapped "like a bird in a cage," though the record does not include any details of why he failed to take Jerusalem.

[19] Oswalt, *The Book of Isaiah*, 653.

ing."[20] Confidence in God, confidence in His character, and confidence in His promises are all one and are the foundation of Biblical prayer.

Universal and local. We have had occasion in this book to emphasize the Israelite belief that God is not a local deity, like the pagans thought their gods to be. By contrast, He is universal, in that His reach extends to all people and His sovereignty has no bounds. At the same time, He is also not so transcendent as to be unknown, unknowable, and unknowing. He is creator of the heavens and the earth, sovereign over all the kingdoms of the earth, and yet the resident of the Temple in Jerusalem. Oswalt is helpful here: "God is no idol, a force who exists for us; but, on the other hand, he is not absolutely removed from us. He is, in Isaiah's words, 'God with us.'"[21]

The paradox of God's transcendence and immanence is an important Biblical theme about God's nature and character that should inform our thinking about God, our faith, and our prayer. As Webb says, "Such praying lifts people out of themselves and into the presence of God. And in that context, present problems are not lost sight of; they are just seen from a new perspective, and the cry for deliverance becomes a cry that God's kingdom may come and his will be done."[22]

The real versus the superficial. The apostle Paul urges Christians to believe that what is truly real is not what we experience with our senses, but what we cannot experience at all: "The things that are seen are transient, but the things that are unseen are eternal" (2 Cor 4.18). To call a full understanding of this a difficulty of our corporeal existence is an understatement of the highest order. We can *only* experience the world around us by our senses and our senses are all we have to know the reality of anything. Trusting that things we cannot experience at all endure the longest will always be a difficulty of life on this side of the resurrection. This scene is another such moment. To say God alone is alive and powerful flies in the face of all the available evidence. His country is small and weak, His cities

---

[20] Chester, *The Message of Prayer*, 107.
[21] Oswalt, *The Book of Isaiah*, 654.
[22] Webb, *The Message of Isaiah*, 152.

have fallen, and the capital is, as Oswalt says, "cowering before an Assyrian Colossus which stands astride the world." Even so, Hezekiah,

> refuses to be deterred from what he knows to be true by evidence which is ultimately superficial. There is a word here for the modern age whose dictum too often is: if it works and if it feels good, it must be right. Had Jesus Christ believed that, there would be no cross and no Church today. What is right is not validated by winning in the short run (Dan 3.16–17).[23]

Hezekiah knew God is transcendent, which made Sennacherib's arguments meaningless. He recognized the difference between the real and the superficial and trusted in what he could not see, in spite of the apparent foolishness of doing so.

True concern for God's glory. In the end, all that mattered to Hezekiah was God's glory. Chester says, "Why should God deliver Israel? Not because the Israelites deserve to be saved—they do not. Not because the Israelites need to be saved—although they do. Deliverance will come for *God's* sake—for the sake of his reputation and to fulfill his promise to David."[24] What happened to Judah was not of ultimate importance to Judah's own king. Rather, what happened to God's name mattered most to him. As Oswalt says,

> How rare this is. We can talk easily of the importance of God's being glorified until we are hurting. Then it is of chief importance that we be delivered, and how God is perceived in it all is of no consequence. Not so with Hezekiah; the chief motive for Judah's being delivered is that the world may know that God alone is God. How often the outcome of our lives and our praying might be different if we focused first upon God's glory and upon his reputation, believing that all would be well with us if his name was well served (Matt 6.33). All too often our well-being is the end and God is only a means to that end. Here Hezekiah demonstrates the opposite: God is the end and deliverance is the means (cf. Phil 1.20).[25]

---

[23] Oswalt, *The Book of Isaiah*, 655.
[24] Chester, *The Message of Prayer*, 105.
[25] Oswalt, *The Book of Isaiah*, 655–656.

Note also that Hezekiah's concern is not merely for God's glory in Jerusalem or for His glory before the Assyrian army, but His glory among "all the kingdoms of the earth" (19.19). Our understanding of God's glory must include His glory not only being revealed to His people or to the people who know His people; rather, God intends for His glory to be known by all people. If Yahweh is the only God over all the kingdoms of the earth (19.15), then it is only natural that He wants His glory to be seen by that very same population—namely, everyone. In short, a proper understanding of God's glory should lead us to reflect upon evangelism and the spread of the gospel. And if the glory of God is central to prayer, so also must our concern about evangelism be central to prayer.[26]

---

[26] Chester, *The Message of Prayer*, 108.

FIFTEEN

How Long Will You Not Hear?
Habakkuk 1.2–4

The God to whom we pray is a God to whom we can complain. In addition to an entire Biblical book named "Lamentations," the Psalter is filled with lament. More than a third of the psalms are laments.[1] The sinful, broken world is an ugly place and we do ourselves no good by pretending in prayer that it is not. Doing so is unhelpful at best and can be downright dishonest. God understands that the world is broken and, by giving so many inspired examples, fully endorses lament language.

Context

Habakkuk is one of the prophets that does not have a specific date indicated in the book. The text itself, however, gives strong hints as to when the events take place. The Babylonian invasion of Judah is just around the corner (1.5–11), which places this book near the end of the period of the divided kingdom.

Hezekiah's reforms were short lived, and idolatry soon returned. Another round of reforms came with Josiah, but his sons did not follow in his paths.[2] Jeremiah's preaching had fallen on deaf ears and wickedness reigned in Jerusalem and throughout the nation. In addition to the gov-

---

[1] Waltke, et al., *The Psalms as Christian Lament*, 1.
[2] Kaiser, *Micah–Malachi*, 152 suggests that the events of Habakkuk occur less than 15 years after the reforms of Josiah.

ernment and the people being wicked, the entire religious structure was wicked as well. The priests were not spiritually astute enough to recognize and respond to evil (Jer 2.8) and false prophets preached their own opinions, giving the people what they wanted to hear (Jer 23.9–40). Yet what seems worse is that God allowed this to happen. To that end, Habakkuk prays:

> O LORD, how long shall I cry for help,
>   and you will not hear?
> Or cry to you "Violence!"
>   and you do not save?
> Why do you make me see iniquity,
>   and why do you idly look at wrong?
> Destruction and violence are before me;
>   strife and contention arise.
> So the law is paralyzed,
>   and justice never goes forth.
> For the wicked surround the righteous;
>   so justice goes forth perverted. (Hab 1.2–4)

Contents

In this short prayer, the key ideas are violence and justice, each occurring twice. Although "violence" provokes in our minds the thought of causing physical harm—and that can be, and likely is included in the events of Habakkuk's day—the Hebrew includes an even broader spectrum of ideas. Even in English, the wider range of meaning can be caught in the etymological connection between "violence" and "violate." Violence is what violates relationships and community standards, whether it involves physical violence or not.[3]

Such violations of covenant and relationship should not be allowed to stand unchecked. God's law spoke explicitly to such abuses, but instead "the law is paralyzed and justice never goes forth" (v 4). These key ideas—violence and justice—do not appear in the relationship they should. The

---

[3] Goldingay, "Habakkuk," 53.

presence of violence should lead to justice, but because the righteous are hamstrung by the prevalence and power of the wicked, *injustice* rules the day; justice is precisely what Habakkuk does not see and he knows "this upside-down world surely cannot be the kind of reality that God authorizes."[4] And yet it is the world that Habakkuk sees, because *God* makes him see it, because *God* idly looks at wrong, because *God* does not hear, because *God* does not save. Further, God's law is powerless to stop it. Habakkuk's complaint is that "violence and suffering abound, justice is perverted, the Torah with its promises of reward for faithfulness is a failure, and God, who is both the origin of Torah and its defender, is silent."[5]

So Habakkuk calls upon the Lord to do something about the injustice. Although "How long?" is a normal question of lament,[6] it likely serves a more literal purpose here than merely indicating genre. That is, Habakkuk does not merely ask "How long?" to indicate he is entering lament, but because he had been pleading long with God about this very matter.[7] God has not responded in the way Habakkuk had hoped. Instead, God seems to sit idly by as His standards, purposes, and law are thwarted. Unrestrained injustice continues and God does nothing about it.

The piling up of terms for sin in verse 3 raises the question of whether there are specific nuanced differences from one to the next or whether it is a rhetorical way of saying "every kind of sin imaginable." If there is some specific distinction in mind, it is the last pair that is particularly noteworthy, as "strife" and "contention" are legal terms, which could indicate that the law is not merely being ignored, but is being used as the very means of oppressing people who are either weaker, poorer, or "less adept at working the legal system."[8]

---

[4] Thomas, *Habakkuk*, 65.

[5] Balentine, *Prayer in the Hebrew Bible*, 184.

[6] See Psalms 6.3; 13.1–2; 62.3; 74.10; 79.5; 80.4; 82.2; 89.46; 90.13; 94.3; Isaiah 6.11; Jeremiah 4.14, 21; 47.5; 47.6. Not all of these citations are identical terms in Hebrew, but all express the same idea.

[7] The literary function may be derived from its literal reality. That is, "How long" has become a standard introduction of lament precisely because those who lament are long in prayer. If God immediately responded as the one who prays hopes every time, there would be no lament.

[8] Goldingay, "Habakkuk," 54. Cf. Thomas, *Habakkuk*, 66.

It is worth noting that, like Abraham in Genesis 18,[9] Habakkuk never makes a specific plea. Abraham and Habakkuk speak to the same issues, but do so from opposite sides. Abraham addresses the character of God, never specifying the wickedness of the Sodomites; Habakkuk addresses the wickedness of the Judeans, never specifying the character of God. In both cases, however, the unspoken assumptions are present. This is the heart of Habakkuk's prayer: the tension between his theological understanding of God's character as just and righteous and his actual experience of God's absence in the injustice and unrighteousness of Jerusalem.[10] Although unspoken, the plea for God to act (or, in Abraham's case, to be merciful) is implied.[11]

Habakkuk follows up his first question with a second: "Why?", another classic question of lament (cf. Pss 10.1; 22.1; 42.9; Jer 15.18; 20.18). Again, the question is not a request for information, but a rhetorical call for action.

God's response will set the context for the next prayer, so we will save our main discussion of it until the next chapter, but it is worth noting in the context of Millar's brief description of Habakkuk's prayer as "…asking him to act in line with his prior covenantal commitments, but to no avail."[12] Millar is surely correct that this is how Habakkuk must feel. What he does not know, however, is that God will, in fact, be acting upon His covenantal commitments. Unfortunately, it will be the full weight of the covenant curses that will be coming (Lev 26.27–39; Deut 28.36–68).

Connections

Covenant and the Character of God. Once again, God's character and covenant come to the foreground in a biblical prayer. In this instance, maybe to the surprise of some, it is specifically because Habakkuk's prayer is a

---

[9] Ibid., 53. See Chapter 1.
[10] Baker, *Nahum, Habakkuk, Zephaniah*, 51. Thomas, *Habakkuk*, 64 calls it "a cognitive dissonance between what Habakkuk knows of God and what his situation reveals."
[11] Miller, *They Cried to the Lord*, 73 says, "Habakkuk's anguished prayers are almost nothing but complaint to God in challenging questions," which, of course, carry the implied request for God to act in light of the complaint.
[12] Millar, *Calling on the Name of the Lord*, 101.

lament. Lament is not merely complaint. Its primary purpose is to take a deeply distressing concern to God for His responsive action[13] and its hope of efficacy is that it is directed to the covenant God of Israel.[14] If there is no just God—or if there is no God who would care about his plight—there is no need to pray.

Lament can be difficult for Christians who are unfamiliar with it, an issue we will return to shortly. For now, it should be said that all biblical lament is founded upon at least three basic assumptions: there is a God; He cares for His people and hears them; He can and will act on their behalf. If any of these is not true, then there is no point in lament prayer. Complaining may continue, but there would be no hope that any situation would ever improve. The one who complains to God is the one who believes in God. As Thomas says, "In a world where the rainbows of paradise lie shattered on the ground, where sin and violence abound, Habakkuk imagines a better world, one in which God will eradicate the devastation, sin, and strife in the present order. This is the persistent hope in lament prayer."[15]

Finally, those with whom God is in covenant are those with whom He has initiated a relationship. Our covenant with God is no mere formality or legal status, but an invitation to fellowship with Him. Everyone would readily agree that their best friends and closest confidants are those who see them at their worst. Those for whom we put on a brave face and from whom we hide our true feelings are those who are, at best, mere acquaintances. If God calls us to relationship, why should we try to hide our true feelings from Him in a misguided attempt at reverence? After all, He already knows what we have been thinking all day; there is no need to pretend when we come to Him in prayer. Prayer is the very place where we should cast our cares upon Him (1 Pet 5.7), not the place to present a phony carefree life to Him.

---

[13] Thomas, *Habakkuk*, 70.
[14] Ibid., 84.
[15] Ibid., 67.

"How Long" and "Why." These questions, and others like them, are at the heart of lament. It may be helpful to recall that the first to ask these questions was not man in suffering, but God in response to sin. Although it is not precisely the same as humankind's "why," God's impassioned "What is this that you have done?" (Gen 3.13; 4.10) carries much of the same emotional burden. And for however long we have been in prayer over suffering, wondering when God will address it finally and fully, He has been even longer in agony over human sin. His "How long?" begins shortly after the Exodus (Exod 16.28), continues into the wilderness (Num 14.11), is repeated in His earthly ministry (Matt 17.17), and surely continues on a daily basis as He watches our ongoing behavior—as do the "saints in perfection," who "are depicted as longing for the righteous retribution that must fall on the wicked" (Rev 6.10).[16]

In other words, when we see the broken world and ask these questions, we are standing beside God and viewing the broken creation from His point of view. But notice that lament prayer does not request deliverance *from* the world, but deliverance *in* the world and, in Habakkuk's case, the redemption and healing of the violence *of* the world.[17]

As I said above, Christians often struggle with lament. It just feels so irreverent. Should we not be people of great faith who fully trust in God in the midst of strife rather than complaining about it? Perhaps this is due to a misunderstanding of lament. As Thomas says,

> Lament can be characterized as irritating complaint, or worse, adolescent whining: moaning about hardships in life instead of facing them head-on, bravely. Lament can be considered speech for the weak when one should put on a brave face during trouble. After all, suffering and trial *produce* something in the life of the believer: patience, perseverance, and other good traits. For this reason, one should not whine about suffering but rather embrace it as a good gift from God! In this way, Christians construe all suffering as 'soul-building.' No time to whine ... God is doing something in the church! Finally, Christians may characterize lament prayer as 'impoverished of faith.'

---

[16] Robertson, *The Books of Nahum, Habakkuk, and Zephaniah*, 138.
[17] Thomas, *Habakkuk*, 84.

In this vein of thought, lament prayer is equated to rebellious protest where the petitioner, in effect, turns away from the Lord.[18]

Far from this perspective, however, is the prayer of Habakkuk and so many of the psalmists.[19] The one who trusts completely in God is the one who can tell Him all things. The one who must put on a fake happy face is the one who has no real relationship with Him. Thomas is correct that lament is relational. It is "not God-denying language but God-affirming language that reveals a radical faith in God and firm understanding of our dependence upon him for all things."[20] Or as Gowan says so well,

> It seems to many that the way of faith is to wait in patience and silence for God's redemption from trouble, but in the Scriptures we find that it is not unbelief but the strength of one's faith that forces one to ask of God impatiently, "How long?" and the reason for this is that God has made it so. It is he who has taught us that his way is a way of justice and righteousness. It is he who has promised us redemption. It is his word that makes us hunger and thirst after righteousness. So if we truly believe the Gospel which has taught us that God is sovereign and righteous, and our Savior, then we *must* ask, "Why?" and "How long?"[21]

---

[18] Ibid., emphasis and ellipsis in original. To be clear, Thomas is enumerating, not advocating, these views.

[19] There are more psalms of lament than any other type of psalm. Further, Psalms shows such pleas were not merely a part of individual prayer, but a part of Israelite worship. They brought these most difficult, deeply personal (or communal) matters before God at the Temple, because, as Gowan says, "they fervently believed he is good and just, that he cared for them and intended to help them" (*The Triumph of Faith in Habakkuk*, 23–24). For more on lament, a good starting point is the short excursus in Thomas, *Habakkuk*, 67–76. A longer entry-level discussion of lament in the context of the Psalter is in Bullock, *Encountering the Book of Psalms*, 123–139. See also Waltke, et al., *The Psalms as Christian Lament*; Wenham, *The Psalter Reclaimed*, 43–50.

[20] Thomas, *Habakkuk*, 76.

[21] Gowan, *The Triumph of Faith in Habakkuk*, 34, emphasis in original. To be sure, these questions can be detrimental for those who obsess about them and refuse to take a position of faith. For a helpful discussion about these questions from the perspective of Christian doubt, see Guinness, *God in the Dark*, 165–214.

SIXTEEN

Why Do You Idly Look at Traitors?
Habakkuk 1.12–2.1

The God to whom we pray is a God who will hear all our prayers—even if they are prayers we have already prayed. The New Testament's injunction against "vain repetitions" does not mean prayers cannot be repeated if they are the sincere and earnest pouring out of our hearts before the only God to whom we can turn. Habakkuk has looked at the world around him and asked "how long" and "why." God responds, which can only lead Habakkuk to take another quick glance at his surroundings, give thought to what God has said He would do, and again ask "how long" and "why."

Context

As discussed in the last chapter, Habakkuk sees wickedness ruling the day in Jerusalem and appeals to God to do something about it. God's response, however, cannot be what Habakkuk had hoped for (Hab 1.5–11). In short, God was not absent from the scene or ignorant of what was transpiring on the ground in Jerusalem. Far from absence or ignorance, God already had a plan to solve the very problem that so deeply concerned Habakkuk: He will destroy Judah with the Babylonian Empire.[1]

---

[1] The text's "Chaldeans" is a reference to the ethnic group that made up the Neo-Babylonian Empire of Nebuchadnezzar's day. See, e.g., Robertson, *The Books of Nahum, Habakkuk, and Zephaniah*, 148–149; Goldingay, "Habakkuk," 57, etc.

The coming Babylonians capture nations (v 6), inflict violence on their path (v 9), take prisoners of war (v 9), and overrun every fortified city (v 10). That they gather captives like sand (v 9) may be especially gut-wrenching, given the larger Biblical context of Abraham's descendants being as innumerable as sand (cf. Gen 13.16; 22.17; 32.14); those who were once promised to be a great nation will instead be captives. The Babylonians' march will be swift, dreaded, and fearsome (vv 7–8), and conquest will be inescapable. Their power is immense and their sword will cut down everything in its path. But, most significantly, the one swinging the sword is not Nebuchadnezzar, but God, the Lord over all nations and human history.[2]

For Habakkuk, God's answer has provided no answer at all. His twofold complaint of "violence" (vv 2–3) is met by God's reply that the Babylonians are coming with even more violence (v 9). His twofold complaint that "justice" never goes forth or, when it does, it goes forth perverted is met by God's reply that the Babylonians' justice is of their own making (v 7). His question of why God "looks" at the iniquity of the Judeans without acting (v 3) is met by God's direction of Habakkuk to look at the judgment He is bringing in the form of the Babylonians (v 5).[3] At every point, God's response does not make the situation better, but worse. Habakkuk sees no real response to his questions, for the cure is worse than the disease. He finds no clarification for his confusion, no comfort for his distress. God's present actions still do not match His known character,[4] so Habakkuk presses on:

> Are you not from everlasting,
>   O LORD my God, my Holy One?
>   We shall not die.
> O LORD, you have ordained them as a judgment,
>   and you, O Rock, have established them for reproof.
> You who are of purer eyes than to see evil
>   and cannot look at wrong,

---

[2] Achtemeier, *Nahum–Malachi*, 38.
[3] Thomas, *Habakkuk*, 62 has a chart of all the verbal interplay in this dialogue.
[4] Ibid., 90.

> why do you idly look at traitors
>   and remain silent when the wicked swallows up
>   the man more righteous than he?
> You make mankind like the fish of the sea,
>   like crawling things that have no ruler.
> He brings all of them up with a hook;
>   he drags them out with his net;
> he gathers them in his dragnet;
>   so he rejoices and is glad.
> Therefore he sacrifices to his net
>   and makes offerings to his dragnet;
> for by them he lives in luxury,
>   and his food is rich.
> Is he then to keep on emptying his net
>   and mercilessly killing nations forever? (Hab 1.12–17)

Contents

Habakkuk's second prayer divides into two basic parts: truths about God's character (vv 12–13) and truths about God's present dealings with Judah through Babylon (vv 14–17). The latter, in Habakkuk's view, seems to be in strange contradiction to the former.

It is clear that Habakkuk understands God. He is, first, Yahweh, the covenant God of Israel. But far from an impersonal national deity, he is "Yahweh, my God." There is relationship and Habakkuk acknowledges the connection between God and His people. He also understands God as holy, judge, and pure, all of which speak to His character and prerogatives as God. But, again, these truths about God only complicate the matter when Habakkuk considers the situation in Jerusalem and God's proposed method of solving it.[5] The essence of Habakkuk's complaint in

---

[5] The statement "We shall not die" is particularly difficult. There are scribal emendations which change it to "You shall not die," which matches the context of God being "from everlasting," but this has no manuscript evidence. Alternately, some see it as a statement of faith (e.g., Robertson, *The Books of Nahum, Habakkuk, and Zephaniah*, 157) and others see it as a rhetorical question, "Shall we not die?", expecting a positive answer (we shall die), thereby contrasting the transience of humanity with the eternality of God (e.g., Thomas, *Habakkuk*, 91–92).

this prayer is quite simple: *they're worse than we are!* The problem is not the fact of judgment; Habakkuk had essentially asked for that very thing. The problem, instead, is the means of judgment: that God will use the Babylonians to accomplish it. And the question shifts from why God idly lets violence prosper in Jerusalem (v 3) to how He could possibly idly let the Babylonians destroy His own people (v 13).[6]

God is not only allowing this to happen, but He seems to have made preparations for it to happen. He has flipped the creation order upside down, with the nations suddenly being like the created animals, completely at the whim of the strength of the Babylonians.[7] Being caught on a hook or in a net is common imagery of judgment (Isa 51.20; Ezek 32.3; Amos 4.2) showing just how powerless the peoples were in the face of Babylon's armies.[8] There may also be a literal element to this too, as there are figures in the Babylonian monuments of captives being led in single-file, strung together with hooks in their lower lips or dragged in a net.[9]

If humans being treated like animals is not topsy-turvy enough for a plan of God, the end of this scene is perhaps the most backwards of all. In celebration of his great victory, the Babylonian victor makes sacrifices to his net (v 16). This worship of the creature (i.e., his own strength) rather than the creator (cf. Rom 1.22–25) is no surprise to God, for He had said as much in His first response to Habakkuk (v 11). Even so, the questions linger. How can God use the wicked to punish His own people? How can He allow His own created order to be flipped so upside down? How can He allow those who do not even acknowledge His existence, much less His role in their success, to be victorious? And, finally, will God let this continue indefinitely?

---

[6] "Idly" is added by the ESV, but is implied. The question is not why God watches it happen, but why God watches it happen without doing anything about it.

[7] Thomas, *Habakkuk*, 94.

[8] Baker, *Nahum, Habakkuk, Zephaniah*, 56–57 points out its presence in the Near East outside the Bible.

[9] Robertson, *The Books of Nahum, Habakkuk, and Zephaniah*, 162–163.

Connections

Patiently awaiting an answer. The first verse of Habakkuk 2 goes with his second prayer, though it seems to be separate from the prayer proper. Here, Habakkuk indicates he cannot determine an answer to this on his own. A prophet has no independent wisdom; he, like us, must await God's revelation. However true that may be in general matters, how much more true it must seem in matters of such perplexity as this! As Robertson says, "Only by revelation can the genuine perplexities of God's dealings with human beings be comprehended."[10]

And waiting is what the believer must do, because faith always dwells in an interim period. It is between promise and fulfillment, between God's message and God's action, between Christ's first and second coming. Faith is, as Guinness says, the gap between the lightning and thunder. He adds,

> Faith's task is to join hands with the past and the future to hold down God's will in the present. The present moment is the disputed territory for faith, a no-man's land between past and future, ground either to be seized by obedience or lost to disobedience. Visionary faith stakes out its possession of the land and does so with energy and enthusiasm that come from its knowledge of what the reclaimed land will one day be.[11]

Why do the wicked prosper? Although this question is never directly asked in Habakkuk's second prayer, it is a related matter and a common question believers wrestle with. Here are a group of people who are known for their violence, make up their own rules to determine righteousness, and worship themselves, their power, and their glory. And these are the agents of God? But God has indicated in many places His willingness to work through the wicked to accomplish His purposes. Besides, "If God worked only through righteous people, this would mean not working through human beings at all."[12]

---

[10] Ibid., 166.
[11] Guinness, *God in the Dark*, 200–201.
[12] Goldingay, "Habakkuk," 60.

This, of course, does not make it easier to bear when the wicked prosper as the righteous suffer, and it is this very matter that can cause some to lose their faith (Ps 73.1–15). But as God will tell Habakkuk in His second reply, He will also bring judgment on the Babylonians. Those who seem to prosper are ultimately "set in slippery places" where God "makes them fall to ruin" (Ps 73.18). The truth of the temporary prosperity of the wicked can only be seen in the greater context of the eternal unseen far surpassing the transient seen (2 Cor 4.18; Ps 73.16–17, 23–26).

Why and How Long. The last chapter did not exhaust all that can be said about the value of lament, nor will this short supplement. But Habakkuk's continued questioning provides another opportunity to touch on this important aspect of faith. And lament is indeed faith. It begins in calling on the name and character of God,[13] showing us yet again that it is not a weak faith that laments, but a perplexed faith.[14] As Gowan says,

> Christian worship tends to be all triumph, all good news. ... And what does that say to those who, at the moment, know nothing of triumph? That they've muffed it, somehow? That their faith hasn't been strong enough to grant them success? That the whole business is a fraud? ... [H]as the Christian gospel completely eliminated the need, which Israel recognized so clearly, to lay all the failures of this life very openly before God himself and ask him, as a believing, worshipping community, Why and how long? ... [P]ain and oppression and injustice are still with us and it is not enough just to say to one suffering the present hurt of all that, "Christ is the answer." We need to cry with them first and plead with God a good bit. "Smile, God loves you," is too little to offer, but most of our corporate worship, I fear, does not move beyond that level.[15]

Repeating the same prayer. Whether the wicked prosper or not, the reality is that we frequently find ourselves in a position where God does

---

[13] Kaiser, *Micah–Malachi*, 156.

[14] Robertson, *The Books of Nahum, Habakkuk, and Zephaniah*, 156. Thomas, *Habakkuk*, 90 says, "[Q]uestioning God is not a faithless action but rather a radically faithful response by those who know and love God."

[15] Gowan, *The Triumph of Faith in Habakkuk*, 38.

things we simply do not understand. We believe that God is working in history and is firmly in control of it, but "at the present what God is doing seems incomprehensible or may even seem to be counterproductive."[16] This must be what Habakkuk is thinking as he returns to God asking a nearly identical question to his first prayer. So he prays yet again. There is no reprimand of Habakkuk for asking again, nor is there a divine lecture on "vain repetition" or anything of the sort. The soul vexed by trouble has the freedom to go to God as frequently as is needed. The darkest lament in the psalter tells the story of one who cries out to God day and night (Ps 88.1–2). He calls upon God every day (v 9) and when his call is unheard yet again, he rises the next morning calling on God once more (v 13). There is no understanding. There is no answer. There is no happy ending. Just a man who refuses to give up on God and a God who is willing to constantly hear his plea.

---

[16] Ibid., 37.

SEVENTEEN

In Wrath Remember Mercy

Habakkuk 3

The God to whom we pray is a God of both justice and mercy. These concepts, however paradoxical the pairing may seem, run throughout the Bible as two fundamental and certain truths about God. Due to the wickedness of the world around him and the certainty of the judgment to come, Habakkuk has come face to face with the former and desperately needs the latter. Even so, he will not appeal for God not to be just, only for the equally-true trait of mercy to be present in the judgment.

Context

The book of Habakkuk begins with his lament over the injustice and violence done and God's apparent absence, asking "How long?" and "Why?" God responds that He will indeed be present, but it will be in the form of judgment at the hands of the Babylonians. Habakkuk sees this as worse than the original situation and returns to God asking again, "How long?" and "Why?" and situates himself to receive God's final answer.

Far from being upset at Habakkuk's continued questioning, God brings more information. This time, He clarifies that Babylon will not escape His judgment. Although He will still use them to judge His own people, they will in turn be judged as well. And though it might seem like it will take a while for this to happen, it will certainly come and Habakkuk will see it if he just waits (2.3). The bulk of chapter 2 is a series of five woes pronounced on Babylon for their extortion and theft (6–20), their unjust and illegal gain (9–11), their violence (12–14), their drunkenness and related shameful behavior (15–17), and their idolatry (18–19).

The woes are interrupted twice to emphasize truths about God in contrast with the surrounding language about the Babylonians. The Babylonians will be shamed and humiliated, but the knowledge of the glory of God will be spread through the earth (2.14). Further, in contrast with the lifeless, powerless idols the Babylonians have built and speak to, the Lord sits in His holy temple and those before Him should be silent (2.20).

With this, God has made His final response to Habakkuk. He has said all that He will say on the matter, and Habakkuk seems to realize this, for his own final prayer reflects a different tone and perspective than the first two. He says,

> O Lord, I have heard the report of you,
>   and your work, O Lord, do I fear.
> In the midst of the years revive it;
>   in the midst of the years make it known;
>   in wrath remember mercy.
>
> God came from Teman,
>   and the Holy One from Mount Paran.   *Selah*
> His splendor covered the heavens,
>   and the earth was full of his praise.
> His brightness was like the light;
>   rays flashed from his hand;
>   and there he veiled his power.
> Before him went pestilence,
>   and plague followed at his heels.
> He stood and measured the earth;
>   he looked and shook the nations;
>   then the eternal mountains were scattered;
>   the everlasting hills sank low.
>   His were the everlasting ways.

I saw the tents of Cushan in affliction;
    the curtains of the land of Midian did tremble.
Was your wrath against the rivers, O LORD?
    Was your anger against the rivers,
    or your indignation against the sea,
when you rode on your horses,
    on your chariot of salvation?
You stripped the sheath from your bow,
    calling for many arrows.   *Selah*
    You split the earth with rivers.
The mountains saw you and writhed;
    the raging waters swept on;
the deep gave forth its voice;
    it lifted its hands on high.
The sun and moon stood still in their place
    at the light of your arrows as they sped,
    at the flash of your glittering spear.
You marched through the earth in fury;
    you threshed the nations in anger.
You went out for the salvation of your people,
    for the salvation of your anointed.
You crushed the head of the house of the wicked,
    laying him bare from thigh to neck.   *Selah*
You pierced with his own arrows the heads of his warriors,
    who came like a whirlwind to scatter me,
    rejoicing as if to devour the poor in secret.
You trampled the sea with your horses,
    the surging of mighty waters.

I hear, and my body trembles;
    my lips quiver at the sound;
rottenness enters into my bones;
    my legs tremble beneath me.
Yet I will quietly wait for the day of trouble
    to come upon people who invade us.

> Though the fig tree should not blossom,
>   nor fruit be on the vines,
> the produce of the olive fail
>   and the fields yield no food,
> the flock be cut off from the fold
>   and there be no herd in the stalls,
> yet I will rejoice in the LORD;
>   I will take joy in the God of my salvation.
> God, the lord, is my strength;
> he makes my feet like the deer's;
>   he makes me tread on my high places. (Hab 2.2–19a)

Contents

Several Old Testament prayers take the form of a psalm, but Habakkuk 3 is probably the single most psalm-like prayer in the Bible outside the Psalter. Verses 1 and 19b frame this with psalm-like technical language and the threefold appearance of "selah" clearly indicate the genre of this prayer.[1]

The prayer itself divides into three basic parts: Habakkuk's acceptance of God's message (v 2); Habakkuk's vision of the warrior God coming in judgment and victory (vv 3–15);[2] Habakkuk's fear and faith at prospects of what the future holds (vv 16–19).

Habakkuk's immediate response is twofold. In his acceptance of God's message, he fears. At the same time, however, he trusts. Habakkuk knows that God is a God of justice, yet he also knows that He is a God of mercy, and so he appeals to the latter in the midst of the former. Habakkuk's fear of what God will do does not prevent him from calling on God to go ahead and do it; he only pleads that God would remember mercy as He pours out His much-needed wrath. The appeal to God to "remember" might have its own importance here, as the word never refers to mere

---

[1] *Shiggaionoth* occurs in its singular form in Psalm 7. The "according to …" language is present in the superscriptions of Psalms 8, 81, and 84. "To the choirmaster" and *"selah"* appear in too many places to cite here. The precise meanings of *shiggaionoth* and *selah* are not known, though speculation abounds.

[2] Hill, "Prayer in the Minor Prophets," 81 divides this section into two parts: a theophany (vv 3–7) and a victory hymn lauding God's triumph over nature and the nations (vv 8–15).

intellectual recall when used of God. Instead, God's remembrance always has a covenant connotation, where He acts on behalf of an established relationship (e.g., Gen 8.1; Exod 2.24; Ps 98.3; etc.). If this is the intended nuance in Habakkuk's appeal, then his prayer is not merely for reprieve in wrath, but for God's covenant faithfulness to His people to be manifest through an active bestowal of mercy.

The bulk of the prayer describes God as a conquering warrior coming in awesome power and wrath.[3] The opening verses contain extensive Exodus imagery. The references to God's coming from Teman and Mount Paran likely refer to the wilderness journey, where God led and helped the people from Sinai to Canaan (cf. Deut 33.2; Jdg 5.4–5).[4] Similarly, the journey ends at Cushan and Midian, terms that refer to the southern end of the Transjordan region.[5] Plague and pestilence are also associated with the Exodus (Exod 9.3, 14; Ps 78.40, 50) and God's meeting with Israel at Sinai (Exod 5.3; Num 14.12). In the context of God's victory, the images of river, sea, horse, and chariot recur in relation to both Exodus and Conquest (Exod 13.17–14.31; Deut 11.4; Josh 3.13–17; 4.21–24; 24.6; Isa 10.26; 43.16; 50.2).[6] God has gone forth to war before and has shown Himself to be victorious—not merely over small Canaanite city-states, but over Egypt, the mightiest nation in the world at the time. It is because of this history that Habakkuk can be certain that the warrior God will be victorious yet again, whether He fights for or against His people.[7]

Similarly, when God comes in judgment, Habakkuk says, nature is impacted. The earth is split, the mountains writhe, the sun and moon stop in their tracks, and even the nations feel the effects. This, of course,

---

[3] For more on this Old Testament theme, see Longman and Reid, *God is a Warrior*. See Goldingay, "Habakkuk," 82–85 for a more thorough summation of the imagery used throughout this section of the text.

[4] Smith, *Micah–Malachi*, 116.

[5] Thomas, *Habakkuk*, 145. Cushan is not to be identified with Cush (Ethiopia), but Midian. Robertson, *The Books of Nahum, Habakkuk, and Zephaniah*, 228 notes that Moses' Midianite wife is called a Cushite in Numbers 12.1 and Judges 3.8–11 reports a Midianite king named Cushan-Rishathaim.

[6] Baker, *Nahum, Habakkuk, Zephaniah*, 71.

[7] See Longman and Reid, *God is a Warrior*, 31–60 for more on these contrasting purposes of God's warring.

is figurative language, but it speaks of the great truth of God's unconquerable power. Again, nothing can prevent the warrior God from victory when He comes in judgment.

In the woes on Babylon, two verses stand alone as statements about God. Similarly, in the midst of this depiction of the warrior God's judgment, a half-verse stands out against that backdrop: "You went out for the salvation of your people, for the salvation of your anointed" (v 13a). This has been called the key to understanding the relationship between this chapter and the entire book, and there is truth in that assertion. We find here that Habakkuk has come to understand that God neither ignores wrongdoing as he once feared (1.2–4), nor will God allow His people to go unpunished, as Habakkuk briefly hoped (1.12–17). Even so, God acts out of covenant loyalty and for the best interest of His people and His purposes.[8]

In other words, Habakkuk is speaking about a Day of Yahweh—any occasion where God breaks into time and space to judge the wicked and vindicate the righteous—although he does not use that terminology. Habakkuk has come to "understand the flow of salvation history in a new way" and to see that there can be "salvific purposes" even in judgment.[9] God's people will indeed be saved, but not without first going through the purifying fire (cf. 1 Pet 1.5–7). Deliverance will come for the righteous, but it cannot come without judgment for the wicked.

Finally, Habakkuk comes to his declaration of faith. He returns to the fear he expressed initially, adding more detail to just how terrified he truly is. Yet, in spite of the fear, he will wait, he will trust, and he will rejoice. Even in the worst possible scenario—siege warfare where every possible food source is cut off—Habakkuk will rejoice. He will do this, because his existence is not based on these things, but on God.

Connections

When prayer based on God's character fails. More than anything else, this book has emphasized—and will continue to emphasize—prayer accord-

---

[8] Baker, *Nahum, Habakkuk, Zephaniah*, 74–75.
[9] Millar, *Calling on the Name of the Lord*, 102–103.

ing to God's character, covenant, and specific promises. There is no better way to be sure that our prayer aligns with God's will than to base it on these fundamental matters, which, as has been said, are all intertwined. Habakkuk has done that very thing. He appeals to the God of justice to bring justice. He appeals to the God of purity not to let those who are impure be the instruments of correction. And yet God's justice appears unjust and God will use the impure to accomplish His pure purposes. In short, Habakkuk has appealed to God's character and God has rejected Habakkuk's appeal. At times, it seems, our understanding of God—however technically accurate it may be—does not match the reality of what God is doing. In such a situation, our only recourse is to continue to trust that God will eventually make sense of the world around us.

In Wrath Remember Mercy. Habakkuk's opening statement of acceptance, fear, appeal, and faith is something of the theme of this entire prayer. God the warrior is coming in justice, His coming will not be stopped, and the results are terrifying. Habakkuk, and any other who must experience that justice, can only fear and plead for mercy. Yet mercy is what God constantly desires to give. As Baker says,

> The love of God is so strong that even when he is flagrantly ignored, deserted or rejected, he is drawn ... to love in spite of the actions of the other (cf. Isa 1.2, 18–20; Hos 11.8–11). The wrongs are real, but so too are the compassion and the desire to forgive, if the "condition" for restoration—a renewed desire to acknowledge God—is present to allow the floods of his mercy to be unleashed.[10]

Baker is correct that this statement is a summation of the entire book and itself a model of prayer to an ever-just but ever-compassionate God.[11]

Rejoicing in Trial and Covenant. Habakkuk's ability to rejoice in spite of the trial that is coming—to paraphrase, "Even though I will starve to death, I will rejoice"—is amazing and difficult to comprehend. This perspective comes from two equally important truths. First, a joyful attitude

---

[10] Baker, *Nahum, Habakkuk, Zephaniah*, 69–70.
[11] Ibid., 70.

is not the same thing as emotional happiness. Perspectives and emotions are not the same and should not be equated. It is wrong to say that Christians should always be happy, because emotions inevitably wax and wane. A set perspective and attitude, however, should be more fixed and sustainable. It is this joy that can, in fact, coexist with suffering and trials.

Second, Habakkuk's joy is rooted not in his physical circumstances, but in his relationship with God. As Thomas says, "Even if the violence of the day seems to have won sway over Yahweh's world, the prophet affirms that Yahweh nonetheless remains his hope, joy, and salvation. If death comes, Yahweh is the hope beyond death."[12] For anyone for whom this is the case, only the (mis)perception of God's abandonment can threaten joy, because even if stripped of all else, we can never be deprived of God. As long as we recognize that our relationship with God is built on the firm foundation of God's covenant promises of an abiding relationship with His people rather than being based on mere emotion or a passing human whim, we know the relationship is sure and solid and we will be able to endure far more than we may presently be able to imagine.[13]

From Lament to Trust. Without retreading the ground of the last two chapters, I will say one last word about lament: it is fundamental to finding trust. Balentine makes this point well, saying that for people who struggle in uncertain times,

> …prayers of lament constitute an inevitable and necessary part of the action and passion of faithfulness. Such praying is inevitable because of the mystery of who God is—at times unquestionably present, and on other occasions inexplicably aloof. Such praying is also necessary. Without it, waiting for relief would threaten to stagnate and leave one in despair. Without it, one's feet could not begin to traverse the path that Habakkuk describes as the way of faith.[14]

---

[12] Thomas, *Habakkuk*, 153.

[13] Baker, *Nahum, Habakkuk, Zephaniah*, 77.

[14] Balentine, *Prayer in the Hebrew Bible*, 188–189.

Thomas makes a similar point, saying that Habakkuk's wrestling with God in complaint and prayer is what paved the path for God to "[open] up to him the wonder of the Lord's ways," going on to say, "God has opened up Habakkuk not *to* faith, as the prophet *already* believed his God, but *to a fuller, richer* faith."[15]

Hope Rooted in History. One of the key truths of God's people throughout history is that their hope for the future is based on God's actions in the past. More than anything else, in fact, the Exodus is repeated throughout the Old Testament as evidence of the faithfulness and power of God.[16] The point they constantly make is that God is known not merely through visions and revelations, but through events in history which they have experienced and remember. In short, God is known by what He has done.[17]

This basic truth does not end with the Old Testament. For Christians, however, the great historical truth is not the Exodus, but the incarnation, crucifixion, resurrection, ascension, and enthronement of Jesus. Gowan makes this point well:

> [God] provides no theophanies for us in our churches. When we gather we do not see him or hear him speak aloud. But we know God by what he *has done,* and on that basis we believe in what he will do, in the future. When questions arise about God, about whether he even exists or about whether he cares anything for his people if he does exist, the way we answer such questions is to remember real events from the past, and those things that really happened—which we believe God was responsible for—give us something to depend on that is more than speculation. Whatever anyone may say about God, his existence or his nature, there *was* an Exodus and there *was* a Jesus of Nazareth, and nothing can change that. So on history we build our theology, and this we Christians have learned from Israel.[18]

---

[15] Thomas, *Habakkuk,* 152. Emphasis in original.
[16] The Psalter is an obvious place to look for this theme (cf. Pss 78.12–16, 42–55; 106.7–11; 111.4; 114.1–6; 135.8–12; 136.10–16), but also the "new Exodus" language used in the restoration themes of the prophets and the Exodus echoes present in Ezra's telling of the return make this even more clear.
[17] Gowan, *The Triumph of Faith in Habakkuk,* 82.
[18] Ibid., 82–83. Emphasis in original.

EIGHTEEN

Nothing Is Too Hard for You
Jeremiah 32.17–25

The God to whom we pray is a God of restoration. In spite of the sin of the people and impending judgment, He continually promises that His purposes will not be thwarted by their evil. He will restore them to the land and start anew with a remnant of the people. This is rooted in His basic character, a God whose anger lasts but for a moment (Isa 26.20; 54.7–8, 16–19; Jer 3.5, 12; Mic 7.18–20), but whose steadfast, merciful, covenant love and faithfulness lasts forever (Ezra 3.11; Pss 100.5; 106.1; 107.1; 118.1–4; 136.1–26; Jer 31.3; 33.11; Hos 2.19).

Context

Jeremiah is among the most hopeless books in the Bible—at least, it feels that way when you read it. Most of the pre-exilic prophets include indictments for covenant breaking accompanied by the assurance of coming judgment, pleas for repentance to avoid the judgment, and brief glimpses of a future restoration.[1] In Jeremiah, the indictments and judgments are nearly unmitigated and God specifically tells Jeremiah not to pray for the people (Jer 7.16; 11.14). In fact, the glimpses of future restoration are largely grouped in a very small part of the book (chs 30–33).

---

[1] Hays, *The Message of the Prophets*, 63–69 summarizes this three-part message concisely. See also, Roberts, "The Prophets," 81–94 for a more detailed summary.

One of the reasons for the hopelessness is that the long-predicted judgment is arriving. By the time of this prayer, Babylon had already come and carried of the children of the nobles (Isa 39.7; Dan 1.1–6) and was exerting control through Zedekiah, whom they installed as their puppet king (2 Kgs 24.17). Zedekiah rebels, however, which will bring Nebuchadnezzar's army back full force this time. They will destroy the city, tear down the temple, terminate the monarchy, and carry the last king and the people into captivity (2 Kgs 24.20–25.21). Given the clear teaching of Leviticus 26, Deuteronomy 28, and a host of the pre-exilic prophets, this is no surprise at all; Nebuchadnezzar and Babylon are acting as the vehicle of divine judgment against God's own people. As hopeless as all this seems, restoration is promised and this chapter lies in the middle of the hope and restoration section of the book—the part that speaks of the ultimate rebuilding of Jerusalem, reconstruction of Israel, and new relationship between God and His people.

As Jeremiah 32 begins, Jerusalem is besieged (v 2). A relative of Jeremiah from Anathoth comes to visit him, urging that he buy a field, because the right of redemption fell to Jeremiah, and God told Jeremiah to buy it (vv 6–8). This practice of redemption was designed to keep the familial land (a blessing from God) in the family (Lev 25.13–17, 23–28). There is, however, multifaceted absurdity about the request. First, a people who have shown no regard for God's law at all are now suddenly concerned with keeping it to the letter (likely because it suited their purposes in the moment). Second, this is the precise moment when the land was the most worthless and the prospect for productive use of the land was absolutely nil.[2] Babylon had destroyed everything in the southern kingdom and was currently besieging Jerusalem. The old realtor's adage "location, location, location" would suggest that "three miles from the Babylonian army" will not likely be in high demand. Third, requesting that a prisoner buy land makes little sense, both in terms of his resources or need for property. Finally, the last word we heard

---

[2] Brueggemann, *Great Prayers*, 69.

about Anathoth was that the people there—including his own relatives (12.6)—wanted to kill Jeremiah (11.21–23).

Ultimately, the purchase of the land was an object lesson. God tells Jeremiah, "Houses and fields and vineyards shall again be bought in this land" (v 15), much as He had earlier said that although He plucks up and tears down, He will also plant and build (31.28). In short, the land is indeed now worthless, but it will be valuable again because the God who dispatched the Babylonian army will return His people back to their land one day. In a sense, Jeremiah's field serves a similar purpose to Abraham's cave: just as the bones of the patriarchs gave witness to their faith in the promise that their descendants would one day return,[3] so also this field indicates that God will restore His people to their land, what Wright calls "a public, written, verified, enduring prophetic signpost, points to a future beyond the immediate catastrophe."[4]

In response to God's command and assurance, Jeremiah prays:

> 'Ah, Lord God! It is you who have made the heavens and the earth by your great power and by your outstretched arm! Nothing is too hard for you. You show steadfast love to thousands, but you repay the guilt of fathers to their children after them, O great and mighty God, whose name is the Lord of hosts, great in counsel and mighty in deed, whose eyes are open to all the ways of the children of man, rewarding each one according to his ways and according to the fruit of his deeds. You have shown signs and wonders in the land of Egypt, and to this day in Israel and among all mankind, and have made a name for yourself, as at this day. You brought your people Israel out of the land of Egypt with signs and wonders, with a strong hand and outstretched arm, and with great terror. And you gave them this land, which you swore to their fathers to give them, a land flowing with milk and honey. And they entered and took possession of it. But they did not obey your voice or walk in your law. They did nothing of all you commanded them to do. Therefore you have made all this disaster come upon them. Behold, the siege mounds have come up to the city to

---

[3] Kidner, *Genesis*, 145.
[4] Wright, *The Message of Jeremiah*, 344.

take it, and because of sword and famine and pestilence the city is given into the hands of the Chaldeans who are fighting against it. What you spoke has come to pass, and behold, you see it. Yet you, O Lord God, have said to me, "Buy the field for money and get witnesses"—though the city is given into the hands of the Chaldeans.'" (Jer 32.17–25)

Contents

Jeremiah's prayer has a simple structure. It begins with doxology (v 17) before discussing the way God governs, first in general (vv 18–19) and then with His people in particular (vv 20–24), before concluding with the statement of the situation (v 25)—which amounts to Jeremiah's question.

First, God is praised for His creation power, for in His making the heavens and earth, He has proven there is nothing too hard for Him. This is a vital point, as it seems Jeremiah's fundamental question is why God would ask him to do such a thing and how it is that God will turn such an impossible situation around.

Before getting to that question, Jeremiah speaks to how God has historically dealt with the world and His people. The twin principles upon which God governs are gracious fidelity and uncompromising sovereignty[5]—or, to put it in simpler terms, mercy and judgment. This brings us back to themes we have seen throughout this book, both the presence of God's "steadfast love"—the same covenant term we have discussed at length elsewhere—and the juxtaposition of His great mercy and His great justice.

This steadfast love of verse 18a is elaborated on in verses 20–23a. God delivered His people in the Exodus and gave them the land in the Conquest, the most significant moments in Old Testament history—and God was behind it all: "You showed … You brought … You gave." But God also repays guilt in His justice (vv 18b–19), an idea clarified in verse 23b. Israel responded to God's graciousness by refusing to do anything that He told them to do ("But they…") and provoking God to keep the covenant curses. In this we again see the tension between mercy and judgment.

---

[5] Brueggemann, *Great Prayers*, 71.

God is indeed a God of gracious faithfulness and mercy, but He is a God who will not be mocked. He is a God who calls to account, yet is a God of immense forbearance.[6]

Finally, the prayer comes to its crux: the purchase of the field. In verse 25, Jeremiah quotes God's instruction (v 15) and implicitly looks back to his own declaration of God's ability (v 17). Whatever else Jeremiah may be feeling, there is surely a quiet confidence in this statement, an amazement about the divine assurance that things will be completely contradictory to how they are now.[7]

Connections

Covenant and Promise. There is no explicit reference to the covenant or promises in Jeremiah's prayer, yet this common idea is implicitly present yet again. The reference to "steadfast love" is enough on its own to make the reader connect to the covenant, but the further connections to Exodus and Conquest surely make the link clear. Beyond this, the entire point of the purchase is that the current state of affairs will not be the final state of affairs, which makes Jeremiah realize the divine command contains an implicit commitment to honor the promise to Abraham. In other words, prayer is intricately linked with the outworking of God's covenant commitments.[8] Or as Widmer says well, "Through the darkest hours that the Old Testament records, it becomes clear that no disaster, suffering, or judgment would ultimately cut off Israel from their covenant God. … It is this loving commitment ['steadfast love'] to the covenant relationship that is the foundation of all prophetic hope and prayer."[9]

Familiarity with History. As we said in the last chapter, God's people base their hope for the future in God's actions in the past. We see this again in the present prayer, where Jeremiah's faith is not expressed in vague abstractions and theological constructs, but in direct, concrete

---

[6] Ibid., 74.
[7] Ibid., 75.
[8] Millar, *Calling on the Name of the Lord*, 84.
[9] Widmer, *Standing in the Breach*, 431.

historical terms.[10] In particular, Jeremiah speaks of God's creation, God's deliverance in the Exodus, and God's giving of the land in the conquest. But such blessings were not unique to ancient history, for "God continued to make his gracious power known to his people up 'to this day.'"[11]

Familiarity with Scripture. As we get deeper into Old Testament history, we see that those who pray are not only familiar with God's promises, character, and historical deeds, but are also familiar with Scripture itself. The people of God are already growing to be a people of the book. Notice how much of the language of this prayer echoes other Old Testament texts. The creation and Exodus language permeates all of Hebrew Scripture, "and the feasts, festivals, and songs of the Temple constantly recalled them."[12] Beyond that, the reference to steadfast love to thousands again echoes Exodus 34.6–7, the "outstretched arm" shows up repeatedly, particularly in Deuteronomy (4.34; 5.15; 7.19; 9.29; 11.2; 26.8), though its origin is in Exodus 6.6 (cf. 1 Kgs 8.42; 2 Kgs 17.36; 2 Chron 6.32; Ps 136.12), "signs and wonders" show up repeatedly in reference to the Exodus (Exod 7.3; Deut 4.34; 6.22; 7.19; 26.8; 29.3; 34.11; Ps 135.9), and "milk and honey" shows up four times in Exodus and six in Deuteronomy.[13] Thompson's summary that much of the prayer "is in the form of stereotyped phrases"[14] may well be overstatement, but the point is well-taken: Jeremiah's prayer is thoroughly informed by what he has read.

Mercy and Judgment. By this point in Jeremiah, judgment is certain. It almost seems as if the Judeans had gone through the book of Deuteronomy, created a checklist of all the covenant rules, and gone out of their way

---

[10] Blackwood, *Commentary on Jeremiah*, 235. The theological constructs are there, as even Blackwood goes on to point out (236) Jeremiah acknowledges God's omnipotence ("nothing is too hard for you"), omniscience ("whose eyes are open to all the ways of men"), and omnipresence ("in the land of Egypt ... in Israel and among all mankind"). But even these principles are based on history, not philosophy.

[11] Longman, *Jeremiah, Lamentations*, 217.

[12] Thompson, *The Book of Jeremiah*, 591.

[13] Blackwood, *Commentary on Jeremiah*, 236. Goldingay, *The Book of Jeremiah*, 465 points out that much of these echoes comes from Deuteronomy 26.8–9, 15. Given the strong echoes of the covenant curses (Deut 28) that permeate Jeremiah, it is not unreasonable to suppose that he is thinking specifically of Deuteronomy 26 in this prayer.

[14] Thompson, *The Book of Jeremiah*, 592.

to violate every single one. But the God who judges is also the God who is merciful as His fundamental trait (Exod 34.6–7; 1 John 4.7–8) and is forgiving beyond our comprehension (Isa 55.6–9).

Kidner refers to this as the "paradox of God's simultaneous yes and no," where the "yes" is implied in the purchase of the field and the "no" is seen in the falling city. Further, he argues that this is "a fine example of the way to pray in a desperate situation," for it acknowledges God's power, faithfulness, and justice, remembering His great redemptive acts, "and then with this background, laying before God the guilt of the past (23b), the hard facts of the present (24), and the riddle of the future (25)."[15] Wright says similarly, "At the very moment when the guilty past has crashed into an inescapable present, God asks Jeremiah to invest in an almost inconceivable future." The question that must reverberate through Jeremiah's mind is whether the wrath of God in judgment through Babylon is the "final denouement" or if it will be the love of God in a new act of redemption. But, as it turns out, "the answer was that it would be both, for only in exercising both wrath *and* redemption would the Judge of all the earth, for whom nothing was too hard, do right."[16]

The Ability of God. As we will see again in chapter 33 of this book, God's ability far outstrips our feeble imaginations, and it is God's ability that governs what He is able to do in our world and in response to our prayers. He is not limited to what we think He can manipulate out of the way things are, because nothing is impossible for Him. Our prayers need not conform to our present circumstances, for we pray to a God who made the heavens and earth by His great power and can again make all things new. God is faithful, God is powerful, and God is free to do what He wants, which means we can pray boldly against our present circumstances. Along these lines Brueggemann says,

> The church, in much of its prayer life, has been cowardly and anemic, daring to pray only for that which the world regards as possible. Jere-

---

[15] Kidner, *The Message of Jeremiah*, 113.
[16] Wright, *The Message of Jeremiah*, 346.

miah's prayer, so typical of Israel's bold faith, exhibits the way in which faith hopes beyond circumstance. Faith knows that new life—in ancient Anathoth or anywhere in the world—arises not from what is given in the world but from the God who makes all things new. Jeremiah is grounded in old miracles and fully acknowledges present judgment. After all of that, however, he says, "And now." He waits for gifts from [Yahweh] that the world does not expect.[17]

Obedience before Counsel. Harrison seems to link Jeremiah's prayer with some sort of buyer's remorse, the cropping up of second thoughts about the wisdom of purchasing the field after having done so.[18] Although it does seem as if Jeremiah is seeking more information and assurance about his purchase, I would argue it is not a result of second-thoughts, but first-obedience. Jeremiah, who once complained to the point of incurring God's anger (15.15–21), is now at the point where he obeys first and asks questions later. God is indeed "great in counsel" (v 19), but Jeremiah knows He need not explain Himself at every point. Our task as His people is to obey and trust, not to seek to understand and be convinced.

The difficulty we all face is not in acknowledging God's ability in principle, but truly trusting it in practice. But such practical trust is what turns faith from an interesting theory into an actual reality. Far from being a mere hypothetical, faith believes in God's ability, bases all else on that, and acts accordingly. Commenting on this prayer, Guinness says,

> God's word is normative and all else is judged by it. The waters may be dark and swirling, but faith steps from one stepping stone of God's word to another. Visibility may be poor, but faith pursues the vision from one glimpse to another, undeterred by whatever stands across its path. If God says so, God must know why. Then the argument is not with God, but with the contradictions of the situation that deny his lordship.[19]

---

[17] Brueggemann, *Great Prayers*, 77.
[18] Harrison, *Jeremiah and Lamentations*, 142.
[19] Guinness, *God in the Dark*, 205–206.

NINETEEN

Because of Your Great Mercy
Daniel 9.3–19

The God to whom we pray is a glorious God of covenant faithfulness and mercy. As Chester says, "Hezekiah 'argues' with God in prayer on the basis of the reputation or glory of God. The people in Nehemiah 9 present before God his promise and his mercy. Daniel 9 brings together these three great arguments—the promise, mercy, and glory of God."[1] Although some might see these great truths as reasons not to pray—what is the point if He has already promised and is merciful? how could I come before a God so glorious as this?—Daniel embraces them as the very foundation and reason for prayer.

Context

Daniel's prayer arises from living in the tension between two competing realities. On the one hand, there is *the reality of imperial overlords*. Daniel had lived through the entirety of the Babylonian captivity, being carried off in the very first wave of exiles (Dan 1.1–7). Now, the Jewish people are under the thumb of the Persians, at the very beginning of their reign (9.1).[2]

---

[1] Chester, *The Message of Prayer*, 111.
[2] How the Bible's Darius the Mede (Dan 5.31; 9.1) correlates to a historical figure outside the Bible is highly debated. A thorough discussion that concludes he is King Cyrus is offered in Steinmann, *Daniel*, 290–296. The primary opposing view (also discussed in Steinmann) is he was one of Cyrus' generals who was reigning over the city of Babylon in Cyrus' absence.

Their present captivity is due to their sin. All the way back in Leviticus, God had promised that breaking His covenant would result in a series of judgments culminating in the land being taken away (Lev 26.14–39). The earlier judgments were designed to bring the people back to God, but if they continued to rebel, the punishment would escalate. The prophets, drawing from the covenant curse passages (cf. Deut 28), preached a message that the covenant had been broken and judgment was coming unless they repented. Their refusal to repent had brought this captivity.

The second aspect of the context of this prayer is *the prophetic hope* of return from captivity. First, as Leviticus predicted the captivity, it also prescribed the way out of captivity:

> But if they confess their iniquity and the iniquity of their fathers in their treachery that they committed against me, and also in walking contrary to me … then I will remember my covenant with Jacob, and I will remember my covenant with Isaac and my covenant with Abraham, and I will remember the land. (Lev 26.40, 42)

Sin brought them into captivity; a prayer of confession indicating repentance and seeking forgiveness is the way out.

Second, Jeremiah had twice prophesied—against the false prophets of his day who were predicting a short captivity—that they would remain away from their homeland for 70 years (Jer 25.11–12; 29.10).[3] Daniel 9.2 indicates he had been reading this text. He, however, does not pray for a return but instead confesses the iniquity of the people, suggesting it is the joining of Jeremiah and Leviticus that serve as the impetus of Daniel's prayer.[4]

Finally, as seen in chapter 6, Daniel prays facing Jerusalem. This is surely drawn from Solomon's Temple prayer (1 Kgs 8.48) and God's af-

---

[3] This number is best understood as either symbolic or an estimate or both. See, e.g., Thompson, *Jeremiah*, 513–514 for a brief discussion.

[4] As noted before, the balancing of God's plan and human request is a deep, possibly unknowable matter this book is not the place to fully unpack. The Bible is clear, however, on two things: God is sovereign and He will make sure His will is accomplished; human prayer impacts God. Along these lines, Baldwin, *Daniel*, 165 says, "Divine decree or no, the Scriptures never support the idea that God's purpose will be accomplished irrespective of the prayers of His people."

firmation of it (1 Kgs 9.3–9), which further shows his familiarity with Scripture and covenant. Indeed, both Kings and Jeremiah feature God's promises and, grounded on that sure foundation, Daniel prays:

> Then I turned my face to the Lord God, seeking him by prayer and pleas for mercy with fasting and sackcloth and ashes. I prayed to the LORD my God and made confession, saying, "O Lord, the great and awesome God, who keeps covenant and steadfast love with those who love him and keep his commandments, we have sinned and done wrong and acted wickedly and rebelled, turning aside from your commandments and rules. We have not listened to your servants the prophets, who spoke in your name to our kings, our princes, and our fathers, and to all the people of the land. To you, O Lord, belongs righteousness, but to us open shame, as at this day, to the men of Judah, to the inhabitants of Jerusalem, and to all Israel, those who are near and those who are far away, in all the lands to which you have driven them, because of the treachery that they have committed against you. To us, O LORD, belongs open shame, to our kings, to our princes, and to our fathers, because we have sinned against you. To the Lord our God belong mercy and forgiveness, for we have rebelled against him and have not obeyed the voice of the LORD our God by walking in his laws, which he set before us by his servants the prophets. All Israel has transgressed your law and turned aside, refusing to obey your voice. And the curse and oath that are written in the Law of Moses the servant of God have been poured out upon us, because we have sinned against him. He has confirmed his words, which he spoke against us and against our rulers who ruled us, by bringing upon us a great calamity. For under the whole heaven there has not been done anything like what has been done against Jerusalem. As it is written in the Law of Moses, all this calamity has come upon us; yet we have not entreated the favor of the LORD our God, turning from our iniquities and gaining insight by your truth. Therefore the LORD has kept ready the calamity and has brought it upon us, for the LORD our God is righteous in all the works that he has done, and we have not obeyed his voice. And now, O Lord our God, who brought your people out of the land of Egypt with a mighty hand, and have made a name for yourself, as at this day, we have sinned, we have done wickedly.

"O Lord, according to all your righteous acts, let your anger and your wrath turn away from your city Jerusalem, your holy hill, because for our sins, and for the iniquities of our fathers, Jerusalem and your people have become a byword among all who are around us. Now therefore, O our God, listen to the prayer of your servant and to his pleas for mercy, and for your own sake, O Lord, make your face to shine upon your sanctuary, which is desolate. O my God, incline your ear and hear. Open your eyes and see our desolations, and the city that is called by your name. For we do not present our pleas before you because of our righteousness, but because of your great mercy. O Lord, hear; O Lord, forgive. O Lord, pay attention and act. Delay not, for your own sake, O my God, because your city and your people are called by your name."

Contents

The prayer itself divides neatly into two parts, confession (vv 4–14) and petition (vv 15–19).[5]

Confession (vv 4–14). These verses are what Brueggemann calls "a stringent, unrelenting admission of guilt on the part of Israel, fully and without reservation acknowledging that the destruction of Jerusalem was deserved as divine punishment."[6] This is seen in the string of verbs Daniel uses throughout the beginning of the prayer—sinned ... done wrong ... acted wickedly ... rebelled ... turning aside ... not listened ... treachery ... treachery ... sinned ... rebelled ... not obeyed ... transgressed your law ... turned aside, refusing to obey ... sinned (vv 5–10). There are no excuses offered, no mitigating circumstances pointed to, no attempt to shift blame or dodge culpability, only direct and repeated acknowledgment of wrong.[7]

With such a complete acknowledgment of wrong comes the full acceptance of the weight of the punishment as fully deserved. The open

---

[5] Although the ESV breaks the paragraph at verse 16, the break should be at 15. This is seen in two ways: first the characteristic "now" introducing the petition in so many Old Testament prayers; second, verse 15's dual focus on God's history of deliverance and great name, which are the foundation for the request the follows, not a conclusion of the confession that precedes.

[6] Brueggemann, *Great Prayers*, 112.

[7] As is often the case in lists like this, the significance is likely not the distinct nuanced definitions of each word, but the rhetorical impact of the accumulation of them: "We have sinned in every way possible."

shame they feel is "because we have sinned against you" (v 8). The curse being poured out on them is "because we have sinned against him" (v 11). The calamity continues upon them because "we have not entreated the favor of the LORD our God, turning from our iniquities" (vv 13–14). This last point should be seen in the context of Leviticus 26, where God had promised restoration when they repent.

Daniel clearly acknowledges what sin is. There is nothing vague about his understanding of it, some enigmatic "doing wrong" abstraction that is difficult to pin down. Instead, sin is rebellion against God by not obeying His voice and walking in His laws (vv 9–10). In particular, Daniel frames his acknowledgment that Israel deserves the punishment she is receiving (vv 11–14) by a reference to them "not listening."[8] The book-ending around a subsection of the text points to the significance of this word, which is not surprising since it is the opening word of one of the most famous Old Testament texts. Modern Jews know this text by that very Hebrew word—the *Shema:* the affirmation of the singularity of God and the fundamental commandment to love Him with our all, beginning with the imperative to *hear*. The admission that Israel and Judah did not hear is not simply an indication that they failed to listen to the words of God, but that they failed at this most foundational of levels.

Daniel's conviction of their guilt and the fullness of their sin is met with a counter-conviction about God that will eventually lead to the second part of the prayer. Verses 4–11 contain three sets of contrasts between the people and God, with verses 4, 7, and 9 beginning with a statement about virtues belonging to God, followed by the people's lack of righteousness.[9] The Lord is a God of covenant and steadfast love (v 4), a God of mercy and forgiveness (v 9), and a God of truth (v 13).[10] The significance is twofold: first, God's trustworthiness is in direct contrast with Israel's unreliability; second, it gives Daniel the basis for an appeal. If God were not such a God, there is no reason whatsoever to plead with

---

[8] Brueggemann, *Great Prayers*, 113. The ESV translates the word as "obey" in both cases.
[9] Balentine, *Prayer in the Hebrew Bible*, 105.
[10] Brueggemann, *Great Prayers*, 115.

Him for forgiveness and restoration; fully disqualified from ever making such a request (v 18b), Daniel can only dare to proceed based on the character of God Himself.

Petition (vv 15–19). As we have seen previously, the petition is headed by "And now," which seems to be a marker of transition in these prayers. Before getting to the actual petition itself (hence the need to repeat "now" in verse 17), Daniel further lays the groundwork for the basis of the appeal: God's ability to deliver and God's great name that needs to be protected. With that said and the counter-conviction fully laid out, Daniel appeals to God on a variety of fronts—almost as rapid-fire as his confession had been: let your anger turn away … listen … make your face shine … incline your ear … open your eyes … forgive … listen … act … do not delay.

Daniel asks God to relinquish the very anger He is fully justified in having.[11] But even this informs Daniel's prayer. God's anger is fully justified because they have broken the covenant; however, that same covenant promises forgiveness if they repent. That God judged as He promised proves He can be counted on to forgive as He promised.[12]

Finally, notice Daniel's concern with God's glory throughout the prayer (vv 15, 17, 19). God's name is great, but *His* temple had been destroyed, *His* city is in ruins, and *His* people are in captivity.[13] To a pagan world, this pronounced loudly that He was not such a great God after all, for no truly great God would allow such a thing to happen. The gods of Babylon and Persia must be stronger, for they are the people who are ruling the world. In that context, Daniel appeals to God to protect His own reputation by restoring His people and (by implication) rebuilding His city and Temple—not because of their righteousness, but because of His mercy; not for their sake, but for the sake of His own name.

---

[11] Brueggemann, *Great Prayers*, 116.

[12] Kaiser, *I Will Lift My Eyes*, 143.

[13] Miller, *They Cried to the Lord,* 257 rightly points out that this serves "to ground the appeal implicitly in the relationship between God and the people, Zion, and the temple," asserting "a connection between the fate of the people and God's reputation."

Connections

God's Promises. As so many of the prayers we have considered, this one is rooted in the promises of God—though maybe even to a larger degree than any other. The covenant, "one of the most potent and pervasive theological themes of the Old Testament," is at the heart of this prayer.[14] That this prayer grows out of Daniel's reading of the promises in Jeremiah and knowledge of the pronounced curses of Leviticus means that it is, from beginning to end, rooted in what God has already told His people. As Wallace says, turning to Scripture and finding "a living voice" in it helps prepare the believer to pray in response to the promises of God and challenges of life.[15]

Intertwined throughout this covenant context are references to the character of God Himself—a God of steadfast love, graciousness, fidelity, who can deliver, whose name is Great. From beginning to end, Daniel's prayer is not driven by what he thinks is important but by what God has already revealed to him as being important. Daniel makes his appeal not on what he has decided should be done, but on what God said would be done. Daniel's basis for asking has nothing to do with the people's merits, but the character and promises of God Himself. Again, we who want a firm footing for an appeal before God can find no firmer ground than the promises and character of the One to whom we pray.

God's Glory. Daniel's prayer is concerned greatly for God's glory, another repeated theme of Biblical prayer. Daniel prays not for their comfort alone, but for God's reputation to be guarded. He prays not merely for their return, but for God's name. Because the people are called by His name, their fate and His glory are bound up in one another. God's name has been dishonored by the disciplinary action His people have forced

---

[14] Longman, *Daniel*, 230. See Millar, *Calling on the Name of the Lord*, 117–120 for a longer discussion of the covenant-focus of this prayer. It could be added to this point that, like others already studied, this prayer is saturated with the language of earlier Scripture, particularly Deuteronomy. For example, Wallace, *The Message of Daniel*, 154 calls it a "mosaic of phrases taken from all over the books he had been studying," and many others make similar points. See, e.g., Hamilton, *With the Clouds of Heaven*, 105–109 for a discussion of Daniel's use of earlier Scripture. On the practical applications of this, see chapters 13 and 18 for discussion on knowledge of Scripture and prayer.

[15] Wallace, *The Message of Daniel*, 154.

Him to take.[16] Daniel knows this and is concerned enough with God's glory in the world that he makes it a foundational part of his appeal. Such a concern for God's reputation should so shape our prayers that our "petitions should be sprinkled with the incense of pleading his honor."[17]

Sin and forgiveness. This prayer shows a proper view of our relationship to God. It does not whitewash sin nor does it show the sinner as hopelessly lost. It acknowledges that the only way we ever come to God is in our failure; even so, the basis upon which we pray is not our guilt but the same counter-conviction held by Daniel: the promises and character of God. Our hope is only who He is as the reality of our sin is overwhelmed by the even more fundamental reality of the faithfulness and forgiveness of God.[18] At the same time, this does not mean that God's holiness and justice should be overlooked. Duguid says,

> [M]any people have denied or ignored God's holiness and imagined for themselves a god of grace alone, who would never judge anyone. It may be comforting to think about such a god, who makes no demands and will easily forgive everything we have ever done, but if he is not the true God, his supposed forgiveness doesn't help us. It is like the comfort of those who imagined that the *Titanic* was unsinkable. That thought was certainly very comforting and reassuring to the passengers—right up until the moment when the ship experienced its disagreement with an iceberg![19]

God is, indeed, a God of grace, mercy, and kindness beyond our imaginations. This does not mean, however, that we take this for granted and presume upon Him. As Veldkamp says, "What distinguishes us from the world is not that we are less wicked but that by the grace of God we have learned to see our wickedness for what it is and that we confess our sins."[20]

---

[16] Baldwin, *Daniel*, 167.
[17] Davis, *The Message of Daniel*, 121.
[18] Brueggemann, *Great Prayers*, 121.
[19] Duguid, *Daniel*, 158.
[20] Quoted in Davis, *The Message of Daniel*, 119.

The innocent pleading for the guilty. Daniel models true leadership in this intercessory prayer. Daniel, who has consistently shown himself to be a man of faith and integrity, does not seek to exclude himself from the indictment. Instead, 39 times in this prayer he identifies himself with the sinful people. Truly godly people do not try to maintain their godliness by contrast to those who are not godly; they join with their people and help bring them to godliness. A good leader does not point fingers and cast blame at the people who need to be led to repentance, but joins in with his people and leads them to repentance. In this prayer, "Daniel stands alongside the great Old Testament prophets, the appointed faithful who identified with their people in their worst moments and interceded for them."[21]

The sovereignty of God. Finally, this text shows how the knowledge of God's sovereignty should impact the believer. Everyone has heard or thought, "Why should I pray if God already knows what I need?" It is a natural question and an important one to consider. The Bible never gives a detailed response to such a question; it just shows people of faith praying. Perhaps no one short of Jesus better knew the sovereignty of God than Daniel. Nearly every chapter of his book can be summarized under the thrice-repeated refrain of chapter 4: the Most High rules in the kingdoms of men (Dan 4.17, 25, 32). He has experienced first-hand the sovereignty of God in a variety of ways over the course of his life. As Duguid says, "To the question, 'If God is a sovereign God, why should you pray?' Daniel would have responded, 'It is *because* God is a sovereign God that I pray.'"[22] Daniel's praying does not come because of his fear that God's promise would fail, but because he was confident God would do exactly what He said. Likewise, Goldingay says, "The fact that God has spoken through the prophets does not mean that all the believer does is sit, newspaper in hand, awaiting the outcome. The appropriate response to prophecy is prayer."[23] Along these lines it should be noted that Gabriel stands ready

---

[21] Widder, "Prayer in Daniel," 143. In an endnote, Widder cites Moses (Exod 32–33), Samuel (1 Sam 12), and Jeremiah (Jer 4.13–26) as other examples of this.

[22] Duguid, *Daniel*, 151. Emphasis in original.

[23] Goldingay, *Daniel*, 263.

to respond immediately (vv 20–23).[24] The very moment Daniel begins to pray, God responds. Seeing God as ready-but-waiting to respond brings to full force the weight of James' statement "You do not have because you do not ask" (Jas 4.2b). One must wonder how many times God has been waiting and wanting to answer a prayer that no one ever bothered to pray.

---

[24] Gabriel's response—the 70 weeks—is beyond the scope of this chapter. For an excellent discussion of various interpretations and a reasoned approach, see Roberts, "The Seventy Weeks of Daniel 9.24–27."

TWENTY

We Are Before You in Our Guilt

Ezra 9.6–15

The God to whom we pray is a holy God—a God of such holiness that He cannot look upon evil (Hab 1.13), a God before whom we cannot stand in our sin (Isa 6.5). Such holiness could eternally sever our relationship with Him, except that He is also a God of love and mercy beyond our comprehension (Isa 55.6–9) who will purify His people so they can stand before Him (Isa 6.7). Ezra's prayer of confession fully recognizes the guilt of the people, while leaving the question of mercy entirely in God's hands.

Context

The people of Israel had returned from captivity. Although it was a mere remnant and primarily the people of the southern kingdom of Judah who returned, the book of Ezra emphasizes that it was indeed Israel (e.g., Ezra 2.2b, 70; 3.1). The return itself is told as a second Exodus (1.5–11; cf. Isa 4.5–6; 10.26–27; Jer 50.33–38; etc.),[1] which further emphasizes this continuity. Both ideas—the reality that they are a remnant and the continuity with a larger Israel—are significant in connecting these people with God's promises. The former brings to mind the promises of a remnant who would return (e.g., Isa 10.20–22; Jer 23.3; Mic 2.12; etc.); God had

---

[1] A thorough discussion of the New Exodus idea can be found in a variety of sources, including Gary Yates, "New Exodus and No Exodus in Jeremiah 26–45: Promise and Warning to the Exiles in Babylon."

been true to His word and these people are experiencing the fulfillment of those promises. The latter connects this small remnant to God's greater promises going all the way back to Abraham, Isaac, and Jacob; the promises to Israel still stand, because Israel herself still stands.

Ezra was the second of three postexilic rebuilders in the Judean remnant community. Zerubbabel led the first group in the work of rebuilding the Temple (Ezra 1–6; Hag) and Nehemiah led a later group in rebuilding the wall of the city (Neh 3–6). Ezra's work, though more abstract, was a rebuilding work in seeking to bring the community back to an informed relationship with God.

The people needed to be taught. Although the problem of idolatry (in the sense of physical statues of foreign deities) seems to have been solved by the exile, other problems lingered. The preexilic issues of injustice and religious ritualism continue to persist (e.g., Zech 7.4–14; Mal 1.6–14). Further, the temptation to idolatry continues because the Jews begin to intermarry with foreign women (Ezra 9.1–2; Neh 13.23–31; Mal 2.10–16).[2] Ezra, the priest and scribe (Ezra 7.1–6), seeks to rebuild the community (cf. Neh 8) in this context of continued sin and ignorance. Ezra, as much as anyone, stamps the Jewish people with its lasting character as a people of the book. He is seen as an authoritative teacher and interpreter of the Law, who, by his work, helps put the remnant community back on a sure footing with God.[3]

Ezra's work makes the people realize their shortcomings, which they bring to him (Ezra 9.1–2). They had intermarried with foreign women—and the leaders of the community were the worst culprits.[4] This is the immediate cause of this prayer. The Jews, called to be a holy people, had mixed with non-Jews, which violated God's commands and their man-

---

[2] The Old Testament intermarriage prohibitions are religious, not racial. The Gentile women highlighted in Matthew's genealogy of Jesus make this clear. Even at the very beginning of the national history, a mixed multitude comes out of Egypt (Exod 12.38). God's concern was the influence of the foreigners' religion on His people.

[3] Brueggemann, *Great Prayers*, 90–91 says rabbinic Judaism sees him as the second most important figure (after Moses).

[4] Ancient marriage was frequently more concerned with advantageous political alliances than the modern focus of romance and emotional fulfillment, which is probably why the leaders were more guilty.

dated identity as a set-apart people. Ezra describes this as "faithless" behavior (9.2, 4; 10.2, 6, 10), a word that always appears in texts that reflect on Israel's exile and describes the sins of the covenant community.[5]

Ezra is appalled, tears out his hair, rips his clothing, and fasts (9.3–5), showing just how distraught he is.[6] Finally, at the time of the evening sacrifices, Ezra rises from his mourning and prays:

> O my God, I am ashamed and blush to lift my face to you, my God, for our iniquities have risen higher than our heads, and our guilt has mounted up to the heavens. From the days of our fathers to this day we have been in great guilt. And for our iniquities we, our kings, and our priests have been given into the hand of the kings of the lands, to the sword, to captivity, to plundering, and to utter shame, as it is today. But now for a brief moment favor has been shown by the LORD our God, to leave us a remnant and to give us a secure hold within his holy place, that our God may brighten our eyes and grant us a little reviving in our slavery. For we are slaves. Yet our God has not forsaken us in our slavery, but has extended to us his steadfast love before the kings of Persia, to grant us some reviving to set up the house of our God, to repair its ruins, and to give us protection in Judea and Jerusalem.
>
> And now, O our God, what shall we say after this? For we have forsaken your commandments, which you commanded by your servants the prophets, saying, 'The land that you are entering, to take possession of it, is a land impure with the impurity of the peoples of the lands, with their abominations that have filled it from end to end with their uncleanness. Therefore do not give your daughters to their sons, neither take their daughters for your sons, and never seek their peace or prosperity, that you may be strong and eat the good of the land and leave it for an inheritance to your children forever.' And after all that has come upon us for our evil deeds and for our great guilt, seeing that you, our God, have punished us less than our iniquities deserved and have given us such a remnant as this, shall we break your commandments again and intermarry with the peoples who practice these abominations? Would you not be angry with

---

[5] Throntveit, *Ezra-Nehemiah*, 52.
[6] See Miller, *They Cried to the Lord*, 50–54 for more on gestures and acts of prayer.

us until you consumed us, so that there should be no remnant, nor any to escape? O LORD, the God of Israel, you are just, for we are left a remnant that has escaped, as it is today. Behold, we are before you in our guilt, for none can stand before you because of this.

Contents

Ezra, like Daniel before him, identifies himself with the people. He is more deeply ashamed than any of the people, which makes him all the more fitting to be their spokesperson in this matter,[7] serving in a mediatorial role similar to Moses, Ezekiel, and others in the Old Testament.[8] He remembers their deserved punishment, which is clear in his references to captivity, slavery, and remnant, yet that last word also speaks to his realization of God's mercy, another matter he is acutely aware of.

They are, however, in a tenuous situation. They have been destroyed, plundered, and shamed (v 7) and their return is a "brief moment" of favor and "a little reviving in our slavery" (v 8). Even the "protection" (v 9) is literally "wall," but not a city wall or fortification. The word instead denotes a dry stone wall, made from loose stones with no mortar.[9] This raises the question of how secure a hold Ezra thinks they have. The word here that most translations render as "a secure hold" (v 8) means peg or pin,[10] and is frequently used to refer to tent stakes. Such a stake can indeed add security over no such peg at all, but it is hardly an image of permanence, providing only the slightest amount of stability.[11] Add to this the faithlessness Ezra sees so clearly—since that piles up higher than their heads and reaches up to the heavens (v 6)—and Ezra's feeling must be one of insecurity. It may even be that, to Ezra, the fate of the remnant seems to hang in the balance.[12]

---

[7] Kidner, *Ezra and Nehemiah*, 69.

[8] McConville, *Ezra, Nehemiah, and Esther*, 63.

[9] HALOT, 181. Throntviet, *Ezra-Nehemiah*, 55 suggests, "'fence' or 'hedge' better captures the idea of impermanence."

[10] BDB, 450; HALOT 450–451.

[11] Throntveit, *Ezra-Nehemiah*, 53. For an argument that it indicates security, see Williamson, *Ezra, Nehemiah*, 135–136.

[12] Millar, *Calling on the Name of the Lord*, 121.

Yet despite their apparently-tenuous position and their heaped-up sins, God has been merciful to them, not forsaking them in their slavery, instead extending his "steadfast love" to them. As always, the word here speaks of love, mercy, kindness, and covenant loyalty. He has done so by bringing them back, by allowing them to rebuild the Temple, and by providing them with a "wall" of safety.[13]

In Biblical prayer, the use of "now" always marks the supplication of the prayer. In Ezra's case, however, he acknowledges that there is nothing they can say. There is no reason they should be able to make an appeal. And so, he instead doubles down on their guilt: we are guilty of the very thing you specifically commanded us not to do (vv 10–12, quoting Deut 7.1–3).[14] The rhetorical questions he follows this up with must be understood as directed to the community who heard Ezra's prayer (vv 13–14), for the impact of such questions are not necessary for the God to whom he prays. Instead, he tries to reinforce the imperatives of verse 12,[15] and drive home the dire consequences of their continued rejection of God's commands.

Finally, Ezra concludes with confession. He confesses God is just. He confesses God has kept His promises. He confesses they are guilty. He confesses they have no hope of acquittal before God.

Connections

The place of confession. The greatest significance of this prayer is its absolute focus on confession. No excuses are offered, no mitigating circumstances suggested. There is no complaint about the Law being too hard to follow, too confusing to understand, or forgotten until Ezra's work began.[16] Instead, there is humble acceptance of guilt, acknowledgement of wrongdoing, and owning of the consequences that come with it. Indeed, one of

---

[13] A metaphor for God's protection, not a reference to Nehemiah's wall.

[14] See Fensham, *The Books of Ezra and Nehemiah*, 131 for a list of other Scriptures verses 10–11 echo.

[15] Brueggemann, *Great Prayers*, 96.

[16] Miller, *They Cried to the Lord*, 255–256 compares the postexilic prayers of confession to lament, but notes, "they lack the strong element of complaint, the questioning of God's actions," instead replacing that with the confession of sin. Or, perhaps, the complaint is now directed at themselves instead of God.

the most striking features of this prayer is that no petition is ever made—no request for God to continue His gracious provisions, no request for Him to be true to His character of being slow to anger and abounding in steadfast love, not even a basic appeal for forgiveness. Instead, it is pure confession from beginning to end, an awareness that, yet again, this remnant has solidarity with Israel of the past—though this time, the shared trait is its rejection of God's law. That shared history with Israel's past is heightened by the appearance of a list of nations that comes from Israel's ancient history—back to the time of the conquest and Abraham before that (e.g., Gen 15.21; Exod 3.8; Deut 20.17; Josh 3.10; etc.). The various people who inhabited the land in Abraham's day were to be driven out in Joshua's time, but were allowed to stay and led the people astray. Such intermarriage is happening again.

The purpose of confession may raise the same kinds of questions as the purpose of petition: why tell God if He already knows? Confession's purpose, however, is not about sharing facts, as if God needs to be informed, "but it is rather a spiritual activity; *we* need to be reminded of our own condition, and the willingness or otherwise to go on our knees with our confessions says something about how we truly stand with God."[17] In short, those who struggle to admit they are wrong do not have the penitent spirit that should accompany such moments as this.

Intercessory prayer. As noted above, the confession in this prayer is intercessory. Ezra is not the guilty party, but joins with his people and identifies himself as part of the guilty. Like Daniel before him, he does not try to heighten his righteousness by contrasting it with the dregs of faithlessness in the community. Far from that perspective, "The Bible's examples of intercession are all based on the powerful feeling of the unity of God's people, whereby the intercessor desires with all his being the good—and the righteousness—of the *whole*, because he cannot ultimately distinguish himself and his interests from it."[18] Such intercession should still be present in the prayer of believers.

---

[17] McConville, *Ezra, Nehemiah, and Esther*, 64. Emphasis in original.
[18] Ibid., 63. Emphasis in original.

Rooted in covenant and promises. Ezra's prayer, though it never makes a request of any kind, is still rooted in covenant and promises and desires covenant renewal.[19] As we have seen before, "steadfast love" is a covenant term. Also, Ezra's recognition of the group as a remnant draws on those prophetic promises, indicating that he is aware of God's kept promises—in particular, promises that are about His forgiveness and restoration of His people.

Confidence in God's holiness. Ezra was as confident in God's holiness as he was in Israel's wickedness. This confidence stands behind his shame to lift his face to God as he considers the people's sin (contrast Jer 6.15; 8.12). The God who keeps His promises is also a God of pure holiness and justice. Ezra's understanding of Israel's sin and God's holiness allows no room for any sort of cheap grace. Clines, speaking of the danger of cheapening God's grace, says, "It is no doubt a weakness of modern spirituality that it regards a real fear of God's wrath which does not immediately lead to assurance of God's forgiveness as somewhat fanatical."[20] Because their faithlessness is not shrugged off and because God's holiness and faithfulness is equally acknowledged, this prayer speaks to the need for every follower of God to meditate deeply on the holiness and mercy of God and the utter sinfulness of sin.

The role of exhortation in prayer. A common pet peeve of Christians is prayers that are too "preachy." While such an annoyance is understandable on a superficial level—"you're supposed to be talking to God, not preaching at the members"—it fails to take into account biblical prayers that are clearly "preachy." Ezra's rhetorical questions are for the benefit of his audience, and his discussion of their sin, God's holiness, and their precarious position are informative to the group around him as well. To the person who leads a public prayer, it should be said that prayers should probably not be sermons from beginning to end and that not all prayers need an element of exhortation. But the congregant grousing in the pew because the one who prays "should leave the preaching to the preacher" is simply wrong. Ezra shows us how impactful (and scriptural) such prayers are.

---

[19] Millar, *Calling on the Name of the Lord*, 122.
[20] Clines, *Ezra, Nehemiah, Esther*, 122.

Turning over everything to God's mercy. Finally, this prayer concludes in a surprising way. With no request of any kind, Ezra concludes with an acknowledgment of who God is and who they are in comparison. They stand before God, even though none in their condition can stand before God. Here is the irony all believers face: we cannot stand before the God before whom we must stand. We have nowhere to turn, so in our destitute dependence, we must turn to the very one we have turned away from. But here also is the great promise of the Bible: we have never turned so far that we cannot turn back; the prodigal never travels so far from his father that he is not welcome home again. And even when, in our sin, we cannot stand before God, He urges us to do that very thing.

In a way, this reminds me of the conclusion of Jehoshaphat's prayer. There, surrounded by enemies, Jehoshaphat concludes not with a strong request, but with the acknowledgment that he does not know what to do and he turns everything over to God instead (2 Chron 20.12).[21] Here, Ezra does something similar, except he is surrounded by sin. "Here we are," he says. "Here we are in our guilt. Here we are in our need. Here we are in our uncleanness. Here we are in our slavery. But here we are. Do with us as you will."[22]

---

[21] See chapter 12.
[22] Brueggemann, *Great Prayers*, 97.

TWENTY-ONE

Let Your Ear Be Attentive

Nehemiah 1.5–11

The God to whom we pray is a God who uses people to accomplish His will. Humans become the tools in His hands to accomplish His purposes in a variety of ways, from foreign kings and armies who execute His judgment or restoration to young maidens He selects to deliver His people or His Son. In Nehemiah's case, God placed one of His people in direct contact with the Persian monarch whose permission would be needed to continue work on rebuilding the city of Jerusalem just as word arrives that the city needs rebuilding.

Context

As the last several chapters have discussed in varying degrees of detail, the Babylonian exile is a key part of the backdrop of this chapter. If Ezra's work that leads to his prayer happens relatively quickly, this is about 13 years after Ezra's prayer (Ezra 7.7–8; Neh 1.1). At this point, it has been nearly a century since Cyrus sent the captives home.[1] The work of Zerubbabel and Haggai had been completed and Erza's task was well underway.

The book of Nehemiah begins with a message brought back from Jerusalem by Hannani, a brother of Nehemiah. In short, the wall and gate of the city still lie in ruins. The success in rebuilding the Temple was not

---

[1] This is based on a 539 BC return of exiles and a 464 BC beginning point to the reign of Artaxerxes. See Yamauchi, "Ezra-Nehemiah," 571–572 for a proposed chronology of events.

duplicated in the walls and gates. What's more, a letter from Artaxerxes—the same king Nehemiah now serves under—instructed them to stop building (Ezra 4.17–23), and those who enforced the letter may well have been a part of destroying and burning what progress had been made.[2] As a result, shame fell upon the city of Jerusalem (and the God whose name was upon that city) and the residents had no protection.

Nehemiah responds by weeping, mourning, fasting and praying. It may be significant that he "sat down and wept" (v 4), as those are the same words used to describe the deportees in Psalm 137.1.[3] His reaction to the ongoing state of disrepair in Jerusalem is the same as the exiles when they reflected upon its initial destruction. In a sense, the exile was not yet over.

In any event, Nehemiah is more open with his emotion than a typical 21st-century Westerner. More than that, however, his emotion is a result of his deep care for the city and what it meant. As McConville says, in Nehemiah we see "the trauma of one who has made God's cause his own and who sees it scorned."[4] In other words, Nehemiah and many other of the faithful refuse to be indifferent to the purposes of God in the world.

It is also clear that Nehemiah understands at least two key points as he enters this prayer. First, he understands that God has not fully kept his promise. This is not to indict God, but to say that Nehemiah could see the reality of the situation on the ground and immediately know there was more yet to come. God had promised He would restore Jerusalem, and as long as the walls and gate lay in ruins, the promise had not been fulfilled. The promise was more than merely relocating a group of people to a particular geographical area, but a restoration of the nation itself and the rebuilding of the city.[5] This fact gives Nehemiah the clear basis for his appeal to God.

---

[2] Allen "Ezra–Nehemiah," 87–88.

[3] Brueggemann, *Great Prayers*, 100; Brueggemann, *The Message of the Psalms*, 76.

[4] McConville, *Ezra, Nehemiah, and Esther*, 62, where he says this about Ezra's openly emotional response, which equally applies here.

[5] Clines, *Ezra, Nehemiah, Esther*, 138.

Second, Nehemiah understands the people have not wholly returned to God as they ought. The promise—from Leviticus and Deuteronomy to Solomon's Temple Prayer and throughout the prophets—was that God would restore them when they had repented. The implications were not merely about what *God* had to do, but about what *they* had to do as well. Daniel's penitential prayer was an important first step in the process of repentance and the work of Ezra progressed it even further. Nehemiah now takes up the mantle and, with this understanding, focuses on the people's sin and need for repentance.

The sentence immediately following the prayer tells us that Nehemiah was the cupbearer to the king. Yamauchi lists the following as key to understanding what this meant about Nehemiah: he was a "convivial companion" to the king; he had the closest access to the king; he enjoyed the unreserved confidence of the king.[6] In short, Nehemiah would have been physically and relationally close to Artaxerxes. It is striking that this information is withheld until the last possible moment of this scene, allowing instead the prayer to take center stage. This may reflect a theological viewpoint that minimizes the role of the king to maximize the role of God, and that Nehemiah's trust lies more in his God than in his own influential position.

Finally, a word must be said about the timeline of this chapter. Nehemiah's brother arrives in the month of Chislev (November/December) and his reaction is immediate (vv 1, 4). Nehemiah's appearance before the king that results in his trip to Jerusalem occurs in Nisan (March/April) (2.1). Apart from these time references, the narrative seems to progress quickly. However, several months pass and Nehemiah has a prolonged period of prayer as he looks for the right opportunity to make his request. Whether this is the same prayer he repeated daily, the first prayer he prayed, the last prayer he prayed, or a text that is representative of a variety of different prayers prayed over the intervening months cannot be known.[7]

---

[6] Yamauchi, "Ezra-Nehemiah," 683. See there for his full list of six different items.

[7] Allen's supposition —"It summarizes from later recollection his praying over that period"—is a reasonable guess ("Ezra–Nehemiah," 89).

O LORD God of heaven, the great and awesome God who keeps covenant and steadfast love with those who love him and keep his commandments, let your ear be attentive and your eyes open, to hear the prayer of your servant that I now pray before you day and night for the people of Israel your servants, confessing the sins of the people of Israel, which we have sinned against you. Even I and my father's house have sinned. We have acted very corruptly against you and have not kept the commandments, the statutes, and the rules that you commanded your servant Moses. Remember the word that you commanded your servant Moses, saying, "If you are unfaithful, I will scatter you among the peoples, but if you return to me and keep my commandments and do them, though your outcasts are in the uttermost parts of heaven, from there I will gather them and bring them to the place that I have chosen, to make my name dwell there." They are your servants and your people, whom you have redeemed by your great power and by your strong hand. O LORD, let your ear be attentive to the prayer of your servant, and to the prayer of your servants who delight to fear your name, and give success to your servant today, and grant him mercy in the sight of this man. (Neh 1.5–11)

Contents

The structure of Nehemiah's prayer is inversely parallel, beginning and ending with petition (vv 5–6a; 11) with confession making up the bulk and center: of Israel's sin (vv 6b–7); of God's promises and faithfulness (vv 8–10).[8] The prayer draws from earlier texts. In addition to those discussed below, Solomon's Temple Prayer also plays a key role, which reminds the reader of God's promise to mercifully respond to such a prayer (2 Chron 7.14).[9]

The opening petition contains several echoes of Deuteronomy—"Yahweh God," "great and awesome," "keeps covenant and steadfast love"—building his prayer on the foundation of covenantal relationship. The petition itself is simply that God would hear the prayer he prays day and night.

---

[8] See Throntveit, *Ezra-Nehemiah*, 65 for a similar structure.
[9] Duguid, "Nehemiah: The Best King Judah Never Had," 263. See his essay for a detailed description of the similarities.

With that, Nehemiah quickly transitions to the heart of the prayer: confession. The confession of the people's sin comes first, but almost seems out of the blue. After all, there has been no reference to Israel's sin, and the last information about it on the scroll was their repentance and confession.[10] At the same time, it seems quite sensible. As mentioned above, if God has not fulfilled His promise of restoration, it must be because the people have not fulfilled their obligation of repentance. Thus, Nehemiah begins confessing the sins of the nation. His descriptions of their sin with comprehensive terms—not keeping the commandments, statutes, and rules of God—indicates they have failed in every way possible. As we have seen with Daniel and Ezra, there is no blame shifting. Rather, reflecting on the imperfection of the people inevitably reminds Nehemiah of his own sin, and "his own sinfulness is a part of that broad canvas of wrong which accounts for all the displeasure of God which His people has known."[11]

As important as the confession of sin is, so also is Nehemiah's confession of God's promise. Here, Nehemiah explicitly appeals to the covenant, paraphrasing Deuteronomy 30.1–5 and also echoing a variety of other passages in Leviticus and Deuteronomy. The very nature of covenant itself teaches something about both God and humankind. Regarding God, it shows that He keeps covenant and steadfast love; regarding humankind, it shows the obligation to love God and keep His commandments. These dual themes of covenant permeate Scripture and always appear in that order, for God always loves us before we love Him (cf. 1 John 4.19; John 14.15).[12] It is to this promise of restoration—and this covenant love and faithfulness—that Nehemiah clings as he prays. If this is not enough, he has the evidence of God's historical dealings with His people, for they are the very people He redeemed with His great power and strong hand, language evocative of the Exodus (e.g., Exod 13.3, et al.), which is fitting for

---

[10] I reference "the scroll" here, because Ezra and Nehemiah were originally a single scroll of Ezra-Nehemiah. From this perspective, Ezra's prayer and the people's repentance immediately precedes Nehemiah 1. See Williamson, *Ezra, Nehemiah*, xxi–xxiii for a discussion of the unity of Ezra-Nehemiah.

[11] McConville, *Ezra, Nehemiah, Esther*, 76.

[12] Ibid.

the restoration from captivity, often seen as a second Exodus. Nehemiah also understands that without God's action, there can be no restoration at all. A future for Israel can only exist if God acts.[13]

Similarly, the promise to "gather them" (v 10) is frequently repeated throughout the Old Testament.[14] This gathering would happen to "your servants and your people, whom you have redeemed by your great power and your strong hand," a strong echo of Ezra's concern for God's reputation that hangs in the balance before the nations.[15]

If it is true that the exile they experienced was due to their disobedience to the covenant, the loving promises of God for restoration were just as certain.[16] As Kidner says, "He is empty-handed, but not uninvited. He knows the threats and promises of Scripture well enough to make a strong, not a tentative plea."[17] Notice, however, that Nehemiah does not merely cite God's promises but pleads with God to remember them, another word with covenant significance, especially when used of God. God's remembrance has little to do with intellectual recall and instead marks occasions when He acts on behalf of one with whom He is in covenant.[18]

Finally, Nehemiah returns to petition, bringing it all together for the moment he is in now: "Give success to your servant." In addition to the basic request for success, two key words require reflection in the petition. "Today" is when Nehemiah hopes to find success. Presuming it was an ongoing part of his prayer, he does not find immediate success, but keeps hoping that every day is the "today" where this will materialize.[19] "This man" is Artaxerxes, which is quite possibly the most understated way that one could possibly describe the most powerful human in the world at that

---

[13] Brueggemann, *Great Prayers*, 103.
[14] In addition to Deuteronomy 30.1–5, the primary text behind Nehemiah's prayer, see Isaiah 11.12; Jeremiah 23.3; 29.14; 31.8–10; Ezekiel 11.17; 16.37; 20.34, 41; 36.24; Micah 2.12.
[15] Miller, *They Cried to the Lord*, 257.
[16] Kaiser, *I Will Lift My Eyes unto the Hills*, 121.
[17] Kidner, *Ezra and Nehemiah*, 79.
[18] See Genesis 8.1; 9.14–15; 19.29; 30.22; Exodus 2.24; 6.5; 32.13; Judges 16.28; 1 Samuel 1.19; Job 14.13; Psalms 8.4; 9.12; 74.1–3; 98.3; 105.8; 106.45; 111.5; Jeremiah 2.2; 15.15; 31.20.
[19] Allen, "Ezra–Nehemiah," 90.

time. If nothing else, it is a reminder that even the Persian monarch is a mere man before God, subject to His will.[20]

Connections

God's covenant and character. It is easy to misunderstand the nature of God's covenant, as if God is nothing more than a computer program who dispenses certain results if we feed in other certain input. Throntveit says,

> A simplistic understanding of the covenant as a pact that somehow obligates God to dispense forgiveness so long as Israel keeps covenant obviously will not do, if for no other reason than that Nehemiah has just confessed to Israel's failure in this regard. But a more theologically astute understanding that would allow the covenant people to demand forgiveness on the basis of God's promise also seriously misreads the situation. The covenant does not set up a business transaction between two parties. In its essence, the covenant establishes a relationship. More importantly, the covenant does not dispense with the need for mercy, indeed the covenant itself grows out of God's mercy, grace, and steadfast love.[21]

Nehemiah sees the punishment that has come upon the people as evidence of God's power. This is strikingly different from how much of the ancient world viewed gods and their nations. To them, a defeated city meant a defeated god, which indicated that the victorious army had the stronger god. Nehemiah, however, sees the conditions under which the people are suffering as evidence that God was powerfully present in judgment, not absent due to His weakness.[22] Similarly, the New Testament teaches that the suffering endured by Christians is not due to God's absence in defeat, but His presence in victory. In particular, it is precisely because Satan is cast down and knows his time is short that he takes out his wrath on "those who keep the commandments of God and hold to the testimony of Jesus" (Rev 12.20). Morris says well, "The troubles of the persecuted righteous arise not because Satan is too strong, but because he

---

[20] Clines, *Ezra, Nehemiah, Esther*, 139–140.
[21] Throntveit, *Ezra-Nehemiah*, 65.
[22] Williamson, *Ezra, Nehemiah*, 173.

is beaten."²³ This perspective changes how we view the world around us. The greater God becomes in our eyes, the smaller the problems and issues we have will seem.²⁴

Every "today" is an opportunity to be the agent of God's will. What are we to do when we pray for a response "today" and do not receive it? Some continue in prayer, never once questioning his or her motives and whether the prayer is proper in the first place. Others presume the answer is "no" and move on without a thought as to whether there is need for endurance in prayer. Nehemiah seems to do neither. He continues in prayer and does so with confidence that his prayer is according to God's will. More than that, he continues watching for the opportunity to arise—in part, because his prayer was ambiguous enough that he had to watch carefully. His ongoing prayer was his ongoing motivation to act when the moment was right. As a result, he was aware when it was.

This means Nehemiah understands that God frequently acts through human agency. Although God does not ever *need* human assistance to accomplish His purpose, He will regularly use it, whether someone is for, against, or ambivalent to that purpose. Nehemiah prays for God to act and then is constantly ready to be the agent whereby He does. This long process of prayer is the background it gives for the so-called "arrow prayer" of 2.4, where Nehemiah silently prays so quickly that it is not recorded.²⁵ The brevity of prayer in that moment stands not in insolation, but is built upon this sustained, enduring foundation of pleas before God for this day to be the "today." It shows Nehemiah "had incorporated the habit of prayer into every aspect of his life."²⁶ And when the king responded positively, Nehemiah knew the hand of God was behind it (2.8).

Confidence and commitment. As mentioned above, Nehemiah was aware of the facts on the ground and how dire the situation was. So he submitted the situation to the God of heaven. Nehemiah, and those who

---

²³ Morris, *Revelation*, 158.

²⁴ Kasier, *I Will Lift My Eyes Unto the Hills*, 118–119.

²⁵ Kidner, *Ezra and Nehemiah*, 78–79. Cf. Nehemiah 5.19; 6.14; 13.14, 22, 29, 31 for a series of brief "remember me" and "remember them" prayers in Nehemiah.

²⁶ Mariottini, "Prayer in 1–2 Chronicles, Ezra, and Nehemiah," 161.

pray like him, "trust that the will of the God of heaven will be visibly enacted in the earth. The life of the world depends, so they confess, on the 'great mercies' of God."[27] Or, as McConville says, "Nehemiah's prayer, therefore, which he believes is shared by other faithful Jews, can strike a note of confidence, mixed with commitment (v 11). The same combination (confidence and commitment) can characterize the prayer of any Christian today."[28]

---

[27] Brueggemann, *Great Prayers*, 110.
[28] McConville, *Ezra, Nehemiah, Esther*, 77.

TWENTY-TWO

Turn Back Their Taunt

Nehemiah 4.4–5

The God to whom we pray is a God who reserves judgment for Himself and the one to whom all vengeance belongs. His people are called to love their enemies and turn the other cheek, not returning reviling for reviling or cursing for cursing. It is surprising, then, that the Bible contains several prayers where a faithful man of God invokes God's judgment on an enemy. Nehemiah's prayer against his enemies provides us an opportunity to discuss this difficult matter.

Context

Cyrus sent the Israelites home when he conquered Babylon and came to power. Artaxerxes listened to Nehemiah's appeal and granted him not merely informal permission, but letters of authorization and a military escort (Neh 2.7–9). All this was according to God's promises that go back long before the exile, and should be seen as His active fulfillment of those very promises.

These facts, however, do not mean that all would be smooth sailing for Nehemiah upon his arrival. His work was met with opposition from a variety of leading individuals nearby Jerusalem, most notably Sanballat the Hornonite, Tobiah the Ammonite, and Geshem the Arab (2.10, 19). Sanballat was the governor of Samaria, to the north of Nehemiah's work. Tobiah was part of a powerful family in Ammon, to the east of Jerusalem.

Geshem and his son ruled a league of Arabian tribes which controlled Moab and Edom and parts of Arabia and the approaches to Egypt, with his influence ranging from the southeast to the southwest of Judah. In short, Nehemiah is surrounded by powerful enemies.[1]

The threat of opposition does not stop Nehemiah from beginning his work, and chapter 3 describes how the work is divided and how it commences. Upon learning this, Sanballat and Tobiah try a new tactic, and one that we have already seen in this book. Like the Rabshakeh taunting the city of Jerusalem while it was besieged by Assyria (2 Kgs 18.19–25, 28–35),[2] so also Nehemiah's foes engage in a verbal warfare (Neh 4.2–3). Taunting and mockery is the oldest trick in the book, and far more effective than the "words can never hurt me" cliché lets on. Further, its effectiveness relies not on any factual ammunition or logical argument, but simply on chipping away at the emotional and psychological well-being of the target.

"What are these feeble Jews doing?" they ask, suggesting that they are such a withering lot of people that they could not accomplish anything worthwhile. "Will they sacrifice?" a question that refers not to the Temple and altar, which are already built, but how they plan on accomplishing this great building task. In other words, "Are you going to *pray* the wall up? Because that's your only hope of accomplishing it—and we all know that's not how walls get built."[3] And so forth.

The motivation of such an approach is transparent. Sanballat knows he has no legal recourse to stop Nehemiah, for Artaxerxes is on the side of the builders. If, however, he can convince the builders to give up on their own, the wall will never be built. But if any of these accusations were true—if they were so feeble and incapable, or if the wall were so fragile that a fox climbing it would knock it back down—there would be no reason to spend time jeering at the builders. In other words, despite his bra-

---

[1] Most commentaries discuss the extrabiblical sources that inform our understanding of these individuals. See, e.g., Kidner, *Ezra and Nehemiah*, 81–82, 84.
[2] See chapter 14.
[3] Kidner, *Ezra and Nehemiah*, 90.

vado and insults, Sanballat and his allies are afraid of their success—and they are powerless to stop it.

In response to this, Nehemiah prays:

> Hear, O our God, for we are despised. Turn back their taunt on their own heads and give them up to be plundered in a land where they are captives. Do not cover their guilt, and let not their sin be blotted out from your sight, for they have provoked you to anger in the presence of the builders. (Neh 4.4–5)

Contents

The meaning of this short prayer is straightforward. Nehemiah asks that God turn the evil of these people back upon themselves, not granting them any forgiveness. He prays urgently, recognizing the real threat of the enemies' words. He prays honestly, not hiding his true feelings from the God to whom he prays. Similarly, he prays passionately, pouring out his emotions rather than bottling them up. He prays realistically, knowing that the true object of their scorn is not himself and his workers, but the God who supports the rebuilding project. Finally, he prays dependently, knowing that they relied on God for their success.[4]

This prayer reflects the fact that Nehemiah takes the verbal attacks of his enemies seriously. He understands that they are an effort to demoralize him and his workers, but even more, he realizes it means they are hostile to God's word and will.[5] Whether Sanballat and the others are thinking of being active foes against God or not, Nehemiah understands his work is God's will, so anyone who stands against it stands against God.

Nehemiah's prayer contains a play on words, as he considers how they are despised (*bûzâh*) before asking that his enemies would be given up to be plundered (*bizzâh*), a punning that reflects the reversal Nehemiah is asking God to enact.[6] Otherwise, there are no other obscurities or text critical issues in this prayer to consider and the message is clear. With

---

[4] Brown, *The Message of Nehemiah*, 73–76.
[5] Allen, "Ezra–Nehemiah," 105.
[6] Clines, *Ezra, Nehemiah, Esther*, 161.

this prayer, the theological implications are what have troubled Christians through the centuries.

Connections

For God, to hear is to act. Miller, writing about a variety of prayers including this one, points out how frequently God is called upon to "hear" or "see," "incline your ear" or "open your eyes"—that He will pay attention to the plight and plea of the petitioner. He says, "There is an implicit assumption that God's attention means God's help. To catch God's eye and ear … is to be able to expect God's help."[7] This recalls what we have said previously about God "remembering." For God to remember is not merely His intellectual recollection of a particular set of data. Rather, for God to remember is for Him to act on behalf of covenant relationship. Similarly, to ask for God to see or hear is to ask for Him to remember—to ask for Him to act. The believer who trusts that God sees and knows can trust that He will do what is best.

The compatibility of faith and works. The old faith and works debate goes back centuries within Christendom—Calvin and Arminius, Luther and Catholicism, Augustine and Pelagius stand among the noted combatants in the fight. My own view is that faith and works are not incompatible and that the Bible reflects this constantly. "Trust in me for salvation when the flood comes," God tells Noah, "and go build the ark that you will survive it in." And, "Watch the salvation I bring," God tells Israel at the edge of the sea, "and now walk across the dry land I have made for you." And, "I will give you the land," God tells Joshua, "so now muster your army and go take it." And, "Work out your own salvation," Paul writes to the Philippians, "because it is God who works in you."

The intersection of divine initiative and human response is where success and salvation are invariably found in Scripture. Nehemiah reflects this in a different sort of way. He is a man of action, a take-charge leader who can be relied upon to get things done. And yet he is a man of ac-

---

[7] Miller, *They Cried to the Lord*, 87.

tion who responds to the circumstances in his life by turning to God in trusting prayer.[8] He consistently trusts not his own ingenuity, but his God—and yet he then acts in such a way that is consistent with, but not negating of, such trust.

Vengeful, cursing prayers. This prayer, along with the so-called imprecatory psalms, call for God to curse, harm, or otherwise attack the enemy of the one who is praying. Because Jesus calls upon His followers to turn the other cheek rather than responding in kind (Matt 5.38–40), Peter directs that we not repay evil for evil or reviling for reviling (1 Pet 3.9), and Paul says to bless the ones who curse you, doing good for your enemies, knowing that vengeance belongs to God (Rom 12.14, 19–21), Christians are frequently uncomfortable with these prayers, and they have been explained in various ways through the years.

Some see imprecatory prayers as a blight on the Bible.[9] In this view, they are evil and embarrassing and *certainly* do not provide the modern Christian with an example of how to pray. One problem with this approach is that it has a low view of inspiration. It is surely possible to argue that Christians should not pray these things, but I would hesitate at saying they were inappropriate in their original context. If so, how can we have faith in the inspiration or appropriateness of the rest of the Psalter? If we draw lines based merely on what offends our particular sensitivities, where can we not draw a line? On the other hand, if Scripture is inspired and profitable to equip us, then we should find use for the text, not dismiss it out of hand.

Others embrace the opposite extreme, pointing to the inspiration of the Biblical authors. Since they were inspired, the reasoning goes, there is no problem at all with what they did. We, however, are not inspired, so we cannot pray such things now.[10] Although this view clearly has a higher

---

[8] Williamson, *Ezra, Nehemiah*, 217.

[9] See Craigie, *Psalms 1–50*, 41; Lewis, *Reflections on the Psalms*, 20–33.

[10] I have not found the argument put this starkly in print, but I have heard people make it in conversation. Perhaps the closest thing to this among scholarship is the idea that the imprecations are to be understood as prophecy of future judgment rather than requests for judgment. Regarding Nehemiah, the closest thing to this may be Brown, *The Message of Nehemiah*, 76 who suggests, "Nehemiah's prayer is descriptive not prescriptive."

view of inspiration, it joins that to a low view of the practicality of the Bible. Or, perhaps more accurately, a buffet-style view of the practicality of the Bible: "the Bible is a practical example for us to follow, as long as I'm not offended by what it's modeling." To be sure, there are examples in the Bible that are not for us to follow (e.g., murder, idolatry, rape, etc.) and the narrator does not always stop to offer moral evaluations, expecting the reader to know the difference without being hand-held through the process. The problem, however, is that Biblical prayer, including the Psalter, is not the same thing as narrative. This entire book is about modeling our prayer after theirs, because that is a valid approach to the topic. The Psalter is frequently pointed to as one of the most personally applicable books in the Bible, because it teaches us to pray. This brings us back to needing an objective standard for drawing lines. No one would argue that the Psalms of Praise, Trust, or Thanksgiving are inappropriate for Christians to pray, and few, if any, would argue that Lament is not valuable.[11] But if Biblical prayer and the psalms are examples of how to pray, are they not *all* examples of how to pray? On what basis—other than what offends our sensitivities—can we wall off one type of prayer as inappropriate while pointing to all the rest as models to the modern reader?

One way some find this basis is to distinguish the Old and New Testaments.[12] This sort of prayer, it alleges, was fine for Old Testament believers, but not for us. After all, Jesus, Peter, and Paul had not taught love of enemy and refusal to retaliate during the days of David or Nehemiah. To its credit, this view neither minimizes inspiration nor practicality in its effort to wrestle through these difficult texts. The problem, however, is that the Old Testament does teach love of enemy (e.g., Exod 23.4–5) and the New Testament includes curse language (Matt 21.19; 26.23–24; 1 Cor 5.5; 16.22; Gal 1.8–9; 5.12; 1 Tim 1.19–20; 2 Tim 4.14) and quotes some of the imprecatory psalms (e.g., Pss 69; 109). Perhaps an even larger problem is the caricature of an Old Testament God of Vengeance and a New Testament God of Love, unintentional though it may be. God does not

---

[11] See chapters 15 and 16 for some discussion of lament.
[12] Lewis, "Difficult Texts from the Psalms and Proverbs," 315.

display disparate personalities in the two testaments of Scripture; even if the covenant has changed, and with it some specific commands within it, the God of the covenant has not. He has been, is, and always will be a God of mercy and justice, a God of reward and punishment.

How, then, can imprecatory prayers be an example for Christians? First, the objects of Biblical imprecatory prayer are wholly unjust, chronically disobedient, ferociously violent, and stubbornly wicked. They practiced injustice and barbarous slaughter against the Israelites. They returned hatred and evil toward the blessed line of Abraham. Against each of these transgressions stands a firm foundation in God's law for God cursing these people. Indeed, God would have proven Himself not to be good had He chosen to overlook their actions. In fact, God had long before promised a curse to anyone who cursed Abraham's offspring (Gen 12.3). The Biblical imprecatory prayer reminds God of His promises and asks Him to be true to them.

Second, the focus of much Biblical imprecatory prayer is God's glory. Their primary sin is not against the one who prays, but against the God of the one who prays. Many individuals have known the natural anger that arises when a spouse, family member, or close friend is unfairly maligned. Believers should have such a relationship with and reverence for God that we are filled with righteous indignation when God is maligned by unbelievers, or they seek to undermine His will. Imprecatory prayers are the proper place to express this, as they are yet another way of seeking, above all else, God's glory in our prayer.

Finally, the ones who pray imprecatory prayers defer vengeance to God. They acknowledge their enemies and how their enemies have wronged them. They acknowledge that God knows who their enemies are and what they have done. Then, they turn the matter over to Him for judgment. The prayer is for vengeance and justice, never angry retribution. They consistently pray that God will repay to their enemies what is due them. Likewise, by understanding that vengeance does not belong to us and God will repay our enemies as they are due, we can turn the issue over to God to deal with, leaving ourselves to love them while hating their sin (cf. Jude 23).

And this is the key: we cannot justify using the imprecatory prayers as a model to hate our enemies. Nor can we gleefully pray against them while longingly looking forward for their demise. This is particularly important in light of Clines' warning that it is "fatally easy" to deceive ourselves and thereby identify our ambitions with God's will when the two do not correspond.[13] McConville, too, urges, "Clearly, in seeking to derive edification from such sentiments, we must in no way diminish the force of Christ's command to 'love your enemies' (Matt 5.44); for if there *can* be godly hatred, there is no doubt whatsoever that *un*godly hatred is a powerful temptation in stressful situations."[14]

Selflessness is never to be set aside; we should love our enemies. We should turn the other cheek. But we also must go to God with our concerns. And it is better for us to express the evils of our enemies to Him, turn the matter over to Him, and move along with our lives than it would be for us to think it improper to pray about these matters and stew in hatred, wishing that we could take vengeance ourselves.[15]

---

[13] Clines, *Ezra, Nehemiah, Esther*, 160.

[14] McConville, *Ezra, Nehemiah, Esther*, 93.

[15] For other helpful approaches to imprecatory language (including other suggestions on how to reconcile imprecatory language with Christian love), see Bullock, *Encountering Psalms*, 221–232; Brueggemann, *Praying the Psalms*, 63–81; Estes, *Handbook on the Wisdom Books and Psalms*, 172–177; Wenham, *The Psalter Reclaimed*, 129–145.

TWENTY-THREE

You Have Dealt Faithfully

Nehemiah 9.5–37

The God to whom we pray is a God who has a long history of dealing with faithless covenant partners. Even the best of His people have broken covenant in shocking ways, but entire generations sometimes turn their back on God. Whether the Exodus generation in the wilderness, multiple generations of the Northern Kingdom from Jeroboam until the fall of Samaria, or most of the Southern Kingdom until the Babylonian captivity, God's people have done a poor job of living up to their obligations as His people. And yet, God is not only willing to forgive when they repent, but He never repays faithlessness with faithlessness. In spite of human sin, God is always faithful to His promises, whether for blessing or curse.

Context

This prayer has two possible backdrops.[1] First, this may be connected to the prayer in Ezra 9. The separation from foreigners in verse 2 and the presence of Ezra's teaching work in chapter 8 are the best evidence for this view. Additionally, this is not the prayer of Nehemiah himself, but a group of Levites.[2] Since those most guilty of the sin in Ezra 9 where the

---

[1] A fuller discussion of this matter, including the issue of timeline based on the dates noted in these books, can be found in Clines, *Ezra, Nehemiah, Esther*, 189–90.

[2] A few translations, most notably the RSV and NRSV, follow the LXX in inserting "And Ezra said." See Williamson, *Ezra, Nehemiah*, 304 for a brief discussion on why this is not likely to be original. Commentaries that uncritically accept Ezra as the speaker (e.g., Yamauchi, "Ezra-Nehemiah,"

leading men (Ezra 9.2), this could be seen as their penitence to parallel Ezra's prayer in the previous book.

How far removed it is from that earlier scene and how well it fits with the immediate context of the book of Nehemiah makes this view less likely. Ezra is indeed present in Nehemiah 8, and his teaching of the Law made the people weep over their sin (Neh 8.9–11). In this case, however, they are instructed not to weep, because it was a time for a festival. They celebrated the Feast of Booths before this prayer (Neh 8.11–18) and engaged in a covenant renewal after it (Neh 10).

Instead, this latter backdrop—a covenant renewal[3]—fits best with the prayer. First, the grief they did not have a chance to express can now be brought to the foreground. That initial anguish over sin must not be forgotten in the delight of the feast, and the people must return to face the facts of the past as they approach the challenge of the future.[4] Second, the separation from foreigners need not be seen as separation from foreign marriages. If marriage is the problem here, it is the one place in all the postexilic writings where it is so ambiguously described. Elsewhere, it is not foreigners in general that they need to separate from but what is explicitly described as foreign marriages or foreign wives (Ezra 9; Neh 13; Mal 2). In addition, the Feast of Booths is not necessarily an exclusively Israelite festival; if foreigners were interested in celebrating it, they could have done so. Repenting of national sin, however, is something foreigners should be excluded from, not because of nationalistic pride, but as North says, "It's not really separatist to exclude others from our acknowledgement of faults whose guilt we do not wish to imply extends to them."[5] Finally, although the chronology of Ezra and Nehemiah admittedly overlap, and there can certainly be gaps of time between chapters (cf. Neh 8.2; 9.1), it is much more natural to read Nehemiah 9 in the context of Nehemiah 8 unless there is compelling reason not to do so.

731–738; McConville, *Ezra, Nehemiah, and Esther*, 123–128) likely do so due to the constraints of the series they are writing in, viz., assigned translation and limited space to interact with critical issues.

[3] Balentine, *Prayer in the Hebrew Bible*, 110.

[4] Kidner, *Ezra and Nehemiah*, 110.

[5] Quoted in Clines, *Ezra, Nehemiah, Esther*, 190.

And so, the grief that they had not previously been able to express is now poured out both in physical terms (fasting, sackcloth, dirt on their heads) and in prayer:

> Stand up and bless the LORD your God from everlasting to everlasting. Blessed be your glorious name, which is exalted above all blessing and praise.
>
> You are the LORD, you alone. You have made heaven, the heaven of heavens, with all their host, the earth and all that is on it, the seas and all that is in them; and you preserve all of them; and the host of heaven worships you. You are the LORD, the God who chose Abram and brought him out of Ur of the Chaldeans and gave him the name Abraham. You found his heart faithful before you, and made with him the covenant to give to his offspring the land of the Canaanite, the Hittite, the Amorite, the Perizzite, the Jebusite, and the Girgashite. And you have kept your promise, for you are righteous.
>
> And you saw the affliction of our fathers in Egypt and heard their cry at the Red Sea, and performed signs and wonders against Pharaoh and all his servants and all the people of his land, for you knew that they acted arrogantly against our fathers. And you made a name for yourself, as it is to this day. And you divided the sea before them, so that they went through the midst of the sea on dry land, and you cast their pursuers into the depths, as a stone into mighty waters. By a pillar of cloud you led them in the day, and by a pillar of fire in the night to light for them the way in which they should go. You came down on Mount Sinai and spoke with them from heaven and gave them right rules and true laws, good statutes and commandments, and you made known to them your holy Sabbath and commanded them commandments and statutes and a law by Moses your servant. You gave them bread from heaven for their hunger and brought water for them out of the rock for their thirst, and you told them to go in to possess the land that you had sworn to give them.
>
> But they and our fathers acted presumptuously and stiffened their neck and did not obey your commandments. They refused to obey and were not mindful of the wonders that you performed among them, but they stiffened their neck and appointed a leader to return to their slavery

in Egypt. But you are a God ready to forgive, gracious and merciful, slow to anger and abounding in steadfast love, and did not forsake them. Even when they had made for themselves a golden calf and said, 'This is your God who brought you up out of Egypt,' and had committed great blasphemies, you in your great mercies did not forsake them in the wilderness. The pillar of cloud to lead them in the way did not depart from them by day, nor the pillar of fire by night to light for them the way by which they should go. You gave your good Spirit to instruct them and did not withhold your manna from their mouth and gave them water for their thirst. Forty years you sustained them in the wilderness, and they lacked nothing. Their clothes did not wear out and their feet did not swell.

And you gave them kingdoms and peoples and allotted to them every corner. So they took possession of the land of Sihon king of Heshbon and the land of Og king of Bashan. You multiplied their children as the stars of heaven, and you brought them into the land that you had told their fathers to enter and possess. So the descendants went in and possessed the land, and you subdued before them the inhabitants of the land, the Canaanites, and gave them into their hand, with their kings and the peoples of the land, that they might do with them as they would. And they captured fortified cities and a rich land, and took possession of houses full of all good things, cisterns already hewn, vineyards, olive orchards and fruit trees in abundance. So they ate and were filled and became fat and delighted themselves in your great goodness.

Nevertheless, they were disobedient and rebelled against you and cast your law behind their back and killed your prophets, who had warned them in order to turn them back to you, and they committed great blasphemies. Therefore you gave them into the hand of their enemies, who made them suffer. And in the time of their suffering they cried out to you and you heard them from heaven, and according to your great mercies you gave them saviors who saved them from the hand of their enemies. But after they had rest they did evil again before you, and you abandoned them to the hand of their enemies, so that they had dominion over them. Yet when they turned and cried to you, you heard from heaven, and many times you delivered them according to your mercies. And you warned them in order to turn them back to your law. Yet they acted presumptuously and did not obey your commandments, but sinned against your rules, which if a person does them, he shall live by them, and they turned a stubborn shoulder and stiffened their neck and would not obey. Many years you bore with them and warned them by your Spirit through your prophets. Yet they would not give ear. Therefore you gave them into the hand of the peoples of the lands. Nevertheless, in your great mercies you did not make an end of them or forsake them, for you are a gracious and merciful God.

Now, therefore, our God, the great, the mighty, and the awesome God, who keeps covenant and steadfast love, let not all the hardship seem little to you that has come upon us, upon our kings, our princes, our priests, our prophets, our fathers, and all your people, since the time of the kings of Assyria until this day. Yet you have been righteous in all that has come upon us, for you have dealt faithfully and we have acted wickedly. Our kings, our princes, our priests, and our fathers have not kept your law or paid attention to your commandments and your warnings that you gave them. Even in their own kingdom, and amid your great goodness that you gave them, and in the large and rich land that you set before them, they did not serve you or turn from their wicked works. Behold, we are slaves this day; in the land that you gave to our fathers to enjoy its fruit and its good gifts, behold, we are slaves. And its rich yield goes to the kings whom you have set over us because of our sins. They rule over our bodies and over our livestock as they please, and we are in great distress.

Contents

The prayer itself is a survey of Israel's history intended to instruct its hearers. It considers the creation (v 6), Abraham (vv 7–8), the Exodus (vv 9–11), the wilderness wandering (vv 12–23), and Israel's time in the land (vv 24–31) before finally considering their present condition as a result of their sin (vv 33–37). This confession, moving from acknowledgment of who God is, to the extent of their unfaithfulness, to their current state due to that faithlessness will lead to a covenant renewal (v 38; ch 10).

The confession is twofold: a confession of God's glory and grace and a confession of their own ingratitude. Such an acknowledgment lies at the root of any true confession: God's glory and grace is ever present and never changes; human ingratitude is always true of sin. This pairing does more than just acknowledge the reality of God and sin, for it does not allow a mere exultation in God's grace without self-reflection. It does indeed produce worship, but it also treats sin seriously. It produces necessary introspection, but does not allow for wallowing in self-reproach.[6]

The prayer itself has an inverse parallel structure:[7]

  A Praise (5b)
      B Confession (historical retrospect) (6–31)
          C Petition (32)
      B' Confession (present circumstance) (33–35)
  A' Lament (36–37)

The prayer begins with a consideration of God's blessing (vv 6–15), with God underscored as the subject of every sentence in this section.[8] God is praised as the creator and sustainer of His creation. The covenant with Abraham is introduced and Abraham's faithfulness is highlighted (set in contrast to Israel's faithlessness). Further, it recalls God's saving acts in Egypt, both because it is the formative moment for Israel as a nation and it emphasizes God's power over even the strongest of nations.

The historical sin of Israel comes to the foreground and is set in contrast with God's blessing in the back-and-forth pairing of God's great acts and His people's disobedience. First, God blesses in spite of their rebellion (vv 16–25) and then they rebel in spite of God's blessing (vv 26–36).[9] The contrast between God's love and care and their disobedience cannot be any clearer, particularly with "nevertheless they" (v 26) and "nevertheless you" (v 31) bookending this paragraph.[10] It is a history of their disobedience and total rejection of God's commandment. Yet in spite of their sin,

---

[6] Kidner, *Ezra and Nehemiah*, 111.

[7] Throntveit, *Ezra-Nehemiah*, 102. For an alternate, more detailed structure, see Balentine, *Prayer in the Hebrew Bible*, 111–112. Balentine's entire exposition of this prayer is especially helpful, but far more detailed than the restrictions of the present book allow.

[8] Kidner, *Ezra and Nehemiah*, 112.

[9] McConville, *Ezra, Nehemiah, and Esther*, 126–127 points out that "presumptuously" in verse 29 is the same Hebrew word as Pharaoh acting "arrogantly" in verse 10, giving clear grounds for judgment and indicating that Israel is no better than Egypt.

[10] Kidner, *Ezra and Nehemiah*, 112.

God never abandoned them, for as He told Moses, He is "a God ready to forgive, gracious and merciful, slow to anger and abounding in steadfast love" (v 17; cf. Exod 34.6–7). As they say later, God has acted faithfully even as they have acted wickedly (v 33).

Finally, they appeal for deliverance and meditate on their current state (vv 32–37). As we have seen so frequently, the petition is marked with "now" (v 32), though the request may not be what we would expect. It surely has far-reaching implications, but the simple request that their hardship not seem little to God is as modest a request as can be imagined. Even as Ezra had made confession with no petition, so now the Levites of Nehemiah 9 make confession with the most unassuming petition imaginable. In both cases, it must be the acute awareness of their perpetual wickedness as a people that mitigates again any sort of grand request they might otherwise conceive. Yet notice that in spite of their covenant breaking, the request is rooted in the covenant loyalty of a "God who keeps covenant and steadfast love" (v 32). The prayer comes to a conclusion with an acknowledgment of their current distress, but leaving God to act according to His will.

Connections

Great is your faithfulness. As we have already seen repeatedly, recognition of God's glory is a key feature in prayer. Although this prayer does not contain the overt doxology that frequently appears, the retelling of God's role from the very creation throughout the history of Israel can only point toward His greatness, making praise foundational to this prayer. It is most explicit at the beginning, where He alone is the creator and the host of heaven worships Him (v 6) and in the Exodus, where He makes a name for Himself by His saving acts (v 10). Most significantly, perhaps, God's greatness is seen in His faithfulness, an idea constantly present in this prayer. God's faithfulness is an aspect of His greatness that we sometimes forget is praiseworthy. His magnificence is not just found in His power to create and destroy, His ability to rule nature and nations, or His ability to give life and overthrow death. Beyond those great actions—and sometimes by means of them—God's greatness is that He is always true to His nature, He is always true to His word, He will never break His covenant. This aspect of God's greatness should not be taken for granted by His people, and we should regularly laud Him for and remind ourselves of it.

It is here that our recurring theme of covenant returns yet again. God, in this prayer, is one who keeps covenant and steadfast love and who deals faithfully even when humankind is faithless (vv 32–33). He has been true to His promises to Abraham and Israel, and this known character of God as deliverer and forgiver stands behind every word of this prayer.

The place of confession. Likewise, confession is a theme we have encountered before. Here, the confession speaks to how thoroughly and consistently they have failed. They are no different from their fathers. And the people here are deeply moved by their sin—so much so that they do not presume upon God's mercy. As said above, they are not wallowing in self-reproach, but they are not merely exulting in God's grace without reflection either. It can be difficult to find this balance. Serious reflection on and sorrow for sin should be a part of the believer's life, but it can be easy to allow sorrow to become an ongoing burden and stumbling block to future progress. Likewise, we should have complete confidence in the grace God has promised to show, but taking His grace for granted is far too easy a habit to slip into. Perhaps Paul's discussion of godly sorrow as opposed to worldly sorrow is the best corrective to the extreme positions (2 Cor 7.8–11).[11]

Praise and confession. It is easy to categorize how we pray. A common acronym turns adoration, confession, thanksgiving, and supplication into "The ACTS of Prayer," which can be helpful, so long as it is not seen as an all-encompassing theology of prayer. In addition to leaving out key elements like lament,[12] it makes dividing lines where none should exist. McConville speaks to this very well, saying, "The note of praise which prefaces the confession (v 5) heralds what will in fact be the tone of the

---

[11] See Ward, *Daybreak*, 95–101.

[12] See our discussions of Habakkuk's prayers in chapters 15 and 16.

prayers, namely that, despite the sin of Israel, the relationship with Israel's God is a continuing one, and that praise and confession belong intimately together, both appropriate because of the greatness of God."[13] So also it should be in our praying: praise should spill over into confession and repentance with gratitude infusing ever word and idea.

Prayers of exhortation. Nearly every author I have read on this prayer (including several not cited in this chapter) makes note of how much of it is for the benefit of the hearers. As we said regarding earlier prayers, there is nothing wrong with prayers that can be a little "preachy." Very few prayers should be dominated by sermon-like material and not every prayer should include such content, but the annoyance that some have at that occasional feature of public prayers is misplaced.

Know your own history. An important element of this prayer we should not miss is the historical retrospective, especially considering how much of the prayer it comprises. To recount past failings in a present prayer is not to deny the efficacy of God's grace, but to remind ourselves of how dependent we are on it, to remind ourselves we cannot make it on our own and it is only His enduring faithfulness that gives us any kind of hope. Further, it reminds us we are part of a long history of God's people who have lived lives of failing and dependence—and yet in thousands of years of failures in covenant history God has not once failed to keep His word or pour out His grace when it is sought. This sort of reflection—on self, on covenant history, and on God—will inevitably change the nature of prayer. Prayer, Clines says, is "not simply a matter of speaking to God, but also of critical self-reflection in the light of God's demands and his grace." He says, therefore, this prayer "cannot conclude with a superficial appeal for deliverance from misery, but must end simply on a note of confession (vv 33–35) and distress (vv 36–37). It does not jog God's elbow, but leaves Him entirely free to act according to His own free will."[14] Prayer of this sort will produce acknowledgment of failure, praise for who God is, and an appeal to God's continued faithfulness even when we are faithless.

---

[13] McConville, *Ezra, Nehemiah, and Esther,* 124.
[14] Clines, *Ezra, Nehemiah, Esther,* 199.

Adding a chapter to the story. As remarkable as this prayer is in highlighting God's faithfulness and mercy over against the faithlessness and sin of His people, the story does not end in Nehemiah's generation. Indeed, the sin continued through the rest of pre-Christian history and has continued for two thousand years since Christ walked on the earth. In response, God has not merely continued to be faithful in a grudging sense, but has brought His covenant promises to fruition in the Incarnation and atoning sacrifice of Jesus. As Chester says, "The God who created all things, the God who keeps His promises, the God who saves His people, the God of compassion and love has brought all these things to a climax in the gift of his Son and in the love of the cross." [15]

---

[15] Chester, *The Message of Prayer*, 111.

TWENTY-FOUR

Now My Eye Sees You

Job 42.2–6

The God to whom we pray is a God of wisdom, a God in whom we can trust because He knows the answers we cannot know. As much as we might question His ways—even as the laments show us we may—our ultimate position must be one of trust. He is the creator of all, His understanding is far beyond our meager comprehension, and He is the source of the paltry amount of wisdom we are ever able to obtain. The book of Job deals with the question of wisdom differently than the other wisdom books,[1] ultimately showing us a man who, far from beaten down by God's torrent of questions, has come to catch a glimpse of God's knowledge and trust Him.

Context

A key piece of context is the genre of the book of Job. Many readers of Job expect the book to answer the problem of evil, making suffering its primary theme. Although undeniably a major theme in Job, the book itself is wisdom literature, and its primary theme is wisdom. This can be seen in many ways. First, the central point of the book is chapter 28, a poem about the divine origin of wisdom.[2] Second, Job 28 provides a

---

[1] See Kidner, *The Wisdom of Job, Proverbs, & Ecclesiastes*, 116–124 and Longman, *How to Read Proverbs*, 79–91 for helpful discussions of the interrelation of Biblical wisdom literature.

[2] See Dorsey, *Literary Structure*, 170 for one example of a chiastic structure that places Job 28 at the center.

definition of wisdom: to fear the Lord and turn away from evil (v 28), the same definition found in other Biblical wisdom (cf. Ps 111.10; Prov 1.7; 9.10; Ecc 12.13). This definition also functions as God's description of Job (Job 1.8). Third, as Job and his friends debate the nature of Job's suffering (4–27; 32–36), the primary debated point is who has an accurate knowledge and understanding of the matter; each presents himself as a wisdom teacher, and they debate whose wisdom is correct. Fourth, God's speeches (38–41) pick up this theme, asking Job repeatedly what he can accomplish with his wisdom, knowledge, and understanding, and Job ultimately replies that he has spoken beyond his knowledge (42.3).[3]

The rest of the context is simply the entire book of Job. Consider Job throughout the book. Before his trial, he is the epitome of righteousness and wisdom. His children and possessions are enumerated in multiples of 7 and 10, indicating a "perfect" family and wealth. Then, due to Satan's machinations, he faces trials. He loses his possessions, his children die, his body is struck with boils, and his wife turns her back on him and their faith. Although he refuses to curse God, he no longer desires to live. In chapter 3, his lament curses the day of his birth and asks why he must continue to live. His friends, who until now have been silent, begin to speak and Job responds to each of them, clinging to his integrity and refusing to admit sin. As the speeches continue, he speaks less with the friends and more to God, contending with Him.

The friends' role is important to consider as well. After sitting with Job in silence, they speak when Job expresses his wish to die, perhaps because they see this as evidence of his wickedness (11.20; cf. 6.8). This, after all, is their main point: Job must have sinned to bring this calamity upon himself. All accuse him of some wrongdoing. Zophar concludes the first round of speeches by saying Job deserves worse than he is getting (11.4–6). In the second round of speeches, each of them urges Job to acknowledge his wrong by describing "the wicked man," a series of thinly disguised descriptions of Job himself. Finally, in the last

---

[3] See Habel, "Wisdom in the Book of Job," 303–315 for a further discussion of the presence of wisdom themes throughout the book.

round of speeches, Eliphaz accuses Job of endless wickedness (22.5) and produces a list of specific sins that Job had supposedly committed. Job concludes the speeches with a final declaration, speaking of his former happiness (29) and his present humiliation (30), before issuing an oath of innocence (31).[4]

Finally, God responds. He opens by asking who dared to "darken counsel by words without knowledge" (38.2) and has arrived to test Job's knowledge with His own questions (38.3; 40.7). God does not engage Job's pain or Job's challenge. He does not address Job's unjust suffering, his ongoing questions, his affirmations of innocence, or the problem of evil. Rather, God's questions answer the question of wisdom. Job, overwhelmed by the first round of questions, can only speak to his smallness, admit he has said too much, and cover his mouth so that he will say no more (40.4–5). God, however, is not done, and the barrage of questions continues. After the second wave (tsunami!) of questions finally passes, Job will speak more fully, saying,

> I know that you can do all things,
>> and that no purpose of yours can be thwarted.
> "Who is this that hides counsel without knowledge?"
> Therefore I have uttered what I did not understand,
>> things too wonderful for me, which I did not know.
> "Hear, and I will speak;
>> I will question you, and you make it known to me."
> I had heard of you by the hearing of the ear,
>> but now my eye sees you;
> therefore I despise myself,
>> and repent in dust and ashes. (Job 42.2–6)

---

[4] Elihu (chs 32–36) is a fascinating character and is harder to pin down than the other friends, making him too much for the limited scope of this chapter. At times, he sounds like a precursor to God's speeches and at times he sounds like a retread of the friends. Views of Elihu vary widely. For example, Hartley, *The Book of Job*, 427 says, "Elihu makes a significant contribution to the core issue of the book," while Longman, *Job*, 367 says, "Elihu says nothing new and therefore can safely be ignored," with other nuanced views between.

Contents

Job's prayer[5] follows a very simple outline.

> Job's statement (v 2)
> Quotation from God (v 3a)
> Job's statement (v 3b)
> Quotation from God (v 4)
> Job's statement (vv 5–6)[6]

The first statement is a doxology, acknowledging the wonder, splendor, and power of God, a matter Job had already acknowledged in the earlier speeches (9.5–12). This opening is a far cry from his initial response of silence. Instead, it is a spontaneous outburst of unrestrained admiration, the cry of a liberated man, not a broken one.[7]

God's first speech opens with the question of who spoke without knowledge, but does not specify to whom He spoke. Most naturally, it might be Job, as he was the direct conversation partner at the moment. Or it could be Elihu, who spoke most recently before God. Or the friends, who God will later say did not speak right concerning him (42.7). Or it could be all five of the humans who opened their mouths, claiming knowledge far beyond what they had. Whoever God had in view when He asked the question, Job takes ownership of it here. Humility and introspection lead Job to admit that he spoke out of his ignorance.

God opened His second speech with the demand that Job instruct Him. Job had been asking questions and expecting answers. God's appearance puts things in their proper perspective. Job had taken the role of interrogator, a role which was not his to have, so God resituates Job. By becoming the interrogator, God makes Job realize who is who and Job takes a posture of prayer as a creature in submission to his creator.[8] In

---

[5] There is more prayer in Job than many initially suppose. Many of Job's responses to his friends gradually turn away from them and to God. By the end, he hardly speaks to them at all. For a brief summary of Job's prayer language outside of this particular prayer, see Millar, *Calling on the Name of the Lord*, 108–114.

[6] Brueggemann, *Great Prayers*, 126.

[7] Anderson, *Job*, 291–292.

[8] Brueggemann, *Great Prayers*, 117.

this encounter, Job gains essential knowledge: knowledge of God, about whom he had only previously heard but now sees; knowledge of himself, because seeing God changed his entire perspective—"Therefore I despise myself, and repent in dust and ashes" (42.6).

This last phrase is simultaneously most important of all and the hardest to ascertain its meaning. It is ambiguous and can be interpreted in at least a couple of different ways, making it difficult to know for certain what Job is saying. First, the verb *repent* means to be sorry, which could indicate either a repentance of sin or simple regret for a bad choice.[9] If the former, it surely does not indicate that Job is repenting of a sin that led to his suffering, for that would undo the clear affirmations of chapters 1–2; instead, it would refer to a sin committed during the rounds of speeches and his affirmations of innocence[10] or "hubris by claiming to have better insight than God into matters on earth."[11] Or, perhaps Job is not repenting of a sin committed in this book, but is acknowledging his general sinfulness, a reality that inevitably becomes apparent in the presence of God (cf. Isa 6.5; Luke 5.8). If the latter, however, it may mean Job regrets the position he took as litigant in the case against God; he is retracting the case he has made against God[12] or retracting a statement or perspective in light of this new information.[13]

A second difficulty is in understanding how to apply verse 7—God's affirmation that Job has spoken rightly concerning Him—to this repentance. If Job has not been incorrect, then there is no need to repent over sin in his speech. On the other hand, is God speaking in generalities regarding Job's position concerning God's justice more than affirming every single sentence that proceeded from Job's mouth? Or is it referring only to the most recent speech—Job's repentance—and the fact that the friends have not yet followed suit?[14]

---

[9] See BDB, 636–637 or HALOT, 688–689 for its semantic range.
[10] See Longman, *Job*, 448–450.
[11] Hartley, *The Book of Job*. 536. It should be noted that Hartley repeatedly mitigates this, saying Job "approached" this sin, was "in danger of it," and came "dangerously close" to it.
[12] Balentine, *Prayer in the Hebrew Bible*, 180.
[13] Wilson, *Job*, 468.
[14] Walton and Longman, *How to Read Job*, 63–64.

Finally, in the Hebrew text, the verb *despise* has no object, so it must be supplied by the translator. Although most make Job the object (e.g., ESV, quoted above), some direct it to his words—e.g., "I reject my words" (CSB; cf. NASB; NJB).[15]

However we work through those precise details, the core message is clear. Job no longer seeks to be a philosopher of religion but instead a trusting child of God, for God is not accountable to Job but Job to God. As Kidner says, "Job has no such pretensions any longer. Seeing God with newly opened eyes he has no questions, only a confession and a self-abasement that is as deep as his indignation had been high."[16]

Connections

Seeing God changes your perspective. This prayer is not based on covenant as so many have been, but it is based on God's self-revelation. Whether you decide Job sinned and repented or changed his view and recanted, it is clear that seeing God impacted the way he viewed the situation. At the same time, this subheading seems so obvious as hardly to be worth saying. And yet it is easy to forget. Because we have never had such an experience, we imagine ourselves asking trivial questions upon our arrival to heaven (at best) or demanding of Him explanations for why the world works as it does. Skeptics whose atheism has led to a shallow understanding of God can perhaps be excused for thinking they will make the sorts of accusations they claim they will make if they end up standing before Him, but believers should know better. Whether Job, Isaiah, Peter, or Paul all who encounter God have their entire perspective realigned. What was once important is no longer so in comparison to what they now know. This leads naturally to the next point.

Seeing God is better than knowing answers. We frequently comfort ourselves with the thought that it will all make sense one day. As the old hymn says, "Farther along, we'll know all about it. Farther along, we'll

---

[15] Balentine, *Prayer in the Hebrew Bible*, 179 says this verb is never used in a genuinely reflexive sense, though the abundance of translations which render it that way indicates translators still see it as a viable option.

[16] Kidner, *The Wisdom of Proverbs, Job, & Ecclesiastes*, 72.

understand why." The book of Job seems to stand against this idea; Job is never given any answers (and I'm not sure he would have been satisfied with them if he had). Job anticipates as much, with his great declaration of faith being "I will see God," not "I will understand all of this" (19.26). When he does see God, the vision overwhelms him, and Job's response is not "At last I understand,"[17] but a realization that all his complaints are utterly insignificant.[18] Likewise, Paul finds comfort in the midst of present trials not in the answers we will receive, but "in the glory that will be revealed" (Rom 8.18). As much as we might think we need answers to the difficulties of this life, a far greater comfort is that the revelation of God's glory will make the worst things we ever experience so dim a memory that we wonder why it ever upset us so much. If seeing *something* of God in this life can so change the perspective of all who encounter Him, how much more will seeing Him *as He is* (1 John 3.2) completely reshape our outlook on everything we have ever known!

Humility regarding God. Job, his friends, and Elihu all spoke with great confidence regarding God's dealings with humankind. Job admitted he spoke beyond his knowledge and God told Eliphaz that he and the other two did as well. In reality, this charge is one that would indict us all:[19] how much—and how confidently—have we spoken about God in matters where He has not revealed what He is doing? Surely we need to be confident about what God *has said* He is doing, but just as surely we need to be humble about what God has not revealed. The believer must find that balance between hope and expectation on the one hand and humbly allowing God to be God on the other. Such a commitment to humility regarding God's sovereignty need not be seen as a lack of faith.[20]

---

[17] Carson, *How Long, O Lord?* 153.
[18] Hartley, *The Book of Job,* 537.
[19] Alden, *Job,* 408.
[20] See Ward, *God Unseen,* 125–134.

TWENTY-FIVE

My Eyes Have Seen Your Salvation
Luke 2.29–32

The God to whom we pray is a God who accomplishes all His purposes. If He says an elderly, barren woman will have a child, she will. If He says a prophet will see a child before he dies, he will. If He says His Messiah is coming to establish a kingdom, it will be established. Simeon was able to experience just a small taste of this in his life and his prayer reflects his gratitude to God for His faithfulness and great purposes in this world.

Context

The gospel of Luke contains more information about Jesus' childhood than any other early source without a close second. It also includes information about the months before Jesus' birth which the other gospels do not include. This material includes two key poems of praise to God. First, shortly after the annunciation of Jesus, Mary speaks what has come to be called her Magnificat (1.47–55), which strongly echoes Hannah's poetic prayer (1 Sam 2) and concludes with a reference to God's loyalty to Israel and His promises to Abraham (1.54–55). Second, Zechariah prophesies after the birth of John (1.68–79), a prophecy (called the Benedictus) that includes reference to David, the prophets, and Abraham (1.69–73). From the very beginning of his gospel, Luke shows the faithful looking to God to keep His promises.[1]

---

[1] Millar, *Calling on the Name of the Lord*, 168.

Second, a subtle, but important element of Luke's gospel is Jesus' devotion to Old Testament Law. Although Luke does not record Jesus' "I came not to destroy, but to fulfill" declaration about the Law (Matt 5.17–20), he does record many accounts of Jesus exemplifying obedience to it.[2] This scene follows on the heels of the obedience of Jesus' parents to the Law. After Jesus was born, He was circumcised on the eighth day (v 21; cf. Lev 12.3) and His parents went to Jerusalem to offer a sacrifice for her purification (vv 22–24; cf. Exod 13.2, 12; Lev 12.8).[3] Thus, we see an obedient Jewish family, conforming to Jewish law, acknowledging that their child is a gift from God. Moreover, this trip brings them to Jerusalem for their meeting with Simeon.

Third is the background of Old Testament Scripture, particularly the book of Isaiah. At least three significant texts stand as backdrop to Simeon's prayer, which will be discussed in more detail below:

> And the glory of the Lord shall be revealed,
>   and all flesh shall see it together. (Isa 40.5)

> I will give you as a covenant for the people,
>   a light for the nations. (Isa 42.6)

> The Lord has bared his holy arm
>   before the eyes of all the nations,
> and all the ends of the earth shall see
>   the salvation of our God. (Isa 52.10)[4]

Finally, we should consider Simeon himself. Many picture Simeon as an old priest on the verge of death who has waited his entire life to see the Messiah. Except for his waiting to see the Messiah, the text says none of this explicitly,[5] though it is a natural reading. The similarity of this scene

---

[2] See Hays, *Echoes of Scripture in the Gospels*, 207–212.

[3] It is also noteworthy that Joseph and Mary offer the sacrifice allowed for the poor who were not able to offer a lamb.

[4] Green, *The Gospel of Luke*, 147 also includes Isaiah 46.13; 49.6; 56.1; 60.1.

[5] Morris, *Luke*, 87. On his waiting to see the Messiah, Millar, *Calling on the Name of the Lord*, 169 says this depicts him as "one who epitomizes faithful Israel."

to 1 Samuel 1–2 provides a contextual echo that recalls a priestly blessing, and his presence at the Temple offering a blessing may well suggest that he is a priest, though he may simply be a prophet. The promise to him that he would see the Messiah before his death and his statement that he can "depart in peace" (vv 26, 29) may well suggest that he is near death and has waited a long time for this moment, though it may simply be a figurative way of saying that his life is complete—many people far from death's door have said, "Now I can die in peace," to indicate such accomplishment.[6] Even if he is older, the text certainly does not imply that he is going to die later that afternoon.

Simeon is a man who is filled with the Spirit (v 25) and led by the Spirit (vv 26–27). To be filled with the Spirit in a pre-Pentecost context recalls various Old Testament heroes who were suddenly and temporarily filled with the Spirit for a specific moment's need (e.g. Jdg 6.34; 11.29; 14.19; 1 Sam 10.6, 10; 11.6; etc.). Something like this has already happened in Luke's gospel to Elizabeth (1.41) and Zechariah (1.67). Simeon, however, was said to have the Holy Spirit "upon him," which might indicate that the Spirit's presence with him was more permanent.[7] Whatever the case, he had been informed by the Spirit that he would see the Messiah before his death and he had a divine appointment at the Temple that day to meet Jesus.[8] Upon seeing Jesus, he turns to God and says,

> Lord, now you are letting your servant depart in peace,
>   according to your word;
> for my eyes have seen your salvation
>   that you have prepared in the presence of all peoples,
> a light for revelation to the Gentiles,
>   and for glory to your people Israel.

---

[6] Green, *The Gospel of Luke*, 147 argues that the word can mean "to discharge." If this is the meaning, it means not that he is necessarily near death, but his task is complete.

[7] See Nolland, *Luke 1–9.20*, 118–119; Morris, *Luke*, 87–88.

[8] Here, "Temple" must refer to the Temple Mount and the larger compound rather than the Temple structure proper, as Mary would not be allowed beyond the Court of the Women.

Following his prayer, Simeon also issues a prophecy that we will also briefly consider in this section.

The Prayer. The prayer itself is reminiscent of hymns in the Psalter, those psalms which are wholly made up of praise. They begin with a call to praise God, offer reasons to praise God, and end with a concluding call to praise God.[9] Similarly, Simeon begins by blessing God (v 28) before elaborating as to why he is offering this praise.

Simeon's prayer is rooted in promise. First, it focuses on the promise that was made to him. God had assured him that he would see the Messiah before his death and that is coming to pass. Simeon begins his prayer with an acknowledgment that God had indeed kept His word to Simeon in this regard. Notice, however, that Simeon does not focus on having seen the Messiah, but having seen God's salvation. To the Christian reader, these two ideas seem interchangeable, as they would have to a first century Jew as well. This maneuver allows Simeon to subtly move from God having kept his personal promise to Simeon to God keeping His promise to the people of Israel. Isaiah had promised that all the nations would see the salvation of God (Isa 52.10; cf. 46.13; 56.1), and Simeon sees that coming to pass in Jesus.

This is closely related to another echo of Isaiah that appears in this prayer. Israel had been commissioned to be a light to the nations (Isa 42.6; 49.6) and had failed miserably in that regard, instead glorying in their unique salvation rather than sharing the light with the world; Jesus, however, would take up that task and succeed where Israel had failed (cf. Luke 24.44–47; Acts 1.8). Strikingly it is at the Temple, "the center of the world of Israel" where it is revealed that "salvation for Israel includes salvation for the Gentiles."[10]

Finally, this light that would be for revelation to the Gentiles would be for glory to the Jewish people (cf. Isa 40.5; 60.1). Their glory is to be found in the arrival of their long-awaited Messiah and His work in bringing the

---

[9] Longman, *How to Read the Psalms*, 24.
[10] Green, *The Gospel of Luke*, 146.

promised blessing to all the nations of the earth. The long-developing special purpose of the people of God in being the conduit through whom the Messiah would come is reaching its culmination. Salvation to the nations is the full realization of Israel's glory.[11]

Simeon's prayer, though brief, is filled with theologically-loaded ideas that say far more than just the words on the page. For example, the Isaianic background of his prayer roots Simeon's message in the purpose of God, particularly Isaiah's vision of divine restoration and healing while emphasizing the universal reach of God's redemption and indicating that Isaiah's Servant of the Lord is a proper background for interpreting the rest of Jesus' life.[12] Beyond this, Simeon's references to God's salvation, God's revelation, and God's glory are all ideas that take up entire chapters in systematic theology texts and one can only presume Simeon's thoughts go far beyond his words as he ponders these ideas and how they relate to the arrival of Jesus.

The Prophecy. According to Simeon, Jesus would be three things: the cause of rising and falling, a sign that is opposed, and a cause of pain to Mary. These three things, however, are probably closely related. Jesus' arrival is always received in one of two ways: acceptance or rejection, and that reaction reveals one's heart before God (cf. Heb 4.12–13, where it is God's word that is the sword which reveals). Those who accept Jesus will rise; those who reject him will fall, though not before their opposition leads to His death, which will surely be the greatest piercing of Mary's heart.[13] Though it does not use the language of Psalm 118.22, this parallels the idea: one either builds on Jesus or stumbles because of Him; one either finds a firm foundation that will support or a rock that will crush and destroy. In the larger context of Luke's writings, it may be significant that one volume tells of the rejection and crucifixion of Christ ("falling") while the second tells of the spread of the gospel of Christ and multiplication

---

[11] Morris, *Luke*, 88.

[12] Green, *The Gospel of Luke*, 147.

[13] See Garland, *Luke*, 137 for a brief summary of various interpretive options of the sword piercing Mary's heart.

of Christians ("rising"), with it being especially noteworthy that the latter includes the revelation being shared with the Gentiles.[14]

Connections

God keeps His promises. Luke begins his gospel tolling this bell over and over again: God can be counted on to do what He said He will do. And this is emphasized throughout Scripture. In fact, of all the characters in the Bible, God is the only one who can be consistently counted on to do what He says He will do. This is all the more remarkable, considering that it is God who says the most outlandish and unbelievable things of all! Between promises of a 90-year-old woman giving birth, a virgin maiden giving birth, and the dead coming back to life, God's promises border dangerously on the edge of preposterous. And yet He always comes through. It is on this basis that believers live their lives and it is on this basis that we offer our prayers. Our trust in this track record of kept promises directs our walk and our talk with God.

Prayer rooted in prophecy. Although Simeon does not explicitly cite any promise or prophecy of God, as we have seen so frequently, his prayer is rooted in promise—this time, in Isaiah. It is not merely God's promise to Simeon that he would see the Messiah that has come true, but His promises about His salvation, revelation, and glory that He would work out in this coming servant that would come true. Rather than an appeal based on God's promises, Simeon issues praise to God for having kept His promises. This reminds us that God's promises are not only the foundation we stand upon when we appeal to God, but the foundation upon which we trust in general and the basis of our thanksgiving and praise to God for what He has done and who He is.

Seeing Jesus impacts the rest of your life. It is impossible to walk away from an encounter with Jesus unchanged. Sure, we may meet a Jesus of our own devising—a god made in man's image—and find ourselves placated and all our beliefs affirmed by such an encounter. But no one meets the real Jesus without it significantly impacting him or her. For Simeon,

---

[14] Garland, *Luke*, 139.

the change was in his role—no longer waiting for the Messiah, he rejoices in having seen Him and prophesies about Him. For everyone else, an encounter with Jesus reveals the heart and one either builds or stumbles on Him. To truly comprehend a message of selfless love and a crucified Christ demands a choice of anyone who would wear His name: acceptance or rejection; there is no middle ground. We deny self and take up a cross or we cling to self and avoid sacrificial service; we build on the foundation laid by Jesus or we trip on it and find ourselves crushed by it.

Short prayers can speak volumes. There are times for long prayers and there are times for short prayers. Not every prayer needs to be the same as every other one; indeed, circumstances of life demand that they are not the same. Short prayers, like Nehemiah's unspoken one (Neh 2.4–5), have a legitimate place in our lives and speak far more than the words that are included in the prayer. Simeon's prayer is yet another example of this: only four verses in the Biblical text, yet packed with ideas that could fill pages of exposition. His prayer is undoubtedly far longer than the few words that he speaks.

There is a practical side of brief, theologically deep prayers. In addition to situations like Nehemiah's where the occasion simply does not allow for a long prayer, many people struggle with their evening prayers—namely, struggling to stay awake as they pray. Some may well be comfortable with the idea of talking to God until they fall asleep, but others' consciences may not allow for such a view.[15] Aside from the eminently practical advice of not attempting to say your day's longest prayer after a long day of work flat on your back on the most comfortable piece of furniture you own with the lights off, I might add that such an occasion is ready-made for a short, theologically-loaded prayer. Instead, save your longer prayers for occasions better suited to that type of praying.

---

[15] There may be some merit to the idea of feeling guilty for falling asleep during prayer. In addition to Jesus' warning to the disciples not to do that very thing (Mark 14.37–38, though the circumstances of that particular hour may allow for a limited application), a friend put the potential offense in relatively stark terms: "Yeah, I just love it when people fall asleep when they're talking to me." On the other hand, if in the evening one of my children fell asleep while sitting in my lap telling me about his day, his joys, and his concerns, it would not bother me at all.

TWENTY-SIX

Teach Us to Pray

Matthew 6.9–13; Luke 11.2–4

The God to whom we pray is a God who teaches us to pray. His instruction is not merely the command that we should or must speak to Him. Rather, in His incarnation He modeled prayer, both by His example as a prayerful person and then by teaching His apostles specifically, and the multitudes more generally, how to pray. This prayer is likely the best-known prayer in history, which makes it fraught with preconceptions and misconceptions, as well as other potential theological baggage arising from the idiosyncrasies of various traditions within Christendom at large.

Context

The beginning of Matthew contains multiple echoes of the Exodus: a trip to Egypt for safety and return that is framed in the context of an Exodus verse (Matt 2.15), a crazy king killing children (Matt 2.16), temptation in the wilderness overcome by quotations from Deuteronomy (Matt 4.1–11), and a man ascending a mountain to present the charter of the kingdom, the "rules" of a new covenant, many of which explicitly echo old covenant regulations.[1]

---

[1] The use of the word "rules" here is to emphasize the connection between the imperatives of the Old Covenant and the imperatives of the New, not to suggest that Jesus taught salvation by works or that Christians remain under law rather than under grace (Rom 6.14). Similarly, my understanding of the explicit references to the Old is not that Jesus is contrasting Old and New, but contrasting His contemporary teachers' perversions of the Old with what God has, in fact, always wanted. For a brief overview of the latter point, see Earnhart, *Invitation to a Spiritual Revolution*, 39–41.

As Jesus makes His way through this sermon, contrasts abound. As He comes to prayer, He zeroes in on two problems: the self-aggrandizing hypocrisy of the pharisees and the pagan ignorance of trying to catch the attention of the gods by their many words.[2] Rather, prayer is to be a function of faith. Believers should pray to God knowing He already knows, which is the reason—as we have seen repeatedly—prayer should be rooted in His promises, not our whims. As we become more conformed to His image in spiritual growth, we find that His desire for us is increasingly the same as our own desires. This focus on God's will and conforming the earthly reality to match the heavenly is a major feature of this prayer.

Luke records a similar, but shorter prayer. In Luke, it comes in a different context: a conversation between Jesus and the apostles rather than the middle of a sermon.[3] It is impossible to know whether the conversation or the sermon came first. Perhaps Jesus first gave the apostles the shorter version, and elaborated further for His sermon; or, perhaps, the longer version was first and the shorter is intended to jog their memory about what He already taught. In either case, this prayer serves as a model of how to pray in both texts:

> Therefore, you should pray like this:
>
> Our Father in heaven,
>> Your name be honored as holy.
>> Your kingdom come.
>> Your will be done
>>> on earth as it is in heaven.
>>
>> Give us today our daily bread.
>> And forgive us our debts,
>>> as we also have forgiven our debtors.
>>
>> And do not bring us into temptation,
>>> but deliver us from the evil one. (Matt 6.9–13, CSB)

---

[2] See Appendix B for a brief discussion of these principles.

[3] See Carson, "Matthew," 166–168 for a discussion of the relationship between the two texts. In this book, this chapter is an oddity in that that it does not take its title from a phrase in the prayer itself. Rather because it is a model—both in Matthew and Luke—its title comes from the apostles' well-known request to Jesus.

Contents

Before Jesus begins the prayer, He says that what follows should be a model for prayer: "pray like this." This excludes using these precise words in every prayer; neither should it be studiously ignored.[4] The prayer itself is divided into two parts: three petitions related to God; three petitions related to the one who prays.

Our Father in Heaven. The prayer begins with the address of a child to his or her father, with all the rights and privileges that such a relationship brings, and with the full confidence that God will do what is in His children's best interest, just as we will do what is in the best interest of our children (cf. Matt 7.9–11). Although Christians may take this relationship for granted, it is a new perspective of the New Covenant. God was occasionally referred to as a father in the Old Testament, but only by analogy and not in direct address.[5] Although there may have been other factors at play, Jesus' teaching shifted the way people think about their relationship with God. Even so, the request is made to a *heavenly* Father, reminding the one who prays of God's capacity to give and of God's pure and right intentions when He does give. It also emphasizes another aspect of our relationship with Him: not only father and child, but creator and creature. There is balance here: we address God intimately as Father while recognizing His infinite greatness in heaven.[6]

Your name be honored as holy. Your kingdom come. Your will be done. These three phrases are parallel in their structure in Greek, which is obscured by English translations that follow the traditional "Hallowed be your name" translation. In addition to being grammatically parallel, they are conceptually parallel as well, particularly if we understand the next phrase—*on earth as it is in heaven*—as being connected to all three, not

---

[4] See Appendix B.

[5] Carson, "Matthew," 169. See Marshall, "Jesus—Example and Teacher of Prayer," 127 for statistical data on the use of "father" in the Old Testament.

[6] Morris, *Matthew*, 144. Carson, "Matthew," 169 points out that the Jewish tendency was to multiply titles of God's sovereignty in prayer, concluding, "Unfortunately, many modern Christians find it very difficult to delight in the privilege of addressing the Sovereign of the universe as "Father" because they have lost the heritage that emphasizes God's transcendence." Stott, *The Message of the Sermon on the Mount*, 146 emphasizes the power at God's command to give what we ask.

just the last. God's name is honored as holy in heaven; God's reign is complete in heaven; God's will is always done in heaven. The prayer asks that the reality on earth would match the reality of heaven, not merely as it relates to the last clause, but to all three.[7]

The CSB's "your name be honored as holy" is a clearer rendering of the more archaic "hallowed." God's name is not merely the designation by which we call Him, but the fullness of His character and His identity. It is God Himself whom we honor as holy, putting Him on the throne of our own hearts, where He belongs as God of all.

The coming kingdom is a matter of confusion and consternation to many, particularly as a debated end-times issue in theology. It is greatly simplified with the realization that the word most frequently refers not to the governmental concept of a kingdom, but the broader concept of royal power.[8] In this case, it is God's reign and rule that we pray for.

The will of God encompasses both of the previous phrases: it is God's will that He be recognized as God, not because of a divinely bloated ego, but because it is the truth and He is a God of truth; it is God's will that His reign be expanded throughout the world. Again, these three phrases go together, and all are governed by the final "on earth as it is in heaven"; all of this is already true in the heavenly realm, and our prayer is that the earthly will come into conformity with the heavenly.

Give us this day our daily bread. This is the most difficult sentence in the entire prayer, largely because of the word translated "daily" and its possible meanings.[9] It is a rare word and its etymology is debated. Some see it as connected to the idea of it being necessary for our existence, others as being for the current day (or the following day), and still others as

---

[7] This is known as ellipsis, a figure where words are intentionally left out to avoid redundancy, but should be supplied by the reader (e.g., Psalm 50.10, where "are mine" is understood as being added to Line B based on the fuller statement of Line A). In this case, "on earth as it is in heaven" is the line to be supplied throughout. See Stott, *The Message of the Sermon on the Mount*, 147 for one of the few writers who takes this phrase to apply to all three.

[8] BDAG, 168–169.

[9] See Hemer, "ἐπιούσιος," 81–94 for a thorough discussion and Yamauchi, "The 'Daily Bread' Motif in Antiquity," 145–156 for background on the topic. BDAG, 376–377 gives a briefer summary of the lexical data.

connected to the idea of a more general coming. As a result, it is hard to pin down exactly what Jesus means by "daily bread." Most see it as literal bread, though perhaps metonymically referring to a variety of physical provisions. Others see it as spiritual bread, such as the bread of the great messianic banquet, an idea that may fit well in a kingdom-centered sermon that has just featured a kingdom-centered petition.

It is worth noting that this would be the only petition in the prayer for physical concerns if it refers to literal bread. This is not insignificant, but only including three petitions does not give a sufficiently large sample size to be certain. Further, "your Father knows what you need" (v 8) can clearly refer to physical needs as well as spiritual (v 32). On this view, the prayer for *daily* bread would further draw from the Exodus imagery (i.e., the daily manna) and focus on our dependence on God for ongoing physical sustenance, and emphasize that we pray "for our needs, not our greeds." [10] On the other hand, if the bread is spiritual—not specifically the eschatological banquet, but a more generally spiritualized bread—it creates a coherent triad of spiritual requests: sustenance, forgiveness, deliverance. Of course, praying for any of these kinds of bread is a legitimate concern for the believer.

And forgive us our debts, as we also have forgiven our debtors. Forgiveness from sin is a necessity for every human. The link between the two phrases does not indicate that we earn forgiveness points by forgiving others, but that there is a natural connection between being forgiven and forgiving others. God's blessings are never given to be selfishly kept, but come with the responsibility to be generously passed along.[11] As Stott says,

> [O]ne of the chief evidences of true penitence is a forgiving spirit. Once our eyes have been opened to the enormity of our offence against God, the injuries which others have done to us appear by comparison extremely trifling. If, on the other hand, we have an exaggerated view of the offences of others, it proves that we have minimized our own.[12]

---

[10] Carson, "Matthew," 171.
[11] France, *Matthew*, 137.
[12] Stott, *The Message of the Sermon on the Mount*, 149–150.

And do not bring us into temptation. This phrase can be difficult as well. On the one hand God does not directly tempt anyone (Jas 1.13) and, on the other, He will lead us into a place where temptation can occur (cf. Matt 4.1). Some have tried to reconstruct what the Aramaic original may have been and have plausibly proposed that the meaning is more likely "don't let us succumb to temptation" or "don't abandon us to temptation."[13] Similarly, a Qumran document suggests to "enter into temptation" means to "yield to temptation." Thus, the negative in "bring us not to enter into temptation" means "cause us not-to-succumb to temptation" rather than "do not cause us to succumb to temptation."[14]

But deliver us from the evil one. Translations differ on whether to treat the Greek as reference to an individual (i.e., "the evil one"; e.g., CSB, NET, NIV, NKJV)[15] or a concept (i.e., "evil," e.g., ESV, NASB, RSV).[16] Both are grammatically possible, and the difference is minimal. Whether it is the place of evil where temptation is found or the personification of evil and the one who tempts us, the result is largely the same: deliverance from temptation and sin.

Yours is the kingdom. The final doxology, found in the KJV and NKJV is likely not original, as it is not found in the oldest manuscripts, differs in the manuscripts in which it appears, and is precisely the sort of liturgical addition that later scribes would add.[17]

Connections

Praying in community. There may be significance in Jesus' instruction to pray *our* Father, rather than *my* Father. Although it is certainly true that Jesus distinguishes His own unique relationship with God from the relationship others have with Him,[18] the plural may serve to remind us "that

---

[13] Blomberg, *Matthew*, 120.
[14] Turner, "Prayer in the Gospels and Acts," 66.
[15] See Carson, "Matthew," 173–174.
[16] See Morris, *Matthew*, 148–149.
[17] See Metzger, *Textual Commentary*, 13–14 for the detailed textual evidence. Morris, *The Gospel According to Matthew*, 149 acknowledges that it is likely a later addition, but says the case for it being original is stronger than is regularly assumed.
[18] See Carson, "Matthew," 169.

our praying ought to reflect the corporate unity, desires, and needs of the entire church."[19] In an effort to be more personal, it has become fashionable to pray public prayers in the singular. While there are surely times where this is appropriate, we should remember—particularly in the context of public congregational praying—that we should speak not merely for ourselves, but for the group. As Carson says,

> Christians are not to pray in splendid isolation, and not to construe spirituality in terms of rugged individualism which stamps so much Western thought. ... There is, no doubt, a place for praying as an individual to God; but the general pattern of our praying must be broader than that. Therefore, when I as one follower of Christ among many, address *our* Father, my concern is to embrace *our* daily bread, *our* sins, and *our* temptations—and not just *mine*.[20]

Pray like this. Throughout this book, we have been extrapolating principles on how to pray from examples of prayer. This is the one place where a prayer is given with the explicit command to pray in the manner of this prayer. Although I have dedicated an entire appendix to this idea, a word should be said about it here. Whatever the imperative means, it does not necessarily exclude prayers that are not like this. For instance, this prayer is short, but longer prayers are also acceptable (Luke 6.12).[21] This prayer is largely general in its focus, but specific prayers are also acceptable (Acts 4.29).

Why pray if He knows? This question has come up already, but seems appropriate to raise again in the context of this prayer. Jesus twice tells His hearers that God already knows what they need (Matt 6.8, 32). To many who hear this, it raises the question, "Then why should we pray?" To the faithful in the Bible, however, this is the very reason they must pray. Jesus

---

[19] Blomberg, *Matthew*, 119.

[20] Carson, *Sermon on the Mount*, 62. Emphasis in original.

[21] Marshall, "Jesus—Example and Teacher of Prayer," 126 rightly points out that this brief prayer is in the context of Jesus saying not to pray like the heathen, who try to impress God with their long prayers. In another context, he says, "[T]o speak in such deterministic terms is inconsistent with the freedom which the Bible itself assigns to God's children, and it wreaks havoc upon the biblical idea of the personal relationship which exists between God and his children" (*The Epistles of John*, 244).

does not say, "God already knows, so there's no real point in praying, I don't guess." Instead, immediately on the heels of saying God knows, Jesus says, "Therefore pray." Whatever prayer is, then, its purpose is not to inform God. Marshall helpfully says, "Human parents often know what their children are going to ask them for, but it doesn't affect the fact that they respond to the children's desires."[22] Prayer is a way of communicating our desires even as we seek to better align ourselves with God's desire. It is a means of pouring out our hearts before the throne of the only one who can make a real difference in our lives. It is the way we come to realize that what we think is best may not after all be what is best. But it is not to inform God, and should not be abandoned because He already knows our needs and desires. As Chester says, "God sovereignly chooses to use our passionate, persistent prayers as an appointed means by which things happen.... In prayer we cooperate with God in his great plans of deliverance."[23]

The order of prayer. There is no prescribed order of prayer in the Bible. Even the priority of praise we have so frequently seen is neither universal nor commanded. A common approach in some congregational praying is to begin with penitence. The idea, sometimes even expressed as such, is that we must first rectify our relationship with God before we can proceed with the rest of the prayer. This is, to some degree at least, logically sound, and can even be helpful to reflect upon the seriousness of the sin in our lives. At the same time, however, Wright is correct when he says, "[T]he church is not instructed by the Lord to approach its father with 'Sorry' as its first word. Even the Prodigal Son began his speech with 'Father.' ... There is a time for penitence, but its location within the Lord's Prayer suggests that it should not take pride of place."[24]

Our relationship with God. Throughout the Bible, our relationship with God is described through a variety of metaphors. It is striking that this single prayer reflects several of those:[25]

---

[22] Ibid., 130.
[23] Chester, *The Message of Prayer,* 252–253.
[24] Wright, "The Lord's Prayer," 149.
[25] Foster, *Studies in the Life of Christ,* 862.

Our Father	father and child
Hallowed be your name	God and worshipper
Your kingdom come	king and subject
Your will be done	master and servant
Give us this day	benefactor and suppliant
Forgive our debts	creditor and debtor
Lead us not to temptation	guide and pilgrim
Deliver us	redeemer and redeemed

Although such a cataloging of relationships is not the point of this prayer (and some may seem more stretched than others to different readers), it is always wise to reflect upon who our God is and who we are by comparison. Doing so—and seeing our utter dependence in such a variety of ways—can only positively affect the content of our prayers by bringing us to the appropriate humility, devotion, and confidence we should have when we approach such a God.

TWENTY-SEVEN

The Hour Has Come
John 17

The God to whom we pray is a God who wants us to be united to Him. Even as there is pure unity within God, He desires unity within the body of His people leading to oneness between the body and the Head. He cares so much about this, in fact, that it was a chief concern in His final prayer, a deeply personal prayer He shares with the apostles—and with anyone who reads John's gospel.

Context

Jesus' prayer in John 17 occurs immediately after the Passover meal He shared with the disciples before His arrest.[1] Following the meal, they leave the upper room where they had eaten and go to the Mount of Olives (Matt 26.30; Mark 14.26). Much of Jesus' so-called Farewell Discourse that followed (John 13–17) must have happened on the walk (14.31). This is the His final night with the disciples, His last occasion for teaching and fellowship before the cross. Throughout, His concern is for the twelve, not His own impending fate, even though He knows well what is coming (13.1–3; 17.1). He teaches, warns, and encourages them to prepare for it. Nearly a quarter of John's gospel (by chapter count) is taken up with this one evening and Jesus' teaching that night.

---

[1] This prayer is sometimes called Jesus' Priestly Prayer (or High Priestly Prayer), a title that was given to it in the 1500s and has since been both embraced and eschewed by various writers.

In addition to the immediate context of the prayer, the fuller gospel needs to be considered.[2] In this prayer, Jesus uses several words that John has used frequently throughout. How John uses these words in the rest of the gospel is vital to understanding this prayer. "The hour" in John is something that for quite some time had not yet come (2.4; 4.21, 23; 7.6, 8, 30; 8.20), but arrives when Gentiles seek Jesus (12.23). From this point forward, the hour has come (12.27; 13.1; 16.32; 17.1). John connects the hour coming with Jesus' departure (13.1) and glorification (12.23; 17.1); in John, Jesus is glorified in the cross. As Morris says, "Christ reigned from the tree. The cross was not defeat but victory. He exercised authority in bringing men life even as He hung, apparently helpless, on the cross."[3] Finally, this prayer greatly concerns "the world." Jesus uses the word eighteen times in this prayer alone, clearly indicating its significance.[4] "The world" can refer to the creation (1.10), the earth (16.33), or the people who inhabit the earth (12.19), but most frequently John uses it to refer to humankind in opposition and hostility to Christ (cf. 1 John 2.15–17 for the definition spelled out).

This prayer is a passing of the baton. Jesus' time on this earth is complete and He is entrusting His work to the twelve. He has overcome the world (16.33) and will be departing it. The apostles will remain in the world, but must not be of it even as they try to win it to God. To that end, Jesus prays:

> Father, the hour has come; glorify your Son that the Son may glorify you, since you have given him authority over all flesh, to give eternal life to all whom you have given him. And this is eternal life, that they know you, the only true God, and Jesus Christ whom you have sent. I glorified you on earth, having accomplished the work that you gave me to do. And

---

[2] Carson, *The Gospel According to John*, 551 says, "In some respects the prayer is a summary of the entire Fourth Gospel to this point."

[3] Morris, *The Gospel According to John*, 719.

[4] Ibid., 126 points out that the word occurs 185 times in the entire New Testament. Of those 185 occurrences, 105 are in John's writings (78 in the gospel). The Synoptics account for only 14 uses. The word is clearly important to John. To the point of this prayer, it occurs more here than in Matthew, Mark, and Luke combined, and its presence here accounts for nearly ten percent of its total usage. See Morris, 126–128 for a larger discussion of the word.

now, Father, glorify me in your own presence with the glory that I had with you before the world existed.

    I have manifested your name to the people whom you gave me out of the world. Yours they were, and you gave them to me, and they have kept your word. Now they know that everything that you have given me is from you. For I have given them the words that you gave me, and they have received them and have come to know in truth that I came from you; and they have believed that you sent me. I am praying for them. I am not praying for the world but for those whom you have given me, for they are yours. All mine are yours, and yours are mine, and I am glorified in them. And I am no longer in the world, but they are in the world, and I am coming to you. Holy Father, keep them in your name, which you have given me, that they may be one, even as we are one. While I was with them, I kept them in your name, which you have given me. I have guarded them, and not one of them has been lost except the son of destruction, that the Scripture might be fulfilled. But now I am coming to you, and these things I speak in the world, that they may have my joy fulfilled in themselves. I have given them your word, and the world has hated them because they are not of the world, just as I am not of the world. I do not ask that you take them out of the world, but that you keep them from the evil one. They are not of the world, just as I am not of the world. Sanctify them in the truth; your word is truth. As you sent me into the world, so I have sent them into the world. And for their sake I consecrate myself, that they also may be sanctified in truth.

    I do not ask for these only, but also for those who will believe in me through their word, that they may all be one, just as you, Father, are in me, and I in you, that they also may be in us, so that the world may believe that you have sent me. The glory that you have given me I have given to them, that they may be one even as we are one, I in them and you in me, that they may become perfectly one, so that the world may know that you sent me and loved them even as you loved me. Father, I desire that they also, whom you have given me, may be with me where I am, to see my glory that you have given me because you loved me before the foundation of the world. O righteous Father, even though the world does not know you, I know you, and these know that you have sent me. I made known to them your name, and I will continue to make it known, that the love with which you have loved me may be in them, and I in them. (John 17.1b–26)

Contents

The prayer breaks down into three basic parts: Jesus prays for Himself (vv 1b–5); Jesus prays for His apostles (vv 6–19); Jesus prays for His future disciples (vv 20–26).[5]

Regarding the first section, it should be said that Jesus prayer for Himself is not at all the kind of praying we tend to do for ourselves. His only concern is that He be glorified in His hour. Since both of those words refer to the cross, Jesus' prayer is about His own impending sacrifice. The cross can mean glorification in two different ways. First, the cross is the culmination of God's plan to save humanity from its sin. Thus, in accomplishing God's plan, there is glory, regardless of how the world may view it (cf. 1 Cor 1.18–25). Second, the cross is not merely the cross, for the cross alone is meaningless (1 Cor 15.14–19). Rather, the cross is shorthand for the death-burial-resurrection-ascension-enthronement of Jesus, the latter three of which clearly glorify Jesus.

The heart of the second section of the prayer may be verse 11b: "keep them in your name, which you have given me, that they may be one, even as we are one." Jesus prays this for them because He will no longer be with them to protect them with His own teaching and acts that reveal the Father (vv 6–8, 11a, 12–13). This is particularly necessary, because the world hates them (v 14).[6] To that end, Jesus prays that they be sanctified in truth, which is not significantly different from God keeping them in His name. As they remain in the world that is hostile to them, the disciples must be set apart for God's purposes, and that can only come by embracing the truth of God in the midst of the world's lies.

Finally, Jesus prays for the unity of future believers so that the world can see that God sent Jesus (cf. 13.35). This unity is not unity-for-the-sake-

---

[5] In addition to the commentaries which give detailed discussion, a helpful, shorter discussion of this prayer (though more thorough than I can give it here) is found in Turner, "Prayer in the Gospels and Acts," 77–80.

[6] Turner, "Prayer in the Gospels and Acts," 78.

of-unity, because it is nice when people agree, or some other trivial matter. Rather, this unity is for the benefit of the watching world, so that those who hear the message from believers "will be caught up in the sweeping work of God,"[7] because they see something special in Christians.

The key theme of the prayer is fellowship. Notice this in a variety of topics repeated through the various sections. Regarding glory, there is the mutual glorification of the Father and Son (vv 1, 4–5) and the glorification of the Son by the disciples (vv 9–10). In the context of the shared glorying by the Father and the Son, it is remarkable to think that the disciples are able to participate in such an action. But throughout this prayer, glory is given and received, shared between the Father and Son, mutually given to each other, and even the disciples may participate.

Joy is also shared. In this prayer, the disciples are able to share in the Son's joy (v 13). Earlier in this night, Jesus had given another key piece of information on this topic: the Son's joy is rooted in the Father's joy (15.11). Thus, Jesus desires to share His joy—the very joy He receives from the Father—with the disciples, and for that joy to be fulfilled in them.

Further, love is shared. Jesus prays that the world will understand that the Father loves the disciples with the same love with which He loves Jesus and has since before the foundation of the world (vv 23–24). Jesus desires this same love that the Father has always poured out on the Son to be in the disciples (v 26).

Unity of fellowship is the essence of all of these points, an idea made explicit throughout the prayer (vv 11, 21–23). The prayer, then, is not merely for unity between believers, but that the believers would have unity with God. We are invited not to be *like* God, but to be *in* God, to share in the fellowship in which glory, love, and joy are freely shared with one another.[8] In this prayer, Jesus describes the kind of fellowship and unity that characterizes His relationship with His father, and then opens the doors of that relationship and invites us to come share in it fully.

---

[7] Millar, *Calling on the Name of the Lord*, 182.

[8] Lincoln, "Prayer in the Fourth Gospel," 169 says that instead of merely mirroring God's unity, "the unity of the believing community actually participates in the unity that defines the relationship between Jesus and God."

Connections

Prayer for God's purposes. As this prayer focuses on Jesus being glorified in His hour and sharing that glory—and the resultant love and joy—with the disciples, it is clear that this prayer is about God fulfilling His eternal purposes. As Millar says, "It is highly appropriate, and consonant with all we have seen, that Jesus' longest and richest recorded prayer focuses on 'the work of the gospel'—it is a thoroughly salvation-historically motivated cry to His Father to continue to work out His purposes through Jesus."[9] Or, in the terms we have used throughout this book as we have encountered this theme so frequently, we might say that it is highly appropriate and consonant with all we have seen that this prayer focuses on God's promises and character.

Prayer for God's glory. Jesus' prayer begins with a focus on God's glory. The opening petition that God would glorify the Son is not in isolation, but "that the Son may glorify you" (v 1), just as Jesus constantly did throughout His life and ministry (v 4). This focus on God's glory defined how Jesus thought about everything, and should also define us and our praying. Turner expresses this well, saying, "Our prayers are too often centered on ourselves and spread out in concentric circles of our (often legitimate) interests, responsibilities, loves, and imagined needs. Jesus' prayer puts the *Father's* glory at the center, and spreads out in concentric circles of *his* will and purpose."[10]

The importance of prayer. A mental exercise that people frequently play is, "If I had one day to live...." In such a scenario, some turn to frivolities and others to relationships: we consider various "bucket list" items that we have not checked off that we might like to complete or various people with whom we might like to be one last time. Jesus, upon knowing that His hour had come, prays. Not just here, but as we will see in the next chapter, again in Gethsemane. In short, His final evening is dominated by prayer. The importance of prayer to Jesus cannot be over-

---

[9] Millar, *Calling on the Name of the Lord,* 182.
[10] Turner, "Prayer in the Gospels and Acts," 80. Emphasis in original; British spelling Americanized.

stated. It permeated His life. He prayed in joy, in sorrow, in need, and in anticipation of His most difficult hour.[11]

The importance of unity. Paul says that in Christ, God created a new society by tearing down the wall of hostility between Jews and Gentiles (Eph 2.11–22). This new society, he said, must be a society characterized by unity (Eph 4.1–16). Paul, of course, emphasizes unity because his Lord did. Here, unity is chief in the mind of Jesus. Such unity is found not in suppressing doctrinal differences, because it is a unity that is rooted in the truth.[12] Similarly, it is "not in some special sense of *camaraderie,* nor in a superficial ecumenical patching over of differences (far less, *contra* Pollard, in a boasting in our ecclesiastical diversity!), but in a belongingness and mutual love that spring from unity with Jesus."[13] As we are united with God, we will be united with each other.

The importance of unity in Jesus' farewell discourse is that it promotes evangelism. Milne says,

> The biggest barriers to effective evangelism according to the prayer of Jesus are not so much outdated methods, or inadequate presentations of the gospel, as realities like gossip, insensitivity, negative criticism, jealousy, backbiting, an unforgiving spirit, a 'root of bitterness,' failure to appreciate others, self-preoccupation, greed, selfishness, and every other form of lovelessness. These are the squalid enemies of effective evangelism which render the gospel fruitless and send countless thousands into eternity without a savior.[14]

Jesus prayed for you. The final section of this prayer concerns "those who will believe in me through their word" (v 20), and there is no ex-

---

[11] In the previous chapter, I pushed back against the trend of leading public prayers in the first person singular. It is only appropriate to acknowledge that Jesus here prays in just that manner as He publicly prays. I previously acknowledged that it may well be appropriate at times to include a personal reflection in a corporate prayer, but I do not believe that this prayer is justification for it as a thoroughgoing practice. Jesus is not here leading the apostles in a shared prayer, but sharing with them His own prayer. Rather than bringing them into the act of praying itself, He reveals to them the prayer He prays for them.

[12] Chester, *The Message of Prayer,* 185.

[13] Turner, "Prayer in the Gospels and Acts," 20.

[14] Milne, *The Message of John,* 250–251.

piration date attached to that statement. Jesus, in His concern for the church of the future, prayed for all of His disciples to come. This means He prayed for you and me, and the work we do in spreading the gospel (v 21). When we work in the world, we have not only Jesus' commission, but the backing of Jesus' prayer, a truth that should shape how we think and what we do as it provides greater reassurance that God is with us in our task. This is the ultimate source of an ongoing confidence that our "mission remains God's cause and God can be entrusted with it. For just as God has given Jesus what it took to accomplish his role, so now Jesus summons God to give what it will take for his followers to complete theirs."[15] We will undoubtedly face opposition, for so did our Lord. But we are never without His watchful care and keeping.

In the world but not of the world. This is a constant teaching in the New Testament (vv 11, 14), but it should not be thought to be effortless simply because it is pithy. This is evident by even a brief survey of the history of Christendom. Some have tried to extract themselves from society and live secluded, holy lives, but this is in clear violation of our call to be witnesses, salt, and light. Others who embrace the call move so close to the world that they become too comfortable with its sin and are slowly but surely enticed by it to the point of falling. By contrast, Jesus prays not that they be withdrawn from the world or assimilated to it, but protected from it (v 15). What this looks like may vary slightly from one generation to the next, but the principle is important. Turner says,

> That perhaps needs pondering: have we become so spiritually superficial that we no longer recognize the different dimensions of the activity of the powers that seek to entice us, and the dangers they pose to our lives before God? Subtly, and in myriad ways, the ruler of this world attempts to keep us in, or move us into, conformity to 'the world' he has woven. We recognize it at a distance, but not so easily in ourselves. We are the first to spot the white South African brother trapped in racism, or to be horrified by yesterday's Christian captain composing hymns on the deck

---

[15] Lincoln, "Prayer in the Fourth Gospel," 171.

of a slaver; but we do not so readily perceive where *we* are in danger of becoming entangled![16]

At this point, Turner stops, leaving me to wonder why he did not get specific in the various ways we face this danger. I suspect that it is because naming the dangers either puts him in a place where he will be called out by one person or another or because the temptations of today are not necessarily the temptations of tomorrow. For example, his reference to South African apartheid may not register with younger readers unaware of the history of that country. Even so, every generation of Christians faces the same basic temptation: conformity with the world that surrounds it. And this is something we must absolutely avoid, in part, by not allowing ourselves to become spiritually superficial. Further, the concern to develop a "not of this world" mindset should permeate our prayers.

An incomplete disciple is still a disciple. The way Jesus speaks about His disciples in this prayer is remarkable: what they have done, what they have believed, how they have accepted Jesus. As Bruce says,

> [T]heir unintelligent questions and interruptions as he talked to them in the upper room shows how far they still were from appreciating their Master's purpose or the seriousness of the hour which had now come for him—and for them. But he looked at them with the insight of faith, hope, and love, and realized their present devotion and their potential for the future.[17]

The disciples, who had just argued about who was the greatest and who would soon abandon Jesus in His hour of need—Peter, who had just argued with Jesus about what He should and shouldn't be doing and would soon openly deny any association with Him—these are the ones Jesus claims as His own and entrusts with the future of His work. To follow God does not require flawlessness, but faith. We will not be saved by our rightness of understanding or behavior any more than they were; we will be saved if we trust in God to save us and seek to do His will in our lives.

---

[16] Turner, "Prayer in the Gospels and Acts," 79. Emphasis in original; British spelling Americanized.
[17] Bruce, *The Gospel of John*, 331.

TWENTY-EIGHT

Not My Will But Yours Be Done

Matthew 26.39–44; Mark 14.32–41; Luke 22.39–46

The God to whom we pray is a God who will uphold us in trial and temptation. Just as Jesus prayed for Peter in light of his impending temptation (Luke 22.31–32), so also He prays for Himself in light of His own impending trial—and urges Peter, James, and John to do likewise. All of this can only be due to His certainty that divine assistance is the key factor to any human success in spiritual warfare.

Context

From the upper room and the last supper, Jesus proceeded with His disciples to Gethsemane.[1] This was the night of the betrayal, and Jesus knew His time on earth was short (John 13.1–4, 27). Having prayed for His followers (John 17), Jesus now seeks a place to pray for Himself and the trial He will soon face. The end He had always anticipated is upon Him and He knows He will need strength to endure what lies ahead.

Just as the betrayal does not surprise Jesus, His location does not surprise Judas. As far as we know, Jesus did not give the disciples an itinerary for the evening, but Gethsemane was a frequently visited site for Jesus and the twelve (John 18.1–2). He could have attempted to foil Judas' plan by

---

[1] "Gethsemane" is a transliteration of two Hebrew words meaning "oil press." In all likelihood, this was an enclosed field or orchard on the Mount of Olives (Matt 26.30), on which an oil press stood.

going somewhere else. For that matter, Jesus could have foiled the plan by clearly identifying Judas as the betrayer at the Supper and clearly identifying "betrayal" as intentionally turning Him over to be killed.[2]

Upon arriving in the garden, Jesus takes Peter, James, and John—the three disciples who had been particularly close to Him and allowed to witness things others were not (Mark 5.37; 9.2; cf. 13.3)—to the place He would pray, indicating to the reader that something important is about to happen.[3] Even more, these three had specifically boasted of their readiness to share in Jesus' fate (Matt 20.22; 26.35) and are now called to share with Him in preparing for it.[4] In addition, Jesus may have simply wanted their companionship. He was "very sorrowful, even to death" (Matt 26.38), a truth He revealed to them, baring before them His deepest emotions, giving them the most compelling reason to do what He asks in the moment.[5] In what must be a one of the most supreme examples of the paradox of Jesus' incarnation, the Son of God seeks the moral support of three Galilean fisherman[6]—though, in the end, they fail to provide even the slightest help in that regard.[7]

As these four separate from the remaining eight, Jesus instructs them to wait while He goes to pray.

> And going a little farther he fell on his face and prayed, saying, "My Father, if it be possible, let this cup pass from me; nevertheless, not as I will, but as you will." And he came to the disciples and found them sleeping. And he said to Peter, "So, could you not watch with me one hour? Watch and pray that you may not enter into temptation. The spirit indeed is will-

---

[2] The apostles' all asking "Is it I?" may indicate that they think Jesus is saying one will make some mistake and unintentionally betray Him, leading to His arrest.

[3] Brooks, *Mark*, 233.

[4] France, *Matthew*, 372. Mark 14.31 indicates that the entire group had made the same boast concerning their loyalty to Jesus, but theirs may be different inasmuch as it is in response to Peter's initial claim. Do they mean it as fervently as Peter does, or are they merely mimicking his claim?

[5] Carson, "Matthew," 543.

[6] France, *Matthew*, 373. By contrast, Hurtado, *Mark*, 242 sees this as a "sentimental suggestion" that "has no basis in the text, for Jesus turns to God and not to them." Instead, he sees their presence entirely as an effort to prepare them for what lies ahead. This seems to me to be a false dichotomy, as prayer need not negate the role of human support (cf. Rom 12.15; Gal 6.2).

[7] Brooks, *Mark*, 234.

ing, but the flesh is weak." Again, for the second time, he went away and prayed, "My Father, if this cannot pass unless I drink it, your will be done." And again he came and found them sleeping, for their eyes were heavy. So, leaving them again, he went away and prayed for the third time, saying the same words again. (Matt 26.39–44)

Contents

Unless Jesus' "one hour" (v 40) is an exorbitant hyperbole, we are given only the general tenor of Jesus' prayer rather than the full text of it. Even so, it is an exceedingly important prayer to consider, for we see in it two distinct attitudes Jesus has toward the cross.

First, Gethsemane reveals Jesus' emotional anticipation of the cross. In this prayer Jesus prostrates Himself before God, something He does only here in all the gospels,[8] and He pleads that the cup would pass.[9] The position Jesus takes is in contrast with the usual Jewish prayer posture of standing and surely reflects the anguish He feels.[10] Emotionally, Jesus does not want to endure the cross. But what exactly is Jesus asking for: not to have to die? If nothing else is clear, Gethsemane indicates that Jesus above all wants God's will to be done. Whatever Jesus might be asking, the question is never whether or not He should accept God's purposes. Instead, it may be that Jesus is asking whether the cup must include the cross.[11] Must they be one and the same, or is there another way for the cup of God's wrath to be poured out?

Jesus' emotion is overruled by His will, for the second attitude seen is His willing anticipation of the cross. The posture of prostration may reflect not merely the emotional anguish, but also the submissive spirit of bowing. In addition to the bow, the address clearly speaks to Jesus' submission. Although it is likely lost on a 21st Century westerner, in the near-Eastern context of Jesus' day, to acknowledge God as father is to

---

[8] Morris, *Matthew*, 668n79.

[9] For a short, helpful introduction to the cup imagery in the Bible, see Gary Fisher, "This Cup," 95–98. See Carson, "Matthew," 543 for a concise list of relevant Old Testament texts.

[10] Turner, "Prayer in the Gospels and Acts," 61.

[11] France, *Matthew*, 373.

acknowledge a submissive role and "to confess God's claim to true filial obedience."[12] Beyond that, Jesus' request explicitly includes the acceptance that it might not be granted. As deeply as He desires not to endure the cross, He more deeply desires to do the Father's will. Jesus' prayer explores the limits of God's will without ever seeking to break outside them:[13] what specific options are there within God's general will? At its most basic level, Jesus' prayer is not "let this cup pass" but "your will be done." In other words, Gethsemane is where the battle is fought and won. Although Jesus does not drink the cup in Gethsemane, here He consents to drink it.[14] The decision is made and nothing will stop Him from accomplishing God's purpose.

Between the first and second prayers, Jesus comes back to find the disciples asleep and chastises them for not being able to stay awake due to their grief (Luke 22.45). He urges them to pray, lest they fall into temptation. This temptation must refer not to the temptation to sleep, but instead spiritual defection (cf. v 31). Only urgent prayer will save them from falling in the coming temptation (cf. Luke 22.31–32). Their failure in this preparation foreshadows their failure in the ordeal ahead (vv 56–62). Far from living up to their boasts of being willing to die for or with Jesus, they cannot even remain awake for an hour.[15] When Jesus returns the second time, He finds them asleep again, a state He leaves them in until He rouses them at the arrival of Judas and the soldiers (v 46). At that point, it is too late for prayer: "The sleepers for whom He would die have lost their opportunity to gain strength through prayer. By contrast Jesus has prayed in agony but now rises with poise and advances to meet His betrayer."[16]

Connections

Your will be done. If nothing else is clear in this prayer, it is that Jesus puts the will of the Father above His own will. His desires must be submitted

---

[12] Turner, "Prayer in the Gospels and Acts," 62.
[13] France, *Matthew*, 373.
[14] Morris, *Luke*, 311.
[15] Morris, *Matthew*, 669.
[16] Carson, "Matthew," 545.

to God's, as He acknowledges in a variety of ways. This, as said above, is at the very heart of the prayer and the fundamental message of it.

It is frequently said that in response to prayer, God sometimes says "yes," sometimes says, "no," and sometimes says "not yet." Whether or not this is true depends entirely upon how one prays. In which of these three ways did God answer Jesus' prayer in Gethsemane? One might suggest that the answer depends on which part of the prayer is being referred to, but if the overriding request is not "let this cup pass" but "your will be done," then God answers this prayer in the affirmative. And so also, if we always pray in such a way, then we can be confident that God will always answer our prayer in the affirmative as well.

This does not mean that the one who prays does not tell God what he or she feels and desires. Throughout the Bible, prayer often involves asking God to change His mind or act differently than He has revealed. As Garland says, "Prayers asking God to have a change of mind are not considered insubordinate but actually exude trust that God listens to prayer and grants requests that can be reconciled 'with overall Providence.'"[17] Even so, in this prayer Jesus subjugates His will to the Father's, knowing that some requests cannot be "reconciled with overall Providence," and in such cases it is God's will that must prevail. Our prayers should absolutely involve a full pouring out of our hearts before God, but they should also involve the full realization that God knows far better than we do what is best, and God has plans we may not yet understand. Therefore, our fundamental, overriding prayer should always be, "nevertheless, not as I will, but as you will." If this is always our prayer, there are no answers of "no" or "not yet," but God will always answer "yes" (cf. 2 Cor 1.19–20).

A contrast of gardens. At the other extreme is the person who prays with the primary goal of his or her own will being done. We see this in the various ways people try to manipulate God—making promises of more devoted service, praying certain "special" prayers that the pray-er

---

[17] Garland, *Mark,* 540.

thinks have a special power, rounding up hundreds of "prayer warriors" in an attempt to bowl God over, etc. The problem with all "my will be done" prayers is that they place us in the wrong garden. In Eden, "not your will but mine" led to the curse and brought about the necessity of Gethsemane. In Gethsemane, "not my will but yours" led to redemption, the breaking of the curse, and the very right hand of God.[18] Shall we stand alongside Adam and Eve or Jesus?

Spiritual battles are won on your knees. Strength to overcome is found in prayer. In Luke's account, Jesus' statement to "pray that you not enter into temptation" frames the entire section (vv 40, 46), suggesting it is central to the scene and showing the significance of this moment to Jesus as well.[19] In short, strength to overcome is found in prayer. Paul's later description of spiritual warfare reflects this same truth. After describing the armor God gives Christians, Paul urges them not to wage war, but to pray (Eph 6.10–20). Jesus here fights and wins the battle with temptation, and He will go out and succeed when He faces the cross.

The disciples, however, fail to pray—and they will fail when the crisis arises. They do not realize just how crucial this moment is and they allow their heavy eyes and grief to distract them from what is the most important thing they could be doing, and so "when they finally rise, they go off in every direction but the one that Jesus leads."[20] Garland continues:

> The hour has come, and the disciples are found snoozing. They fail miserably in their responsibilities. A nameless woman anoints Jesus for his burial over the objections of friends. A bystander carries his cross. A pagan centurion who supervises his execution makes the public confession that he is the Son of God. A council member who probably participated in his condemnation obtains the body and buries it in his tomb. Women followers watch him die on the cross and go later to anoint the body. By contrast, the male disciples doze while he shudders in horror, betray him,

---

[18] Carson, "Matthew," 545.
[19] Turner, "Prayer in the Gospels and Acts," 60.
[20] Garland, *Mark,* 544.

flee for their lives when he is hauled away, and deny him when he is being condemned to death. They do not keep watch but fall asleep.[21]

The truth of this did not end two thousand years ago in Gethsemane. Strength to overcome still comes through prayer. Success in prayer leads to success in temptation, and failure in prayer leads to failure in temptation. The weakness of the flesh is a permanent problem, which is why vigilance and prayer is a constant need.[22] Those who do not pray, trying instead to succeed on their own power, will collapse and fail.[23]

---

[21] Ibid., 543.
[22] France, *Matthew*, 373.
[23] Garland, *Mark*, 552.

TWENTY-NINE

Grant Your Servants Boldness

Acts 4.24–30

The God to whom we pray is a God whom the world rejects. From the very beginning, the vast majority of people cared little to nothing about what God would have them do. Even many who claimed to believe and love God either secretly or openly followed their own selfish desires. It is not surprising, then, that He is ignored, His Messiah rejected, and His followers proclaiming His message persecuted. It is never in question that people will oppose what God is doing. The only question is how members of His community will face such opposition.[1]

Context

After the initial success of Peter's sermon (Acts 2.41), the church continued to grow. Their daily fellowship and building of community surely played a part in their early strength, as did the continued preaching of the apostles. This success, not to mention the miracles being performed (3.1–10) and Peter's continued preaching of the resurrection in the Temple (3.11–26), irritated the Sadducees (4.1–3), which led to the arrest of Peter and John and their trial before the Sanhedrin (4.5–21).[2]

---

[1] Bock, *Acts*, 208.

[2] Regarding the various groups mentioned in Acts 4.1–5: The Sadducees were descendants of the Hasmoneans, and the priests allied with them. The captain of the temple guard commanded the temple soldiers; at the Temple, he ranked second only to the high priest and was responsible for maintaining order at the Temple. The rulers, elders, and scribes together, made up the Sanhedrin

This same council that had tried and condemned Jesus is now trying two of the most prominent apostles.

The Council, however, had a problem: a miracle had been performed publicly, and they had no way of denying it. Rather than considering what that miracle might mean, they were concerned with stopping the apostles' preaching. After deliberating, they decided the best they could do was to forbid them to teach about Jesus again (4.16–18). Peter and John replied that they must follow the will of God rather than the Sanhedrin and that they could not possibly stop talking about Jesus (4.19–20), for whatever authority the Council had was subject to a higher authority, and "the edicts of man cannot overturn the decrees of God."[3] Thus, they were further threatened and released (4.21).

Upon their release, Peter and John returned to their friends and reported what had happened at the trial. Their immediate reaction was a united prayer that, despite opposition, they would continue witnessing boldly.

> And when they heard it, they lifted their voices together to God and said, "Sovereign Lord, who made the heaven and the earth and the sea and everything in them, who through the mouth of our father David, your servant, said by the Holy Spirit,
>
> 'Why did the Gentiles rage,
> > and the peoples plot in vain?
> The kings of the earth set themselves,
> > and the rulers were gathered together,
> > against the Lord and against his Anointed'—
>
> for truly in this city there were gathered together against your holy servant Jesus, whom you anointed, both Herod and Pontius Pilate, along with the Gentiles and the peoples of Israel, to do whatever your hand and your plan had predestined to take place. And now, Lord, look upon their threats and grant to your servants to continue to speak your word with all boldness,

---

Council, which is surely what Luke refers to in verse 5 and the subsequent trial (note "council" in verse 15). See Longenecker, *Acts*, 97–98 and Bruce, *Commentary on the Book of Acts*, 95n4, 5, 97n9 for more on these groups.

[3] Stott, *The Message of Acts*, 99.

while you stretch out your hand to heal, and signs and wonders are performed through the name of your holy servant Jesus." (Acts 4.24–30)

Contents

The early Christians did not see the persecution they experienced as a personal attack, but looking to Scripture, saw it as continuation of the ongoing attacks made by human rulers upon God and His anointed.[4] What was first spoken of in Psalm 2 was later fulfilled in Herod, Pilate, and the Jewish leaders against Jesus. This imprisonment and threatening of Peter and John was a continuation of the same attack.

Their prayer focuses on two key truths before they make their petition: the power of God and the futility of human rebellion against Him. God's power is doubly emphasized in the opening line, first by calling him "Sovereign Lord" and also by referring to Him as the creator God. The word "sovereign" was a common word for rulers in that time, but was not used frequently to speak of God. In this context, emphasizing God as the master was fitting, as it emphasizes the servant nature of His people: David (v 25); Jesus (vv 27, 30); Christians (v 29).[5] That He is the God of creation provides the foundation for their certainty of God's powerful control.[6]

The futility of human rebellion is emphasized by the quotation and interpretation of Psalm 2. In its original context, the psalm speaks of a new king's coronation as a time of unrest and rebellion. To such a Davidic king, it serves as a reminder of God's promises: his enemies will be overthrown if he trusts in God. In light of Jesus, the apostles see a new interpretive context: the fruitlessness of the people and their rulers to plot against the Messiah and, by extension, His ambassadors.[7] In uniting against Jesus, they carried

---

[4] Marshall, *Acts*, 103.

[5] Longenecker, *Acts*, 104.

[6] Marshall, *Acts*, 104 sees an echo of Hezekiah's prayer in the apostles' words, saying that it "has supplied the general pattern and suggested some of the phraseology."

[7] Marshall, *Acts*, 105–106; cf. Chester, *The Message of Prayer*, 143–144. Jewish methods of re-interpreting a passage in light of a new divinely-revealed context is called *midrash*. For a popular-level introduction to this, see Pickup, "The New Testament's Exegesis of Old Testament Passages." For a more academic treatment, see Pickup, "New Testament Interpretation of the Old Testament."

out the foreordained counsel of God that the Messiah must suffer.[8] In this, the apostles found comfort. God knew persecution would come. Far from proof of God's weakness or the strength of evil, God remains in control.

Finally, in view of God's power and foreknowledge, they brought their situation to Him, confident that it, too, was under His control.[9] From their initial response until now, their resolve has not been shaken. It never crosses their minds to stop preaching. Instead, they see persecution as a given and pray for strength to carry on through it. They do not pray for their opponents to be brought to nothing or even for an end to the persecution they faced. Rather, they pray for increased boldness in speech and God's continued working through them. Their overriding concern was that God's word would go forth and Christ's name would be glorified, leaving what might happen to them entirely to God.[10] They understood that the threats called not for fear and silence, nor for pleas for peace, but increased boldness in speech.[11]

In response the place they were in was shaken, which, "made them the more unshaken,"[12] and they received a "fresh" filling of the Spirit. Since earthquakes were a common Old Testament sign of a theophany (e.g., Exod 19.18; Isa 6.4), they would have seen this as an immediate response to the prayer, an interpretation confirmed by the Spirit's descent. In light of God's immediate response to their prayer, they "continued to speak the word of God with boldness" (v 31) and "signs and wonders were regularly done among the people by the hands of the apostles" (5.12).

Connections

As we have seen so frequently already, this prayer begins with praise and focuses heavily on God's word as a foundation to prayer. For now,

---

[8] Bruce, *Acts*, 106.

[9] Marshall, *Acts*, 106–107. Stott, *The Message of Acts*, 100 describes this succinctly: "This, then, was the early church's understanding of God, the God of creation, revelation, and history, whose characteristic actions are summarized by the three verbs 'you made' (24), 'you spoke' (25), and 'you decided' (28)."

[10] Longenecker, *Acts*, 105.

[11] Bruce, *Acts*, 107.

[12] Chrysostom, Homily XI, 73.

we will allow this brief note of those lessons so thoroughly emphasized already to suffice.

The power of God and futility of rebellion. God's power is not seen merely in the note of God as sovereign and creator, but in His providential working as it was directly related to their unique circumstances. The God who created the universe was at work in their lives. Many Christians today tend to see God as either a cosmic micromanager who turns traffic lights green and opens parking spaces, or as an uninterested, hands-off deistic God. The Bible affirms neither of these, and righteous people speak frequently of God's activity without presuming to know exactly what He is doing at every moment.[13] God is indeed at work, and He frequently uses the actions of humankind to accomplish His purposes. From the human perspective, one can work with God, work against Him, or be ambivalent toward Him. In all cases, however, God will use that work to accomplish His purpose. It is futile for humankind to scheme against a God who not only created the whole universe, but foresaw their scheming,[14] for even opposition to God is subject to His will. If even the cross was ordained by God, then everything we pray for should be "conditioned by the fact that God is continuing to work out His purposes."[15]

The reality of suffering. The early Christians were not at all surprised to suffer for the cause of Christ, because Jesus had told them that this very thing would happen (John 15.19–21). Rather, they saw their suffering as a reason for rejoicing (Acts 5.41), because the suffering of believers is directly related to the suffering of Christ.[16] In the twenty-first century West, we have lived in peace and luxury for so long, we feel entitled to it and are shocked to hear of persecution. This cannot be due to the apostles not passing along this message of Jesus, for they do so unequivocally

---

[13] See Ward, *God Unseen*, 125–134.

[14] Marshall, *Acts*, 105.

[15] Millar, *Calling on the Name of the Lord*, 193. Peterson, *Acts*, 201 points out that in each of the first four chapters of Acts, Peter expresses confidence that "God is able to carry out his purpose even through rebellious human beings who do not accept his revealed will (1.16–20; 2.23–36; 3.13–15)."

[16] Longenecker, *Acts*, 105.

(e.g., Rom 8.17; Col 1.24; 2 Tim 3.12; 1 Pet 2.20–25; 3.14–4.2; 4.12–13). Rather, this reflects either an ignorance of or unbelief in the Bible at worst, or a careless complacency at best. Both are dangerous places for Christians to find themselves.

The importance of prayer in trial. In the previous chapter, we saw Peter and John, along with James, failing to pray in preparation for a trial that they failed, while Jesus' success in prayer led to His success when tried. This scene suggests that they have learned the lesson Jesus intended to teach them: the importance of prayer in the midst of trials.[17] Now they pray and their prayer leads to their success.

Prayer for resolve not relief. Surely, praying for peaceful times is not wrong, for Paul directs us to do that very thing (1 Tim 2.1–4). I might add two caveats, lest we thoughtlessly cite this Scripture. First, why do we pray for peace? In 1 Timothy, "a peaceful and quiet life" is not the end goal. Instead, our peaceful and quiet lives are pleasing to God "who desires all people to be saved and to come to the knowledge of the truth." Paul urges prayer for peace so that the gospel may be spread. In our context, our prayer for peaceful times must not be to continue our middle-class status quo unabated; if it is, we have constructed a false god. Second, peace is not what is most needed in the midst of the persecution itself. To be sure, relief is always desired in the midst of persecution, but resolve is most needed.

Turn the other cheek. The apostles petition God for their own boldness and not their enemies' defeat. Although imprecatory praying does have a legitimate place in the lives of Christians,[18] we must not be too hasty in seeking the destruction of our enemies, especially if we are driven by anger and personal vengeance, rather than God's righteous justice. In the context of this prayer, McGarvey makes the point well:

> These men were not in danger of losing some merely political power or privilege; but the dearest and most indisputable right they had on earth was denied them, and they were threatened with death if they did not

---

[17] Green, "Persevering Together in Prayer," 192.
[18] See chapter 22.

relinquish it: yet in their prayer they manifest no vindictive or resentful spirit; but they pray in reference to their enemies only this, "Lord, behold their threatenings," while they leave the Lord without suggestion or request, to do as might appear good in his sight. By such prayers as are often uttered at the present time men seek to make God a partisan in all their angry contentions, as though he were nothing more than themselves.[19]

God gives strength. Many who do not identify with Pentecostal movements have become so afraid of the Holy Spirit, miracles, and God's activity that we minimize God's working. We pray for various things, but scarcely believe He gives them. We receive the things we have asked for and write it off as a coincidence or otherwise explain it away. Although God may not shake the room we are in or pour out His Spirit on us in any sort of tangible way, we must not disbelieve that God gives what He promises and that He is indeed active in our lives.

---

[19] McGarvey, *Acts*, 77.

THIRTY

Increase and Abound in Love

1 Thessalonians 3.9–13

The God to whom we pray is a God who helps us grow. Growth is necessary for life, especially fledgling life. Newborns are incapable of providing for and sustaining their own life, and need something greater than themselves to keep them alive and progressing toward maturity. In the case of Christians, human teachers and support play a part in the process, but the Bible regularly points to God as playing the key role.

Context

Paul chose Silas as a companion for his second missionary journey. After visiting the churches he established on the first trip, Timothy joined them and God led them to the region of Macedonia (Acts 15.39–16.10).[1] In Philippi, Paul met with some success, but he and Silas were arrested, beaten, and imprisoned before God sent an earthquake that freed them, leading to the conversion of the jailer (Acts 16.11–40). From Philippi they traveled to Thessalonica, where they encountered more adversity. There, Paul reasoned from the Scriptures with the Jews for three Sabbaths before being thrown out of the synagogue, though not before converting some. Paul's opponents, however, formed a mob, attacked the house of Jason,

---

[1] Based on the first person plural pronoun in verse 11, it seems that Luke joined them at Troas. Luke will apparently stay behind in Philippi, as the first person plural drops off here and picks up again when Paul returns to Macedonia on his third journey (Acts 20.6).

and dragged him and some other Christians before the city authorities, ultimately leading to Paul and the others leaving for Berea (Acts 17.1–9).[2]

After Thessalonica, Paul had success in Berea until the Jews from Thessalonica followed him there and continued to cause problems. Paul traveled on, leaving Timothy and Silas behind him to continue the work (Acts 17.10–15). In Athens, he reasoned with the intellectual elite at the Areopagus (Acts 17.16–34) before heading to Corinth, where he spent eighteen months teaching the gospel (Acts 18.1–18). At Corinth, "Silas and Timothy arrived from Macedonia" (v 5).

Throughout all of this, Paul continued to be concerned with the fledgling group in Thessalonica he had been forced to leave so quickly. Indeed, his concerns were so great that "when I could bear it no longer," Timothy returned to exhort them further in the afflictions they were surely continuing to endure (1 Thes 3.1–2, 5; cf. Acts 17.15), willing to be alone in Athens in order to further strengthen them. Now, Timothy has returned and brought "good news of your faith and love and reported that you always remember us kindly and long to see us, as we long to see you—for this reason, brothers, in all our distress and affliction we have been comforted about you through your faith. For now we live, if you are standing fast in the Lord" (1 Thes 3.6–8). This news prompts a spontaneous outburst of thanksgiving and prayer in the next verses. The prayer is twofold: Paul reports what he prays for the Thessalonian Christians and then offers a prayer on their behalf:[3]

> For what thanksgiving can we return to God for you, for all the joy that we feel for your sake before our God, as we pray most earnestly night and day that we may see you face to face and supply what is lacking in your faith?

---

[2] The exact amount of time Paul spent in Thessalonica is hard to pin down. Three Sabbaths can mean as little as two weeks or as many as four, depending on the arrival and departure days around those Sabbaths. Likewise, Paul usually stayed in town teaching the Gentiles after being thrown out of the synagogue, which he may have done here as well. Given the hostility in Thessalonica and Paul's statements in 1 Thessalonians, it seems that their time was brief.

[3] The remaining prayers in this book are from Paul's epistles, a very different sort of prayer than the narrative prayers we have encountered so far. Although different, they are outstanding examples and well worthy of inclusion in such a study. For a systematic discussion of Paul's prayers that discusses various features without engaging in detailed exegesis, see Longenecker, "Prayer in the Pauline Letters," 203–227 or Peterson, "Prayer in Paul's Writings," 84–101.

Now may our God and Father himself, and our Lord Jesus, direct our way to you, and may the Lord make you increase and abound in love for one another and for all, as we do for you, so that he may establish your hearts blameless in holiness before our God and Father, at the coming of our Lord Jesus with all his saints. (1 Thes 3.9–13)

Contents

Even before Paul reports his earnest praying, he says (by rhetorical question) that it is impossible to adequately thank God for them and the joy they bring (cf. Ps 116.12), which is the third thanksgiving Paul issues in the letter (1.2; 2.13). The inability to adequately express thanksgiving does not absolve Paul of the responsibility of expressing it anyway, especially in the ancient world where the principle of reciprocity permeated every relationship.[4] The first century Roman Stoic Seneca said, "Not to return gratitude for benefits is a disgrace, and the whole world counts it as such."[5] Regarding situations such as Paul's, he said, "I shall never be able to repay you my gratitude, but, at any rate, I shall not cease from declaring everywhere than I am unable to repay it."[6] Paul apparently feels likewise, declaring openly his inability to sufficiently thank God for the Thessalonians.

In that context, he says that he prays continually for them about two interrelated things: to see them again and to teach them further. Regarding the prayer report, consider first the intensity with which Paul prays. Some debate the meaning of "night and day,"[7] but in either case it emphasizes Paul's deep concern. In addition, "most earnestly" is a translation of a word with a double intensifier,[8] a super-superlative. This is joined to a verb for prayer that could be translated "begging," stronger than the

---

[4] See deSilva, *Honor, Patronage, Kinship, & Purity*, 95–119.

[5] Seneca, *De Beneficiis*, 3.1.1.

[6] Ibid., 2.24.4.

[7] It may simply refer to constant prayer (e.g., Morris, *First and Second Thessalonians*, 104–105; Green, *The Letters to the Thessalonians*, 173) or, if echoing the Psalms (Pss 42.8; 63.6; 77.2; cf. 2 Macc 13.10), it could indicate a sign of deep concern to pray at night (Marshall, *1 and 2 Thessalonians*, 98; Witherington, *1 and 2 Thessalonians*, 96).

[8] Bruce, *1 & 2 Thessalonians*, 68: "Paul is found of compounds expressing superlativeness."

normal word for prayer, frequently connoting a sense of personal need.[9] To this, Paul adds his desire that they "increase and abound" in love. All of this speaks to the urgency of Paul's prayer.

Second, Paul desires to "supply what is lacking" in their faith. This could refer to some negligence on their part,[10] but more likely speaks to the simple reality of the paucity of teaching that could be done in such a short visit, which led to the need for more teaching.[11] In either case, the prayer that follows indicates they still needed growth in love and holiness—two topics Paul discusses in the next chapter (4.3–12). After all, both are lifelong endeavors that cannot be perfected on this side of eternity. This may especially be the case for holiness, since it is a word that is exclusively used of God in the LXX and only used of people one other time in the New Testament (2 Cor 7.1),[12] another text about the need to grow in it. Their love should grow "for one another and for all," likely means both Christians and the world (cf. Gal 6.10).[13] The goal of this growth is their blamelessness before God when Christ returns. Regardless of how peers or the world may judge, blamelessness before God is the only verdict that matters—a verdict that will be rendered at the final judgment day.

Notice that the prayer itself closely mirrors the report of the prayer. The two concerns of the report (visiting them and supplying what is lacking) are mirrored by the two concerns of the prayer (God directing their way to them and their increasing and abounding in love and holiness), clearly joining the two: Paul tells them what he regularly prays regarding them and then proceeds to pray in that very way.[14] The prayer,

---

[9] Malherbe, *The Letters to the Thessalonians*, 204.

[10] Morris, *First and Second Thessalonians*, 106 says that the word is used, among other things, for "deficiencies in spiritual matters." Further its grammatical plurality "points us to the fact that more than one thing needed rectification" and although Paul was delighted about the state of the Thessalonians, "that did not mean that he was blind to their failings."

[11] Bruce, *1 & 2 Thessalonians*, 68; Malherbe, *The Letters to the Thessalonians*, 205; Marshall, *1 and 2 Thessalonians*, 98; Witherington, *1 and 2 Thessalonians*, 97.

[12] Morris, *First and Second Thessalonians*, 110.

[13] Beale, *1–2 Thessalonians*, 109 suggests that "everyone else" ("all" in ESV) could refer to Christians outside of Thessalonica based on the same word's use in 4.9–10.

[14] The prayer is in the third person instead of a second person, vocative prayer. Even so as Bruce, *1 & 2 Thessalonians*, 74 says, "there is no difference in principle between saying, 'O God our Father

then, is not merely an expression of thanks and request to God, but also benefits the Thessalonians who hear it. First, it serves as an immense encouragement, a topic we will consider in the next section. Second, it provides an exhortation to them to let the Lord continue to work in their lives to fulfill His purposes.[15]

Both petitions are ultimately answered. Although Thessalonica is not specified in the text, Acts 20.1–2 reports Paul returned to Macedonia and traveled through the region giving them much encouragement. More directly, however, Paul himself commends them for their growth in faith and love: "We ought always to give thanks to God for you, brothers, as is right, because your faith is growing abundantly, and the love of every one of you for one another is increasing" (2 Thes 1.3).

Finally, this prayer says something profound about the identity of Jesus. Paul addresses this prayer to God the Father and the Lord Jesus at its opening and to the Lord [Jesus] directly in the second petition. This is striking not only because of its implications regarding prayer to Jesus,[16] but also because of its very high view of Jesus at a very early stage in church history. Paul writes 1 Thessalonians on his second journey, making it by all accounts one of the earliest New Testament documents. At this point, Jesus is already viewed as a proper object of prayer alongside God the Father. Further, this is not argued, but assumed.[17] It is done incidentally in a prayer, not in the midst of a theological discourse on the nature of deity and Jesus. This proceeds naturally from Paul's understanding of God and Christ.[18] The deity of Jesus was not a doctrine that developed slowly over time; here is evidence it was believed from the very beginning of Christianity.[19]

---

and our Lord Jesus, direct our way...' and saying, 'May God our father and our Lord Jesus direct our way....'"

[15] Marshall, *1 and 2 Thessalonians*, 101.
[16] See Appendix A.
[17] Witherington, *1 and 2 Thessalonians*, 103.
[18] Morris, *First and Second Thessalonians*, 107.
[19] Bruce, *1 and 2 Thessalonians*, 74 also points to the return of Jesus being spoken of in language echoing "those occasions when the God of Israel reveals himself in glory, attended by his heavenly hosts. The unobtrusive spontaneity with which such language is applied to Jesus by more NT writers

Connections

Even good churches need to grow. Perhaps the most remarkable thing about this prayer is that it reflects Paul's earnest desire that the Thessalonians grow in love and holiness. The Macedonian epistles are among the few generally-positive letters Paul wrote to a church. Indeed, Paul has already praised them for their love and rejection of idolatry (1.8–10; cf. 1.3; 3.6; 4.9–10), saying they were an exemplary group others could learn from. Paul is delighted by their spirituality, but he is not satisfied, instead praying that they "increase and abound" (3.12) in the love they have, and that in the ways they are already pleasing God they "do so more and more" (4.1). Whether individually or congregationally, Christians never have occasion to rest on their laurels.

Investing energy in prayer. Many Christians see prayer as a last resort. When we cannot do anything else, well, the *least* we can do is pray for them. One might get the wrong impression that Paul thinks something similar, since he has been so intent on getting back to the Thessalonians in person. Already, he has tried to return only to be thwarted by Satan (2.17–18), and sent Timothy back in his place to establish and exhort them (3.2) and learn about them (3.5). For that matter, this very letter will continue to work for their benefit in Paul's absence. And Paul still desires to visit in spite of all that he has done in lieu of returning. He knew nothing could substitute for being in their presence and teaching them in person.[20]

But if we know anything about Paul's practice of praying it is that he invested as much energy praying for them as he did in trying to get back to them.[21] For Paul, prayer was never a last resort to fill the gaps in what he could not do on his own; rather, it was a first stop, the most important step to take in seeking to help another. In Paul's thinking, there is an intersection between intercessory prayer and his own service; for him, "prayer is

---

than one is more eloquent than any formal creedal statement could be." There is debate as to whether the singular verb accompanying the two subjects is meaningful to this discussion or not. See Bruce for an argument that it is not and Beale, *1–2 Thessalonians*, 108–109 (footnote) for an argument that it is.

[20] Green, *The Letters to the Thessalonians*, 174.

[21] Ibid., 173.

not a substitute for Christian service; it is part of it. And apparently he cannot long pray for believers without longing to serve them himself."[22]

Need for divine assistance in Christian living. The two matters Paul specifically prays about—love and holiness—are basics of Christianity. This is not to say they are easy, but that they are fundamental. And yet how frequently do we make them a priority in our prayers? Barclay makes the point well:

> We often wonder why the Christian life is so difficult to live, especially in the ordinary everyday relationships of life. The answer may very well be that we are trying to live it by ourselves. The man who goes out in the morning without prayer is, in effect, saying, "I can quite well tackle today myself." The man who lays himself to rest without speaking to God is, in effect, saying, "I can bear whatever consequences today has brought myself." ... [I]t may well be that our failure to live the Christian life is due to the fact that we have tried to live it without the help of God—and that is an impossible assignment.[23]

This point echoes what we have said in the last two chapters: failure in prayer leads to failure in temptation; success in prayer leads to success in temptation. If we ever hope to succeed in living the kind of life God calls us to, we must constantly seek His gracious and powerful help.[24]

God gives the increase. This prayer is an excellent illustration of something Paul says in 1 Corinthians about how the spiritual realm works. There, in an effort to dispel contention rooted in rivalries over their connection to Paul, Apollos, Peter, and others, he says, "I planted, Apollos watered, but God gave the growth. So neither he who plants nor he who waters is anything but only God who gives the growth" (1 Cor 3.6–7). In this case, Paul and his compatriots planted the Gospel in Thessalonica. Later, Timothy returned to further establish their faith (3.2) and the

---

[22] Carson, *Praying with Paul*, 70.

[23] Barclay, *Philippians, Colossians, Thessalonians*, 229.

[24] To this we might add the help we provide to others (and vice versa) in intercessory prayer. Barclay also says, "We will never know from how much sin we have been saved and how much temptation we have conquered because someone has prayed for us" (227–228; cf. Luke 22.31–32).

Thessalonians themselves continued in their faith and love (3.6). Even so, God is the one who receives the thanksgiving for their success (v 9) and the Lord Jesus is the one who will make them increase and abound in love and establish their hearts in holiness (vv 11–12).

At the same time, this emphasizes a point I have made throughout about the intersection of divine initiative and human response, which Marshall refers to here as "the paradox of Christian faith and growth which is both due to the working of God by his Spirit and also due to the activity of the believer." He continues,

> Christian growth is not produced "automatically" by divine grace, so that the believer needs to make no effort but rather the believer must be encouraged to show faith and love. Hence Paul can both pray to God for his converts and thank him for their spiritual progress and also urge them to growth in their faith and express his delight when they respond to his urging (or rebuke them when they fail to do so).[25]

Encouraging others in prayer. This prayer not only thanks God and exhorts the Thessalonians, but would serve as an encouragement to them as well. Regarding encouragement, Carson contrasts Paul's prayer with both "the backslapping flatterer [who] constantly compliments everyone," cheapening the value of all compliments, and "the sober theologically precise types [who] are deeply committed to the truth that all praise finally belongs to God alone," so they never thank or praise anyone for what they have done. Paul serves as a contrast to these extremes:

> He encourages Christians by thanking God for his grace in their lives. More precisely, he encourages Christians *by telling them* that he thanks God for his grace in their lives. Thus he has simultaneously drawn attention to the Thessalonians' spiritual growth, thereby encouraging them, and

---

[25] Marshall, *1 and 2 Thessalonians*, 97. Moo, *2 Peter and Jude*, 285 says something similar of Jude's pairing of being kept by God (v 1) and the charge to keep themselves (v 21): "Here we find the typical two sides of the New Testament approach to the Christian life. God has done all in Christ that we need to be saved, yet we must respond to God if we are to secure our salvation. God 'keeps' us; we are to 'keep ourselves.' Both are true, and neither can be sacrificed without missing something essential to the Christian pursuit of godliness." Cf. John 15.9.

insisted that God is the one to be thanked for it, thereby humbling them. There is simply no way that these believers can listen to what Paul says and then smugly pat themselves on the back: God, and God alone, is to be praised for the signs of grace in their lives. Yet nonetheless they cannot help but feel encouraged to learn that the apostle himself has observed God's work in their lives and rejoices because of it.[26]

Such encouragement of one another should be a given among Christians, but it is strikingly absent in many places. "How much would our churches be transformed if each of us made it a practice to thank God for others and then to tell these others what it is about them that we thank God for?"[27]

---

[26] Carson, *Praying with Paul*, 66–67. He goes on to cite prayers in nine other Pauline letters bearing this trait.
[27] Ibid., 67.

THIRTY-ONE

The Lord Glorified in You

2 Thessalonians 1.11–12

The God to whom we pray is a God who will grant our every resolve for good. This is not to say that God is a genie in a bottle or can be treated as a cosmic vending machine. Instead, as we grow in our faith, more closely align ourselves with His will, and better understand what is truly good—as God defines good—our prayers will seek that will, and God will grant our desires for spiritually-minded purposes and God-focused work. Paul's second prayer for the Thessalonians touches on this idea.

Context

Although it is impossible to be precise as to when it was written, it does not seem like much time passes between Paul's first and second letters to the Thessalonian churches, perhaps as little as weeks or months between them.[1] However much time passes, many of the same difficulties facing the Thessalonians since the time of the church's founding and Paul's first letter remain. The church began amid persecution and continued therein. This gives the background for verses 3–10, which serve as the background of the prayer. In the Greek they are one long sentence focusing on two primary matters: Paul's thanksgiving for the Thessalonians (vv 3–4) and

---

[1] Morris, *First and Second Thessalonians*, 14; Malherbe, *The Letters to the Thessalonians*, 350. Alternately, see Wanamaker, *The Epistles to the Thessalonians*, 37–45 for an argument that 2 Thessalonians was written first.

the certainty of divine recompense (vv 5–10). Since Paul explicitly connects his prayer to what he has just said (note the first words in verse 11), it is important to consider them at least briefly.[2]

One thing is certain about Paul's relationship with the Thessalonian Christians: he was thankful for them. In addition to three expressions of thanksgiving in the first letter (1.3; 2.13; 3.9), he expresses the same sort of gratitude twice in the second (1.3; 2.13). The thanksgiving here draws on the prayer in 1 Thessalonians 3.9–13. There, Paul prays for their growth in faith and love, and here he thanks God for that very thing. Further, he says he boasts about them to other churches because of their steadfastness and faith during persecution.

It is striking that Paul commends the Thessalonians for their faith and love without ever mentioning their hope. This triad of virtues commonly occurs together, including the thanksgiving in 1 Thessalonians 1.3. Some have seen the "steadfastness" as an implicit stand-in for hope, but it seems unlikely that Paul would only hint at something he regularly says explicitly. Perhaps it is omitted because it becomes the focus of his discussion in verses 5–10. Even here, however, it remains implicit, which leaves the lingering question of why Paul never says anything about it outright. The answer may be as simple as it not being something he prayed for in 1 Thessalonians 3, which this thanksgiving is designed to echo.

As to the coming recompense, Paul here provides a reason for the Thessalonians to remain steadfast in the persecution, even as they had been doing. The Day of the Lord will come again, and as always happens on that Day, God will intervene in time and space to bring justice to the wicked and deliverance to the righteous.[3] Those who have stood against the Lord and His people will be punished for their impudence and the saints will receive a relief from their sufferings that is far greater than can be imagined.

---

[2] Carson dedicates an entire chapter to this task (*Praying with Paul*, 21–32).

[3] The Day of the Lord is a common theme in the prophets, most frequently in Joel and Zephaniah, and is discussed in some depth in commentaries on those books. For a brief summation of this theme, see Tully, *Reading the Prophets*, 344–350.

It is in this context that Paul prays:

> To this end we always pray for you, that our God may make you worthy of his calling and may fulfill every resolve for good and every work of faith by his power, so that the name of our Lord Jesus may be glorified in you, and you in him, according to the grace of our God and the Lord Jesus Christ. (2 Thes 1.11–12)

Contents

Paul begins the prayer by connecting it to what has just been said. Paul's "to this end" has been the subject of much discussion among commentators, but the general idea is simple: his prayer draws out of the discussion that has preceded it. Part of the significance of this lies in what has just been said: their past progress and the assurance of future judgment in their favor. Much like in 1 Thessalonians, Paul is not satisfied with an ongoing *status quo*, even if the norm is excellent. Christian perseverance must include continued growth, continued prayer, and continued faith,[4] which is why Paul urges this already-excellent group to excel still more (cf. 1 Thes 4.10).

The prayer consists of two basic petitions: that God would make them worthy of His calling and that He would fulfill their resolve and work by His power. In addition to the two petitions, it contains two goals: the glorification of Jesus and the glorification of the Thessalonians.

First, Paul prays that God would make them worthy of His calling. There is some debate as to whether Paul means that God would *make* them worthy[5] or *deem* them worthy.[6] In the final analysis, the difference matters little, for in either case, their worthiness is dependent upon God rather than themselves. As Marshall says, "God cannot deem worthy any whom he himself has not made worthy by his action rather than by their good works."[7] The worth in question is to be "worthy of his calling"

---

[4] Marshall, *1 and 2 Thessalonians*, 181.

[5] CSB; ESV; NIV; Malherbe, *The Letters to the Thessalonians*, 410.

[6] NASB; NKJV. Most commentators seem to favor this option. See, e.g., Morris, *First and Second Thessalonians*, 209; Wanamaker, *The Epistles to the Thessalonians*, 233.

[7] Marshall, *1 and 2 Thessalonians*, 182.

(cf. Eph 4.1), which is to say that they are to live up to their Christianity, living a life that is conformed to God's will.

Second, he prays that God would fulfill their every resolve for good and every work of faith by His power. This statement is remarkable both in its simplicity and its profundity. In short, God is the ultimate source for the good they do and fulfilling their obligations depends on God's powerful presence in their lives.[8] At the same time, however, it urges them to make a commitment to have resolve and be working, rather than expecting God to do everything for them. They are neither dependent upon their own scant resources to accomplish these great tasks nor can they presume upon God's work in their lives to accomplish everything without their participation.

Paul prays these things for an intended result: that Jesus would be glorified and that they would be glorified in him. More precisely, Paul's concern is that the *name* of Jesus would be glorified. The name meant more to the ancients than a mere designation; rather, it included the entire character and reputation of the person.[9] The prayer, then, is that "there may be such virtues manifest in the believers that glory will accrue to him who is ultimately responsible for these virtues."[10] This is much as Jesus Himself prayed: "All mine are yours, and yours are mine, and I am glorified in them" (John 17.10). Further, glorifying God through one's conduct is common in the New Testament (Matt 5.16; 1 Cor 6.20; 10.31; Gal 1.24; 1 Pet 2.12; 4.16).[11] But this is not the end of the matter, because Christians are in Christ, as those who make up the body of Christ. Inasmuch as He is glorified, so are they.

Throughout all of this is God's gracious providing, which is the foundation for the entire prayer and runs through every phrase, from beginning to end. He thanks *God* for their growth and assures them of *God's*

---

[8] Green, *The Letters to the Thessalonians*, 297.

[9] Morris, *First and Second Thessalonians*, 210 points to Revelation 2.17 as an illustration of this, for it speaks of a new name that no one knows but the person given it: "To our way of thinking a name that nobody knows is useless. But in the Revelation the name nobody knows is very much in point. It signifies a new character that is given to the person in question, something that is a secret between his Lord and himself."

[10] Ibid.

[11] Malherbe, *The Letters to the Thessalonians*, 412.

coming vindication before asking that *God* would make them worthy and fulfill their resolve and work so that the *Lord Jesus* would be glorified in them and they in *Him* according to *the grace of our God and the Lord Jesus Christ*.[12] None of this means the Thessalonians are absolved from any obligation, but it is a reminder that any progress they can make begins with God's provision.

Connections

Framework informs focus. As we have seen throughout, understanding the context of a prayer is vital to understanding its application to us. In this case, it also helps shape our understanding of the very essence of prayer. It is easy to get wrapped up in praying for physical things, some of which may indeed be legitimate matters of prayer. But set in the framework of the final judgment, Paul's focus becomes laser-like: "he prays with eternity's values in view."[13] Earthly health, success, wealth, or other values are the farthest things from Paul's mind. Nor does he seek the removal of the present persecution he and the Thessalonians know well. Rather, Paul's focus is righteous living in the interim as they await the return of the Lord in judgment: the behavior and belief of the Christian that is expected by God as we live between the promise and its fulfillment.[14]

The intersection of divine initiative and human response. We have already discussed this concept, but it appears again in this prayer, and the preceding point provides another opportunity to speak briefly about it. Among people who profess Christian faith, there is a tendency to overemphasize one side of this at the expense of the other—some virtually exclude the other, paying lip service to it at best. By contrast, both must be our complete focus. At all times, we must constantly remember that we are utterly dependent upon God's grace, not merely for the initial steps toward our salvation, but at every step along the way as He works

---

[12] Grammatically this last phrase can refer either to the Father and Son (as stated above) or to just the son ("the grace of our God and Lord, Jesus Christ"). Green, *The Letters to the Thessalonians*, 300 is among the few who argue for the latter.

[13] Carson, *Praying with Paul*, 35.

[14] Witherington, *1 and 2 Thessalonians*, 200.

within us to accomplish His purposes. At the same time, we must constantly remember that we are obligated to have a resolve for good and to work in our faith, not merely as some superficial show, but because we will stand before the judgment seat of God and be judged according to our deeds (Ps 62.12; Jer 17.10; 32.19; Ezek 33.20; Matt 16.27; 25.31–46; Rom 2.6–8; 2 Cor 5.10; Gal 6.7–8; Rev 2.23; 22.12; etc.). As paradoxical as it may be, neither truth detracts from or in any way minimizes the other, and either diminishing what we do or what God does stands in opposition to the Bible's clear, repeated teaching.

Our every wish granted. What if we could have our every wish granted? Such a thought seems too good to be true. At the same time, this is essentially what Paul prays for in regard to the Thessalonians: that God would "fulfill every resolve for good and every work of faith by his power" (v 11). Carson makes this point well:

> We may have all kinds of wonderful ideas about what we as Christians might do, yet somehow never get around to doing any of them. Alternatively, we may immediately proceed to organization and administration and never seek, except in sporadic and accidental ways, the decisive approval and blessing of God for our Christian dreams. The truth is that unless God works in us and through us, unless God empowers these good purposes of ours, they will not engender any enduring spiritual fruit; they will not display any life-transforming, people-changing power. "Unless the LORD builds the house, its builders labor in vain. Unless the LORD watches over the city, the guards stand watch in vain" (Ps 127.1). And unless the Lord fulfills our good, faith-prompted purposes, they will remain arid, fruitless—either empty dreams or frenetic activity with no life, but in either case, spiritually anemic.[15]

The question is not what God is willing to give, but whether we have developed spiritually-minded purposes and are engaged in God-focused work.

Prayers of exhortation. We return to yet another previously discussed point: prayer can sometimes serve in a role of exhortation. In this case,

---

[15] Carson, *Praying with Paul*, 38.

it is true both of Paul's thanksgiving and the prayer itself. Regarding the former, his boasting about the Thessalonians to other churches serves a dual exhortative function: for the Thessalonians, it encourages them in what they have been doing and urges them to continue and grow in that behavior; for those to whom he boasts, it provides a model of behavior for them to emulate. In short, Paul's boasting about them and report of the boasting is designed to strengthen both the Thessalonian Christians and those who hear of them.[16] Regarding the latter, it should be remembered that Paul's letters were first read out loud before a full congregation, which gives it the function of persuading the congregation toward making a decision to be the people he urges them to be.[17]

---

[16] Green, *The Letters to the Thessalonians*, 282.
[17] Witherington, *1 and 2 Thessalonians*, 200.

THIRTY-TWO

Know the Hope, Riches, and Power of God

Ephesians 1.16–23

The God to whom we pray is a God who has already given us everything we need. Even so, He is a God who sees greater things for us and expects greater things of us. Possessing every spiritual blessing is not enough if we do not grow therein, and so after affirming the former, Paul turns his attention to the latter.

Context

After the letter's prescript prescript, Ephesians opens with a long statement of adoration to God, a single sentence (in Greek) extolling praise to God for having blessed believers with every spiritual blessing. In short, God has taken incredible initiative in blessing us: He blessed us (v 3); He chose us (v 4); He predestined us to be his sons (v 5); He freely bestowed on us his grace (v 6); He lavished grace upon us according to His wisdom (v 8); He made His will known to us (vv 9–10); He accomplishes all things according to his will (v 11). All this was according to His love (v 4), His will (v 5), His grace (v 6, 8), His purpose (v 9), and His plan (v 10). Just as thoroughly as Paul emphasizes God's initiative, so also He emphasizes that these blessings are through Christ, whom he mentions by name, title, or pronoun some 15 times in the first 14 verses (vv 3–4, 6–7, 9–10, 11–14). In sum, no spiritual blessing has been withheld from the believer.[1]

In some sense, then, this is a surprising prayer. After all, Paul just finished saying that they have been blessed with *every* spiritual blessing. In this context, what more can they possibly need? The answer to this is found in the content of the request: a prayer for "a spirit of wisdom and of revelation in the knowledge of him" (v 17). Having praised God for the presence of the blessing, Paul now prays that God will open their eyes to grasp the fullness of the blessing.

A second context from which this prayer arises is the report Paul had received about the Christians to whom he writes. He had heard of their faith in the Lord and their love toward all the saints (v 15), a commendation speaking to the great commands that govern every other (Matt 22.36–40). In short, they are not only blessed with every spiritual blessing but succeeding admirably in holy living. Even so, Paul is not satisfied.[2] He wants more for them, and of them.

> I do not cease to give thanks for you, remembering you in my prayers, that the God of our Lord Jesus Christ, the Father of glory, may give you the Spirit of wisdom and of revelation in the knowledge of him, having the eyes of your hearts enlightened, that you may know what is the hope to which he has called you, what are the riches of his glorious inheritance in the saints, and what is the immeasurable greatness of his power toward us who believe, according to the working of his great might that he worked in Christ when he raised him from the dead and seated him at his right hand in the heavenly places, far above all rule and authority and power and dominion, and above every name that is named, not only in this age but also in the one to come. And he put all things under his feet and gave him as head over all things to the church, which is his body, the fullness of him who fills all in all. (Eph 1.16–23)

---

[1] This brief summation is drawn from Stott, *The Message of Ephesians*, 33–34.
[2] Ibid., 53.

Contents

Paul prays that God increase their understanding of the blessings He bestowed. The words Paul uses emphasize the point: wisdom; revelation; knowledge; enlightened; know (vv 18–19). Although they are already blessed in every way, Paul prays for their understanding of that blessing to grow.

Interpreters debate whether Paul asks that they receive "a spirit of wisdom" (e.g., NASB, NRSV)[3] or "the Spirit of wisdom" (e.g., CSB, ESV, NIV).[4] Paul uses the same word to speak of both a person's inner spirit or disposition and the Holy Spirit. The connected phrase "and of revelation" may point to the latter, if both are connected to the same "spirit of," as the capital-s Spirit is the one consistently connected with revelation (cf. John 14.26; 1 Cor 2.10–13). There may even be a connection between the two, for the very gentleness which is part of the Spirit's fruit (Gal 5.23) is to be the disposition wherein one believer corrects another (Gal 6.1). In light of this deSilva suggests Paul's prayer is for them to be given a spirit of wisdom and revelation by means of the Holy Spirit.[5]

Paul does not want his readers to have understanding for the sake of understanding, or knowledge only in some general sense. Rather, he prays for their insight to grow in three particular ways.[6] He wants them to better know the hope of God's call, the glory of God's inheritance, and the greatness of God's power.[7]

The first of these seems to refer to the normal Christian hope: the anticipation of eternal life with God. Morris says, "In modern times we seem

---

[3] Witherington, *Philemon, Colossians, Ephesians,* 240–241 translates it as "spirit" and comments that Paul's prayer is that "God will give them both spiritual discernment (wisdom) and revelation."

[4] Lincoln, *Ephesians,* 57; Arnold, *Ephesians,* 104.

[5] deSilva, *Ephesians,* 90–91; cf. Foulkes, *Ephesians,* 60.

[6] The Greek uses an indefinite pronoun to mark off each successive topic. The ESV translates this with "what is." Chester, *The Message of Prayer,* 253–257 sees this as one request divided out into two different ways—i.e., the hope of God's call is the single issue, which can be fleshed out by the other two topics. The pronoun at the front of each clause, however, serves almost as a bullet-list marker, suggesting Paul is discussing three separate (but related) ideas. See Lincoln, *Ephesians,* 58.

[7] On a surface level, these seem like rather simple concepts. Such a superficial view is not sufficient, first because of the vast depths of each idea, which could fill many pages. Beyond that, the grammar—a genitive construction in each case—is ambiguous and could mean different things.

often to have downgraded that word's meaning from the blazing certainty of the New Testament hope to nothing more than a feeble optimism. … For Paul, hope represented the certainty of something not yet present."[8] The second is more debated: does Paul refer to the inheritance that we receive from God or the inheritance that we are to God. The connection to "hope" may point to the former, but there is thoroughgoing Old Testament background of God's people being His heritage.[9] In this view, Paul emphasizes to his readers how deeply God values and cherishes them: "As an earthly king values treasuries full of silver and gold, God values *his people* as his wealth and honor."[10] Finally, the greatness of God's power, although a topic that could be expounded upon endlessly, is rather straightforward.

Even so, the final topic is further elaborated in the end of the prayer. God's power is displayed in three ways: His resurrection of Jesus from the dead, His enthroning of Jesus over every power, and His giving headship over the church to Jesus. There is a natural connection between the first two and third of these. Jesus' headship over the church is an outgrowth of His resurrection and enthronement over all other forces. He is not head of the church merely because of divine fiat (though He could be), but because He is uniquely qualified for the role. The two universal problems over which humankind has no power—sin and death—have been subjected to Christ in His resurrection and enthronement. God has placed Christ over all powers, the world, and the church, and Christ is currently ruling all things for the sake of the church. In short, "The body of Christ is possible in a dark and fallen world because of the resurrection and exaltation of Christ and the subjection of the powers under his feet."[11]

As is frequently the case, the accumulation of synonyms raises the question of whether Paul intends a nuanced distinction in each word or

---

[8] Morris, *Ephesians*, 32.

[9] Deuteronomy 4.20; 9.26, 29; 2 Samuel 21.3; 1 Kings 8.51, 53; 2 Kings 21.14; Psalms 28.9; 33.12; 68.9; 78.62, 71; 94.14; 106.5, 40; Isaiah 19.25; 47.6; 63.17; Jeremiah 10.16; 51.19. Interestingly, Stott argues for this view in verses 11 and 14 and against it here, though he does so on the basis of Colossians 1.12, which he sees as parallel (*The Message of Ephesians*, 56).

[10] Arnold, *Ephesians*, 109, emphasis in original.

[11] Witherington, *Philemon, Colossians, Ephesians*, 239.

is piling up similar words for rhetorical emphasis. This issue arises three times in this prayer, first in the opening request for wisdom, revelation, and knowledge; second with power, working, great, and might; and third with the rule, authority, power, and dominion. Although the words in each case have different semantic ranges and precise definitions can be given, it is likely that Paul is not pressing nuanced difference, but emphasizing the point. In this view, Paul is attempting "to exhaust the resources of the Greek language by piling up four synonyms for power in order to convey an impression of something of the divine might."[12] As Morris says regarding the third example, "Paul is not describing different ways in which Christ may function in heaven, but is saying that whatever sovereignty there may be in the celestial sphere, Christ is above it."[13]

Connections

The importance of a rational religion. The Bible never commends blind faith and constantly speaks of faith and our relationship with God as matters that are intellectually grounded and rooted in knowledge and wisdom, an idea clearly seen in Acts 17: in Thessalonica, most of the Jews rejected any new teaching and drove Paul and Silas out of town (vv 1–9); in Athens, the Greeks were excited about any new teaching and were interested in what Paul brought (vv 16–21); in Berea, however, the hearers are commended, for they neither accepted blindly nor rejected blindly the message, but carefully weighed and evaluated it against the truth they knew (vv 10–15).[14] In short, God wants a well-reasoned faith. Adapting an oft-repeated Platonic aphorism, Barclay correctly says, "The unexamined religion is the religion not worth having."[15]

---

[12] Lincoln, *Ephesians*, 60.

[13] Morris, *Ephesians*, 35.

[14] This theme is also present in all three of the remaining prayers this book will cover and a host of other Biblical texts (cf. Matt 11.2–6; John 20.30–31; Rom 1.19–20; 1 Cor 10.15; Col 2.5; 3.10; 1 Thes 5.21; 1 Pet 3.15; 1 John 4.1). To be clear, this is not to say that Christianity should be a religion of rational*ism*, where human reason plays the starring role, but simply that it should be rational.

[15] Barclay, *Galatians and Ephesians*, 104.

Having everything isn't enough. Paul's prayer should help us refocus our praying. Our prayers regarding spiritual blessings are frequently minimalistic, focusing on only a few things before quickly turning to physical concerns. We may even be oblivious—in practice, if not in reality—to the fact that God has blessed us with *every* spiritual blessing. Or perhaps we are complacent in our faith and knowledge, lacking the desire to know and experience those blessings more completely. This prayer and its context remind us that it is not enough to be blessed by God if we do not grow in that blessing and appreciate to the fullest extent possible the implications of that blessing (cf. Eph 3.18; Phil 1.9; Col 1.9).[16] Growth in understanding is indispensable to growth in holiness, and there will always be room to grow since God's inexhaustible wisdom can never be totally possessed.[17]

The power of God and our spiritual warfare. This text connects to Paul's discussion of spiritual warfare in chapter 6. When Paul speaks of our spiritual warfare in Ephesians 6, he calls us to draw on the "power," "might," and "strength" of the Lord (v 10). These are the very words he uses here of God's power, might, and strength shown in His work of raising Jesus from the dead—the very event that assures the defeat of the enemy (1.19–20). He refers to our enemies as spiritual forces "in the heavenly places" (6.12), but this assures us of their eventual defeat as well, because this is the very realm in which Christ reigns (1.20).[18] In short, we are fighting a battle that is ours for the taking. The better we know the power of God that has been manifested in these ways, the harder we will fight for the victory, because we know the victory has been won and the victor fights for us.

Sharing in Christ's victory. Most Christians are well aware of the parallel between baptism and the death, burial, and resurrection of Jesus (cf. Rom 6.1–4). In this prayer, however, Paul's focus moves to the resurrection, ascension, and enthronement. What's more, he goes on to say that our salvation is parallel to this in the next chapter (2.5–6). Although there

---

[16] These texts will be treated in more detail in the next three chapters of this books.
[17] Lincoln, *Ephesians*, 56.
[18] Stott, *The Message of Ephesians*, 266.

is much to reflect on here, I will limit my comments to two main points. First, this should shape our understanding of the cross. As Paul makes clear, the cross alone is useless, because Jesus' death without a resurrection simply means that Jesus was defeated (1 Cor 15.14–19). But similarly, the resurrection without the subsequent ascension and enthronement is likewise meaningless. Jesus did not rise from the dead merely to live out an earthly existence and die again. Rather, he returned to the throne of heaven where He reigns over every power, good or evil. The death-burial-resurrection-ascension-enthronement, though spread out as we reckon time, is one grand event. Second, in some amazing way—in what must be the epitome of the already-but-not-yet "inaugurated eschatology" of Christianity—believers share in every bit of it, in our baptism and in our salvation. Though we may not be able to fully understand the ins and outs and every implication of this affirmation, we should constantly be amazed at what God has done for us in Christ.

THIRTY-THREE

Exceedingly Abundantly Beyond Our Imagination

Ephesians 3.14–21

The God to whom we pray is a God who is far beyond our comprehension, yet a God who desires us to understand Him. He is a God whose ability to give goes far beyond our imagination, yet a God who does not limit Himself to our musings. He is a God whose power cannot possibly be quantified in human terms, yet a God whose power is already at work within human beings. In this prayer, Paul turns his focus to all of these ideas in an effort to help Christians grapple with—and find faith in—such unfathomable paradoxes.

Context

Since this prayer begins with "for this reason," Paul is building on the immediate textual context. A close reading of the immediate textual context, however, points further back than just the opening thirteen verses of the chapter, because the chapter begins with the same phrase. This phrase also opens the first prayer in the letter (1.15), which makes it reasonable to think that Paul began chapter 3 with the intent to pray. Instead, mentioning his apostleship leads to a brief digression to flesh out his understanding of it before returning to the prayer he intended to express. If this commonly-held reconstruction is correct, it means "this reason" refers not just back to verses 1–13—although those verses are not necessarily excluded—but to what preceded chapter 3. Given the near seamlessness of thought from 1.3–2.22, the question is whether "this reason" points back merely to the last thought of chapter 2 or to the whole letter to this point.

Another part of the context of this prayer may help resolve this difficulty. This prayer wraps up a major section of the epistle. It is commonly said that Paul's letters divide into doctrinal and practical sections, sometimes referred to as indicative (what is) and imperative (what therefore must be). Although an oversimplification of Paul's letters, it is not necessarily wrong, for Paul's letters do focus primarily on principles at the outset and practice in the end. In Ephesians, the division is between chapters 3 and 4, where the great truths of the gospel are proclaimed in chapters 1–3 and the implications to the Christian walk are enumerated in chapters 4–6.

Since this prayer serves as the conclusion to chapters 1–3, it is reasonable to think that Paul has in mind everything that has come before, namely the great spiritual blessings in Christ (1.3–14), including both the reversal of sin's consequences (2.1–10) and the repair of broken human relationships (2.11–22) in Christ, a matter Paul has already prayed his readers will better understand (1.15–23). It is, then, because of the great truth of the gospel, the mystery of God's eternal purposes now made known (3.1–13), that Paul prays:

> For this reason I bow my knees before the Father, from whom every family in heaven and on earth is named, that according to the riches of his glory he may grant you to be strengthened with power through his Spirit in your inner being, so that Christ may dwell in your hearts through faith—that you, being rooted and grounded in love, may have strength to comprehend with all the saints what is the breadth and length and height and depth, and to know the love of Christ that surpasses knowledge, that you may be filled with all the fullness of God.
>
> Now to him who is able to do far more abundantly than all that we ask or think, according to the power at work within us, to him be glory in the church and in Christ Jesus throughout all generations, forever and ever. Amen. (Eph 3.14–21)

Contents

As a result of Paul's reflection on God's great actions taken on behalf of humanity, he bows his head and kneels in prayer, a posture of devotion and humility. His prayer is "before the Father, from whom every family in heaven and on earth is named." Some disagree over whether Paul refers to "each family" (ESV) or "the whole family of believers" (NKJV). The former is more frequent in English translations, but the latter fits well with the context of Ephesians where a dominant theme is the newly united single family of Jews and Gentiles, brought together in Christ (cf. 4.6).[1]

A final point before turning to the prayer itself is the grounds upon which Paul builds this prayer, namely "according to the riches of his glory." Paul is about to pray for a mind-bogglingly amazing thing that will stretch the very bounds of language to express. Such a petition cannot be laid before one with minimal ability. Paul, however, prays to a God whose power has been clearly manifest (1.19–23), and so he has full confidence in the inexhaustible riches at God's disposal and has no doubt that from them, He is able to answer the prayer.

This prayer begins where the last one ended: the power of God. The difference is that the prayer in Ephesians 1 expressed a desire for understanding God's power and this prayer is a petition that God would empower them.[2] This power will come through two closely related things, God's Spirit in one's inner being and Christ dwelling in his or her heart—two items that are best seen as synonymous rather than separate (cf. Rom 8.9–11)—a thought later expanded to include God filling the believer (v 19). The word for "dwell" is not the weaker Greek word, used of living somewhere as a stranger (2.19), but a stronger word denoting settling down in permanent residence,[3] the same word used of deity dwelling in

---

[1] A question remains about the nature of every family "in heaven." If "each family" is meant, it may refer to angelic classes (Lincoln, *Ephesians*, 202–203). If, however, it refers to a single family of believers, it would "indicate that the church militant on earth and the church triumphant in heaven, though separated by death, are nevertheless only two parts of the one great family of God" (Stott, *The Message of Ephesians*, 133).

[2] Arnold, *Ephesians*, 209.

[3] BDAG, 534.

Christ (Col 2.9). This indwelling happens "through faith," Paul says. On this point, Lincoln says well, "Faith involves a relationship of trust between two parties, and so there can be no implication that the notion of Christ living in the center of a believer's personality means the absorption of that individual personality or the dissolving of responsibility."[4]

The second petition[5] is for comprehension of the love of Christ. This petition is based on the believer being rooted and grounded in love, a logically-mixed metaphor that draws from agriculture and architecture: deep roots and a solid foundation, two ideas that fit well together, for both are largely unseen but extremely important for stability. With such a foundation—and empowered by God dwelling in them—Paul prays that they will comprehend Christ's love. Debates over whether the various references to love focus on Christ's love for the believer, the believer's love for Christ, or the believer's Christlike love for others often miss the point that all are interrelated and, more significantly, interdependent. We learn to love by experiencing Christ's love for us, which is then returned to Him and shared with others. Without all three components, love is incomplete. God's love for us is primary, because we will not love Christ or others without Him first loving us (1 John 4.19–21), but any comprehension of His love necessarily includes its reflection and refraction.

This petition is expanded in a few ways. First, it is described in dimensional terms: grasping the breadth, length, height, and depth.[6] These terms

---

[4] Lincoln, *Ephesians*, 207.

[5] Due to the complexity of the Greek, commentators vary on how many petitions there are. Three phrases begin with "in order that," which might normally provide a bullet-like listing, but even here there is disagreement, with some seeing the third as a result of the first two rather than a separate petition (e.g., Carson, *Praying with Paul*, 161; Chester, *The Message of Prayer*, 188) and others seeing an implied "in order that," which is not in the Greek (e.g., ESV's addition of "so that" in verse 17 or Stott's supposition that being "rooted and grounded in love" is a key purpose for which Paul prayed [*The Message of Ephesians*, 136]). The three explicit clauses are: "that ... he may grant you to be strengthened with power"; "that you ... may have strength to comprehend..."; and "that you may be filled with all the fullness of God." deSilva, *Ephesians*, 179 is correct that "the possibility of hearing these petitions as cumulative is attractive," where each builds successively on the previous. For simplicity, I will consider each as a separate petition and the surrounding material as supporting them.

[6] This phrase does not have a direct object, leaving a variety of interpretive possibilities. See Arnold, *Ephesians*, 214–217 for a brief discussion of seven possibilities, including an argument that it refers to God's power. Most commentators see it as a reference to Christ's love, made specific in the following phrase.

have led to a variety of imaginative interpretations, including the ancient Christian commentators who saw it reflected in the cross itself, whose upright pole reached down into the earth and pointed up to heaven and whose crossbar spread wide the arms of Jesus, stretched out as if to invite and welcome the whole world.[7] Others have spoken of each term as having a significant meaning of Christ's love: broad enough to encompass all humankind; long enough to last for eternity; deep enough to reach even the lowest sinner and to extend even into the grave; high enough to exalt all men to heaven.[8] Although there is, to be sure, some level of truth to those various statements, it is unlikely that Paul had them all (or any of them) in mind. Rather, this is characteristic of rhetorical language designed to make an impact and suggests with these dimensional terms the fullness, vastness, and grandeur of Christ's love. Second, this love is understood in the context of "all the saints." This reminds us not only of God's desire for all Christians to understand it, but that such understanding is experienced in fellowship, not isolation. Indeed, no one can fully experience the love of Christ in isolation, for it is impossible to be connected to the head if one is not a part of the body. Finally, this love that Paul desires the believer to comprehend "surpasses knowledge," a deliberate paradox designed to emphasize that however much we may know of Christ's love, there is always more to learn about this inexhaustible topic.[9]

Finally, Paul prays that they be "filled with all the fullness of God." This is the ultimate goal of the prayer, for it is the ultimate goal of Christianity: to be holy like God is holy (1 Pet 1.15–16), to love like He has loved (John 13.34), to be perfect as the Father is perfect (Matt 5.48), to see Him as He is and be made like Him (1 John 3.2). This standard for which we strive directs us to the already-but-not-yet nature of Christianity, for however close we may grow to the goal in this life, it is God who will perfect us in the next (1 Pet 5.10). After all, "God's

---

[7] Arnold, *Ephesians*, cites Origen, Gregory of Nyssa, Jerome, Augustine, Anselm, and Aquinas as among the writers who took this view.

[8] Stott, *The Message of Ephesians*, 137.

[9] Bruce, *Colossians, Philemon, Ephesians*, 329.

purpose for the men and women he redeems is not simply to have them believe certain truths but to transform them in a lifelong process that stretches toward heaven."[10]

The prayer closes with a doxology that returns to God's ability. Just as the requests drew from God's inexhaustible resources at the outset, it closes with a reminder of God's ability, perhaps because the requests themselves are so grand that we need to be reminded of the limitless resources of the God to whom we pray: a God "who is able to do exceedingly abundantly above all that we ask or think" (v 20, NKJV),[11] a topic we will return to shortly.

The doxology closes with a final ascription of glory to God in both Christ and the church. This pairing fits well with the rest of the New Testament's teaching of the church as the bride and body of Christ. Given God's eternal plan to reconcile all people into a single, restored humanity and ultimately back to Himself, Foulkes is correct: "The glory of God is most gloriously seen in the grace of His uniting His sinful creatures to His eternal, sinless Son."[12]

Connections

The immeasurable power of God. God's power and ability frames this prayer and should be a constant companion in our own praying, because "as finite beings we pray as finite beings do. We have no conception of what almighty power can do."[13] This power itself deserves further reflection and considering how Paul builds his sentence makes it even more remarkable.[14] Although such an overly-precise distinction of terms violates my

---

[10] Carson, *Praying with Paul*, 167.

[11] The NKJV was the translation of my late teens and early 20s, and this phrasing has stuck with me. As a result, I used it for the chapter title and the breakdown of this verse below, except there I change its "above" to "beyond," due to my own chafing at the use of "above" and "under" as descriptors of quantity rather than spatial relationships. (My apologies to those who wasted their time reading this footnote.)

[12] Foulkes, *Ephesians*, 107.

[13] Morris, *Ephesians*, 108. Carson, *Praying with Paul*, 179 succinctly says, "To an omnipotent God, there cannot be degrees of difficulty."

[14] Both Stott, *The Message of Ephesians*, 139–140 and Lincoln, *Ephesians*, 216 break down the sentence in this way. The following draws from, but is a modification of, the former.

usual practice of not focusing too much on synonyms, slowing down in this case to see just how thoroughly Paul has amassed superlatives heightens the rhetorical impact.

God has the ability to *do*, itself a remarkable trait when compared with the gods known to the world who cannot even move themselves (Isa 45.20; 46.6–7; Jer 10.5). God can do *what we ask*, for He is not a deistic God, unconcerned with His creation, but a personal one who hears and answers prayer. God can do what we ask *or think*, because He not only hears our words but knows our thoughts. God can do *all* that we ask or think; He answers prayer "according to the riches of His glory," so there is nothing in our imagination that He cannot perform. God can do *beyond* all that we ask or think. His expectations are greater than ours and He is not limited to our imagination; the more we limit God to our imaginations, the feebler our prayers will be. He knows what we do not know and blesses in ways we frequently do not comprehend or even see in the moment. God can do *abundantly* beyond all that we ask or think, because He does not limit the grace and love He pours out upon His people. Finally, God can do *exceedingly* abundantly beyond all that we ask or think, for He is a God of super-abundance. The word Paul uses is a super-superlative he likely coined (cf. 1 Thes 3.10; 5.13) as his "rhetorical ability is stretched to a breaking point"[15] in his attempt to describe the grandeur of God. This prayer, coupling the knowledge-surpassing love of Christ and the imagination-surpassing ability of God,[16] is designed to awe the Christian at just how great God is—far beyond our comprehension, and yet desiring us to comprehend Him.

After all of this, Paul says what might be most shocking of all: this inexpressibly amazing power is already at work within us, which may refer to the transformation process of individual Christians or His empowering of the church for its work on the earth, or both.

Growth to spiritual maturity. Although this, like other Pauline prayers, focuses on knowledge and understanding, such intellectual achievements are never an end in themselves. In this case, the growth in knowledge is

---

[15] Lincoln, *Ephesians*, 216.
[16] deSilva, *Ephesians*, 186.

to be reflected in growth in maturity: strengthened in the inner being; Christ dwelling in your hearts; rooted and grounded in love; filled with all the fullness of God. There is an eminently practical element to this prayer, which is only fitting as Paul transitions to what it means to "walk in a manner worthy of the calling to which you have been called" (4.1). Along these lines, Carson says,

> We quickly learn that God is more interested in our holiness than in our comfort. He more greatly delights in the integrity and purity of his church than in the material well-being of its members. He shows himself more clearly to men and women who enjoy him and obey him than to men and women whose horizons revolve around good jobs, nice houses, and reasonable health. He is far more committed to building a corporate "temple" in which his Spirit dwells than he is in preserving our reputations. He is more vitally disposed to display his grace than to flatter our intelligence. He is more concerned for justice than for our ease. He is more deeply committed to stretching our faith than our popularity. He prefers that his people live in disciplined gratitude and holy joy rather than in pushy self-reliance and glitzy happiness. He wants us to pursue daily death, not self-fulfillment, for the latter leads to death, while the former leads to life.[17]

Gospel-shaped prayer. Our New Testament prayers have not as thoroughly emphasized the practice of praying God's promises as the Old Testament prayers did. Even so, this theme has been present, even if more subtle. Throughout his discussion of Paul's prayers, Millar sees them as "profoundly gospel shaped."[18] In this prayer, for example, he sees Paul praying that "God will supply us with strength in a way that is commensurate with the riches of his glory," concluding that such a request is "shaped by his understanding of what God has already done for us in the gospel."[19] Similarly, Carson says the essential values of the gospel that shaped Paul's praying must shape ours as well, concluding, "It is a wonderful comfort, a marvelous boost to faith, to know that you are

---

[17] Carson, *Praying with Paul*, 177.
[18] Millar, *Calling on the Name of the Lord*, 204.
[19] Ibid., 205.

praying in line with the declared will of almighty God."[20] I believe this understanding is correct, for Paul's whole life was shaped by and centered around the gospel of Jesus. His praying could not possibly veer from that course. A close examination of Paul's prayers—whether this one or any of the others considered in this book (or outside it)—will reflect the same truth: Paul's confessions, thanksgivings, petitions, and doxologies are built out of his understanding of the gospel; in other words, his prayers were rooted in God's promises.

Prayer for God's glory. Another element of prayer we have seen frequently and focused on less recently is praise of God. This facet of prayer cannot be missed in Ephesians 3, which concludes with one of the more remarkable doxologies in the New Testament. This desire should be central to all our praying, for seeking God's glory should be central to our lives. The more central this is to our praying, the less likely we will be to ask God for shallow, selfish, fleshly things, or to be deceived into praying for good things for selfish reasons, "thinking of God's will primarily in terms of its immediate effect on ourselves, still longing for blessings simply so that we will be blessed."[21]

---

[20] Carson, *Praying with Paul*, 177.
[21] Ibid., 180.

THIRTY-FOUR

Pure and Blameless for the Day of Christ

Philippians 1.9–11

The God to whom we pray is a God who desires that we make spiritual progress in our lives. Greater still, He is a God who will help us make spiritual progress. He has the ability to transform suffering into growth (Jas 1.2–4; 1 Pet 1.6–7) and His word is transformative, for it can bring everything into existence out of nothing and replace death with life. Further, this transformative word is enduring and a living tool for His purposes, which equips the believer for every good work (1 Pet 1.22–25; Heb 4.12–13; 2 Tim 3.16–17). In these and other ways, Christians make progress throughout their lives until God, on the Last Day, perfects them.

Context

Paul's letter to the Philippians was written near the end of his first imprisonment in Rome, the house arrest recorded at the end of Acts.[1] He anticipates a positive result of his trial (1.24–26; cf. Phlm 22), but it has been a difficult four years for him: two years in a Caesarean prison on charges of which he was innocent, including two attempts on his life while the

---

[1] For a defense of the Roman provenance of Philippians, see Ward, "Philippians," 275–280. The full essay (272–287) provides a variety of other introductory material.

Roman leaders used him to score political points, followed by a shipwreck and two years awaiting his trial in Rome (Acts 21.27–28.31). This letter to the Philippians, known so well for its positive outlook and focus on rejoicing, was written in a very difficult situation.

As many of Paul's letters do, it begins with an expression of thanksgiving for the church, which shifts seamlessly over into his prayer for them. His thankfulness for them is expressed in prayer (1.3–4), and notice how thorough this is: "…in *all* my remembrance of you, *always* in *every* prayer of mine for you *all*."[2] He is certain that the good that God began in them will be brought to completion (v 6). Perhaps Paul feels like they might see his praise as excessive, because he immediately defends it: "It is right for me to feel this way" (v 7). In particular, Paul praises their partnership with him in the gospel, something they had long participated in (Phil 4.15–17), something for which he also praises them to the Corinthians (2 Cor 8.1–5), and something that continues to be evident in the gift they sent by the hand of Epaphroditus (Phil 4.18). Paul sees this partnership as evidence of their love and commitment to God and His gospel. And so, out of his great thanksgiving and affection for them, Paul prays,

> And it is my prayer that your love may abound more and more, with knowledge and all discernment, so that you may approve what is excellent, and so be pure and blameless for the day of Christ, filled with the fruit of righteousness that comes through Jesus Christ, to the glory and praise of God. (Phil 1.9–11)

Contents

Although the prayer is brief, it is one relatively-long sentence (in Greek) that builds clause by clause to its logical end. Fee offers the following basic structure:

---

[2] "You all" is not the American South's second person plural, but the second person plural "you" followed by another occurrence of a word indicating completeness.

Paul prays (1) for their love to abound yet more and more;
　　that (2) this be accompanied by full knowledge and moral insight,
　　　　so that (3) they might approve those things that really matter,
　　　　　　so that (4) they might be unsullied and blameless when Christ returns,
　　　　　　　　as (5) they are now full of the fruit of righteousness,
　　　　　　　　　　fruit that is (6) effected by Christ Jesus
　　　　　　　　　　　　and (7) for the glory and praise of God.

He concludes, "Items 1, 2, 3, and 5 thus give the *what* of his prayer for them; item 4 gives the *why*, while item 6 offers the *means* to the (ultimate) *end* expressed in item 7."[3]

Similarly, Chester organizes it as follows:[4]

	I pray
request:	for love informed by the gospel
purpose:	so that you can discern what is best
	so that you may be pure and blameless = fruitful
	so that God may be glorified

The difference between the two approaches is minor: what Fee divides out into *why*, *means*, and *end*, Chester sees cumulatively as *purpose*. For both, the fundamental request is love and everything else builds from that.

The request for love is not due to a lack of it on the Philippians' part. As he has already indicated, they do have love, have shown it in the past, and continue to show it in the present.[5] Even so, as with the Thessalonians, Paul is not satisfied with the status quo and expects their love to continue to grow. Interestingly, there is no object attached to the verb. Paul does not specify love for God or for one another or any other possible object. This may be a deliberate ambiguity, as Paul has no intention of limiting love in any way,[6] or it may reflect the fact that all loves overlap: growing love for God necessarily manifests itself in love for

---

[3] Fee, *Philippians*, 96.
[4] Chester, *The Message of Prayer*, 195.
[5] Though some see 2.1–4 and 4.2–3 as possible evidence that there is some problem with love in the group.
[6] Carson, *Basics for Believers*, 20.

others; growing love for others apart from loving God is an empty shell of pseudo-love. Whatever the case, a "mawkish sentimentality"[7] cannot be what Paul has in mind, because his prayer is for a love that increases in knowledge and discernment. Love must be accompanied by wisdom, for love alone can be directed toward the wrong objects or treat proper objects in inappropriate ways.[8] And, of course, knowledge without love is equally flawed (1 Cor 8.1). Silva says, "The apostle cares not for any (false) knowledge that fails to issue in love. But it is just as important to reflect that Paul does not view love as mindless."[9] Another way of putting it is to emphasize that Paul does not pray for a growth in more love *and* more knowledge, but more love of a certain kind: love informed by knowledge and insight.[10]

The point of this growth is to know what is best, and in so knowing, to be blameless and pure for the day of Christ, being filled with the fruit of righteousness. Again, there is an organic connection here. By having the discernment to love as one ought to love, one can know what is best. The one filled with love who knows what is best will inevitably strive to do what is best, which is evident in the fruit he or she bears.[11] This is the one who will be best prepared to meet Christ upon His arrival. To be clear, the point is not that Christians must achieve sinless perfection but that the growth envisioned in this prayer is the path all Christians must be on to be prepared to meet Christ, who will complete the work on that day. At the same time, it does seem that "Paul appears to be thinking of the present condition of his readers and not of some special transformation that will take place in the future. The idea is that whenever the day of Christ comes the readers will be ready for it rather than that the day itself will work some transformation in them."[12] Paul's confidence that God will

---

[7] Carson, *Praying with Paul*, 106.
[8] Marshall, *Philippians*, 16.
[9] Silva, *Philippians*, 50.
[10] Chester, *The Message of Prayer*, 195.
[11] Based on the use of "fruit of righteousness" in the LXX (Prov 3.9; 11.30; Amos 6.12), the phrase has an ethical meaning: the fruit that consists in right conduct.
[12] Marshall, *Philippians*, 17.

ultimately complete the work does not stop him from praying that the Philippians will be pure and blameless for that day.[13]

Finally, the prayer ends with a typical Pauline doxology: "to the glory and praise of God," the sort of statement that is so familiar it is easy to take for granted. Indeed, to categorize it "a typical Pauline doxology" betrays this very complacency, the sort Paul would never have had as he penned the words. Far from a throwaway closing, in Paul's mind this is the very essence of the prayer. In a sense, the fundamental request is not for the Philippians' growth, but for God's glory. As Chester says,

> We should perhaps invert our original analysis. This is not so much a request for love informed by the gospel from which certain results flow. Paul's central request is that God will be glorified, which occurs as the Philippians are pure and blameless, filled with the fruit of righteousness. And that in turn occurs as they grow in love and knowledge, able to approve what is best.[14]

Connections

Prayer for the glory of God. To continue the thought immediately above this, if it is true that the chief end of man is to glorify God, then all sound prayer should reflect this same truth. If so, we must allow this to shape all our praying. This is not to say that we should never appeal to God with our own concerns, for we have seen many prayers so focused already. Rather, our concerns should not merely be submitted to His will, but also shaped around our concern for His glory. As Silva says, "By making the first petition the hallowing of God's name, our Lord taught us to place every other request within the framework of our desire to glorify God."[15] Certainly, in the context of this prayer, our concern for growth should not be about *our growth*, but about Him being glorified through it.

Prayer for the will of God. Although there is no overt reference to God's will, no citing of God's character, and no quoting of God's promises, this

---

[13] Chester, *The Message of Prayer*, 198.
[14] Ibid., 199.
[15] Silva, *Philippians*, 49.

prayer remains firmly fixed in the pattern we have seen throughout this book. This time, however, we find it in the context that leads up to the prayer. God has begun a good work in the Philippians and will bring it to completion (v 6), a foundation upon which Paul stands when he prays that they abound in discerning love and blameless purity, bearing the fruit of righteousness. They will be prepared to meet Christ not only because of their own work, but because of God's work in them (cf. 2.12–13). In other words, "His prayer is doing nothing more than asking God to do that to which he is already committed."[16] Or, as Motyer puts it, "Every other ethical system calls us to the costly effort of becoming what we are *not*. But in the full salvation already bequeathed to us in Christ, the new nature is already ours, waiting for expression, poised in growth, until its full potential is triggered by our obedience to the word of God."[17] Throughout the letter, Paul joins together their free choice and God's working in them.[18]

The connection between love, knowledge, and behavior. As the prayer builds from love to discerning love to discernment to purity, there is a natural connection throughout. Barclay says,

> Love is always the way to knowledge. If we love any subject, we want to learn more and more about it; if we love any person, we want to learn more and more about him or her; if we love Jesus, we will want every day to learn more and more about Him and about His truth. Love is always sensitive to the mind and the heart of the one it loves.[19]

He goes on to say that this makes us increasingly sensitive to His will and tender in our consciences, so that we will shrink from the evil and desire the good. "Real love," Barclay says, "leads to knowledge and obedience increasing every day."[20]

Living with a view of eternity. This idea is seen in different ways at different times throughout Scripture. In 2 Corinthians, it is looking not

---

[16] Millar, *Calling on the Name of the Lord*, 206.
[17] Motyer, *The Message of Philippians*, 55.
[18] Garland, "Philippians," 196.
[19] Barclay, *Philippians, Colossians, Thessalonians*, 22–23.
[20] Ibid., 23.

to the things that are seen but the things that are unseen as a defining principle of Christian living. In Hebrews, the faithful looked to a better country as the homeland they were seeking. In this prayer, we live in light of the day of Christ. As Carson puts it:

> The church is to see itself as an outpost of heaven. It is a microcosm of the new heaven and the new earth, brought back, as it were, into our temporal sphere. We are still contaminated by failures, sin, relapses, rebellion, self-centeredness; we are not yet what we ought to be. But by the grace of God, we are not what we were. For as long as we are left here, we are to struggle against sin and anticipate, so far as we are able, what it will be like to live in the untarnished bliss of perfect righteousness. We are to live with a view to the day of Christ.[21]

If this is indeed how we are to live, then this also must be how we are to pray: with a view to the day of Christ.

---

[21] Carson, *Praying with Paul*, 115.

THIRTY-FIVE

Knowledge to Walk Worthy

Colossians 1.9–14

The God to whom we pray is a God of wisdom. Wisdom, the Bible repeatedly teaches, comes from God alone, and any wisdom not from Him is not truly wisdom at all. As a result, His will is always wise. The believer, then, should seek after both God's wisdom and His will to be done. Or, as Paul prays here, for "knowledge of his will in all spiritual wisdom and understanding."

Context

Paul's letter to the Colossians was written in response to a false teaching that was spreading through the region and threatening the church at Colossae. Although the exact nature of the false teaching cannot be known with certainty,[1] it was rooted in a philosophy of some kind (2.8) and presented a false-appearance of wisdom (2.23). These connections to the prayer—as well as Paul's tendency to introduce items in the openings of his letters that become key points later—suggest that the prayer "has an eye on the alternative teaching being offered."[2]

In addition, Paul points to an immediate context by saying "for this reason" ("and so," ESV) to open the prayer. This points back to verses 3–8,

---

[1] For a discussion of the basic options, see Ward, "Colossians," 299–304. The full essay (288–306) provides a variety of other introductory material.

[2] Lincoln, "Colossians," 592.

which elaborate on Paul's thanksgiving for the Colossians when he prays for them, namely the faith, hope, and love evident in their lives since their salvation. The Colossian church—though presently assaulted by false teaching—was doing well. And yet Paul was not satisfied with the status quo and prayed that, in light of their present success, they grow in continued success—and, by implication, avoid those falsehoods that would lead to failure and disaster. This connection is heightened by several verbal parallels between the thanksgiving and prayer, reminding the Colossians that they must continue on the path they have begun.[3]

Finally, the framing around this prayer is an important context. In addition to "for this reason," which points back to the gospel's effect in their lives, Paul picks up with a gospel focus as soon as the prayer is concluded: redemption and forgiveness through Jesus detailed in verses 13–14.[4] Although I have not used this terminology frequently in this book, Paul's prayers are consistently gospel-focused.[5] This prayer is no different, indicating clearly what Paul finds most important in his prayers for churches. Further, a focus on what God has already accomplished in them can give Paul confidence in what else God will be able to do.[6]

> And so, from the day we heard, we have not ceased to pray for you, asking that you may be filled with the knowledge of his will in all spiritual wisdom and understanding, so as to walk in a manner worthy of the Lord, fully pleasing to him: bearing fruit in every good work and increasing in the knowledge of God; being strengthened with all power, according to his glorious might, for all endurance and patience with joy; giving thanks to the Father, who has qualified you to share in the inheritance of the saints in light. (Col 1.9–12)

---

[3] Moo, *Colossians and Philemon*, 92. See there for a listing of the parallels.

[4] Pao, *Colossians*, 78–79.

[5] Millar, *Calling on the Name of the Lord*, 201–216. See the subsection "Prayer for the Will of God" in chapter 34 for one place we touch on the idea.

[6] Wright, *Colossians and Philemon*, 60.

Contents

The layout of the prayer is relatively simple: in this single Greek sentence, there is one petition elaborated on by one reason, which will result in four different behaviors.

Paul's petition is that the Colossians be filled with the knowledge of God's will in all spiritual wisdom and understanding. Although these words are undoubtedly related to the false teaching infiltrating the area, it is probably best to understand them against their Old Testament background, where wisdom is rooted in the fear of Yahweh (Job 28.28; Ps 111.10; Prov 1.7; 9.10; Ecc 12.13) and is practical in its effect.[7] The nature of the wisdom Paul prays for is "spiritual," which indicates a wisdom that is God-centered rather than a human-derived, fleshly philosophy.[8] Since the Old Testament presents wisdom as coming from God's Spirit (cf. Exod 31.3; 35.31; Isa 11.2) and Paul also connects God's wisdom and His Spirit (1 Cor 2.6–13), it may also mean that it is wisdom received from/by means of the Spirit. Paul does not pray that the Colossians would merely have some wisdom, but that they would be "filled with" it, "a term used in number of locations in Colossians and Ephesians for the redemption now unleashed in the fullness himself, Christ."[9]

Paul asks for this so they may live in a manner worthy of the Lord, fully pleasing to Him. This is a key difference between what Paul prays for and what the heretics seduce the Colossians with. The spiritual wisdom of God can transform behavior, but the fleshly philosophy of man cannot (2.23).[10] Interestingly, the idea of service worthy of a deity was prominent in the region. Again, this would make the point even clearer

---

[7] Wright, *Colossians and Philemon*, 62; Beale, *Colossians and Philemon*, 55–57; Thompson, *Colossians and Philemon*, 23. Witherington, *Philemon, Colossians, Ephesians*, 124 also sees significance in Aristotle marking wisdom and understanding "the highest level of generally recognized civic virtue."

[8] Bird, *Colossians and Philemon*, 42. Colossians 2.18 describes the false teaching as coming from a "sensuous" mind, the same word frequently translated with the English "flesh" and seen as antithetical to a spiritual life. Interestingly, "spiritual" as defined in contemporary western culture (being in touch with one's inner voice or some such thing) is precisely the *opposite* of Paul's point. Such spirituality, as Pao, *Colossians and Philippians*, 81 points out, is but an act of idolatry.

[9] McKnight, *Colossians*, 108. He cites Colossians 1.19, 25; 2.9–10; Ephesians 1.10, 23; 3.19; 4.10, 13; Philippians 1.11; 4.18–19.

[10] Bird, *Colossians and Philemon*, 42.

to the original audience: if pagans understood the importance of giving worthy worship to false gods who cannot actually accomplish anything in the lives of their adherents, how "much more should Christians render the spiritual service of obedient lives to the living and true God and to his Son Jesus Christ."[11]

Such a well-pleasing life is described with four participial phrases that give a brief picture of the result of a knowledge-filled, worthily-lived life. First, it is bearing fruit in every good work. Theologians through the centuries have spilled far too much ink arguing about faith and works when it is abundantly clear that the New Testament embraces both. Indeed a life pleasing to God is a life that bears fruit in the very works for which it was recreated (cf. Eph 2.10).

Second, it is growing in the knowledge of God. This is not a thoughtless retread of the original petition, but an indication that knowledge begets knowledge. As Garland says, "Sin becomes a vicious cycle as it plunges us deeper and deeper into degradation. Knowledge of God becomes a virtuous cycle as it leads us deeper and deeper into fulfilling God's sovereign purposes."[12]

Third, it is being strengthened to display endurance and patience. Although there is no subject specified (who does the strengthening), the answer seems clear enough: the use of a passive in a prayer to God that the Colossians would be strengthened indicates He is the one empowering them. Further, that the text piles up synonyms for power, strength, and might—sometimes obscured in translation[13]—points toward God being the source of the power.

God's power is frequently thought of in terms of Old Testament pyrotechnics, New Testament miracles, or (as Paul would have it) the resurrection, ascension, and enthronement of Jesus (Eph 1.19–23). But its demonstration in believers here is in great patience and endurance—

---

[11] Bruce, *Colossians, Philemon, Ephesians*, 47.

[12] Garland, *Colossians and Philemon*, 73. See Carson, *Praying with Paul*, 87.

[13] Thompson, *Colossians and Philemon*, 25 gives the following as a more literal translation: "being empowered by the power of the might of God's glory."

matters which require God's divine empowering to master. But far from God's empowering being a reason for believers to sit back and do nothing, Christians should be motivated to obey God *precisely because* He has provided the power for them to do so.[14]

Finally, it is giving thanks joyfully to the Father. Paul thanks the One who has qualified them to share in the inheritance of the saints (contrast 2.18). This verse, along with verses 13–14, picks up several Exodus themes and terms and applies them to God's continuing work through Jesus.[15] God is redoing what He once did before, only this time it is an even greater redemption to an ever-greater inheritance. If it is true that the fundamental sin, leading to all other sin, is the failure to recognize God as God and give thanks (Rom 1.21), then it would seem that the fundamental Christian virtue is to be thankful: "When it comes to life, the critical thing is whether you take things for granted or take them with gratitude."[16]

Connections

Ongoing prayer. Paul begins this prayer by saying, "We have not ceased to pray for you." Although there was a growing threat of false teaching—and this prayer is not ignorant of it—this prayer predates it. Its purpose is not the crisis, but "preventative maintenance." It is what Paul previously prayed for regarding the Colossians, what he currently prays for on their behalf, and what he will likely continue to pray. As a result, it provides an exemplary model of the sorts of ongoing concerns Christians the world over should have. Further, it is a reminder that we should not wait until the time of crisis to begin prayer—though, admittedly, all who endure crises will surely intensify their praying in such seasons. As Lewis said to a correspondent, "I specially need your prayers because I am (like the pilgrim in Bunyan) traveling across 'a plain called Ease.' Everything without and many things within are marvelously well at present."[17]

---

[14] Beale, *Colossians and Philemon*, 61.
[15] See Bird, *Colossians and Philemon*, 43–44; Wright, *Colossians and Philemon*, 64–67 for brief discussions of this theme.
[16] Chesterton, *Irish Impressions*, 24.
[17] C.S. Lewis, *Letters of C.S. Lewis*, 232.

Praying for the will of God. The petition in this prayer is for them to know God's will, an idea that is often misunderstood in contemporary culture. Chester makes this point well, saying,

> In the Bible the will of God is not a specific plan for my life—whom I should marry, what job I should do, where I should live. The will of God is the way of life that pleases God. Indeed God's will describes not only how he wants us to live, but 'an understanding of God's whole saving purpose in Christ.' It is knowledge of God himself, of his character and of his saving purposes (see Eph 1.3–14). You may want to know who to marry, but God is more concerned that you be a good husband or wife. You may want to know where to work, but God is more concerned about the type of employee you are.[18]

Carson says it is not intrinsically bad to seek God's will in specific ways, for "there are many ways in which the Lord does lead us and we should not despise them," but the issue is one of focus: "Nevertheless this focus is often quite misleading, perhaps even dangerous, for it encourages me to think of 'the Lord's will' primarily in terms of my future, my vocation, my needs—and that is often another form of self-centeredness, no matter how piously put."[19] Alternately, it is too easy to fall into patterns of seeking God's will in ways not too dissimilar from how pagans sought the will of their gods,[20] flipping through pages in the Bible to find a meaningful verse as if the Bible were a Ouija board.[21] In context, *doing* God's will is virtually synonymous with obedience.[22] Further, *knowing* God's will is quite simple: it is the result of a deep, abiding relationship that is centered on making God's priorities one's own. As a wife knows her husband's wishes by knowing him, so also it is "this kind of knowledge for which

---

[18] Chester, *The Message of Prayer*, 200–201. The internal quote is of Wright, *Colossians and Philemon*, 57.

[19] Carson, *Praying with Paul*, 81. Chester, too, acknowledges this: "We can pray for *anything*. But we should pray for such things with biblical priorities" (204).

[20] Waltke, *Finding the Will of God*, 11–12. See also the comments in chapter 2 on seeking God's will.

[21] Garland, *Colossians and Philemon*, 75.

[22] Carson, *Praying with Paul*, 81.

Paul prays: that we might know God through the gospel so that we can discern His will in different situations."[23]

Wisdom. In the Old Testament, wisdom frequently has a practical element to it. The difference, in this context, would be between knowing Biblical truth and practicing it. As Barclay says, this prayer asks that the Colossians be able to apply the great truths of Christianity "to the tasks and decisions which meet them in every day living." He continues, "A man can quite easily be a master of theology and a failure in living. He may be able to write and talk about the great eternal truths, and yet be quite helpless to apply these truths to the things which meet him every day."[24] Paul realizes that what Christians need most "is to grow in the knowledge that will govern their faith and decisions."[25]

Praying outside our circles. Perhaps the most amazing thing about this prayer and its ongoing nature is that Paul had never met the Colossian Christians (Col 2.1). It is not surprising that he prays with fervor for groups like the Thessalonians, a church that he planted and that had been enduring trials from the very beginning. But the intensity and regularity with which Paul prays for a group he had never seen goes beyond the experience of most Christians I know. We pray regularly for those within our world and occasionally for those outside it, if a third party happens to tell us of some momentary need. No doubt, our primary focus is naturally (and should naturally be) those we are closest to, but Paul shows prayer that regularly reaches beyond such limitations. Carson, again, provides a thoughtful comment on the matter:

> Our prayers may be an index of how small and self-centered our world is. Of course, we cannot pray for all believers everywhere, except in the most general ways. But it will do us good to fasten on reports of Christians in several parts of the world we have never visited, find out what we can about them, and learn to intercede with God on their behalf. Not only is this an important expression of the fellowship of the church, but

---

[23] Chester, *The Message of Prayer*, 201.
[24] Barclay, *Philippians, Colossians, Thessalonians*, 130.
[25] Garland, *Colossians and Philemon*, 72.

it is also a critical discipline that will enlarge our horizons, increase our ministry, and help us to become world Christians.[26]

---

[26] Carson, *Praying with Paul*, 77–78.

THIRTY-SIX

Conclusions

My prayer in writing this book is that it will help you see how much there is to learn from the prayers of the Bible. To be sure, the Bible says more about prayer than just the examples of praying we have discussed,[1] but my own experience is that we narrowly focus on those texts and only rarely talk about the Biblical examples of prayer. From the first time I taught a class on this until the present day, I have seen firsthand how studying the prayers has positively impacted students of the Bible. I have no doubt that we can learn to pray better by seeing how the faithful men and women of history have prayed. In an effort to draw this book to a close, I want to try to systematize some of the key ideas we have seen in our journey.

Types of Prayer

Not every Biblical prayer is the same, which is helpful as the variety of prayers we encounter show us the faithful praying in different contexts for different things. This makes their examples practical to our lives by touching on so many different concerns. In our study, we have seen prayers of intercession (both for those inside the community and those outside), requests for guidance, open lament, imprecation, prayers seeking wisdom (both to rule a kingdom and to know God's will), prayers that are explicitly paradigmatic, and other prayers that may not be quite so easy to designate.[2]

---

[1] See Appendix C for a very brief discussion of some of those key texts.

[2] For a helpful overview of a variety of Biblical prayer types, see Block, *For the Glory of God*, 197–217.

If there is a common thread to Biblical prayers, it is their focus: the prayers recorded in Scripture laser in on a certain idea, rather than being a shotgun blast of every possible concern.

I must admit that most of my praying tends to be more broadly focused. Of course, such prayer isn't wrong, and at times may be exactly what we should be doing. Further, the laser-like focus of Biblical prayer is due to their praying in specific moments for a specific situation that has arisen. But if my prayers are always general and their prayers are specific, it raises a particularly uncomfortable question: do I not pray enough in specific situations—or am I instead trusting myself to get past the obstacles in my path and congratulating myself for the blessings that come my way? To pray like the faithful in Scripture is to pray as constantly as moments demanding prayer arise.

Principles about Prayer

Even though not every Biblical prayer is the same as every other, and they frequently arose in drastically different circumstances, we repeatedly saw the same major themes. At first blush, this may seem remarkable, but after reflection on the themes themselves, it is inevitable—and most certainly instructive. You may add to or modify this list for your own purposes, of course, but here are five ideas I find to be particularly helpful.

Praying the promises. This theme absolutely dominates Old Testament prayer. The faithful who approached God did so on the basis of His promises, His character, and His covenant. They asked God to give what He already promised He would. They asked Him to give because of who He is, fundamentally and unchangeably. They asked God to give because of the special relationship He had initiated between Himself and them, whether nationally or individually. Their requests were not founded upon a momentary whim or desire, but upon God's own revelation of His will. The one who seeks to pray according to God's will can find no better starting place than God's promises. Look again at the epigraph of this book and read the quotes I selected for that space. Calvin, Kaiser, and Carson say it so well.

Praise and humility. Although not every Biblical prayer follows an exact pattern of organization, a high percentage begin with praise of God and humbling of self. In other words, the one who prays seeks to properly orient himself, expressing his own understanding of the identity of the God to whom he prays and, by contrast, his own frailty. This, too, is vital to praying according to God's will. The more we forget who God is, the more we will seek—even if subconsciously and unintentionally—to accomplish our will in prayer. The more we forget who we are in relationship to God, the more we will try to use God as a means to our end. If instead we find time in prayer to honestly acknowledge both His identity and ours, we will inevitably find our desires properly prioritized.

Depth of relationship. Who is the person you have the better relationship with: the one you always put on a smile for or the one who has seen you at your absolute worst, the one you share small talk with or the one you pour your heart out to? The answer is so obvious that asking the question seems absurd. Far from an unapproachable God, the Bible shows us a God we can bring anything to. The faithful in the Bible allow God to see themselves at their worst and pour their hearts out to him in language that can make us uncomfortable. If, however, we are uncomfortable with the idea of being honest with God, that too speaks volumes about our relationship with Him—whether our lack of trust in His love for us, our lack of understanding that He already knows what we are thinking, or something else. Biblical prayer is rooted in relationship—real relationship—with a God who cares.

Trust in God's ability and goodness. There is a word in the Old Testament that combines the ideas of praying according to the promises and praying with a focus on the depth of relationship. Most translations render it as "lovingkindness" or "mercy," but no single English word can do justice to it. It is love and mercy, but it is also brings with it the idea of unwavering loyalty to a covenant commitment. In an attempt to capture all of that, I have consistently rendered it "steadfast, merciful, covenant love and faithfulness." The faithful repeatedly take their stand on this very trait, which indicates their trust in God: trust He is there; trust He hears and cares; and trust He can and will act decisively in their lives. It is universally held that a key to a successful relationship is trust, so it should be no surprise that the faithful who called upon the Lord trusted in Him.

Spiritual before physical. Physical needs are a real and legitimate concern for Christians, and the Bible does show faithful men and women praying about physical concerns. Further, passages urging us to pray do not exclude the physical (e.g., Phil 4.6; 1 Pet 5.7). Even so, it is noteworthy that Paul's prayers for the churches focus almost entirely on their spiritual needs. This is not surprising, given Paul's perspective regarding the physical and spiritual worlds:

> So we do not lose heart. Though our outer self is wasting away, our inner self is being renewed day by day. For this light momentary affliction is preparing for us an eternal weight of glory beyond all comparison, as we look not to the things that are seen but to the things that are unseen. For the things that are seen are transient, but the things that are unseen are eternal. (2 Cor 4.16–18)

This viewpoint is not an easy one to master, as we sensually experience the physical world, while the spiritual is entirely a matter of faith. As a result it is easy—and quite natural—to become spiritually nearsighted, focusing entirely on physical needs and problems and forgetting those things that are spiritual. Consider what Carson says on the matter:

> [W]e must ask ourselves how far the petitions we commonly present to God are in line with what Paul prays for. Suppose, for example, that 80 or 90 percent of our petitions ask God for good health, recovery from illness, safety on the road, a good job, success in exams, the emotional needs of our children, success in our mortgage application, and much more of the same. How much of Paul's praying revolves around equivalent items? If the center of our praying is far removed from the center of Paul's praying, then even our very praying may serve as a wretched testimony to the remarkable success of the processes of paganization in our life and thought.[3]

---

[3] Carson, *Praying with Paul*, 76–77.

Carson's rhetoric at the end may be a little strong—though such a shock to the system may be exactly what we need—but the general idea is right. If it is true that the physical is destined to perish and the spiritual will endure eternally, there is no doubt what our primary concern should be. A disproportionate focus on things that do not ultimately matter reveals much about either our understanding or our faith and will further dull our spiritual perception. As Inge says, "It is quite natural and inevitable that, if we spend sixteen hours daily of our waking lives in thinking about the affairs of the world and five minutes in thinking about God and our souls, this world will seem two hundred times more real to us than God."[4]

One way we can keep the physical from dominating our prayers is to allow those concerns to be a bridge to the spiritual. Consider the following three examples. First, it is good and proper to be concerned about and pray for those who are sick. There is, however, an even greater and more prevalent illness on the spiritual level that we should be even more concerned about. Our prayer for sickness should lead to even more prayer about sin.

Second, it is good and proper to be concerned about and pray for those who are traveling, as there are any number of dangers that such people face. There is, however, an even greater and more dangerous journey on the spiritual level that we should be even more concerned about. Life itself and the decisions we make—choosing the path of wisdom rather than folly (cf. Prov 1–9; Matt 7.13–27)—brings with it countless spiritual dangers. Our prayer about loved ones' physical journeys should lead to even more prayer about our (and their) spiritual journeys.

Third, it is good and proper to pray for the government and peaceful times under it, because Paul commands this very thing (1 Tim 2.1–4). There is, however, an even greater kingdom we have been called to be a part of (Phil 1.27; 3.20)[5] that we should be even more concerned about. Our prayer about the government should lead to even more prayer about the Kingdom, manifest in concern for local congregations, Christians

---

[4] Inge, *Religion and Life*, 4–5.

[5] Philippians 1.27 uses a word that indicates citizenship in its appeal to a worthy life (BDAG, 846). See Ward, "Philippians," 284–286 for a brief discussion of Paul's citizenship theme in this letter.

around the world, the rule of God in the hearts of men and women who have not submitted to Him, and the return of Christ to establish the eternal kingdom in heaven.

The list could continue, but I hope this will suffice to make the point: allow your real and worthy physical concerns to bring you to see the spiritual corollary that should be an even greater concern. In short, there is a balance we must find between having physical concerns and not letting them dominate our lives, between praying about physical things and not letting that dominate our conversation with God. The more we can join with Paul in a view that sees this world as transient and the next as eternal, the more unnatural it will seem to be wholly overcome with anxiety about this life.

Summation. Another way of expressing this is in terms of what the person who prays knows about God. Biblical prayer reveals believers who know who God is, know what God wants, know that God cares, and know that God reigns. The more these ideas undergird our prayer, the more biblically we will pray.

APPENDIX A

On Praying to Jesus

I do not know how widespread the view is among those who claim to follow Jesus, but I know some Christians believe we should not pray to Jesus. The position is often accompanied by what seems like reasonable logic, at least on a surface level. We ought not to pray to Jesus, it is said, because He is our mediator—and if He is our mediator, He cannot also be the object of our prayer. Likewise, we ought not to pray to Jesus because, when He taught His disciples how to pray (Matt 6.9–13; Luke 11.2–4), He prayed to the Father not to Himself. It is best, then, only to pray to the Father through Jesus the mediator.[1] On one level, this line of thinking makes some sense. But it doesn't hold up in the face of Scripture at large.

Jesus taught us to pray to Him. In John 14.14, Jesus encouraged the apostles to petition Him in His name. Someone might respond by pointing out the textual variant that omits "me" and say that it makes better sense to ask the Father in His name (as Jesus also teaches in John 15.16; 16.23–24). The problem with this is threefold. First, the textual evidence itself strongly supports "me" being included.[2] Second, even without the "me," Jesus is still clearly the one being asked ("If you ask … *I* will do it"). Finally, however odd it might seem to us to ask Him in His name, the idea of asking God in God's name is attested elsewhere

---

[1] This view dates at least back to Origen (cf. *Treatise on Prayer,* 15.1), whose view seems a bit inconsistent on the matter in his writings. For a summary, see Gorman, "Prayer," 424–425.

[2] See Metzger, *Textual Commentary,* 208 for information on the text critical issue.

in Scripture (cf. Ps 54.1; 1 Chron 16.8 [LXX]), so asking Jesus in Jesus' name is not nonsensical.[3]

Jesus' apostles prayed to Him. In Acts 1.24–25, the disciples pray to the Lord for revelation of whom He has chosen to be the twelfth apostle in Judas' stead. Although Jesus is not specifically named in the prayer, He is identified as the Lord twice in the chapter (vv 6, 21), including in the immediate context of the prayer. Likewise, the word Luke uses for "you have chosen" is the same word he earlier uses of Jesus choosing the original twelve (Luke 6.13). Their prayer to the Lord to show who He has chosen to be an apostle is most naturally read as a prayer to Jesus.[4]

Stephen prays to Jesus. In Acts 7.59–60, Stephen is being stoned and calls out to Jesus. Although the word "prayer" is not used here, he is calling out to his Deity at the moment of his death; if this is not prayer, I don't know what prayer is. Most significantly, he says two things here that parallel Jesus' prayer to the Father at His death, both of which Luke also records in his gospel. Stephen is clearly imitating Jesus' prayer to the Father and praying it to Jesus. This is either an act of blatant idolatry and blasphemy or it unequivocally shows that Jesus is the fitting recipient of Stephen's dying prayer, just as the Father was the fitting recipient of Jesus' dying prayer.[5]

Paul prays to Jesus. When Paul was afflicted by some sort of physical pain, he appealed to the Lord about it (2 Cor 12.8–10). Again, the Lord is not initially named, but it becomes clear that the Lord is Jesus by the response of the Lord and Paul's expression of confidence at the end: "my grace and power" given Paul by the Lord wind up being "the power of Christ."[6] Likewise, Paul's prayer in 1 Thessalonians 3 is to "our God and Father himself, and our Lord Jesus" (v 11) with the next statement being to the Lord [Jesus] alone (v 12). This prayer is not to the Father *through* the son, but jointly to the Father *and* the Son (cf. 2 Thes 2.16–17).[7]

---

[3] See Carson, *The Gospel According to John*, 496–498 for a discussion of this text.
[4] See Bruce, *Commentary on the Book of Acts*, 51–52 for a discussion of this text.
[5] See Ibid., 170–173 for a discussion of this text.
[6] See Garland, *2 Corinthians*, 507–527 for a discussion of this text.
[7] Bruce, *1 & 2 Thessalonians*, 74 argues (correctly, I believe) that this prayer being in the third person and not in the vocative case does not make it any less a prayer, for "there is no difference in

Finally, Paul says he thanks Jesus in prayer (1 Tim 1.12) and prays to Jesus for His return (1 Cor 16.22).

John prays to Jesus. John continues the practice of praying to Jesus at the end of the final book of the New Testament. His prayer is simple, but that does not thereby render it less of a prayer. Like Paul in 1 Corinthians 16, John prays for the Lord's return (Rev 22.20). Second, although in symbolic terms, John describes prayer to Jesus in this book. In an early scene, "golden bowls full of incense, which are the prayers of the saints" are brought before the Lamb (Rev 5.8).[8]

The Psalmist prays to Jesus. Psalm 102 is indicated as a prayer in the historical superscription ("A Prayer of One Afflicted…") and begins with "Hear my prayer, O LORD," going on to speak of the Lord's creation of the universe. Not only does the New Testament clearly teach that Jesus was the agent of Creation, which would make the connection implicit (John 1.3; Col 1.16; Heb 1.2), but the author of Hebrews explicitly says Psalm 102 is about Jesus (Heb 1.10–12).[9]

Everyone prays to Yahweh. This instance of the Psalmist unwittingly praying to Christ segues to the fact that nearly every major prayer of the Old Testament is to the LORD (=Yahweh). As we have seen throughout this book, Moses, Hannah, David, Solomon, Jehoshaphat, Hezekiah, Habakkuk, Jeremiah, Daniel, Ezra, and more (including the Psalmists) pray to God by His revealed covenant name.

This is significant since the New Testament repeatedly applies Yahweh passages to Jesus. This happens in two ways. First, specific citations of Old Testament Scripture about Yahweh are applied to Jesus (e.g., Isa 40.3/Mark 1.3; Joel 2.32/Acts 2.21/Rom 10.13; Isa 6.1–10/John 12.40–41; Isa 44.6/Rev 1.8, 17; Zech 12.10/John 19.34/Rev 1.7; Ps 68.18/Eph 4.7–10; etc.). Second, clear allusions of what Yahweh does are applied to Jesus (the

---

principle between saying, 'O God our Father and our Lord Jesus, direct our way…' and saying, 'May God our father and our Lord Jesus direct our way.…'"There is debate as to whether the singular verb accompanying the two subjects is meaningful to this discussion or not. See Bruce for an argument that it is not and Beale, *1–2 Thessalonians*, 108–109 (footnote) for an argument that it is.

[8] See Beale, *The Book of Revelation*, 357–358 for a discussion of this text.

[9] See Bruce Waltke, et al., *The Psalms as Christian Lament*, 210–237 for a discussion of this text and McClister, *A Commentary on Hebrews*, 85–87 for the New Testament use of the Psalm.

one who "will give rest," "who is your life," "to whom salvation belongs," etc.). As if this is not enough, Paul asserts that every tongue will confess that Jesus is Lord. Given the Old Testament background of Philippians 2 (cf. Isa 45.22–25), Paul's point is not that people will confess Jesus is master, but that they will confess He is Yahweh.[10]

Although I have known Christians to take issue with praying to Jesus, I have never known one to complain about praying to Yahweh (or "Jehovah" or "the Lord"). Yet it is clear they are one and the same. My point is not to deny that the Father is also Yahweh God, but to emphasize that we divide God up far more than He divides Himself. In John, Jesus says in the same breath that another helper is coming *and* that He Himself is coming to the disciples (John 14.16–18). In Romans, Paul interchangeably speaks of the Spirit, the Spirit of God, and the Spirit of Christ (Rom 8.9–10; cf. 1 Cor 15.45; 2 Cor 3.17; Eph 3.16–17).[11] By contrast, we come dangerously close to being tri-theists rather than monotheists who believe in a triune God—and both Testaments repeatedly affirm that God is one.

Calling on the name of the Lord. Praying to Yahweh connects to the Old Testament passages that speak of calling on His name for salvation. True, the word "prayer" is not used, but again, if calling on a deity's name for salvation is not prayer, I do not know what prayer is. This is significant, because calling on the Lord's name is also applied to Jesus in the New Testament. After Paul's incident on the road to Damascus, Ananias receives a vision from Jesus instructing him to go teach Paul. Ananias refers to Christians as people who call on Jesus' name (Acts 9.14) and encourages Paul to do likewise (Acts 22.16). Indeed, Christians are fundamentally people who call on the name of the Lord Jesus for salvation (Rom 10.12–13; 1 Cor 1.2). In all cases, the Lord upon whom one calls is no other than Jesus.

---

[10] See Nathan Ward, "Philippians," 284–286 for a somewhat fuller exposition of the Paul's point in Philippians 2 and Bowman and Komoszewski, *Putting Jesus in His Place* for an excellent study of the deity of Jesus. See also, McClister, "Paul's View of Jesus Christ," 62–87.

[11] Lincoln, *Ephesians,* 206 says the Pauline view is, "…in believers' present experience there is no real difference between Christ and the Spirit. …Believers do not experience Christ except as Spirit and do not experience the Spirit except as Christ. … [G]reater experience of the Spirit's power will mean the character of Christ increasingly becoming the hallmark of believers' lives."

But what about the Model Prayer? So why, then, doesn't Jesus teach us to pray to Him? It is certainly true that Jesus teaches His disciples to pray to the Father, both in the Model Prayer and in the Farewell Discourse, but it is not true that Jesus does not teach us to pray to Him as well. Not only is it clear in His teaching (John 14.14, above), but in the Biblical record of the early church: praying to Jesus—whether seeking guidance, offering thanksgiving, making petitions, or appealing to Him for salvation, for His return, or in death—was a common part of the Christian life. Further, the earliest Christian records outside the Bible reflect a practice of praying to Jesus.[12]

The Model Prayer is not exhaustive in its scope as a model. That means, practically speaking, that it does not exclude everything not found therein. If the Model Prayer were an exhaustive model of all praying, it not only limits *to whom* we may pray, but also *about what* we may pray. In that case, we would not be able to pray for the sick, each other, our enemies, government officials, or offer any thanksgiving. Yet it is clear from the rest of Scripture that these are perfectly legitimate subjects of prayer (e.g., Jas 5.14, 16; 1 Thes 5.18; 1 Tim 2.1–2; Matt 5.44). Likewise, it is clear from the rest of the Bible that Jesus is a legitimate object of prayer.

But that doesn't apply to us. I have heard opponents of praying to Jesus cite a perceived special relationship the apostles had that allowed them such a conversation with Jesus that no longer applies to us, or a special circumstance the person found himself in that would negate it from being an example for us to follow. Even if it were admitted that there was something different about, say, Stephen's experience in death (since he saw the heavens opened and Jesus standing at God's right hand) or Paul's experience with this thorn in the flesh (because Jesus seems to answer him directly), those exceptions still only address a small fraction of the overwhelming Biblical evidence that supports praying to Jesus. If these were the only examples—if only Stephen and Paul prayed to Jesus only once each and only in special circumstances or only with a special

---

[12] See Gorman, "Prayer," 419–443 for a discussion of some of the early debates in the church about praying to Jesus.

response—such an argument might have some traction. But it fails to account for Paul's more general giving of thanks to Jesus, his prayer to the Father *and* the Lord Jesus, John's and Paul's prayers to Jesus for His return, the apostles' prayer for direction, and the general depiction of Christians as those who call on the Lord Jesus' name for salvation—not to mention the fundamental monotheistic worldview held by every Biblical author, and the Biblical equating of Jesus with Yahweh to whom all believers have always prayed.

Further, this argument against praying to Jesus becomes dangerous. It amounts to picking and choosing which apostolic models we should follow and which we can't even remotely think about following because the apostles were, after all, so incredibly unique. On what basis can we consistently draw such a line? This sort of reasoning frequently winds up mirroring our preconceptions: tossing out things we disagree with and keeping things we agree with.

So can we pray to the Holy Spirit, too? This question often arises in the discussion of this issue, but it is a red herring. It may well be an interesting topic to discuss on its own merits (or lack thereof), but it has no bearing whatsoever on what the Bible says about praying to Jesus. If the Bible says nothing at all on the topic of praying to the Spirit, that does not thereby negate the scriptures that do speak about praying to Jesus.

The need to acknowledge and thank God. A colleague of mine often points out the fundamental sin is the failure to honor God or give Him thanks, and all other sins spring forth from that most basic failing (Rom 1.20–21). With that in mind, is Jesus God or isn't He? If He is—and not just God, but Yahweh God who suffered with us to die for us—how can we not offer Him our endless thanks, starting in this life? With that, we have come to the crux of the matter: the question is not whether we can pray to Jesus, but whether we can afford not to.

APPENDIX B

On the Use of the Lord's Prayer

No prayer in the Bible may be more polarizing than the prayer Jesus gives as an example of how to pray.[1] Some have fully adopted it as an ongoing part of liturgy, where it is regularly quoted in worship assemblies. Some bring that practice into their private lives, quoting it as part of their daily practice of prayer. It is surely true that no prayer has been repeated more than this one, and frequently without understanding.[2]

On the other hand, some avoid the prayer altogether. Some do so to avoid the "vain repetitions" Jesus warned about in this very context. Some, similarly, see this prayer being used as a borderline-pagan magical incantation and want to avoid that at all costs. Some, reacting against dispensational premillennialism, object to the prayer for the kingdom to come, arguing that it has already come in the church, thereby rendering the prayer obsolete. Still others, although likely smaller in number, find problems with it not being "in Jesus' name" or even with calling it "the Lord's Prayer."

To pray or not to pray? Jesus did not intend His instruction to "pray *like* this" in Matthew 6 to be an exclusion of ever uttering the words of this prayer. Although praying the very words of the prayer is technically not praying *like* Jesus teaches—a simile must be different to be a simile—there is nothing inherently wrong with the words of the prayer

---

[1] See chapter 26 for our discussion of this prayer. This brief appendix cannot answer every issue that could possibly be raised, but I wanted to include some discussion on the matter.

[2] Carson, *The Sermon on the Mount*, 61. Carson cites the *Didache*, a second century Christian document that prescribed quoting this prayer three times a day.

Appendix B: On the Use of the Lord's Prayer | 289

themselves that would forbid us from using them. Indeed, in Luke's version, Jesus says, "Pray this" (Luke 11.2).[3]

The problem with praying this prayer is twofold, and both are admittedly variations of a slippery slope argument. There are, to be sure, slippery slope fallacies that must be avoided in argumentation, but there are also slippery slope realities that must be avoided in life. Sometimes the difference between the two is a thinner line than we might care to admit.

First, praying this prayer as an ongoing practice has the very real danger of becoming a meaningless mantra. Recitations of it can easily become thoughtlessly rote, and when done in large groups, it is virtually certain that at least some are giving no thought whatsoever to what they are saying.[4] Such practices pervert it into "the kind of mindless incantation which the Teacher so vehemently abhorred. There is no magic in repeating it, but there is power in understanding it."[5] Second, as hinted at in the second sentence of the above quote, some see it as almost mystical in some way: an incantation that God will readily hear and will result in some sort of blessing; a magic talisman that, if said enough, will win the favor of God. This not only demeans God as one who can be easily manipulated by us, it turns prayer into a means of us getting our way. This mindset is similar to one held by the early Israelites regarding the Ark of the Covenant (1 Sam 4.3), a view that was more like the pagan Philistines (1 Sam 4.7) than it was a true understanding of who God is or what the Ark represented. The Israelites were soundly defeated in their pagan ignorance, and we can hope for no better if we turn this prayer into something similar.

Pray like this, not ignore this prayer. The above problems have had the pendulum effect for many, who react to the religious world's misuse of

---

[3] McKnight, *Sermon on the Mount*, 188 argues from Luke's "Whenever you pray, say this" that it is meant to be recited at set prayer times. See Garland, *Luke,* 460 for an exposition of Luke that argues otherwise. Further, Luke uses the exact same Greek construction in 17.10, and no one has ever interpreted it to mean that we must utter those exact words or be careful to only say words *like* them. Thanks to Evan Blackmore for this final point.

[4] To be fair, improvised prayer is not immune from this problem. Many improvised prayers fall back into stock terminology and phrases that can be just as thoughtlessly rote as a scripted or memorized prayer, to say nothing of the use of "Lord" as a verbal pause.

[5] Earnhart, *Invitation to a Spiritual Revolution*, 93.

this prayer by avoiding it as much as possible. Whatever else we may think of this prayer, it is obvious that it is impossible to pray like Jesus instructs if we studiously ignore His prayer and never learn what it teaches. Unfortunately, reactionary theology like this is all too common throughout the history of Christianity, and this is only one of many examples of the error of overreaction.

In my own experience, objections like "it's not in Jesus' name" and "it can't be 'the Lord's Prayer' because it asks for forgiveness and He was sinless" are outliers. Regarding the former, this objection excludes virtually every prayer in the Bible from use. Perhaps even more significant is that is that it fails to understand that prayer in Jesus' name goes far beyond uttering that particular phrase, and that prayer can be in His name without ever uttering that phrase.[6] Regarding the latter, this objection fails to understand how language works, a problem that many seem to have when it is convenient. In normal conversation, we rarely object to accommodative language or figurative speech of one type or another, but those same rules seem to fly out the window when talking about religious matters and a new set of rules apply (though only when it suits us to invoke those rules). Regarding the objection to its traditional designation, it is called "The Lord's Prayer" because that what folks have called it for centuries. Choosing to use that established title as a designation does not necessarily mean that one brings with it all the baggage that someone else has imposed on the title.

More significant, perhaps, is the objection about the kingdom. Although I am not premillennial, either dispensational or otherwise, I do not find this objection compelling either. First, this matter is resolved by the meaning of the word itself, which most basically refers to reign or rule, kingly authority rather than the institution of a kingdom, complete with territorial boundaries and subjects. Thus, the prayer is for God's rule to expand on the earth, which is an ongoing need. Second, as it could possibly relate to the kingdom in some organizational sense, there is the matter of inaugurated eschatology, the technical term for what is sometimes called

---

[6] See also Crozier, *Plugged In,* 135–138.

the "already but not yet" nature of God's promises.[7] God's kingdom has come, but it has not yet come as fully as it will.[8] Even the church as a manifestation of the kingdom is not present everywhere in the world, and God is certainly not enthroned as king over every human heart. To say that we need not pray for God's kingdom to come is short-sighted, to say the least.

Pray like this—how? The instruction to "pray like this" clearly indicates that this prayer is, in some sense, to be normative. But in what sense should it be normative? It cannot be length or specific content alone, because the Bible contains many longer prayers and many examples of people praying for things not listed in this prayer. Likewise, the order of items in the prayer cannot be the focus, as many other prayers emphasize different things at different points. These preliminary points tell us we are looking in the wrong place, either because we have selected the wrong things to consider as normative or because the normative nature of the prayer is not meant to focus on the mechanical nuances of praying.

It is important to remember that this prayer does not occur in a vacuum. Jesus says, "Don't pray like this, but pray like this." In other words, "pray like this" is not a hard and fast rule for all prayer of all time, but intended to set off a proper kind of prayer with two examples of improper kinds of prayer. The fact that other proper prayers in the Bible do not fit the precise pattern or verbiage of this prayer seems to support that conclusion. This prayer is a model of how to pray that avoids the pitfalls of self-aggrandizing hypocritical prayer and ignorant pagan prayer, praying instead as a citizen of God's kingdom.

---

[7] Wright, "The Lord's Prayer," 135 says, "Where the leader, God's chosen one, was present, the kingdom was already present. But there was, of course still work to be done, redemption to be won. The present and the future did not cancel one another out, as in some unthinking scholarly constructions. Nor did 'present' mean 'a private religious experience' and 'future' mean 'a Star Wars-type apocalyptic scenario.'"

[8] The notion that the kingdom and church are interchangeable is also mistaken. The church is the present, earthly manifestation of the kingdom, but it is not the fullness of what it will one day be revealed to be (cf. Acts 14.22; 2 Tim 4.1; 2 Pet 1.11).

APPENDIX C

Some Important Prayer Passages

The purpose of this book has been to study prayers themselves rather than texts that discuss principles about prayer. Even so, it only seems right to include a brief discussion of some of the key passages about prayer. This appendix, though far from exhaustive, will aim to accomplish that purpose by considering a handful of these verses.

The Example of Jesus

In addition to verses that give commands to pray or elaborate on why we should pray, the gospels consistently depict Jesus as a praying person. Indeed, Jesus prays more than any other character in the Bible. As many before have said, if Jesus—who of all people may have needed prayer the least—shows a recognition of His own need to pray and reflects a constant desire to pray, how much more do we need to make it a part of our daily practice?

The ways and times that Jesus prays are also instructive. He prays when He is in need, such as when He is about to make an important decision, praying at great length (Luke 6.12–13). And He prays for others when they are in need, such as an impending trial (Luke 22.31–32). He prays in His distress, pouring out great emotion, yet subordinates His will to God's, praying with great humility (Matt 26.39–44; cf. Heb 5.7). But even in His humility and submission, He prays with confidence that God hears Him (John 11.41–42). Finally, in the context of Jesus humbling Himself and submitting to God's plan, it is worth noting that Jesus leaves popularity and human success to pray, showing that He cares more about a relationship with God than human acclaim—that He cares more about the cross than an earthly crown (Matt 14.21–23; Luke 5.15–16).

Passages about Prayer

Matthew 6–7. In addition to The Lord's Prayer, discussed in chapter 26 and Appendix B, The Sermon on the Mount has more to say about prayer. Consider briefly the following three principles.

First, pray in secret not for praise (Matt 6.5–6). Jesus here contrasts the prayer God wants with the prayer of the hypocrites, who desire to be heard and thought well of. Instead, pray in secret, seeking to be heard only by God. The point is not that public prayer is inherently sinful (cf. John 11.41–42; 17; Acts 1.24; 3.1; 4.24–26; etc.), but that prayer rooted in ego is. To ensure that our prayer is about God rather than impressing people, Jesus instructs us to pray where no one can hear us.[1]

Second, pray in faith not in human rationality (Matt 6.7–8). The pagans believed the gods cared little, if at all, for human life, so they had to catch their attention in prayer. It is not surprising that some Christians believe God is so transcendent that we fall into the same traps. After all, David expresses a similar awe and wonder that God cares for humankind (Ps 8.3–4). The reality, however, is that God does care about His creation and desires to do good for us. We do not need to catch His attention, as if He would otherwise overlook us, nor do we need to convince Him of our needs. It is not the number of words or the number of people who pray that move God, but the heart of the one who prays.[2]

---

[1] Stott, *The Message of the Sermon on the Mount*, 134–135 says, "Our Lord's emphasis on the need for secrecy should not be driven to extremes. To interpret it with rigid literalism would be guilty of the very phariseeism against which he is warning us. If all our praying were to be kept secret, we would have to give up church-going, family prayers, and prayer meetings. … Rather than becoming absorbed in the mechanics of secrecy, we need to remember that the purpose of Jesus' emphasis on 'secret' prayer is to purify our motives in praying. As we are to give out of a genuine love for people [6.2–4], so we are to pray out of a genuine love for God. We must never use either of these exercises as a pious cloak for self-love."

[2] Carson, *The Sermon on the Mount*, 60–61 speaks to the contrast between this text and the persistent widow of Luke 18. He says, "In the particular example before us, if we absolutize Matthew 6.7f, the logical conclusion is that followers of Jesus must never pray at length, and seldom if ever ask for anything since God knows their needs anyway. If instead we absolutize Luke 18.1–8, we will rea-

Finally, pray with confidence (Matt 7.7–11). Here, Jesus makes a great promise: the one who asks receives! He compares God's giving with our natural parental tendencies to give good gifts to our children. If we, who are sinful and short-sighted always try to do what is best for our children, how much more will a good and perfect God with an eternal viewpoint always do what is best (cf. Isa 49.15). Of course, the illustration Jesus gives—a father will not give a stone instead of bread—cuts both ways, because children are not always wise enough to ask for what is best and a good parent will refuse to give an evil gift. The child who asks for a stone to eat will instead be given bread. This likely provides some answer to prayers that seem to go unanswered: we do not always pray for what is a "good thing," which is what Jesus promises we will receive.[3]

Romans 8. Paul says the *pneuma* (s/Spirit) intercedes in our prayers (vv 26–27). Although this has widely been understood to be a reference to the Holy Spirit, some argue it refers instead to the human spirit.[4] The word can refer to either and in the immediate context it refers to both (e.g., v 16). According to this reading, "he who searches the hearts" is a reference to Jesus (cf. Rev 2.23), who is the Christian's intercessor (v 34; 1 Tim 2.5; Heb 7.25; 1 John 2.1). His knowledge of our spirit allows Him to present our inarticulate groanings to the Father, fulfilling His intercessory role. A key part of this position is the emphasis on Jesus being uniquely qualified to be an intercessor for humanity (cf. Heb 2.14–18; 4.14–16; Job 9.32–33; 10.4–5).

There is much truth to be considered in this view and it should not be discarded as lightly as some do, but there are also difficulties in it. First,

---

son that if we are serious with God we will not only pray at length, but we may expect the blessings we receive to be proportionate to our loquacity. However, if we listen to *both* passages with a little more sensitivity, we discover that Matthew 6.7f is really not concerned with the length of prayers, but with the attitude of heart which thinks it is heard for its many words. Likewise, we find that Luke 18.1–8 is less concerned with mere length of prayers than with overcoming the quitting tendency among certain of Christ's followers. These Christians, finding themselves under pressure, are often in danger of throwing in the towel. But they must not give up."

[3] Motyer, *Studies in the Epistle of James*, 88 says, "If it were the case that whatever we ask God was pledged to give, then I for one would never pray again because I would not have sufficient confidence in my own wisdom to ask God for anything. It would impose an intolerable burden on frail human wisdom if, by His prayer promises, God was pledged to give whatever we ask, whenever we ask, and in exactly the terms we ask. How could we bear that burden?"

[4] See, e.g., Campbell, "Eighth Chapter of Romans," 111–116; Turner, *Reading Romans*, 125–128.

although it is true that Jesus is said to be *the* intercessor, that does not necessarily disqualify others from being *an* intercessor. If Abraham and Moses can intercede for other humans, and if Paul can command Christians to intercede on behalf of everyone (1 Tim 2.1), surely the Spirit of God can at least intercede on a similar level.

Second, this approach makes too sharp a distinction among the persons of God, turning Christianity into a tri-theistic religion where Jesus' human experience is somehow walled off from the rest of the one, triune God. Throughout the Bible, in both Testaments, the inspired authors repeatedly affirm that there is one God (e.g., Deut 4.35; 6.4; Pss 83.18; 86.10; Isa 44.6; 45.18; Rom 3.30; 1 Cor 8.4; Eph 4.6; 1 Tim 1.17; 2.5; 6.15–16; Jas 2.19). I cannot claim to understand the exact mechanics of a triune God, but the Bible's affirmation of it is clear. Indeed, this is suggested in this very chapter where Paul interchangeably speaks of the Spirit, the Spirit of God, the Spirit of Him who raised Jesus from the dead, and the Spirit of Christ (Rom 8.9–11; cf. John 14.16–18; 1 Cor 15.45; 2 Cor 3.17; Eph 3.16–17).[5] Further, in the larger Biblical context, "he who searches the hearts" is not just a reference to Jesus; in fact, since Paul wrote Romans at least 30 years before John wrote Revelation, the only Scriptural references his audience could consult were more broadly references to God (e.g., 1 Chron 28.9; Ps 139; Jer 17.10). Although Revelation 2.23 could be understood as clarifying the earlier passages as referring to Jesus and only Him, it is at least equally likely the overarching Biblical teaching is simply that God (more generally speaking) knows human thoughts. After all, when someone says, "God knows our thoughts," it is rare, if ever, that he or she means "Jesus—and only Jesus—knows our thoughts."

Third, understanding the *pneuma* in question to be the human spirit creates other problems. One difficulty is that it only shifts the problem of an unqualified intercessor. After all, if God's Spirit is not qualified to inter-

---

[5] Lincoln, *Ephesians*, 206 captures this point well, saying the Pauline view is, "...in believers' present experience there is no real difference between Christ and the Spirit. ...Believers do not experience Christ except as Spirit and do not experience the Spirit except as Christ. ... [G]reater experience of the Spirit's power will mean the character of Christ increasingly becoming the hallmark of believers' lives."

cede, how much less is the human spirit fit for the job? It is true that this view suggests that it is ultimately Jesus who intercedes, but that is not what the text says. Paul says "the *pneuma* **himself** intercedes" not "Jesus intercedes by reading our thoughts and then interceding because He's actually the intercessor."[6] As indicated in the opening paragraph of this section, it is possible to get to that reading, but it seems to be a convoluted reading of a sentence that has a simple grammatical construction: a subject, an active verb, and pronoun that clarifies that the verb is connected to the subject. A second difficulty is that the spirit in question is the one interceding when the person in question does not know how to pray. Unless his own spirit is understood as somehow different from his conscious self—which the Bible never otherwise portrays the human spirit as being—it makes little sense for the spirit to intercede for what the self does not know how to do.[7]

A very simple solution presents itself within the chapter and is hinted at above. Paul equates the Spirit with the Spirit of Christ. How can the Spirit intercede (v 26; cf. Eph 6.18; Jude 20) when Jesus is interceding for us (v 34)? Because there is one God, not three. The Spirit is "qualified" to intercede, because the Spirit of God *is* the Spirit of Christ. This also fits with what Paul says in Galatians 4.6, where he explicitly connects the Spirit of Christ crying out on our behalf.[8] In this view, the Spirit in our

---

[6] The repetition of the verb in verse 27 does not contain the subject some translations insert. It either refers back to the same subject as the last time the verb was used (the Spirit) or the most recent subject (he who searches hearts). Even if it is referring to Jesus, this does not necessarily mean that the Spirit does not intercede. Rather, just as verse 9 indicates that the Spirit of God dwelling in a Christian and having the Spirit of Christ are two ways of saying the same thing, so also the Spirit interceding and Christ interceding are two ways of saying the same thing.

[7] Although "spirit" can refer to "a part of human personality ... the source and seat of insight, feeling, and will" (BDAG, 832–836), it more frequently refers to the animating force of life itself or one's breath. "Soul" (Greek *psyche,* immediately recognizable in English as well) would likely have been Paul's choice if he wanted to refer to the "seat and center of the inner human life in its many and varied aspects" (BDAG, 1098–1100). Given the semantic range of both words, however, this point is not ironclad.

[8] The participle ("crying") agrees in number and gender with "Spirit of Christ," not "our," suggesting it is the Spirit who cries out on behalf of the believer (see Longenecker, *Galatians,* 174; but note that the participle is first person plural [i.e., connected to "we"] in Romans 8.15). Additionally, the Spirit was given to be an advocate for the apostles (John 14.16, 26; 15.26; 16.7). Christians debate just how far-reaching Jesus' promises to the apostles in His Farewell Discourse are. Were they intended for the twelve alone, the twelve plus other later apostles and prophets (e.g., Paul, Matthias, Mark, Luke, etc.), or do they extend to all Christians and, if so, how? If the Spirit remains, in some sense, an advocate for Christians today, these promises would apply to our interpretation of Romans 8.26.

hearts—the Spirit, the Spirit of God, or the Spirit of Christ, as Paul interchangeably uses those phrases—knows our needs in those most difficult times when we (and our spirits) cannot find the right words, and He can present our inarticulate groanings to the Father.[9]

One final difficulty of this verse concerns the varying views of just what the Spirit does and how He dwells in believers today. Those who see the Spirit as still performing miraculous deeds through believers will be on one end of the spectrum and those who see the Spirit as little more than knowledge of the inspired word will be on the other end, with varying intermediate views filling the spectrum between.[10]

Ephesians 6. The letter of Ephesians ends with a description of the armor of God, armor designed to help the Christian stand[11] in the spiritual warfare we face. After the preamble that includes both the exhortation (vv 10–11) and description of the terrifying foes (12–13), Paul describes how God has armored us (vv 14–17; cf. Isa 11.4–5; 59.17). Finally, the stage is set and the battle is ready to begin:

> …praying at all times in the Spirit, with all prayer and supplication. To that end keep alert with all perseverance, making supplication for all the saints and also for me, that words may be given to me in opening my mouth boldly to proclaim the mystery of the gospel, for which I am an ambassador in chains, that I may declare it boldly, as I ought to speak. (vv 18–20)

It may be surprising to find Paul saying "Pray!" instead of "Fight!", but spiritual warfare is fought on a spiritual level. Spiritual warfare, Paul says, is fought on your knees.[12]

---

[9] So Morris, *Romans,* 328. Some argue that the groanings are from the Spirit Himself, though this does not seem to fit the context as well. Millar, *Calling on the Name of the Lord,* 210 rightly points to the context of verses 23–25, concluding, "The angst envisaged is 'gospel angst,' not simply struggling to make sense of life in our messy world. Paul anticipates a situation where the tension between what we are now and what we will be brings us to the end of ourselves (or, at least, to the end of our words)."

[10] This appendix is not suited to a full discussion of these issues. For a balanced discussion of the Holy Spirit in the context of Paul's writings, see McClister, "Paul's View of the Holy Spirit," 88–120.

[11] Notice that the word "stand" appears three times in verses 11–14 and "withstand" (a related word in Greek) appears once as well.

[12] Stott, *The Message of Ephesians,* 283–284 points out the "four universals, indicated by the fourfold use of the word 'all.'" He continues, "Most Christians pray sometimes, with some prayers and

Philippians 4. In Philippians 4.6, Paul uses three different words for prayer in one verse to emphasize the need for believing and expectant prayer in Christians.[13] But this emphasis is not merely on prayer for the sake of prayer, but prayer as an antidote to anxiety. Commands not to worry are well known to Christians; Jesus' teaching in Matthew 6 gives even more detail on the matter. If the Bible did not give positive teaching on what to do instead of worry, believers may well be consigned to worry about not worrying. Instead, we are told to pray.

The exhortation to pray "in everything" should surely be understood in a literal sense—i.e., there is nothing about which we should not pray. Perhaps this is said because of how easy it is to make exceptions when prayer seems unnecessary (because things are going well) or ineffective (because the situation seems too difficult) or due to individual apathy (because we are not in the mood).[14] But it seems more likely that "everything" is emphasizing that there is no individual thing that should be withheld from God—namely, matters that cause anxiety. If we should not worry about "anything," the "everything" that we take to God is likely focused on the same matter. In short, Paul urges we pray specifically about those things that worry us. Notice also the emphasis on thanksgiving being a part of such prayer. As we have noted earlier, the failure to acknowledge God and be thankful is the first step toward outright rejection of God (Rom 1.21).

The result of such praying, Paul says, is that God's incomprehensible peace will guard the hearts of the believer in Christ. He does not explain exactly what this means or how it works, but at the very least it is safe to say that God's peace far surpasses human understanding, meaning it will protect the believer "from those very thoughts that lead to fear and distress and that keep one from trusting prayer."[15]

This passage is easy to misconstrue. It can be seen as a promise that problems magically go away with a wish in the right direction. Such a

---

some degree of perseverance, for some of God's people. But to replace 'some' by 'all' in each of these expressions would be to introduce us to a new dimension of prayer."

[13] Bruce, *Philippians*, 143.

[14] Marshall, *Philippians*, 113.

[15] Fee, *Philippians*, 411.

reading will only destroy the faith of the praying one who does not feel this happen in his or her life. As Carson says,

> None of this should be misconstrued as a Pollyannish approach to life. Christians are not ostriches with heads carefully buried in the sand. None of this means that our paths will be smooth and edged with the sweetest smelling roses. There is no hint that we shall live above the pressures of other mortals by escaping them. Far from it. It is precisely in the context of the pressures we all must endure that we find our rest in God. If you worry little simply because Providence has so far blessed you with a relatively easy passage or if you worry little because you have a carefree personality, you know little of the truth of this passage. This passage does not deny the existence of anxieties, it tells us what to do with them. It does not tell us that if we have the right personality, we can live above tension; it tells us where we find strength and grace to help in times of need.[16]

1 Thessalonians 5. One of the more famous short verses on prayer is in Paul's concluding exhortations to the Thessalonian church. "Pray without ceasing," he says (v 17; cf. Rom 12.12; Eph 6.18; Col 4.2). This verse is simple and straightforward and yet difficult at the same time. One cannot unceasingly pray; the human brain is not wired to do such a thing. Even if we could somehow continue in prayer while, say, calculating our family budget, we surely cannot do so while we sleep. The coupling of the clear command with the impossibility of performing it has led some to interpret it as something like, "Have a prayerful attitude." This pious-sounding platitude satisfies many who hear it, but others may wonder just what it means. Something that is so difficult to quantify can hardly be obeyed.[17]

The solution to this text is not so difficult if we paraphrase Paul to say, "Don't stop praying," and hypothetically have him ask the Thessalonians at a later point, "Have you stopped praying?" or, better, "Are you still praying?"

---

[16] Carson, *Basics for Believers,* 113.
[17] The best articulation of this may be from Morris, *1 and 2 Thessalonians,* 107: "It is not possible for us to spend all our time with the words of prayer on our lips, but it is possible to be all our days in the spirit of prayer, realizing our dependence upon God for all we have and are, being conscious of his presence with us wherever we may be, and yielding ourselves continually to him to do his will. Such an inward state will of course find expression from time to time in verbal prayer."

This reconstruction is useful when considered against situations we know. Imagine that a friend known for attention to fitness moved away and a few years later calls to catch up. At some point you might ask, "Are you still working out?" It would never cross his mind to say, "Of course not. That's a weird question. I'm on the couch talking on the phone." He would either respond that he has or has not "ceased" working out, but it would have no bearing on his precise action at any individual moment. Rather, exercise is something that characterizes his life; it is his habit and a trait of who he is. So also prayer must be for us. To pray without ceasing does not mean that one must constantly be in prayer nor does it mean to have some enigmatic "prayerful attitude"; instead, prayer is to be something that characterizes the Christian life, a habit and trait of who we are.[18]

1 Timothy 2. Here, Paul urges intercessory prayer.[19] Although we may be tempted to smile at a perceived naivete of a child's prayer "for everyone," this is exactly what Paul urges in this text, with the repetition of "all people" (vv 1, 4; cf. "all" in v 6) suggesting it is the primary point of the exhortation.[20] Further, praying for everyone is manifest in Paul's own life, as the prayer lists he gives in his letters are monumentally long. And he urges multiple churches and Christians to pray for him as well (e.g., Rom 15.30–32;[21] 2 Cor 1.11; Eph 6.18–20; Col 4.3–4; 1 Thes 5.25; 2 Thes 3.1–2; Phlm 22; cf. Heb 13.18–19). In short, intercession for others—for everyone, for preachers, for fellow Christians, for kings and presidents—should be a hallmark of Christian prayer.[22]

---

[18] See also Crozier, *Plugged In*, 19–20.

[19] Paul's four words for prayer can either emphasize the different nuance of each word or have the rhetorical effect of grouping synonyms "to add luster to the basic concept," as Mounce, *Pastoral Epistles*, 79 says. In this latter view, which I would take, "The point is that all prayers, of all type, should be for all people," just as we saw in Ephesians 6. The alternate view is taken by Knight, *Pastoral Epistles*, 114–115, who defines each term and sees them as four different aspects of prayer.

[20] Chester, *The Message of Prayer*, 212.

[21] See Carson, *Praying with Paul*, 183–201 for a full discussion of this text.

[22] Although there are obvious caveats to the illustration, Stott's point on this verse is striking: "This immediately rebukes the narrow parochialism of many churches' prayers. Some years ago I attended public worship in a certain church. The pastor was absent on holiday, and a lay elder led the pastoral prayer. He prayed that the pastor might enjoy a good vacation (which was fine), and that two lady members of the congregation might be healed (which was also fine; we should pray for the sick). But that was all. The intercession can hardly have lasted thirty seconds. I came away saddened, sensing

It is also worth noting that Paul urges prayer for government leaders "that we may lead a peaceful and quiet life, godly and dignified in every way," which he goes on to connect with God's desire for all to come to a knowledge of the truth. Occasionally, one will hear a Christian say the church needs is a "good round of persecution" to weed out the pretenders. While it is true that persecution can have that purifying element to it, it can also "weed out" those who aren't necessarily hypocrites, but whose faith is not fully formed. More than that, to wish for persecution is to fly in the face of Paul's explicit command to pray for peace and tranquility—to say nothing of the foolishness of American Christians who have no concept of real persecution, wishing for something they cannot begin to fathom. At the same time, it should be noted that Paul expects persecution (e.g., 2 Tim 1.8; 3.12). We do not need to seek persecution; persecution will eventually find those who live a God-centered life in a world that has rejected God. Most importantly, Paul is not suggesting that we seek peace for the sake of peace, but peace for the spread of the gospel (v 4).[23]

James 4–5. The final two chapters of James provide descriptions of both effective and ineffective prayer. In chapter 4, he speaks first of those who do not have because they do not ask (v 2). As God is the giver of all good gifts (Jas 1.17), the one who does not ask will not receive (cf. Matt 7.7). He then turns and speaks of those who do not have because they ask wrongly (v 3). This may be a second category of those who do not receive, or it may clarify what the first statement means—i.e., to ask with evil motives is not to ask at all. In either case, "wrongly" here does not refer to a methodological error, as is clarified by what follows: "to spend it on your passions." Indeed, "wrongly" may not be the best English option for a Greek word that frequently refers to evil or wickedness.[24] As we have seen throughout this book, Biblical prayer is rooted in God's character,

---

that this church worshipped a little village god of their own devising. There was no recognition of the needs of the world, and no attempt to embrace the world in prayer." (*The Message of 1 Timothy and Titus*, 61). At the very least, the notion that we can find ourselves "worshipping a little village god of our own devising" should cause us to ask whether our prayers are so limited and, if so, why.

[23] Millar, *Calling on the Name of the Lord*, 211 and Chester, *The Message of Prayer*, 212 are among those who point out the gospel focus of this text.

[24] Johnson, *James*, 278; BDAG, 502.

will, and promises, not humankind's selfish whims or hedonistic desires. Along these lines, Tasker says, "There is, to be sure, no prayer that we all need to pray so much as the prayer that we may *love* what God commands and *desire* what he promises."[25] On the other hand, those requests that are rooted in our passions are hardly worthy of being called "prayer." As Hort says, "God bestows not gifts only, but the enjoyment of them: but the enjoyment which contributes to nothing beyond itself is not what He gives in answer to prayer; and petitions to Him which have no better end in view are not prayers."[26]

James 5, however, speaks of effective prayer. In the context of sickness, James advocates prayer as the means to a cure, concluding that a righteous person's prayer is effective.[27] As an illustration, he cites Elijah, a righteous man who prayed to great effect.[28] Elijah, as remarkable as he may seem, was just a normal human being, James contends, meaning that any righteous person who prays can expect his or her prayer to have similar efficacy.

1 Peter 5. Peter's well-known depiction of the Christian "casting all your anxiety on him" (v 7; cf. Ps 55.22) has been referred to more than once in the chapters of this book. What we have not discussed is the broader context of this verse, which pairs two Old Testament images of God: God the Mighty Warrior and God the Merciful. Regarding the former, Peter speaks of the mighty hand of God (v 6; cf. Exod 32.11; Deut 4.34; 4.15; 7.19; Dan 9.15) that has the strength to lift you up (v 6) and restore, support, strengthen, and secure (v 10), to whom be the power

---

[25] Tasker, *James*, 88. Emphasis in original.

[26] Hort, *James*, 91.

[27] Whether James refers to moral or physical sickness has been long debated. Good arguments can be made for either side of the issue. The role of anointing with oil has also been widely debated. See Moo, *James*, 238–242 for a discussion of the various interpretive options of anointing with oil. For our purposes in this appendix, understanding the nuance of the situation is not as important as the message that prayer is effective. In addition, the injunction to sing psalms in joy can also be understood as instruction about prayer. Michaels, "Finding Yourself an Intercessor," 237 points out that this too is a kind of prayer and this text is James' equivalent to Paul's instructions in 1 Thessalonians 5.16–18.

[28] For a helpful, popular-level discussion of this text, see Crozier, *Plugged In*, 83–86. For a brief discussion of Elijah as a praying prophet, see Ward, "The Reign of Ahab," 98–99.

forever (v 11). Regarding the latter, God is the one who cares for you (v 7), who is the God of all grace, and who called you (v 10; cf. 1.1–2; 2.9–10). Peter's use of these common images draws attention to the ever-present battle and the merciful God who will emerge victorious.[29]

To cast one's cares upon God is to recognize that victory can only come from His hand. It is how we humble ourselves (v 6)[30] and remain disciplined and vigilant (v 8). It is, as Green says, "a recognition of God's monopoly on justice as well as a deep-seated confession of God's power to accomplish his purposes."[31] It is the process by which we unload ourselves of anxiety even if we cannot do anything about the problem that causes it—the refusal to be burdened with care even in the midst of trials.[32] It is important to recognize the flip side of this assertion as well. If casting one's cares upon God is an example of humility, then clinging to his or her cares and persisting in anxiety is an example of pride. As Schreiner says,

> Worry is a form of pride because when believers are filled with anxiety, they are convinced that they must solve all the problems in their lives in their own strength. The only god they trust in is themselves. When believers throw their worries upon God, they express their trust in his mighty hand, acknowledging that he is Lord and Sovereign over all their life.[33]

1 John 5. As John concludes his epistle, he speaks of the confidence that we can have in a personal relationship and communication with God (vv 14–15). Although it might seem like a blank check to use God as a cosmic vending machine for our every desire and whim, these verses do not exist in a vacuum. In addition to the broader portion of Scripture that speaks of prayer and would qualify the promise, the immediate con-

---

[29] See Green, *1 Peter*, 175–178 for a fuller discussion of these ideas.

[30] Some English translations begin a new sentence in verse 7, but it continues a sentence that begins in verse 6 in the Greek: the imperative in verse 6 ("humble") is elaborated upon by the participle in verse 7 ("casting").

[31] Green, *1 Peter*, 179.

[32] Stibbs, *1 Peter*, 171. Suffering is the major theme in 1 Peter, with the word showing up a drastically disproportionate amount of times in the letter. Of the New Testament uses of various forms of the word, 1 Peter accounts for 4 out of 16 uses of the noun form and 12 out of 41 uses of the verb (Marshall, *1 Peter*, 89).

[33] Schreiner, *1, 2 Peter, Jude*, 241.

text specifies what John is referring to: life for a brother who has sinned. We might even go further. Prayer has not been a main point of John's letter, but sin has. Thus, the issue of sin is not merely an illustration of prayer's efficacy, but the main point John was working toward when he first brought up prayer.[34] In this specific context, then, John is urging that Christians pray for the spiritual health of the congregation by intercessory prayer.[35] This fits well with what we have seen of intercessory prayer in Genesis 18 and Numbers 14.

---

[34] Marshall, *The Epistles of John*, 245.
[35] Jobes, *1, 2, & 3 John*, 246.

BIBLIOGRAPHY

Achtemeier, Elizabeth. *Nahum–Malachi.* INT. Atlanta: John Knox Press, 1986.

Alden, Robert L. *Job.* NAC. Nashville: Broadman & Holman Publishers, 1993.

Alexander, T. Desmond. "Jonah." In *Obadiah, Jonah, Micah: An Introduction and Commentary.* TOTC. Downers Grove: Intervarsity Press, 1988.

Allen Leslie C. "Ezra–Nehemiah." In *Ezra, Nehemiah, Esther.* NIBC. Peabody: Hendrickson, 2003.

———. *Joel, Obadiah, Jonah, and Micah.* NICOT. Grand Rapids: Eerdmans, 1976.

Anderson, A.A. *2 Samuel.* WBC. Dallas: Word Books, 1989.

Anderson, Francis I. *Job: An Introduction and Commentary.* TOTC. Downers Grove: Intervarsity Press, 1976.

Arndt, William, et al. *A Greek-English Lexicon of the New Testament and Other Early Christian Literature.* Chicago: University of Chicago Press, 2000.

Arnold, Clinton E. *Ephesians.* ZECNT. Grand Rapids: Zondervan, 2010.

Baker, David W. *Nahum, Habakkuk, Zephaniah: An Introduction and Commentary.* TOTC. Downers Grove: Intervarsity Press, 1988.

Baldwin, Joyce. *1 and 2 Samuel: An Introduction and Commentary.* TOTC. Downers Grove: Intervarsity Press, 1988.

———. *Daniel: An Introduction and Commentary.* TOTC. Downers Grove: Intervarsity Press, 1978.

Balentine, Samuel E. *Prayer in the Hebrew Bible: The Drama of Divine-Human Dialogue*. Overtures to Biblical Theology. Minneapolis: Fortress Press, 1993.

Barclay, William. *The Letters to the Galatians and Ephesians*. DSB. Philadelphia: The Westminster Press, 1958.

_____. *The Letters of James and Peter*. DSB. Philadelphia: The Westminster Press, 1960.

_____. *The Letters to the Philippians, Colossians, and Thessalonians*. DSB. Philadelphia: The Westminster Press, 1959.

Beale, G.K. *1–2 Thessalonians*. IVPNTC. Downers Grove: IVP Academic, 2003.

_____. *Colossians and Philemon*. BECNT. Grand Rapids: Baker Academic, 2019.

_____. *The Book of Revelation: A Commentary on the Greek Text*. NIGTC. Grand Rapids: Eerdmans, 1999.

Bielby, James K. and Gregory A. Boyd (eds.). *Divine Foreknowledge: Four Views*. Downers Grove: IVP Academic, 2001.

Bird, Michael F. *Colossians and Philemon: A New Covenant Commentary*. NCCS. Eugene: Cascade Books, 2009.

Blackwood, Andrew. *Commentary on Jeremiah: The Word, the Words, and the World*. Waco: Word Books, 1977.

Block, Daniel I. *For the Glory of God: Recovering a Biblical Theology of Worship*. Grand Rapids: Baker Academic, 2014.

Blomberg, Craig L. *Christians in an Age of Wealth: A Biblical Theology of Stewardship*. Biblical Theology for Life. Grand Rapids: Zondervan, 2013.

_____. *Matthew*. NAC. Nashville: Broadman Press, 1992.

Bock, Darrell L. *Acts*. BECNT. Grand Rapids: Baker Academic, 2007.

Brooks, James A. *Mark*. NAC. Nashville: Broadman Press, 1991.

Brown, Francis, Samuel Rolles Driver, and Charles Augustus Briggs. *A Hebrew and English Lexicon of the Old Testament.* Oxford: Clarendon Press, 1977.

Brown, Raymond. *The Message of Nehemiah: God's Servant in a Time of Change.* BST. Downers Grove: Intervarsity Press, 1998.

Bruce, F.F. *1 & 2 Thessalonians.* WBC. Waco: Word Books, 1982.

───────. *Commentary on the Book of Acts.* NICNT. Grand Rapids: Eerdmans, 1984.

───────. *Philippians.* NIBC. Peabody: Hendrickson, 1983.

───────. *The Epistles to the Colossians, to Philemon, and to the Ephesians.* NICNT. Grand Rapids: Eerdmans, 1984.

───────. *The Gospel of John.* Grand Rapids: Eerdmans, 1983.

Brueggemann, Walter. *Great Prayers of the Old Testament.* Louisville: Westminster John Knox Press, 2008.

───────. *The Message of the Psalms: A Theological Commentary.* Minneapolis: Augsburg Publishing House, 1984.

───────. *Praying the Psalms: Engaging Scripture and the Life of the Spirit,* 2nd ed. Eugene: Cascade Books, 2007.

Bullock, C. Hassell. *Encountering the Book of Psalms: A Literary and Theological Introduction.* 2nd ed. Grand Rapids: Baker Academic, 2018.

Calvin, John. *Commentaries on the Four Last Books of Moses, Arranged in the Form of a Harmony.* Translated by C. W. Bingham. 4 vols. Edinburgh: Calvin Translation Society, 1852–1855.

Camp, Phillip G. "Prayer in the Pentateuch." *Praying with Ancient Israel: Exploring the Theology of Prayer in the Old Testament.* Edited by Phillip G. Camp and Tremper Longman III. Abilene: Abilene Christian University Press, 2015.

Campbell, Alexander. "Christianos and the Eighth Chapter of Romans." *The Millennial Harbinger* 1, No. 3 (1830): 111–116.

Carson, D.A. *Basics for Believers: An Exposition of Philippians*. Grand Rapids: Baker Academic, 1996.

_____. *How Long, O Lord? Reflections on Suffering and Evil*. 2nd ed. Grand Rapids: Baker Academic, 2006.

_____. "Matthew." *Matthew, Mark, Luke*. EBC. Edited by Frank E. Gaebelein. Grand Rapids: Zondervan, 1984.

_____. *Praying with Paul: A Call to Spiritual Reformation*. 2nd ed. Grand Rapids: Baker Academic, 2014.

_____, ed. *Teach Us to Pray: Prayer in the Bible and the World*. Grand Rapids: Baker Book House, 1990.

_____. *The Gospel According to John*. PNTC. Grand Rapids: Eerdmans, 1991.

_____. *The Sermon on the Mount: An Evangelical Exposition of Matthew 5–7*. Grand Rapids: Baker Book House, 1978.

Chester, Timothy. *The Message of Prayer: Approaching the Throne of Grace*. BST. Downers Grove: Intervarsity Press, 2003.

Chesterton, G.K. *Irish Impressions*. London: Collins, 1919.

Chisholm, Robert B., Jr. *1 & 2 Samuel*. TTCS. Grand Rapids: Baker Books, 2013.

Chrysostom, John. "Homilies of St. John Chrysostom, Archbishop of Constantinople, on the Acts of the Apostles." *Saint Chrysostom: Homilies on the Acts of the Apostles and the Epistle to the Romans*. Edited by Philip Schaff. Vol. 11. A Select Library of the Nicene and Post-Nicene Fathers of the Christian Church, First Series. New York: Christian Literature Company, 1889.

Clines, D.J.A. *Ezra, Nehemiah, Esther*. NCB. Grand Rapids: Eerdmans, 1984.

_____. *The Dictionary of Classical Hebrew*. 8 vols. Sheffield: Sheffield Phoenix Press, 1993–2011.

Cole, R. Dennis. *Numbers*. NAC. Nashville: B&H Publishing Group, 2000.

Craigie, Peter C. *Psalms 1–50*. WBC. Nashville: Thomas Nelson, 1983.

Crozier, Edwin. *Plugged In: High-Voltage Prayer.* 2nd ed. Chillicothe: DeWard Publishing Company, 2017.

Curtis, Edward M. "Structure, Style and Context as a Key to Interpreting Jacob's Encounter at Peniel." *JETS* 30 (1987): 129–137.

Davis, Dale Ralph. *The Message of Daniel: His Kingdom Cannot Fail*. BST. Downers Grove, IVP Academic, 2013.

deSilva, David A. *Ephesians*. NCBC. New York: Cambridge University Press, 2022.

_____. *Honor, Patronage, Kinship, & Purity: Unlocking New Testament Culture.* Downers Grove: IVP Academic, 2000.

Dillard, Raymond B. *2 Chronicles*. WBC. Waco: Word Books, 1987.

_____ and Tremper Longman III. *An Introduction to the Old Testament.* Grand Rapids: Zondervan, 1994.

Dorsey, David. *The Literary Structure of the Old Testament: A Commentary on Genesis–Malachi.* Grand Rapids: Baker Books, 1999.

Duguid, Iain M. *Daniel*. REC. Phillipsburg, N.J.: P&R Publishing, 2008.

_____. *Living in the Gap Between Promise and Reality: The Gospel According to Abraham.* The Gospel According to the Old Testament. Phillipsburg: P&R Publishing, 1999.

_____. *Living in the Grip of Relentless Grace: The Gospel in the Lives of Isaac & Jacob.* The Gospel According to the Old Testament. Phillipsburg: P&R Publishing, 2002.

_____. "Nehemiah: The Best King Judah Never Had." *Let Us Go Up to Zion: Essays in Honour of H. G. M. Williamson on the Occasion of His Sixty-Fifth Birthday.* Edited by Iain Provan and Mark J. Boda. Leiden: Brill, 2012.

_____. *Numbers*. PTW. Wheaton: Crossway, 2006.

———. *The Rebel Prophet: The Gospel in the Book of Jonah*. Glenside: St. Colme's Press, 2022.

Earnhart, Paul. *Invitation to a Spiritual Revolution: Studies in the Sermon on the Mount*. Chillicothe: DeWard Publishing Company, 2009.

Estes, Daniel J. *Handbook on the Wisdom Books and Psalms: Job, Psalms, Proverbs, Ecclesiastes, Song of Songs*. Grand Rapids: Baker Academic, 2005.

Fee, Gordon. *Paul's Letter to the Philippians*. NICNT. Grand Rapids: Eerdmans, 1995.

Fensham, F. Charles. *The Books of Ezra and Nehemiah*. NICOT. Grand Rapids: Eerdmans, 1982.

Firth, David G. *1 & 2 Samuel*. AOTC. Downers Grove: Intervarsity Press, 2009.

Fisher, Gary. "This Cup." *Beneath the Cross: Essays and Reflections on the Lord's Supper*. Edited by Jady S. Copeland and Nathan Ward. Chillicothe: DeWard Publishing Company, 2008.

Foster, R.C. *Studies in the Life of Christ*. Grand Rapids: Baker Book House, 1971.

Foulkes, Francis. *The Epistle of Paul to the Ephesians: An Introduction and Commentary*. TNTC. Grand Rapids: Eerdmans, 1963.

France, R.T. *Matthew: An Introduction and Commentary*. TNTC. Downers Grove: Intervarsity Press, 1985.

Garland, David E. *2 Corinthians*. NAC. Nashville: Broadman & Holman, 1999.

———. *Colossians and Philemon*. NIVAC. Grand Rapids: Zondervan, 1998.

———. *Luke*. ZECNT. Grand Rapids: Zondervan, 2011.

———. *Mark*. NIVAC. Grand Rapids: Zondervan, 1996.

———. "Philippians." *Ephesians–Philemon*. REBC. Edited by Tremper Longman III and David E. Garland. Grand Rapids: Zondervan, 2006.

Goldingay, John E. *Daniel*. WBC. Grand Rapids: Zondervan, 1996.

_____. "Habakkuk," in J. Goldingay and P. Scalise. *Minor Prophets II*. NIBC. Peabody, Hendrickson, 2009.

_____. *The Book of Jeremiah*. NICOT. Grand Rapids: Eerdmans, 2021.

Gorman, Heather M. "Prayer." *From Celsus to the Catacombs: Visual, Liturgical, and Non-Christian Receptions of Jesus in the Second and Third Centuries CE*. Edited by Chris Keith, et al. Vol. 3 of *The Reception of Jesus in the First Three Centuries*. New York: T&T Clark, 2019.

Gowan, Donald E. *The Triumph of Faith in Habakkuk*. Eugene: Wipf and Stock, 2009.

Green, Gene L. *The Letters to the Thessalonians*. PNTC. Grand Rapids: Eerdmans, 2002.

Green, Joel B. *1 Peter*. THNTC. Grand Rapids: Eerdmans, 2007.

_____. *The Gospel According to Luke*. NICNT. Grand Rapids: Eerdmans, 1997.

_____. "Persevering Together in Prayer." *Into God's Presence: Prayer in the New Testament*. Edited by Richard Longenecker. Grand Rapids: Eerdmans, 2001.

Greenberg, Moshe. *Biblical Prose Prayer*. Berkeley: University of California Press, 1983.

Guinness, Os. *God in the Dark: The Assurance of Faith Beyond a Shadow of Doubt*. Wheaton: Crossway, 1996.

Habel, Norman C. "Wisdom in the Book of Job." *Sitting with Job: Selected Studies in the Book of Job*. Edited by Roy B. Zuck. Grand Rapids: Baker Book House, 1992: 303–315.

Hailey, Homer. *A Commentary on Isaiah: With Emphasis on the Messianic Hope*. Louisville: Religious Supply, 1992.

Hamilton, James M. *With the Clouds of Heaven: The Book of Daniel in Biblical Theology*. NSBT. Downers Grove: Intervarsity Press, 2014.

Hamilton, Victor P. *The Book of Genesis: Chapters 18–50*. NICOT. Grand Rapids: Eerdmans, 1995.

Harris, R. Laird, et al., eds. *Theological Wordbook of the Old Testament*, 2 vols. Chicago: Moody Press, 1980.

Harrison, R.K. *Jeremiah and Lamentations: An Introduction and Commentary.* TOTC. Downers Grove: Intervarsity Press, 1973.

Hartley, John E. *The Book of Job*. NICOT. Grand Rapids: Eerdmans, 1988.

Hays, J. Daniel. *The Message of the Prophets: A Survey of the Prophetic and Apocalyptic Books of the Old Testament*. Grand Rapids: Zondervan, 2010.

Hays, Richard B. *Echoes of Scripture in the Gospels*. Waco: Baylor University Press, 2016.

Hemer, Colin. "ἐπιούσιος." *JSNT* 22 (1984): 81–94.

Heschel, Abraham J. *The Prophets: Two Volumes in One*. Peabody: Hendrickson Publishers, 2010.

Hill, Andrew E. *1 & 2 Chronicles*. NIVAC. Grand Rapids: Zondervan, 2003.

———. "Prayer in Minor Prophets (The Book of the Twelve)." *Praying with Ancient Israel: Exploring the Theology of Prayer in the Old Testament*. Edited by Phillip G. Camp and Tremper Longman III. Abilene: Abilene Christian University Press, 2015.

House, Paul R. *1, 2 Kings*. NAC. Nashville: Broadman & Holman Publishers, 1995.

Hort, F. J.A. *The Epistle of St James: The Greek Text with Introduction, Commentary as far as Chapter IV, Verse 5, and Additional Notes*. London: Macmillan, 1909.

Hurtado, Larry W. *Mark*. NIBC. Peabody: Hendrickson Publishers, 1989.

Inge, William Ralph. *Religion and Life: The Foundations of Personal Religion*. Essay Index Reprint Series. Freeport: Books for Libraries Press, 1968.

Jobes, Karen H. *1, 2, & 3 John*. ZECNT. Grand Rapids: Zondervan, 2014.

Johnson, Luke Timothy. *The Letter of James: A New Translation with Introduction and Commentary*. AYB. New Haven: Yale University Press, 1995.

Jowers, Dennis (ed.). *Four Views on Divine Providence*. Grand Rapids: Zondervan, 2011.

Kaiser, Walter C., Jr. *Have You Seen the Power of God Lately? Lessons for Today from Elijah*. San Bernandino: Here's Life Publishers, 1987.

_____. *I Will Lift My Eyes unto the Hills: Learning from the Great Prayers of the Old Testament*. Wooster, OH: Weaver Book Company, 2015.

_____. *Micah–Malachi*. Mastering the Old Testament. Dallas: Word Publishing, 1992.

Kidner, Derek. *Ezra and Nehemiah: An Introduction and Commentary*. TOTC. Downers Grove: Intervarsity Press, 1979.

_____. *Genesis: An Introduction and Commentary*. TOTC. Downers Grove: Intervarsity Press, 1967.

_____. *The Message of Jeremiah: Against Wind and Tide*. BST. Downers Grove: Intervarsity Press, 1987.

_____. *The Wisdom of Proverbs, Job, & Ecclesiastes: An Introduction to Wisdom Literature*. Downers Grove: Intervarsity Press, 1985.

Knight, George W., III. *The Pastoral Epistles: A Commentary on the Greek Text*. NIGTC. Grand Rapids: Eerdmans, 1992.

Koehler, Ludwig, et al. *The Hebrew and Aramaic Lexicon of the Old Testament*. 5 vols. Leiden: E.J. Brill, 1994–2000.

Leithart, Peter J. *1 & 2 Chronicles*. BTCB. Grand Rapids: Brazos Press, 2019.

_____. *1 & 2 Kings*. BTCB. Grand Rapids: Brazos Press, 2006.

Leupold, H.C. *Exposition of Genesis*. 2 vols. Grand Rapids: Baker Book House, 1942.

Lewis, C.S. *Letters of C.S. Lewis.* New York: Harcourt, Brace and World, 1966.

_____. *Reflections on the Psalms.* New York: Harcourt Books, 1958.

Lewis, Jack P. "Difficult Texts from the Psalms and Proverbs." *Difficult Texts of the Old Testament.* Ed. Wendell Winkler. Hurst: Winkler Publications, 1982.

Limburg, James. *Hosea–Micah.* INT. Atlanta: John Knox Press, 1988.

Lincoln, Andrew T. "The Letter to the Colossians." In *NIB,* vol. 11. Nashville: Abingdon, 2000.

_____. *Ephesians.* WBC. Nashville: Thomas Nelson, 1990.

_____. "God's Name, Jesus' Name, and Prayer in the Fourth Gospel." *Into God's Presence: Prayer in the New Testament.* Edited by Richard Longenecker. Grand Rapids: Eerdmans, 2001.

Longenecker, Richard N. *Acts.* EBC. Grand Rapids: Zondervan, 1995.

_____. *Galatians.* WBC. Nashville: Thomas Nelson, 1990.

_____. "Prayer in the Pauline Letters." *Into God's Presence: Prayer in the New Testament.* Edited by Richard Longenecker. Grand Rapids: Eerdmans, 2001.

Longman, Tremper, III. *Daniel.* NIVAC. Grand Rapids: Zondervan, 1999.

_____. *How to Read Proverbs.* Downers Grove: Intervarsity Press, 2002.

_____. *How to Read the Psalms.* Downers Grove: Intervarsity Press, 1988.

_____. *Jeremiah, Lamentations.* UBC. Grand Rapids: Baker Books, 2008.

_____. *Job.* BCOT. Grand Rapids: Baker Academic, 2012.

_____ and Daniel G. Reid. *God is a Warrior.* OTBT. Grand Rapids: Zondervan, 1995.

MacKenzie, R.A.F. "The Divine Soliloquies in Genesis." *CBQ* 17 (1955): 277–286.

Magonet, Jonathan. *Form and Meaning: Studies in Literary Techniques in the Book of Jonah.* 2nd ed. BLS. Sheffield: The Almond Press, 1983.

Malherbe, Abraham J. *The Letters to the Thessalonians: A New Translation with Introduction and Commentary.* AYB. New Haven: Yale University Press, 2000.

Mariottini, Claude. "Prayer in 1–2 Chronicles, Ezra, and Nehemiah." *Praying with Ancient Israel: Exploring the Theology of Prayer in the Old Testament.* Edited by Phillip G. Camp and Tremper Longman III. Abilene: Abilene Christian University Press, 2015.

Marshall, I. Howard. *1 Peter.* IVPNTC. Downers Grove: Intervarsity Press, 1991.

_____. *1 and 2 Thessalonians.* NCB. Grand Rapids: Eerdmans, 1983.

_____. "Jesus—Example and Teacher of Prayer in the Synoptic Gospels." *Into God's Presence: Prayer in the New Testament.* Edited by Richard Longenecker. Grand Rapids: Eerdmans, 2001.

_____. *The Acts of the Apostles: An Introduction and Commentary.* TNTC. Downers Grove: Intervarsity Press, 1980.

_____. *The Epistle to the Philippians.* EC. London: Epworth Press, 1991.

_____. *The Epistles of John.* NICNT. Grand Rapids: Eerdmans, 1978.

Mathews, Kenneth A. *Genesis.* 2 vols. NAC. Nashville: Broadman & Holman Publishers, 2005.

McClister, David. *A Commentary on Hebrews.* Temple Terrace: Florida College Press, 2010.

_____. "Paul's View of Jesus Christ." *From the Pen of Paul: An Introduction to the Pauline Epistles.* 2nd ed. Edited by Nathan Ward. Temple Terrace: Florida College Press, 2022.

_____. "Paul's View of the Holy Spirit." *From the Pen of Paul: An Introduction to the Pauline Epistles.* 2nd ed. Edited by Nathan Ward. Temple Terrace: Florida College Press, 2022.

McConville, J.G. *Ezra, Nehemiah, and Esther.* DSB. Philadelphia: The Westminster Press, 1985.

McGarvey, J.W. *New Commentary on Acts of Apostles.* Cincinnati: The Standard Publishing Foundation, n.d.

McKnight, Scot. *Sermon on the Mount.* SOGBC. Grand Rapids: Zondervan, 2013.

Metzger, Bruce M. *A Textual Commentary on the Greek New Testament.* 2nd ed. New York: United Bible Societies, 1994.

Michaels, J. Ramsey. "Finding Yourself an Intercessor: New Testament Prayer from Hebrews to Jude." *Into God's Presence: Prayer in the New Testament.* Edited by Richard Longenecker. Grand Rapids: Eerdmans, 2001.

Millar, J. Gary. *Calling on the Name of the Lord: A Biblical Theology of Prayer.* NSBT. Downers Grove: Intervarsity Press, 2016.

Miller, Patrick D. *They Cried to the Lord: The Form and Theology of Biblical Prayer.* Minneapolis: Fortress Press, 1994.

Milne, Bruce. *The Message of John: Here Is Your King.* BST. Downers Grove: Intervarsity Press, 1993.

Moo, Douglas J. *2 Peter and Jude.* NIVAC. Grand Rapids: Zondervan, 1996.

_____. *The Letter of James.* PNTC. Grand Rapids: Eerdmans, 2000.

_____. *The Letters to the Colossians and to Philemon.* PNTC. Grand Rapids: Eerdmans, 2008.

Morris, Leon. *1 and 2 Thessalonians: An Introduction and Commentary.* TNTC. Downers Grove: Intervarsity Press, 1984.

_____. *Expository Reflections on the Letter to the Ephesians.* Grand Rapids: Baker Books, 1994.

_____. *The First and Second Epistles to the Thessalonians.* Rev. ed. NICNT. Grand Rapids: Eerdmans, 1991.

_____. *The Gospel According to John.* NICNT. Grand Rapids: Eerdmans, 1971.

———. *The Gospel According to Luke: An Introduction and Commentary*. TNTC. Downers Grove: Intervarsity Press, 1974.

———. *The Gospel According to Matthew*. PNTC. Grand Rapids: Eerdmans, 1992.

———. *Revelation: An Introduction and Commentary*. TNTC. Downers Grove: Intervarsity Press, 1992.

———. *The Epistle to the Romans*. PNTC. Grand Rapids: Eerdmans, 1988.

Motyer, J. Alec. *Studies in the Epistle of James*. London: New Mildmay Press, 1968.

———. *The Message of Philippians: Jesus Our Joy*. BST. Downers Grove: Intervarsity Press, 1984.

Mounce, William D. *Pastoral Epistles*. WBC. Nashville: Thomas Nelson, 2000.

Nolland, John. *Luke 1:1–9:20*. WBC. Nashville: Thomas Nelson, 1989.

Olson, Dennis T. *Numbers*. INT. Louisville; John Knox Press, 1996.

Oswalt, John N. *The Book of Isaiah: Chapters 1–39*. NICOT. Grand Rapids: Eerdmans, 1986.

Pao, David W. *Colossians & Philemon*. ZECNT. Grand Rapids: Zondervan, 2012.

Payne, J. Barton. "1 & 2 Chronicles." *1 & 2 Kings, 1 & 2 Chronicles, Ezra, Nehemiah, Esther, Job*. EBC. Edited by Frank E. Gaebelein. Grand Rapids: Zondervan, 1988.

Peskett, Howard. "Prayer in the Old Testament Outside the Psalms." *Teach Us to Pray: Prayer in the Bible and the World*. Edited by D.A. Carson. Grand Rapids: Baker Book House, 1990.

Peterson, David G. *The Acts of the Apostles*. PNTC. Grand Rapids: Eerdmans, 2009.

———. "Prayer in Paul's Writings." *Teach Us to Pray: Prayer in the Bible and the World*. Edited by D.A. Carson. Grand Rapids: Baker Book House, 1990.

Pickup, Martin. "New Testament Interpretation of the Old Testament: The Theological Rationale of Midrashic Exegesis." *JETS* 51 (2008): 353–381.

_____. "The New Testament's Exegesis of Old Testament Passages (With Special Emphasis on the Psalms)." *Studies in the Psalms: Essays in Honor of D. Phillip Roberts*. Edited by Daniel W. Petty. Temple Terrace: Florida College Bookstore, 2007.

Provan, Iain. *1 and 2 Kings*. NIBC. Peabody: Hendrickson, 1995.

Reiner, Erica, and Martha T. Roth (eds). *The Assyrian Dictionary of the Oriental Institute of Chicago*. 26 vols. Chicago: The Oriental Institute, 1956–2010.

Roop, Eugene F. *Genesis*. BCBC. Scottsdale: Evangel Publishing House, 1987.

Roberts, Phil. "The Prophets: The Interpreters of Israelite History." *Leaving a Mark: The Lectures of Phil Roberts*. Edited by Nathan Ward. Temple Terrace: Florida College Press, 2013.

_____. "The Seventy Weeks of Daniel 9.24–27." *Leaving a Mark: The Lectures of Phil Roberts*. Edited by Nathan Ward. Temple Terrace: Florida College Press, 2013.

_____. "The Story of the Tabernacle." *Leaving a Mark: The Lectures of Phil Roberts*. Edited by Nathan Ward. Temple Terrace: Florida College Press, 2013.

Robertson, O. Palmer. *The Books of Nahum, Habakkuk, and Zephaniah*. NICOT. Grand Rapids: Eerdmans, 1990.

Ross, Allen P. "Studies in the Life of Jacob, Part 2—Jacob at the Jabbok, Israel and Peniel." *BS* 142 (1985): 338–354.

Schreiner, Thomas R. *1, 2 Peter, Jude*. NAC. Nashville: Broadman & Holman Publishers, 2003.

Selman, Martin J. *1 Chronicles: An Introduction and Commentary*. TOTC. Downers Grove: Intervarsity Press, 1994.

Silva, Moisés. *Philippians*. 2nd ed. BECNT. Grand Rapids: Baker Academic, 2005.

Smith, Ralph L. *Micah–Malachi*. WBC. Nashville: Thomas Nelson, 1984.

Steinmann, Andrew E. *Daniel*. CC. St. Louis: Concordia Publishing House, 2008.

Stibbs, Alan M. and A.F. Walls. *The First Epistle General of Peter: An Introduction and Commentary*. TNTC. Grand Rapids: Eerdmans, 1959.

Stott, John R.W. *The Message of 1 Timothy and Titus: Guard the Truth*. BST. Downers Grove: Intervarsity Press, 1996.

_____. *The Message of Acts: To the Ends of the Earth*. BST. Downers Grove: Intervarsity Press, 1990.

_____. *The Message of Ephesians: God's New Society*. BST. Downers Grove: Intervarsity Press, 1979.

_____. *The Message of the Sermon on the Mount: Christian Counter-Culture*. BST. Downers Grove: Intervarsity Press, 1978.

Stuart, Douglas. *Hosea–Jonah*. WBC. Nashville: Thomas Nelson, 1987.

Tasker, R.V.G. *The General Epistles of James: An Introduction and Commentary*. TNTC. Grand Rapids: Eerdmans, 1983.

Thomas, Heath A. *Habakkuk*. THOTC. Grand Rapids: Eerdmans, 2018.

Thompson, J.A. *The Book of Jeremiah*. NICOT. Grand Rapids: Eerdmans, 1980.

Thompson, Marianne Meye. *Colossians and Philemon*. THNTC. Grand Rapids: Eerdmans, 2005.

Throntveit, Mark A. *Ezra-Nehemiah*. INT. Louisville: John Knox Press, 1992.

Timmer, Daniel C. *A Gracious and Compassionate God: Mission, Salvation, and Spirituality in the Book of Jonah*. NSBT. Downers Grove: Intervarsity Press, 2011.

Tully, Eric J. *Reading the Prophets as Christian Scripture: A Literary, Canonical, and Theological Introduction*. Grand Rapids: Baker Academic, 2022.

Turner, M.M.B. "Prayer in the Gospels and Acts." *Teach Us to Pray: Prayer in the Bible and the World*. Edited by D.A. Carson. Grand Rapids: Baker Book House, 1990.

Turner, Robert F. *Reading Romans.* Temple Terrace: Florida College Bookstore, 1995.

VanGemeren, Willem A., editor. *New International Dictionary of Old Testament Theology and Exegesis.* 5 vols. Grand Rapids: Zondervan, 1997.

Wallace, Ronald S. *The Message of Daniel: The Lord is King.* BST. Downers Grove: Intervarsity Press, 1979.

Waltke, Bruce K. *Finding the Will of God: A Pagan Notion?* Grand Rapids: Eerdmans, 1995.

_____ with Cathi J. Fredricks. *Genesis: A Commentary.* Grand Rapids: Zondervan, 2001.

_____, James M. Houston, and Erika Moore. *The Psalms as Christian Lament: A Historical Commentary.* Grand Rapids: Eerdmans, 2014.

Walton, John H. *Genesis.* NIVAC. Grand Rapids: Zondervan, 2001.

_____ and Tremper Longman III. *How to Read Job.* Downers Grove: IVP Academic, 2015.

Wanamaker, Charles A. *The Epistles to the Thessalonians.* NIGTC. Grand Rapids: Eerdmans, 1990.

Ward, Nathan. *Daybreak: A Guide to Overcoming Temptation.* Tampa: DeWard Publishing Company, 2013.

_____. *God Unseen: A Theological Introduction to Esther.* Tampa: DeWard Publishing Company, 2016.

_____. *The Growth of the Seed: Notes on the Book of Genesis.* Tampa: DeWard Publishing Company, 2007.

_____. "Colossians." *From the Pen of Paul: An Introduction to the Pauline Epistles.* 2nd ed. Edited by Nathan Ward. Temple Terrace: Florida College Press, 2022.

———. "Philippians." *From the Pen of Paul: An Introduction to the Pauline Epistles*. 2nd ed. Edited by Nathan Ward. Temple Terrace: Florida College Press, 2022.

———. "The Reign of Ahab: The Low Point in Israel." *Lessons from the Kings of Israel and Judah*. Edited by Daniel W. Petty. Florida College Annual Lectures. Temple Terrace: Florida College Press, 2014.

Webb, Barry G. *The Message of Isaiah*. BST. Downers Grove: IVP Academic, 1996.

Wenham, Gordon J. *Numbers: An Introduction and Commentary*. TOTC. Downers Grove: Intervarsity Press, 1981.

———. *The Psalter Reclaimed: Praying and Praising with the Psalms*. Wheaton: Crossway, 2013.

Widder, Wendy. "Prayer in Daniel." *Praying with Ancient Israel: Exploring the Theology of Prayer in the Old Testament*. Edited by Phillip G. Camp and Tremper Longman III. Abilene: Abilene Christian University Press, 2015.

Widmer, Michael. *Standing in the Breach: An Old Testament Theology and Spirituality of Intercessory Prayer*. Siphrut: Literature and Theology of the Hebrew Scriptures. Winona Lake: Eisenbrauns, 2015.

Williamson, H.G.M. *Ezra, Nehemiah*. WBC. Waco: Word Books, 1985.

Willis, Timothy. "Prayer in the Deuteronomistic History." *Praying with Ancient Israel: Exploring the Theology of Prayer in the Old Testament*. Edited by Phillip G. Camp and Tremper Longman III. Abilene: Abilene Christian University Press, 2015.

Wilson, Gerald H. *Job*. UBC. Grand Rapids: Baker Books, 2007.

Wiseman, Donald J. *1 & 2 Kings: An Introduction and Commentary*. TOTC. Downers Grove: Intervarsity Press, 1993.

Witherington, Ben, III. *1 and 2 Thessalonians: A Socio-Rhetorical Commentary*. Grand Rapids: Eerdmans, 2006.

———. *The Letters to Philemon, the Colossians, and the Ephesians: A Socio-Rhetorical Commentary on the Captivity Epistles*. Grand Rapids: Eerdmans, 2007.

Wordsworth, Christopher. *The Books of Samuel*. 2nd ed. London: Rivingtons, 1867.

Wright, Christopher J.H. *The Message of Jeremiah: Against Wind and Tide*. BST. Downers Grove: IVP Academic, 2014.

Wright, N.T. *Colossians and Philemon: An Introduction and Commentary*. TNTC. Downers Grove: IVP Academic, 1986.

———. "The Lord's Prayer as a Paradigm of Christian Prayer." *Into God's Presence: Prayer in the New Testament*. Edited by Richard Longenecker. Grand Rapids: Eerdmans, 2001.

Yamauchi, Edwin. "Ezra-Nehemiah." *1 & 2 Kings, 1 & 2 Chronicles, Ezra, Nehemiah, Esther, Job*. EBC. Edited by Frank E. Gaebelein. Grand Rapids: Zondervan, 1988.

———. "The Daily Bread Motif in Antiquity." *WTJ* 28 (1966): 145–56.

Yates, Gary. "New Exodus and No Exodus in Jeremiah 26–45: Promise and Warning to the Exiles in Babylon." *TB* 57.1 (2006): 1–22.

Youngblood, Kevin J. *Jonah: God's Scandalous Mercy*. 2nd ed. ZECOT. Grand Rapids: Zondervan, 2019.

Youngblood, Ronald F. "1 & 2 Samuel." *Deuteronomy, Joshua, Judges, Ruth, 1 & 2 Samuel*. EBC. Edited by Frank E. Gaebelein. Grand Rapids: Zondervan, 1992.

Also By Nathan Ward

God Unseen
A Theological Introduction to Esther

Preachers and commentators often focus on Esther as a story of divine providence. Many go so far as to say that the absence of any mention of God in Esther is proof of his presence—a tenuous foundation upon which to build a case! *God Unseen* argues that Esther is indeed intended to be read in a religious context and that it does speak to God's providence, but shows this by a careful comparison of the text of Esther with many other Old Testament narratives that it echoes, thus setting it squarely in a canonical context. The result of such a contextual reading will give credence to the belief that God should be seen in those silences.

Esther closely parallels life in 21st-century western culture. It tells the story of people who know how to be righteous followers of God, but who are surrounded by a world of paganism and, far too often, find themselves assimilating rather than standing apart. The characters receive no special revelation from God, nor does he seem to be present at all in their lives. Many Christians today live under a similar set of circumstances, so its message is vital. *God Unseen's* argument that the book of Esther is religious and that God is present in the narrative will help give practical shape to modern questions of what it means to live during the apparent silence of God. 188 pages. $14.99 (PB).

Also By Nathan Ward

Daybreak
A Guide to Overcoming Temptation

The sun rose on Jacob after his wrestling match with God. A new day dawned and he had a new name to match his new life. A similar call for daybreak is made for Christians today: come out of the darkness and into God's marvelous light (1 Pet 2.9). As Christians, we must not live in the night. We have experienced our own daybreak and should walk in the light—but far too often, we find the darkness alluring. *Daybreak* examines the call to overcome temptation, a closer look at the enemy, and some practical principles for winning the battle with sin. 108 pages. $8.99 (PB).

For a full listing of DeWard Publishing Company books, visit our website:

www.deward.com

www.ingramcontent.com/pod-product-compliance
Lightning Source LLC
Chambersburg PA
CBHW032147080426
42735CB00008B/615